Individuality and Beyond

Individuality and Beyond

Nietzsche Reads Emerson

BENEDETTA ZAVATTA

TRANSLATED BY
ALEXANDER REYNOLDS

OXFORD
UNIVERSITY PRESS

OXFORD
UNIVERSITY PRESS

Oxford University Press is a department of the University of Oxford. It furthers
the University's objective of excellence in research, scholarship, and education
by publishing worldwide. Oxford is a registered trade mark of Oxford University
Press in the UK and certain other countries.

Published in the United States of America by Oxford University Press
198 Madison Avenue, New York, NY 10016, United States of America.

CIP data is on file at the Library of Congress
ISBN 978–0–19–092921–3

1 3 5 7 9 8 6 4 2

Printed by Sheridan Books, Inc., United States of America

To Paolo,
true friend and educator

CONTENTS

ACKNOWLEDGMENTS

The initial nucleus of the present book took form many years ago out of doctoral research conducted at the Scuola di Alti Studi of the Fondazione San Carlo in Modena, Italy, under the supervision of Giuliano Campioni. My first words of thanks go to him, for having taught me to read Nietzsche as Nietzsche himself asked that he be read, "with delicate eyes and fingers" (D, Preface 5). I also wish to express my thanks to my friends and colleagues of the Seminario Permanente Nietzscheano, a study association founded in 2005, with whom I have had many opportunities over the years to engage on the themes discussed in this book and who were never tardy in expressing their advice and criticism. My thanks go particularly to Maria Cristina Fornari, Luca Lupo, João Constâncio, Maria João Branco, Pietro Gori, and Paolo Stellino. I thank the European Commission, which funded the research that went into the book via a Marie Curie IEF fellowship; the Institut des Textes et Manuscrits Modernes in Paris, where this research was actually conducted; and, with especial warmth and recognition, Nadia Urbinati, who made it possible for me to conduct a part of it as a visiting scholar of the Department of Political Science of Columbia University in New York. I feel a particular debt of gratitude toward the Scientific Committee, and the members, of the International Society of Nietzsche Studies. Taking part in the stimulating annual meetings of this association played an important role in deepening my understanding of Nietzsche's thought and of all that this thought might be construed to imply. Particular thanks go also to all those who encouraged and supported the publication of this book, among whom I shall mention specifically Christa Davies Acampora, Anthony Jensen, and Eduardo Mendieta, and to the authors of those books that have been a special inspiration to me, among whom are George Kateb, John Richardson, and Paul Katsafanas. Finally, very special thanks go to Paolo D'Iorio, who has supported me in my academic career for some fifteen years now and has always, with great generosity, read and discussed whatever I have written. To him this book is dedicated.

INTRODUCTION

Among Nietzsche scholars it is, by now, a fact recognized and beyond dispute that Ralph Waldo Emerson exercised a decisive influence upon the development of the philosophy of his younger German contemporary. Nietzsche began reading Emerson at the age of seventeen, and there can be found not only in the former's published works but also in his private notes and in his correspondence innumerable traces of this reading, right on into the final years of Nietzsche's conscious life. The tone of Nietzsche's remarks on Emerson generally remains, throughout this whole period, a positive one—something quite extraordinary in view of Nietzsche's marked tendency to overturn, in the course of his own development, his intellectual idols. Nietzsche considered the American essayist to be not only a "master of prose" (GS 92) but also the most fertile thinker of their shared century. What is more, Nietzsche's intellectual esteem for Emerson as a philosopher was accompanied by an equally strong sympathy for the elder writer as a human being. In 1881 Nietzsche wrote, in a personal note, of Emerson's collection *Essays: First and Second Series* that he had never "felt so at home in a book; felt so much, indeed, as if the home were my own," and he concluded, "I cannot praise it; it is too close to me [*ich darf es nicht loben, es steht mir zu nahe*]" (NL 1881 12[68], KSA 9: 588). In a letter to his friend Franz Overbeck two years later, he declared that he considered Emerson to be a "*twin **soul*** [Bruder-**Seele**]" and that even the differences between Emerson's philosophy and his own could not undermine the deep affinity he felt with him (KSB 6: 463, n. 477).

Further evidence of the intensity with which Nietzsche read Emerson can be found in his own personal copies of several collections of Emerson's essays in German translation, which feature copious underlinings and notes and comments added in the margins. Nietzsche's personal library, which has been conserved up to the present day, includes a copy of *Versuche* (Hannover: Meyer Verlag, 1858, 448 pp.), a German translation of Emerson's *Essays: First and Second Series* (1841–44);[1] a copy of *Neue Essays* (Stuttgart: Auerbach, 1876, 324 pp.), a German translation of *Letters and Social Aims* (1875);[2] and *Historische Notizen über Lebensweise und Literatur in Massachusetts* (59 pp.), a manuscript translation of *Historic Notes of Life and Letters in Massachusetts*, an article of Emerson's that had appeared in the *Atlantic Monthly* in October 1883.[3] Nietzsche's library had originally included two copies of *Die Führung des Lebens: Gedanken und Studien* (Leipzig: Steinacker, 1862), a German translation of Emerson's *The Conduct of Life* (1860);[4] and a copy of *Über Goethe und Shakespeare* (Hannover: Rümpler, 1858, 116 pp.), a German translation of the essays on these two authors that Emerson had included in *Representative Men* (1850). These last three volumes, however, were lost during the war and are not preserved, as are the others, in the Duchess Anna Amalia Library in Weimar. Nietzsche's *Nachlass* also includes an entire notebook of excerpts from the *Versuche* made in 1882 (M III 7), published in the Critical Edition of Nietzsche's works as "Exzerpte aus Emersons 'Essays'" (NL 1882 17[1–39], KSA 9: 666–672).[5] Some are copied word for word, some summed up or slightly reformulated, others altered from the third into the first person, and yet others blended together with thoughts of Nietzsche's own. Nietzsche also made other sets of excerpts from Emerson's works: there can be dated to 1863 two series of excerpts from *Die Führung des Lebens* (NL 1863 15[36], KGW I/3: 180–182; NL 1863 15A[5], KGW I/3: 227–228), and among the notes of Nietzsche's "Middle Period," above all those of the year 1878, there are to be found many excerpts from the *Versuche* and from *Über Goethe und Shakespeare*.

Among the books that make up what was Nietzsche's personal library, the copy of *Versuche* stands out as a singular case: its pages are literally covered with various traces of Nietzsche's reading and rereading of them, ranging from underlinings, exclamation marks, question marks, and dog-eared pages right through to numerous annotations and philosophical comments written in the margins. The editors of the Critical Edition of Nietzsche's works, Giorgio Colli and Mazzino Montinari, decided to publish only a selection of these marginal comments and annotations (*Emerson-Exemplar*, NL 1881 13[1–22], KSA 9: 618–622).[6] This selection consists of the longest of the remarks and annotations and those possessing a fully developed significance of their own (i.e., those whose meaning could be grasped without there having to be published beside them the text of Emerson's to which they referred). Most of Nietzsche's glosses, however, consist in short comments, exclamations, and expressions of approval or dissent (*Ja!, bravo!, Alles falsch!*, etc.), and these do indeed yield no meaning except where considered alongside a specific passage from Emerson. These traces of Nietzsche's reading of Emerson's works have, as yet, been neither fully deciphered nor published, let alone drawn into consideration in the interpretation of the relationship between the two thinkers. Curiously, neither the selection of marginal annotations nor the notebook full of excerpts from

Emerson which were published as part of the Critical Edition have been taken into account in those monographs that have hitherto appeared in English on the Emerson-Nietzsche connection.[7] Nietzsche's reactions to the ideas of Emerson have mostly simply been surmised on the basis of scholars' general knowledge of the two authors' respective philosophies; while his real reactions—manifestly and materially expressed in the form of his underlinings, crossings-out, exclamation points, and marginal comments appended to Emerson's books—have been ignored.

The aim of this book is to provide an interpretation of the influence exerted by Emerson on Nietzsche's thought which will, finally, be an interpretation founded upon a solid philological basis: that is to say, an interpretation founded upon a careful consideration and contextualization of the signs and traces left by Nietzsche's actual reading of Emerson and of the specific selection of excerpts that he made from the essays of this latter. With this work I aim to demonstrate the truth of Mazzino Montinari's contention that philology, far from being the antithesis, is in fact the necessary premise and precondition of philosophical reflection. Retracing the exact paths and details of Nietzsche's reading of Emerson not only makes it possible finally to evaluate the real reception of the latter author's ideas by the former; it also helps to clarify the genesis of certain key ideas in Nietzsche's own philosophy. This, in turn, allows us to disentangle several hitherto intractable interpretative knots in Nietzsche's philosophy—that is to say, to find answers to questions that have so far remained unresolved or to look in new and different ways at some widely discussed themes of Nietzsche's thought.

In the first chapter of this book I investigate the reasons why the Emerson-Nietzsche relationship tended to be played down, where it was not frankly and entirely denied, for almost a century. Already during the early years of the 20th century a number of scholars became aware of the affinity between the philosophies of Nietzsche and Emerson. It was, however, only in the 1990s on that the relationship between the two philosophers began really to be explored. I argue that this is not just a matter of chance but rather a symptom of a long-protracted cultural and political hostility between Germany and the United States for whose respective cultural traditions Nietzsche and Emerson, each on his side, had come gradually to be exalted to the status of summary icons.

In the study's second chapter I consider a topic that is central to Nietzsche's philosophy from his first adolescent essays right up to his very last works, namely, the topic of fate and free will. It is a theme that is closely linked to two other central themes in Nietzsche's philosophy: the theme of moral responsibility for one's own actions, and that of the construction of one's character, or self-creation. What Emerson offered Nietzsche was a quite different notion of the subject's relationship to his or her "fate" than the one that Nietzsche would have been familiar with from the tradition of German Romanticism. If the "hero" as conceived of by this great cultural movement in which Nietzsche, as it were, had been raised was one who proved his own moral superiority by hurling himself with tremendous energy against the order of Nature, tragically aware that this could only end in his inevitable defeat, the "hero" as personified in the American pioneer was a figure who proved able to use Nature to his own advantage and succeeded, as it were, in "riding the wave" of those natural forces by which he might otherwise have been crushed. In the last analysis, the idea that Emerson proposes to Nietzsche, and that is broadly developed by Nietzsche in the works of his middle period, indeed already in writings as early as those from 1862, is that freedom does not consist simply in the absence from one's life of immutable given facts. Freedom, Emerson informs Nietzsche, consists in having a sense of oneself as an agent—that is to say, as a being who actively takes up some position vis-à-vis such "immutable given facts." While rejecting the metaphysical assumptions on which Emerson personally chose to base this contention (specifically, the thesis that the subject is capable of taking a position in this way inasmuch as his or her thought and will are essentially and unconditionally free), Nietzsche nonetheless made use of the idea in order to work out a philosophical account of human freedom that was, paradoxically, alternative to the traditional conception of freedom as unconditionedness. Those, argued Nietzsche, who attain to the mastery of their own drives and act on the basis of their own values are not, indeed, free in the sense of being "absolutely unconditioned" but have, nonetheless, a sense of themselves as free beings inasmuch as they are agents of their own actions.

In the book's third chapter, however, I consider the position that Nietzsche adopts vis-à-vis Socratico-Christian morality, or the "morality of customs," and his elaboration of a model of morality alternative to this. Examining what his reading of Emerson contributed to Nietzsche's thoughts on the realization of the self through the development of one's own distinct individuality makes it possible to clarify the exact nature of this alternative model of morality. It is a model of morality concerned solely with the manner in which values are posited, not with their specific content. Put more precisely, this model of morality is concerned with the development of the individual up to the stage in which he or she finally becomes capable of "transvaluing" the values he or she has inherited from the tradition and of living on the basis of values of his or her own creation. My examination of the contribution made by Emerson to Nietzsche's treatment of this theme in the various phases of the latter's philosophy is intended to throw light on how Nietzsche recognizes there to inhere in the virtue that Emerson called the virtue of "self-reliance" a key test and criterion of this "transvaluation of values." This "transvaluation of values" as Nietzsche conceives of it comprises several different attitudes which are personified in a series of invented personalities representative of Nietzsche's thinking on morality and moral questions in just those three phases of his thought in which the influence of Emerson is most substantial and perceptible, namely, the figure of "Schopenhauer as educator" in the third *Untimely Meditation*; the "free spirit" qua "wanderer" of the works of the middle period; and, finally, Zarathustra, eponymous protagonist of the most emphatically poetic of Nietzsche's works. In other words, these three figures highlight the qualities that are essentially required in order for individuals to prove capable of separating and freeing themselves from the morality of custom and of positing their own self-created values. The three just-mentioned figures represent incarnations, respectively, of the reverence for one's own self as a unique and unrepeatable individual which serves to incline one toward originality and nonconformism; the willingness to place one's own self in question and to confront viewpoints and ways of life different from one's own so as to enlarge one's personal vision; and the ability, finally, to let go even of the feelings of resentment and guilt, as well as of all the other "reactive" feelings, that may have arisen in one in and through the very process of separating and liberating oneself from the morality of customs, so as to attain to a state of "divine indifference" in which one can express oneself entirely freely.

Whereas in the book's third chapter I examine the development of the individual, in the fourth I look at this individual in his or her relation to society. Nietzsche avails himself of Emerson's reflections in order to draw a distinction between, on the one hand, egoism as this is traditionally understood and, on the other, a healthy egoism that is more suitably denominated "individualism." If, in Europe, the term "individualism" tended to evoke a shutting oneself away within one's own private sphere and a refusal to participate in social and political affairs, in the American democratic tradition that was inaugurated by Emerson "individualism" represented the very highest form of social and political commitment. In Nietzsche, the "transvaluation of the value" of egoism goes hand in hand with the critique of compassion and of the altruistic actions that are founded upon it. Here too Emerson's reflections played a fundamental role for Nietzsche in helping him to work out a distinction between, on the one hand, the aid that an individual offers to another individual only in order to flee from his or her own self and, on the other hand, another type of "interest in the other," one that is compatible with the healthy desire to stay centered on and in oneself. This latter type of "interestedness," moreover, differs from mere compassion in being sincerely oriented to promoting the well-being of the other, a well-being that for Nietzsche consists not in the absence of pain but in the invigoration of character.

The relationship par excellence in which this second type of "interestedness" in the other manifests—that is to say, an authentic interestedness in the other's well-being—is the relationship of friendship. In order to describe the characteristics that any relationship worthy of this name needs necessarily to possess Nietzsche draws very heavily upon the essay of Emerson's that bears this title, just as Emerson, in his turn, had drawn heavily upon Aristotle's treatment of the notion of friendship in book 8 of the *Nicomachean Ethics*. But in contrast to Aristotle, who considered friendship to be one of the fundamental prerequisites for the construction of a political community, Emerson is extremely skeptical of that ideal of a "community of friends" which had emerged, in his day, in New England as a form of social protest. Emerson's keen-sighted criticism of the very idea of "community" awakened Nietzsche from that dream of establishing little "monasteries for free spirits" all over Europe which he had conceived around 1876, after turning away from his academic career in Basel and from the Wagnerian pseudo-religion centered on Bayreuth. After 1883, indeed, Nietzsche resolved to extend the bond of friendship to embrace society as a whole, with the consequence that this bond would cease to be characterizable in any way as a merely personal one.

In the fifth chapter I examine the role played by Emerson in the evolution of the positions taken by Nietzsche on the topics of history and historiography, from the period of the second *Untimely Meditation* on the "uses and disadvantages of history for life" through the works of the middle period on into those of the late. Highlighting the appreciation expressed by Nietzsche for Emerson's position on these topics allows us to understand and to evaluate more correctly certain of Nietzsche's affirmations regarding "active forgetting" as a remedy against the rampant historicism of his age. Specifically, it allows us to situate and relativize these well-known affirmations and to recognize them as being valid really only for the Nietzsche of the early works. Essential in this regard were those thoughts and ideas that Nietzsche found in Emerson's work that had been ripened and developed in the course of the older American author's reading of Goethe but which Emerson had reworked into forms that were all his own. The image of Goethe elaborated by Emerson—that of a mind and personality providing a representative example of how to establish a genuinely fruitful relationship to the historical tradition—came gradually, for Nietzsche, to replace the image of the real Goethe, becoming a model for Nietzsche's portrait of the ideal historian in the works of his middle and late periods. In this portrait Goethe takes on the traits of that supremely potent nature the possibility of which Nietzsche had envisaged already in the second *Untimely Meditation*, namely, a nature endowed with so great an assimilative capacity that it would have no need to limit its historical horizon but would be able to welcome into itself the past of humanity as a whole. The reading of Emerson was of fundamental importance for Nietzsche also in respect of both writers' critiques of the metaphysical notion of genius and of the "cult of the hero" that tended to arise on the basis of this metaphysical notion. By collecting the traces of Nietzsche's reading of Emerson here we can situate the genesis of Nietzsche's version of this critique already in a period anterior to *Human, All Too Human*—that is to say, at a time when Nietzsche still "officially" maintained, through the energetic support he offered to Wagner's Bayreuth project of cultural renewal, a position apparently far from critical of such a cult. We can also clarify hereby Nietzsche's position in respect of the theory of perfectionism.

The nature of the topics discussed is such that there are inevitably certain overlappings in the themes and arguments of the various chapters. The process of acquiring liberty in the sense of agency, a topic forming the theme of chapter 2, necessarily involves that realization of true individuality which we focus on in chapter 3. And the "virtuous individual," the individual who embodies the law in his or her own person, whose portrait forms the culmination of chapter 3, is not indeed just the "free individual" described in chapter 2 but also and at the same time the "great man" on whom we focus in chapter 5—that is to say, the person who has discovered, and developed to the highest potency, his or her own distinctive talent. In other words, the process of self-cultivation or self-creation which leads one to achieve liberty is one and the same with the process through which one attains to autonomous moral conduct and to the expression of one's own distinctive genius. The process of the development of one's own character described in chapter 2—a process in the course of which one seems to transform oneself successively into a whole series of individuals, each one different from the next—is a process that is shown here to occur only in and through a confrontation with the views and opinions of others (as described in chapter 3), with one's own friends/enemies (as described in chapter 4), and with the "great men" of history (as described in chapter 5). Individuality is a merely momentary result of this process which is produced as a synthesis of a whole multiplicity of agencies and factors that are often mutually contradictory and countervailing. It tends to be temporarily lost upon contact with new stimuli, only to be subsequently reconquered in some other form (that is to say, in one's reemergence as a new "individual"). The individual described in chapter 4, who is focused on himself or herself and on his or her own task and who refuses to yield to the temptations of compassion and of altruism, is one and the same with the individual who has attained dominion over himself or herself and a consciousness of his or her own self-created values—that is to say, one and the same with the "free individual" (chapter 2) and with the "virtuous individual" (chapter 3). Such an individual will be able to ignore, with magnanimity, the mass of humanity (as described in chapter 3), establish loyal and loving relationships with his or her friends/enemies (as described in chapter 4), and learn from the "great men" of the past, without thereby subordinating himself or herself to these latter (as described in chapter 5).

The present study, by revealing the influence exerted by Emerson on Nietzsche, also aims to point up the contribution that the former writer, through the latter, made to European philosophy of the 20th century. Nietzsche was one of the subtlest and most acute interpreters of Emerson, perhaps the best of all his interpreters. For this reason, to look at Emerson with the eyes of Nietzsche, that is, to cast light on the reasons Nietzsche found Emerson so interesting, is to make a decisive contribution also to understanding Emerson's philosophy and its relevance to philosophical debates of the present day. Discovering Emerson, as he did, only in 1862, the young Nietzsche came directly into contact with the "second" Emerson, specifically with the collection of essays *The Conduct of Life*, which Emerson had published just two years before, in 1860. This fact is of decisive importance for understanding the profound satisfaction that Nietzsche found in Emerson's work. The "first" Emerson—that is to say, the Nature-transfiguring mystic whose credo is stated most fully and clearly in the essay *Nature* from 1836—remained a figure entirely unknown to Nietzsche.[8] Nietzsche, indeed, did later come to read the *Essays: First and Second Series* (1841–1844) in which there still persist certain metaphysical ideas, such as the "Oversoul" or a Providence-like conception of "Compensation" first formulated by the "mystic" that Emerson had been in his youth; to such ideas, however, Nietzsche always showed the most resolute opposition. It was in fact this "second" Emerson, who was the first Emerson that Nietzsche discovered and the only Emerson that he really made use of in his own work, who was to become the subject of the "Emerson renaissance" that made itself felt from the 1980s onward and is still developing today (see Buell 1984; Wilson 1997). From this perspective, Emerson's thought reveals itself both as an existentialism *ante litteram*—which, through Nietzsche, influenced Heidegger and French poststructuralism—and as a lucid cultural, social and political critique of the modern world that is in no respect inferior to Marx's (see Packer 1982; West 1989; Robinson 1993; Lopez 1996; Porte and Morris 1999; Kateb 1992, 2002; Zakaras 2009). This "new" Emerson, on whom Nietzsche was throwing light already in the middle of the 20th century, today demands his rightful place in the very forefront of the contemporary philosophical scene.

ABBREVIATIONS OF NIETZSCHE'S WORKS

A   *The Antichrist*, translated by Judith Norman. Cambridge, UK: Cambridge University Press, 2005.

AOM   *Assorted Opinions and Maxims*, translated by R. J. Hollingdale. Cambridge, UK: Cambridge University Press, 1986.

BGE   *Beyond Good and Evil*, translated by Judith Norman. Cambridge, UK: Cambridge University Press, 2002.

BT   *The Birth of Tragedy*, translated by Ronald Speirs. Cambridge, UK: Cambridge University Press, 1999.

CW   The Case of Wagner, translated by Walter Kaufmann. New York: Vintage Books, 1967.

D   *Daybreak*, translated by R. J. Hollingdale. Cambridge, UK: Cambridge University Press, 1997.

EH   *Ecce Homo*, translated by Judith Norman. Cambridge, UK: Cambridge University Press, 2005.

FH   *Fate and History*, translated by George Stack in "Nietzsche's earliest Essays. Translation and Commentary on "'Fate and History' and 'Freedom of Will and Fate'"", *Philosophy Today* 37 (1993): 153–169, 154–156.

FWF   *Freedom of the Will and Fate*, translated by George Stack. *Philosophy Today* 37 (1993): 153–169, 156–158.

HH   *Human, All Too Human*, translated by R. J. Hollingdale. Cambridge, UK: Cambridge University Press, 1986.

HL   *On the Uses and Disadvantages of History for Life*, translated by R. J. Hollingdale. Cambridge, UK: Cambridge University Press, 2005.

KGB   *Briefwechsel, Kritische Gesamtausgabe*. Berlin: de Gruyter, 1975.

KGW	*Werke, Kritische Gesamtausgabe.* Berlin: de Gruyter, 1967.
KSA	*Sämtliche Werke, Kritische Studienausgabe.* 2nd rev. ed. Berlin: de Gruyter, 1988.
KSB	*Sämtliche Briefe, Kritische Studienausgabe.* 2nd rev. ed. Berlin: de Gruyter, 2003.
GM	*On the Genealogy of Morality,* translated by Carol Diethe. Cambridge, UK: Cambridge University Press, 1994.
GS	*The Gay Science,* translated by Josefine Nauckhoff and Adrian Del Caro. Cambridge, UK: Cambridge University Press, 2001.
Moods	*On Moods,* translated by Graham Parkes. *Journal of Nietzsche Studies* 2 (1991): 5–10.
PTAG	*Philosophy in the Tragic Age of the Greeks,* translated by Marianne Cowan. Washington, DC: Regnery, 1962.
SE	*Schopenhauer as Educator,* translated by R. J. Hollingdale. Cambridge, UK: Cambridge University Press, 2005.
TI	*Twilight of the Idols,* translated by Judith Norman. Cambridge, UK: Cambridge University Press, 2005.
WB	*Richard Wagner in Bayreuth,* translated by R. J. Hollingdale. Cambridge, UK: Cambridge University Press, 2005.
WEN	*Writings from the Early Notebooks,* translated by Ladislaus Löb. Cambridge, UK: Cambridge University Press, 2009.
WLN	*Writings from the Late Notebooks,* translated by Kate Sturge. Cambridge, UK: Cambridge University Press, 2003.
WS	*The Wanderer and His Shadow,* translated by R. J. Hollingdale. Cambridge, UK: Cambridge University Press, 1986.
Z	*Thus Spoke Zarathustra,* translated by Adrian Del Caro. Cambridge, UK: Cambridge University Press, 2006.

Section or chapters that are not numbered but given a title in Nietzsche's text are quoted accordingly: e.g., EH, Why I Am So Clever 10 (Ecce Homo, section: Why I Am So Clever, paragraph: 10).

Letters are quoted as follows: KGB or KSB volume and section, pages, number of the letter; e.g., KSB 6: 463, n. 477.

References to the *Nachlass* are given as follows: NL year, note, KSA or KGW volume, pages; e.g., NL 1881 12[68], KSA 9: 588. When available, references to a translation are given after NL year and note, as follows: NL 1885–1886 1[122], WLN, 63. Notes from the *Nachlass* not available in WEN or WLN have been translated by the book's translator, Alexander Reynolds.

ABBREVIATIONS OF EMERSON'S WORKS

Note: The volume *Versuche* read by Nietzsche was the German translation of the first and second series of *Essays* published by Emerson, respectively, in 1841 and 1844. The first series of the *Essays* bore on its title page only the word *Essays*, since Emerson, at this time, did not yet envisage writing a second series. This first edition, which had an extremely small print run of only 1,500 copies, was out of print already by 1845. Before republishing this volume in 1847, Emerson wanted to make some corrections to it, and on this occasion he also altered its title to *Essays: First Series*, in order to distinguish it from the second series of short pieces which he had in the meantime (in 1844) published under the title *Essays: Second Series*. Aside from the correction of a misprint, no further modifications were made to this 1847 reedition of the *Essays: First Series*, which was subsequently reprinted several times and has been included in both Critical Editions of Emerson's works which have hitherto appeared (Houghton Mifflin, 1803, and Harvard University Press, 1971–). For this reason, whereas, when citing the *Essays: Second Series* we can use the Harvard University Press Critical Edition, in order to cite the *Essays: First Series* we are obliged to make use of the text of the first edition of this work (James Munroe, 1841).

CL	*The Conduct of Life.* Vol. 6 of *Collected Works.* Cambridge, MA: Harvard University Press, 2004.
E I	*Essays.* Boston: James Munroe, 1841.
E I 2nd edition	*Essays: First Series.* Vol. 2 of Collected Works. Cambridge, MA: Harvard University Press, 1980.
E II	*Essays: Second Series.* Vol. 3 of *Collected Works.* Cambridge, MA: Harvard University Press, 1984.
EL I	*Early Lectures, vol. I: 1833–1836.* Cambridge, MA: Harvard University Press, 1959.

EL II | *Early Lectures, vol. II: 1836–1838.* Cambridge, MA: Harvard University Press, 1964.

EL III | *Early Lectures, vol. III: 1838–1842.* Cambridge, MA: Harvard University Press, 1972.

ET | *English Traits.* Vol. 5 of *Collected Works.* Cambridge, MA: Harvard University Press, 1994.

HNLLM | "Historic Notes of Life and Letters in Massachusetts." *Atlantic Monthly* 52 (1883): 529–543.

JMN | *Journals and Miscellaneous Notebooks.* Cambridge, MA: Harvard University Press, 1960–1982.

LSA | *Letters and Social Aims.* Vol. 8 of *Collected Works.* Cambridge, MA: Harvard University Press, 2010.

NAL | *Nature, Addresses, and Lectures.* Vol. 1 of *Collected Works.* Cambridge, MA: Harvard University Press, 1971.

RM | *Representative Men.* Vol. 4 of *Collected Works.* Cambridge, MA: Harvard University Press, 1987.

SS | *Society and Solitude.* Vol. 7 of *Collected Works.* Cambridge, MA: Harvard University Press, 2008.

Emerson's Works in German Translation

FL | *Die Führung des Lebens,* translated by E. S. von Mühlberg. Leipzig: Steinacker, 1862.

NE | *Neue Essays (Letters and Social Aims),* translated by J. Schmidt. Stuttgart: Auerbach, 1876.

UGS | *Über Goethe und Shakespeare,* translated by H. Grimm. Hannover: C. Rümpler, 1857.

V | *Versuche (Essays: First and Second Series),* translated by G. Fabricius. Hannover: Carl Meyer, 1858.

A NOTE ON THE APPENDIX

A companion website with an appendix of images is available at www.oup. com/us/individualityandbeyond

It houses digital copies of Emerson's *Versuche* (*Essays: First and Second Series*) with Nietzsche's underlinings, comments, and marginalia. Please visit this site to view the figures mentioned in this book.

1

The Reception of the
Emerson-Nietzsche Relation

1.1. A "Collective Amnesia"

Already during the early years of the 20th century a number of scholars became aware of the affinity between the philosophies of Nietzsche and Emerson.[1] It was, however, only from the 1990s on that the relationship between the two authors began really to be explored. This appears somewhat curious given their importance for their respective cultural traditions and the great mass of critical studies devoted to their bodies of work considered in separation. The first writer to point out the strange paucity, throughout the 20th century, of critical studies dealing with Nietzsche's reading of Emerson was Stanley Cavell. "Why is it," asked Cavell (1995, 95) provocatively, "that Emerson's decisive philosophical importance for Nietzsche evidently cannot be remembered by philosophers?" Michael Lopez (1997, 4–5) also speaks here of a "collective amnesia" and comments, "It is extraordinarily ironic that commentators have so regularly and easily forgotten the historical linkage of two such dominant, such iconic and influential, figures" (7). It is, then, surely incumbent on us to retrace the history of the persistent failure to recognize the importance of this relationship and to ask just what factors this may be due to.

Charles Andler, the first scholar to carry out a systematic study of Nietzsche's sources, secured for Emerson, already in the 1920s, a recognized place as one of Nietzsche's (to adopt Andler's own phrase) "précurseurs." He shed light on how important a role the reading of Emerson played in the maturation of the young Nietzsche's sense of a philosophical vocation. In this period, says Andler (1920, 228), Emerson was for Nietzsche "one of those beloved writers whose thoughts he absorbed so fully that he no longer always distinguished them from his own." But Andler was of the view that Emerson's influence on Nietzsche was basically restricted to the latter's youth. He considered that when Nietzsche, from 1876

1

on, began to adopt positions opposed to German Romanticism, this meant that he rejected Emerson's philosophy as well:

> Emerson is a Platonist and a mystic. He abandoned himself so care-
> lessly to the currents of German Romanticism that he found him-
> self inevitably set adrift upon the waters of that revived Platonism
> in which the doctrine of a Fichte, a Novalis or a Schopenhauer es-
> sentially consisted. . . . Exposing himself to Emerson, Nietzsche was
> sucked back, in his turn, into these bewitching waters. Around 1876
> he had sworn no longer to believe in any metaphysical chimeras.
> But Emerson thrust him once again into this dark and shifting
> element. (247)

Andler, in short, believed that the American Emerson, an enthusiastic reader of the German Romantic philosophers, had merely allowed Nietzsche to draw once again on this tradition strong in Nietzsche's own native land. Andler set limits, in other words, not only to the duration of Emerson's influence on Nietzsche but also to this influence's real significance.

1.2. The "American Goethe": The Reception of Emerson in Germany

This judgment of Andler's is perfectly in line with the general reception accorded to Emerson in Europe. Emerson was indeed looked upon, in Germany and other European nations, as "the American Goethe." That is to say, he was received and appreciated only to the extent that his philosophy recalled the philosophies of figures who played important roles in German Romanticism: Goethe himself, indeed, but also Schelling and Novalis. The diffusion of Emerson's philosophical ideas in Germany was promoted by a small circle of intellectuals headed by Herman Grimm, a renowned art historian based in Berlin,[2] and his wife, Gisela von Arnim.[3] Gisela was the daughter of Achim von Arnim and Bettina Brentano von Arnim, who was remembered particularly for her close friendship with Goethe. Already in the opening lines of the preface she wrote for the German translation of Emerson's *Essays: First and Second Series*, Gisela von Arnim (1858, iii) emphasized just this closeness of Emerson's thought to the German cultural tradition: "Emerson brings back to us only the flowers whose seeds he gathered through his study of the German people and of their spiritual and intellectual productions."[4] Von Arnim surely intended this observation as high praise of the American writer. But it was inevitable that such a reading of

Emerson should eventually provoke the reaction "Why do we need Emerson when we already have Goethe?" (Simon 1937, 117–118). In any case, what most of all stood in the way of Emerson's reception in Germany was the fact that the philosophies of Romanticism and Idealism had, by the middle years of the 19th century, fallen out of intellectual grace. Emerson could plausibly use the philosophy of Nature developed by Schelling, Novalis, and other thinkers—a philosophy in which reality is conceived of as the projection of an omnipotent Subject—to interpret the reality of his own country, the United States. This country was, in fact, growing easily and rapidly wealthy thanks to the enormous natural resources at its disposal. Moreover, in the still young society of America, unburdened by bureaucracy or consolidated social privileges, each individual seemed able to aspire to a social position and a fortune corresponding to his or her own capacities and effort. In Germany, however, the situation was completely different. The Industrial Revolution had signaled the rapid decline of the Romantic and Idealist philosophies, the place of which was taken by the new ideology of Positivism.[5] Moreover the German people were exerting a huge collective effort to bridge the technological and economic gap which still separated them from other, more advanced European nations. This effort gave rise, in turn, to enormous social and political tensions which finally exploded in the insurrectionary movements of 1848. The swift and bloody suppression of these revolts caused many German intellectuals to lapse into the deepest pessimism and to begin to think that nothing would ever change. The success enjoyed in this post-1848 period by the philosophy of Schopenhauer, and by Eduard von Hartmann's popularization of Schopenhauer, is representative of the mood of disappointment and apathy into which the entire middle class of the German-speaking countries tended to fall in these years. In such a cultural climate Emerson, whose thought was characterized by trust in the limitless potential of every human being and in a moral order guiding and governing the world, tended to be looked on with antipathy as an American who lacked all understanding of the way things were going in Europe (Simon 1937, 119–121). In 1858 Herman Grimm, the husband of Gisela von Arnim, published a German translation of a part of Emerson's essay collection *Representative Men*, specifically the essays dealing with Goethe and Shakespeare (UGS). In an essay from 1874 on Emerson, however, Grimm expressed his own awareness of how nigh-impossible an undertaking it was to try to gain an audience for Emerson's philosophy in this Germany of the post-1848 period. He tells of how a friend of his reacted to the news that he planned to translate Emerson into German: "As far as I am concerned [his friend had said] it is absolutely irrelevant whether you translate Emerson or not. I see that he is a poet, a poetic orator, but he is not akin to my nature. He is an American, he is no German and will never become a

German, no matter how well you may translate his works" (Grimm 1874, 439). As the response of Grimm's friend reveals, the greatest obstacle to the spread of Emerson's ideas in Germany was not a problem of language. The obstacle consisted rather in the enormous cultural difference. What is more, the markedly rhetorical, indeed rhapsodic style of Emerson's writing also made it harder for him to be accepted as a philosopher by the German reading public of these "sobered-up" years after 1848.[6]

The reception of the works of Emerson in Germany continued to be beset by these difficulties during the whole latter half of the 19th century. The situation changed completely, however, toward the end of the century, when there burst onto the cultural scene powerful "irrationalist" tendencies in art and literature.[7] Emerson was taken up and restored to significance by this fin de siècle generation as a defender of intuition and inspiration and as an antidote to the Positivism and materialism that had pervaded the culture of the immediately preceding decades. Many of the earliest comparisons between Nietzsche and Emerson were drawn on the basis of this stereotypical understanding of Emerson as a typical Romantic. Régis Michaud ([1910] 1924, 23), for example, in his 1910 book on Emerson, speaks of him as the theoretician of a superior type of man, a type of man guided by an "intuitive and emotional reason, a 'reason of the heart,'" and suggests that Nietzsche might have drawn from this Emersonian "superman" inspiration for his own *Übermensch*. Both the Emersonian and the Nietzschean "superman" were perceived at this time as placing high value on force and strength, defending the primacy of instinct over reason, and adopting an affirmative attitude to war and to the values and virtues of the warrior.

Besides as a defender of the primacy of feeling and intuition over reason, Emerson was also embraced, in these closing years of the century, as the representative of a "new humanism" (Francke 1907, 110), being classed here together with Kant, Schelling, Fichte, Goethe, Schiller, and Novalis. Different as these personalities may have been in terms of their specific goals and ideals, it was felt that they could be grouped together by virtue of their cheerful optimism and unwavering faith in humankind's value and potentialities. Their works were regarded as a fundamental resource for the eagerly awaited "spiritual awakening" of Germany, that is, the project of winning the masses back to spiritual hope and moral faith. "They believed in the future. They believed in eternity. They believed that humanity was slowly advancing toward perfection . . . and they derived their highest inspiration from the feeling that they themselves were workers in the service of this cause" (Francke 1907, 111–112). Emerson's deep interest in Man, his belief in moral freedom and the moral order of the universe, his pantheism, optimism, and confidence in the perfectibility of humankind were finally appreciated as responding to the spirit of the time. Even Emerson's style of writing was reevaluated. His works were now praised for their "simplicity and strong, direct appeal to the popular heart"—qualities sorely lacking in German literature, the typical form of which was, as this new generation complained, "thoroughly aristocratic" (Francke 1907, 113).[8] The writer Maurice Maeterlinck (1987, 270), in the preface to the German edition of *Representative Men*, defined Emerson as a master in the "science of human greatness, the most notable of all sciences," and welcomed his essays as a blessing at a time when people needed to believe that human beings are "greater and deeper" than they had hitherto shown themselves to be. "Without such a belief," Maeterlinck concluded, "we could not, nowadays, live" (277). Oddly, we do not see, in these years, attempts to point up affinities between the philosophies of Emerson and of Nietzsche; on the contrary, the former was often invoked as a kind of safeguard against the pessimism and cynicism of the latter. Emerson was seen as the founder of a "philosophy of joy, based on observations that are, for Nietzsche, rather sources of sadness" (Michaud [1910] 1924, 420). Whereas Emerson—so ran a view widely shared by his European readers and admirers during the turn of the century—was a philosopher of affirmation, Nietzsche was nothing more than "a pessimist and a sick man" (420). The cultural-philosophical watchword of these early years of the 20th century in Europe might, then, be expressed as "less Nietzsche and more Emerson" (Francke 1907, 126).

But one factor which tended to discourage the reception in Europe of the markedly "American" traits in Emerson's ideas, and thereby to hinder any really fruitful confrontation with the ideas of Nietzsche, was a deep-seated prejudice of European intellectuals which made them doubt the capacity of Americans to practice philosophy at all. Typical in this regard is an article authored in 1902 by the German emigrant to the United States, Georg Biedenkapp. While noting Nietzsche's abiding interest in Emerson, Biedenkapp (1902, 240) struggles to understand why Nietzsche should have found a "Yankee" writer worthy of interest at all: "The qualities which we admire in the Yankee are hardly such as to lead us to believe that these dollar-hunters, these shoeshine-boys-become-millionaires, these cattle-barons, or any other variety of Yankee 'self-made man,' would be capable of writing even a single line of philosophy." In other words, the general tendency not only in Germany but also in France was to believe that Nietzsche, for some strange reason, had overestimated Emerson's originality and that, if the former owed anything at all to the latter, it was, at most, the opportunity the American had given the German of reacquiring elements of his own German intellectual tradition. Behind this overt contempt for Americans expressed by many European intellectuals there doubtless lay a broader preoccupation with, in Biedenkapp's phrase, an impending "Americanization of the world [*Amerikanisierung der Welt*]" (241). Indeed, by this time, the United States had achieved an unquestionable superiority in many fields, above all that of technology, thanks to the invention of the steamboat, the railroad, the telephone, the telegraph, etc. German intellectuals observed with concern the increasing power and influence of the United States over the modern way of life and feared that, sooner or later, Europe would also have to cede its position of cultural leadership to this new society rising on the far side of the Atlantic.

1.3. Emerson and American Transcendentalism

At home, Emerson enjoyed a very different reputation. He was venerated already in his own lifetime as the first great American intellectual, as the man who had liberated his countrymen from cultural subjection to the mother country, Britain, and established a tradition of thought entirely native to the United States. In the words of Joel Porte (1999, 1), "it was Emerson who, in literary terms at least, really put America on the map." Or, as George Kateb (2002, 197) has put it, Emerson, like a sort of "American Shakespeare," gave voice "to almost all the general thoughts and recurrent sentiments that have since arisen in American culture." Nourished though it was by many different cultural traditions, Emerson's thought responded specifically to the demands of his country and his age. It was Josiah Royce (2005, 206) who said of him, "He was himself no disciple of the Orient, or of Greece, still less of England and Germany. He thought, felt, and spoke as an American."

Emerson received his education at Harvard Divinity School, which at that time was a seedbed for the spread of Unitarian ideas in America. In the words of the first historian of American Transcendentalism, Verner Louis Parrington (1927, 327), Unitarianism was a "humanistic religion, rational, ethical, individual, yet with deep and warm social sympathies." It was, Parrington went on, actually more an "attitude of mind than a creed" (327). Unitarians were critical thinkers who refused the very idea of dogma and claimed that the Bible should be studied in a rational spirit just like any other text. Respect for differences and freedom of opinion was one of the main tenets of their ethics. Unitarians also opposed the Calvinist dogma of the fundamental depravity of Man. They insisted rather on the perfectibility of human nature and accorded to each individual the recognition of certain natural, inalienable rights. Parrington tells of how, "under its discreet disguise, Unitarianism accomplished for New England what Jeffersonism had accomplished for the South and the West—the wide dissemination of eighteenth-century French liberalism" (322). William Ellery Channing was the foremost proponent of these new ideas. Channing insisted particularly on the potential inherent in each human being and described religious and spiritual life as essentially a matter of cultivating this potential, the disclosure of which should give to the individual the feeling of a "divine presence within" (Robinson 1999, 15).[9] Channing's preaching was extremely important in the formation of Emerson's mind and sensibility. Even after quitting the ministry, the younger man continued all his life to preach self-cultivation, self-perfection, and self-expression.[10] Emerson, however, remained thoroughly unsatisfied by the empiricist and sensualist philosophy on which Unitarianism was based. In 1832, during a long journey through Europe, he had had the opportunity to become better acquainted with the philosophy of Romanticism and German Idealism (Porte 1988, 71). The spread of knowledge about this philosophy in the United States dated from 1829, the year of the publication of Marsh's American edition of Coleridge's *Aids to Reflection*, and it was a Harvard contemporary of Emerson's, Friedrich Henry Hedge, who published a significant essay on Coleridge's book four years later, in 1833.[11] Just back that year from his lengthy stay in Europe, Emerson immediately understood that he could find in Hedge a spiritual and intellectual ally. Together with another Harvard contemporary, the minister George Ripley, the two young men founded a private association, the Transcendental Club. "What precisely we wanted it would have been difficult for either of us to state," Hedge observed, but "there was a promise in the air of a new era of intellectual life" (Cameron 1945, 199).[12] Those who gathered around these three founders of the Transcendental Club to read and discuss together the works of the new German philosophers were not, philosophically speaking, people of great erudition.[13] The academic training of even the best educated among them had consisted mainly in the theological studies required to become a Christian minister. None of the members had been educated as a philosopher. Hedge, who was the exception here, wrote, "How the name Transcendental . . . originated I cannot say. It certainly was never assumed by the persons so called. I suppose I was the only one who had any first-hand acquaintance with the German transcendental philosophy, at the start" (Cameron 1945, 199).[14] In the essay *Historic Notes of Life and Letters in Massachusetts* (1883), Emerson describes the cultural and social milieu in which he lived and worked and that saw the birth of the Transcendental Club. He explained that none of the members had intended to found a literary or philosophical school. It was a matter merely of friends who "from time to time spent an afternoon at each other's houses in serious conversation" (HNLLM, 534). Aside from these rare moments when they shared ideas with one another, he went on, the members' reading was "solitary" and had "the American superficialness" (534).[15]

The official organ of the Club was the journal *The Dial*. This journal was published from 1840 to 1844, with Margaret Fuller as its main editor, and Emerson, George Ripley, and Bronson Alcott all involved in the planning and management process (Robinson 1999, 20). It was host to a diverse range of writing: book reviews, translations, theological discourses, literary essays, as well as poetical texts. What all these texts had in common, however, was the emphasis they placed on religious and moral feeling.[16] The journal's editors were in fact fully aware that their potential audience consisted not of academics but of social and cultural reformers.

American Transcendentalists displayed, in general, little enthusiasm for German theoretical philosophy, whose mysteries most of them did not possess the skill, nor indeed the inclination, to fully penetrate. Whereas Kant's *Critique of Pure Reason* was essentially misunderstood as a kind of intuitionism,[17] the works of post-Kantian thinkers like Hegel were so foreign to the pragmatic American mind as to be considered nothing but "wonderful specimens of intellectual gymnastics" (Wellek 1965, 171).[18] Works that dealt with religious and moral issues, on the other hand, such as Kant's *Critique of Practical Reason* and certain writings of Fichte and Jacobi, were enthusiastically welcomed. One author who found immediate and unconditional approval among the Transcendentalists was Goethe, whose principal spokesman in the English-speaking world was Thomas Carlyle. "The pages of *The Dial* abounded in references to (Goethe's) ideas and writings. No author occupied the cultivated New England mind as much as he did" (Frothingham 1959, 57). Goethe's ideal of *Bildung*, in particular, was not long in enflaming the souls of the Transcendentalists, engaged as they were in the spiritual and cultural reform of their society. The Transcendentalists also absorbed with great interest the philosophy and literature of Asia, above all the sacred texts of Hinduism and Buddhism. They looked on these texts as moral authorities no less important than the New Testament—although (as has been argued) the Transcendentalists' assimilation of them was very often a selective one governed by the desire to find there confirmation of ideas and sentiments already present in the Transcendentalists' own Occidental culture (Versluis 1993, 5).[19] Nevertheless Emerson and Thoreau in particular were passionate readers of the sacred writings of the Orient and acquired, with time, a deep and thorough knowledge of them.[20]

Though drawing sustenance from these old and weighty texts, the character of American Transcendentalism was "rather spiritual and practical than metaphysical" (Frothingham 1959, 40). The contributions made by the Club's members to the development of culture consisted not so much in treatises or philosophical systems of special density or profundity as in a dedication to testing out, practically, new ways for human beings to live together inspired by new principles. "It was felt at this time, 1842, that in order to live a religious and moral life in sincerity it was necessary to leave the world of institutions, and to reconstruct the social order from new beginnings" (164). Certain Transcendentalists founded self-sufficient agricultural communities as a form of protest against the inhumane character of the capitalist mode of production and against the general tendency toward dehumanization displayed by the emerging "mass society" of the modern age. The first of these was George Ripley, who was ordained a Unitarian minister as a young man but quit the ministry some 15 years later, in May 1840, with the intention of finding "a more concrete means of reforming American society" than was afforded him by the sermons he delivered in chapel (Richardson 1995, 337). In April 1841 Ripley bought a dairy farm near West Roxbury in Massachusetts and founded the agricultural commune Brook Farm. This commune was intended not only to allow its members to directly enjoy the fruits of their own labors but also to establish more authentic relationships with each other and with the environment (340). Following Ripley's example, some 40 such cooperative communities were founded in New England during the 1840s, some of which were later adapted to fit the Fourierist model of social cooperation, which was just then being popularized in the New World by Fourier's American disciple Albert Brisbane. Henry James was later to look back somewhat sardonically, in his novel *The Bostonians*, on this "heroic age of New England" as an "age of plain living and high thinking, of pure ideals and earnest effort, of moral passion and noble experiment" (Porte 1999, 1). But despite their rapid and predictable failure, these New England social experiments profoundly affected the American way of life and laid the basis for a new political awareness (Frothingham 1959, 105). They marked the beginning of a new era, one in which the prosperity of the state was finally subordinated to the education of the individual (HNLLM, 529).

Emerson was the spiritual guide of this cultural and social revolution. Although he never openly espoused any particular political cause—with the one exception of the abolition of slavery—nor ever personally participated in any of the era's many experiments in communal living, he expressed and defended in his writings and public lectures the principles that inspired these political movements and revolutionary social projects of his day. It was Emerson, argues Kateb, who laid the cornerstones of the philosophy of democratic individualism. He "was the first to say what individualism means in a modern democratic society, and no one has done it better since" (Kateb 2002, xliii). Emerson celebrated "the age of the first person singular" (JMN 3: 70) and "the infinitude of the private man" (7: 342). In other words, Emerson shed light on how the reform of society and culture has necessarily to begin with the reform of the inward life and consciousness of each individual. Just shortly after his death John Dewey (1903, 412) anointed Emerson "the philosopher of democracy" on the grounds that, in his essays, he was the first major author to identify and celebrate the values and the qualities indispensable to democratic life. And this position of the supreme and exemplary "philosopher of democracy" is one that Emerson has retained, in the collective imaginary of his American countrymen and -women, right up to the present day.

1.4. The Hostility between the United States and Germany

In view of the absolutely central position that American intellectuals accorded, right from the start, to Emerson within—or rather at the very source of—their own cultural tradition, and seeing the decisive contribution they recognized him to have made to the furtherance of the culture of democracy, it is not surprising that these American intellectuals proved very reluctant to investigate even the possibility that Emerson might have exerted an influence on Nietzsche. Around 1900 Nietzsche was widely perceived in the English-speaking world as one of the sources of inspiration for the autocratic power politics pursued by Germany during the chancellorship of Otto von Bismarck. Any apparent similarities between the main ideas of Emerson's philosophy and those of Nietzsche's, then, tended to be dismissed by democratically minded Americans as misunderstandings arising from a merely superficial reading of the two authors, a kind of optical illusion the spell of which would be broken as soon as one probed even a little way into the respective contexts of the two bodies of work. The American poet and academic Lewis Worthington Smith, for example, in a 1911 study entitled "Ibsen, Emerson and Nietzsche: The Individualists," takes great pains to trace the commitment to "individualism" that the two latter writers appear to have in common back to aspirations that were in fact of entirely different kinds. Emerson's praise of "self-reliance," argues Worthington Smith, represents a development of the Christian principle of the equal dignity and worth of all human beings, but the emphasis Nietzsche placed on the moral autonomy of the individual was a matter, he continues, of glorifying individual strength and power and of justifying the indiscriminate use of these qualities to achieve one's own particular ends. Whereas the "self-reliant" individual set up as a model by Emerson is respectful of others even in his or her self-possession, Nietzsche's "select man," as Worthington Smith denominates him, is "a man who takes tribute of other men and lives gladly and freely and fully, obeying his instincts and ignoring the common priest-taught, slave-born distinction between good and evil" (151–152). The "mark of excellence" of this Nietzschean individual is "the power . . . to conquer others, to use men of less power for his own ends" (152).[21]

In the immediately subsequent period, that between the two world wars, Emerson and Nietzsche were even more tightly embraced as icons of their respective cultural and political traditions and thereby driven still further apart from one another in the eyes of those embedded in these traditions. "Both men became cultural icons, one sanctified and dismissed, the other idolized and demonized," writes Lopez (1997, 14). The idolization of Nietzsche is clearly seen in the Nazis' adoption of him as their spiritual precursor and guide. During the rise of Nazism and the Third Reich, many short collections of Nietzsche's sayings were printed, popularizing a distorted version of his thought, promoting militarism and physical toughness as supposed core "Germanic" values. The demonization correlative to this idolization we see in the Allies' war propaganda's direct reflection of these crude distortions, for example, the newspaper headlines in Britain and the United States which depicted Nietzsche as the source of a merciless German barbarism and as Hitler's favorite author. Certain phrases and formulations of Nietzsche's, such as "the Superman," "the blond beast," "master morality," and "the will to power," were torn, on both sides, out of context and turned into slogans supposedly illustrating Nietzsche's identification with German militarism and imperialism (Golomb and Wistrich 2002, 5). The fate of Emerson, as Lopez and others argue, was similar but also different. He too was sanctified within his own cultural tradition as the representative figure of a particularly glorious moment in American history, but this very sanctification meant his practical dismissal as a figure of living relevance. His image was tainted with an "an aura of bland impracticality, of something quite harmless and perhaps permanently outdated" (Nicoloff 1961, 5).[22] This tended to discourage and discredit still further any impulse that might have arisen to explore the possible connections between Emerson's thought and Nietzsche's since, in this period of ascendant militaristic supremacisms, Nietzsche appeared to be the least "outdated" and certainly the least "harmless" of philosophers. In short, then, this establishment in the early twentieth century of certain stereotypical images of the two thinkers rendered a serious consideration of the possible real connections between their ideas almost impossible. How, it was thought, could the "sage of Concord" possibly be significantly related to "the Nazi Chief's favorite author" (see Brinton 1941, 205)?

Particularly vivid testimony of how the cultural and political hostility between the United States and Germany hindered investigation into the real relationship between Nietzsche and Emerson is borne by the dramatic story of Eduard Baumgarten. Baumgarten had studied philosophy, economics, and history at the universities of Freiburg, Munich, and Heidelberg. Through his uncle Max Weber, who was at the time one of the most important voices of German liberalism, he had acquired a keen interest in American culture. This led him, once he had obtained his doctorate, to move to the United States, where he taught as a visiting professor at various institutions from 1924 through 1928. When he returned to Germany in 1929 he began the process of *Habilitierung* (qualification as a tenured professor) at the University of Freiburg, starting to write, as his required "*Habilitierung* thesis," a study of John Dewey under the supervision of the eminent Freiburg philosopher Martin Heidegger. Baumgarten and Heidegger worked together for several years and became good friends.

In the end, however, the project of Baumgarten's *Habilitierung* at Freiburg foundered. In 1931 Heidegger chose another of his students as his teaching assistant, and Baumgarten transferred to the University of Göttingen, where he finally achieved *Habilitierung* in 1936. It was at Göttingen that Baumgarten taught in 1933, a course titled The Intellectual Foundations of American Society (*Die geistigen Grundlagen des amerikanischen Gemeinwesens*). He then expanded the material into a two-volume book published in 1938. In the second volume of this huge study, dealing with the philosophical origins of Pragmatism, Baumgarten (1938, 81–96) devoted an entire section to Emerson and, in a detailed appendix, emphasized the many striking similarities between Emerson's thought and Nietzsche's. Baumgarten gave expression here to his conviction that no non-American author displayed a closer affinity to the American mind than Nietzsche and that, conversely, no American author stood closer to German culture than Emerson. In fact 1933 was also the year of Baumgarten's first attempt at gaining tenured professorship in Göttingen. This attempt was blocked, however, by a letter written by his former teacher and friend Heidegger to the president of the university's National Socialist faculty association. Heidegger claimed in this letter that Baumgarten was linked, by blood and upbringing, to a circle of liberal-democratic intellectuals and for this reason could never become a good National Socialist. Heidegger also maintained that Baumgarten lacked all real scholarly training and talent and that it had surely only been thanks to his ties with the Jewish professor of Classics at Göttingen, Hermann Fränkel—who had himself recently been expelled from the university—that he had secured a teaching position there at all. In conclusion, Heidegger insinuated that, due to his long stay in the United States, Baumgarten had become "Americanized." For all these reasons, Heidegger wrote, to grant Baumgarten's application for tenure would be very ill advised (see Farias 1987, 234–236; Ferry and Renaut 1990, 26).[23] Even the head of the National Socialist faculty association at Göttingen found Heidegger's letter too obviously malicious to be usable and set it aside. Some time later, however, in 1935, this letter was taken out of the files again and used to seriously endanger the continuation of Baumgarten's career at Göttingen.

In the end, Baumgarten succeeded in holding on to his university position and did eventually become a full professor at Göttingen (see Farias 1987, 236). He did not abandon the idea that Emerson had had an important influence on Nietzsche's thought, and in the hope of discovering some concrete evidence of this fact, he applied, in the winter 1938–1939, for a research stay at the Nietzsche-Archiv in Weimar. The Archiv's director at the time, Max Oehler, was skeptical of Baumgarten's thesis but nonetheless allowed him to consult the papers forming Nietzsche's *Nachlass*. This enabled Baumgarten to make a sensational discovery: not only had Nietzsche owned several books of Emerson's in German translation; he had also heavily annotated all of them on many of their pages. Moreover, examining Nietzsche's private notes, Baumgarten also became aware of two further important facts: first, that Nietzsche was an assiduous reader of Emerson not just in his youth but continued to frequent the American writer's pages almost without interruption throughout the whole twenty-five and more years of his active intellectual life; second, that Emerson's works had not just been the inspiration for a few well-turned metaphors but had exerted a decisive influence on the formation of all the most important concepts in Nietzsche's philosophy.

This amazing discovery, however, awoke hardly any interest at the time. World War II had just begun, and nobody wanted to hear about possible connections between the culture of Germany and that of America. In 1939 Baumgarten was able to publish only a short summary of his research. He postponed the publication of the entirety of his work on Nietzsche's marginal glosses and notebooks until after the war. Even this extensive study, however—published in German in 1956 under the title *Das Vorbild Emersons im Werk und Leben Nietzsches* (*Emerson as a Model in the Life and Work of Nietzsche*)—enjoyed little resonance among scholars.[24] Its sole effect within the German-speaking philosophical community was to prompt Stanley Hubbard, a student of the eminent German Swiss philosopher Karl Jaspers, to put Baumgarten's theses to the test by once again going over all the material on which Baumgarten had worked 10 years before. The conclusion Hubbard arrived at in his own study, published two years after Baumgarten's, was a harsh one. He claimed that Baumgarten had deliberately omitted to take account of those comments and underlinings appearing in Nietzsche's personal copies of Emerson's works which indicated disagreement, rather than agreement, with the views of the annotated author. Where these dissenting signs and comments were also drawn into the interpretative equation, argued Hubbard, the comparison of Emerson's positions with Nietzsche's revealed the philosophical positions of the two men to be, at bottom, irreconcilable with one another (Hubbard 1958, 173). This negative judgment was enough to discourage any further investigation into the Emerson-Nietzsche connection by German-speaking scholars from this immediate postwar period right up to the present day.

As for the scholarly community in the United States, Baumgarten's researches received not even the minimal and negative recognition that they received in the German-speaking world. His book is conspicuous by its absence, for example, from the lengthy bibliography of writings on and around Nietzsche that Crane Brinton included in the 1941 study of the philosopher that he wrote on commission from Harvard University Press. This is all the more grave an omission in view of the fact that Brinton specifically devotes a whole section of this bibliography to "Nietzsche's relations with other thinkers." If, while failing to mention

Baumgarten's work, Brinton had listed other publications addressing this same topic of Nietzsche's relation to Emerson the omission might be forgiven as an oversight. But the bibliography appears to systematically ignore all the several works in print at the time that dealt with this relation, suggesting that Brinton was deliberately exercising a kind of censorship, doubtless intended to protect Emerson's good reputation. Indeed during that whole period of American intellectual life in which the myth of Nietzsche as the inspiring force behind National Socialism—"the German monster Nitzky" (Marcuse 1951, 333)—had not yet been gotten out of the way, no interest was shown by anyone in exploring the possibility of there existing a connection between this "monster" and Emerson. Of all the intellectual biographies of Nietzsche that were published in the United States in the immediate post–World War II decades not a single one took account of Nietzsche's lifelong frequenting of the pages of Emerson. Emerson's name does not appear even once in the book that founded the American tradition of Nietzsche studies, namely Arthur Danto's (1965) *Nietzsche as Philosopher*, nor does it appear in Alexander Nehamas's (1985) *Nietzsche: Life as Literature*. In fact, up until the 1990s the only scholarly works published in the United States that included a (brief) mention of Nietzsche's relation to Emerson were Kaufmann (1950) and Carpenter (1953). As for American works of Emerson scholarship, those published between 1950 and 1980 either fail to mention Nietzsche at all or mention him only in passing.

The American work that is remembered as first raising a voice of objection and opposition to this myth of Nietzsche as a philosopher compromised by a complicity with Nazism is Walter Kaufmann's (1950) landmark study *Nietzsche: Philosopher, Psychologist, Antichrist*. This one book, however, was not enough to eradicate the cloud of prejudice obscuring Nietzsche's philosophy for most Americans. In any case, as far as our specific topic is concerned, even Kaufmann mentions Emerson only in passing. It is above all in his introduction to the American edition of *The Gay Science* that Kaufmann (1974) speaks of Nietzsche's reading of Emerson. Here he does justice to the love that Nietzsche surely felt for Emerson's works, citing the many positive remarks he made about them. Kaufmann remains skeptical, however, regarding the substantial similarities that many scholars who had studied this topic believed they had discovered between the two men's respective philosophies. "It seems to me," concludes Kaufmann, "that most of those who have written on this subject have exaggerated the kinship of these two men, and that the differences are far more striking" (11).

It was only with the publication in the 1970s and 1980s of the *Kritische Gesamtausgabe* (*Complete Critical Edition*) of Nietzsche's works, posthumous notes, and letters that it was revealed to scholars all over the world how serious a falsification of Nietzsche's philosophical writings had been perpetrated by his sister Elisabeth, the initial proprietor of the Nietzsche-Archiv and an anti-Semite and Nazi sympathizer.[25]

Once Nietzsche's image had been rehabilitated and his thought had become an important focus even of philosophy as it was practiced on the other side of the Atlantic, Cavell (1972) had the idea of using the relationship proven to have existed between Nietzsche and Emerson to point up the continuing importance of the thought of the by this time comparatively neglected Emerson. Deploring "American philosophy's repeated dismissal" or even "repression" of the thought of Emerson because of a style deemed overly "literary", Cavell (1990, 4) took up a contrary stance and argued that Emerson's work deserved a place at the very forefront of the late 20th century inasmuch as, like Nietzsche, Emerson had distanced himself from the traditional form of the "systematic philosophical treatise" and had thereby performed all the more successfully that task which Heidegger was, some decades later, to propose as the true task of philosophy, namely, "the task of onwardness."

Cavell's pioneering studies had the merit of finally bringing to the scholarly community's attention the need for a systematic confrontation and comparison between the two philosophies of Emerson and Nietzsche—a task that was finally tackled by Stack in 1992. *Nietzsche and Emerson: An Elective Affinity* is the first monograph in English devoted to the relationship between the two philosophers. Stack's aim in this monograph is the same as Cavell's in his: he wants to demonstrate how, through Nietzsche, Emerson exerted an important influence on European Existential philosophy (Stack 1992, VII), above all on Heidegger (see 30–31). Being in the uncomfortable position of having to set himself against a long tradition of failures or refusals to acknowledge the importance of this relationship, Stack does everything possible to demonstrate the proximity of Emerson's ideas to Nietzsche's—with the ultimate result, unfortunately, of departing too far from the philosophical identities of both authors. The Emerson that emerges from Stack's monograph is closer to that stereotype who has often stood in for Nietzsche than he is to Nietzsche himself: the great American essayist is portrayed here as an aristocratic elitist (see 267–268, 274) who replaces faith in God with a faith in "great men" (271). Stack's Nietzsche, conversely, emerges as an "Emersonized" Nietzsche, the advocate of a sort of naturalistic spiritualism (see 199), a "nature-mysticism" (198), a "voluntaristic idealism" (143), even the proclaimer of a "new religion" (36, 158). Many readers will be surprised, to put it mildly, by Stack's portrait of a Nietzsche who is not even as hostile as he is usually taken to be toward the hypothesis of the existence of God (see 15, 159). Stack, moreover, perpetuates the stereotypical image of the two philosophers that had become established by writers and commentators early in the 20th century. Still, in Stack's study, Emerson and

Nietzsche are portrayed as champions of a "philosophy of spontaneous life" (189), which envisages both freedom from social conditioning (see 187–188) and creativity itself (see 279) as being attainable by bypassing rationality and trusting simply to one's instincts.

David Mikics's (2003) monograph *The Romance of Individualism in Emerson and Nietzsche* is, to date, the latest word on the relationship between the two authors. Unfortunately, however, Mikics chooses to point out similarities between the philosophies of the two authors just in a general manner, without concerning himself with the question of exactly what Nietzsche had read and of exactly how he had received and interpreted it. While surely containing certain valuable insights, then, Stack's and Mikics's monographs do not meet the need for a systematic interpretation of Nietzsche's reception of Emerson based on that broad and deep knowledge of the thought of the two writers which we now possess and on the close philological examination of the texts available to us.

2

The Struggle against Fate

Regarding the question of the relationship between fate and freedom, Katsafanas (2016) has argued that Nietzsche passes from an account of human willing that is incompatibilist and eliminativist, which we find him propounding in his early and middle works, to an account that is rather compatibilist and is developed only in the late works—to be precise, in those composed after 1883. "Incompatibilism is the claim that the will is free only if it is causally undetermined," while "eliminativism is the claim that the will does not exist" (Katsafanas 2016, 138).[1] The compatibilist account of the will, by contrast, is one that insists that our actions can be at the same time causally determined and free (see 139).

According to Katsafanas, in the works of his youth and of his so-called middle period Nietzsche is of the view that the claim "X has a will" means "X has a capacity for reflective choice that is undetermined by prior events." And since Nietzsche holds that the will is always determined by something other than itself—that is to say, that it can in no case ever be undetermined—he is obliged, in the end, to conclude that the will simply does not exist. "He moves from the claim that we lack free will to the claim that we lack will" (Katsafanas 2016, 139). In the period of *On the Genealogy of Morality* and *Beyond Good and Evil*, however—so Katsafanas goes on to argue—Nietzsche abandons this way of seeing things and works out a more sophisticated account of the will, namely a compatibilist account. In other words, as Katsafanas reads him, Nietzsche's final conclusion was that determinism does not exclude the possibility that our actions are free. Clearly, such a change in position must have involved a redefinition on Nietzsche's part of the very meaning of the notion "freedom." The "free" agent becomes for the late Nietzsche (on Katsafanas's reading of him) no longer the agent whose action is undetermined or unconditioned by any prior event but rather the agent whose action is performed deliberately, that is to say, through a process of reflective choice. According to Katsafanas, the late Nietzsche considers that action to be "free" which fulfills the following two conditions: (1) it is deliberate, that is to say, it differs from mere "behaviour"

17

(Katsafanas 2016, 165), and (2) it is performed autonomously, that is to say, it is not informed by the "morality of custom" (171).

Here, however, I want to present a reading alternative to Katsafanas's. By examining the various stages of Nietzsche's reading of Emerson and by showing the influence that this exerted on Nietzsche's reflections regarding the relationship between free will and determinism, I will demonstrate that Nietzsche's redefinition of freedom as agency and his compatibilist approach to the problem of the will were already basically sketched out in the very earliest of his philosophical writings, set to paper when he was a 17-year-old Gymnasium pupil, and were already fully formed by the time of his writing *Human, All Too Human*. The thesis that I wish to demonstrate, in other words, is one to the effect that Nietzsche, during the entire course of his philosophical production, on the one hand denied the existence of a "free will" understood as an unconditioned and undetermined will—that is to say, as a "causa sui" (BGE 21)—while on the other hand redefining the concept of "freedom," understanding it in terms of agency: for Nietzsche, from the very beginning, the "free" action is the action that proceeds from a true volition, that is to say, from a deliberate choice that is guided by values that are truly the agent's own.

In this chapter I will also be offering additional evidence in support of Pippin's (2009) thesis that Nietzsche is interested in the question of human freedom not so much from a theoretical as from a psychological point of view. Nietzsche defines the feeling of being free as the feeling of acting in the absence of all coercion, that is to say, as the feeling that one's own power is preponderant over the powers inherent in all external circumstances. I will show how Nietzsche came already in the writings of his adolescence to define the feeling of freedom as a feeling of power and to recognize the compatibility of this feeling with the perception of necessity, that is, of the presence within one's life of certain immutable facts. Nietzsche achieved these initial insights, I will further argue, thanks to his reading of Emerson and then, continuing to draw on the thoughts of the American writer, went on to further develop his position on these questions in the course of his own subsequent philosophical production. In particular, I will show how Nietzsche's reading of Emerson influenced two key cornerstones of his philosophical thought, (1) the Eternal Return and (2) the "gay science" (*gaya scienza*), and how recognizing this Emersonian influence allows us to interpret both these concepts as expedients devised in order to intensify just this feeling of power or freedom.

2.1. The Young Titan

Nietzsche began reading Emerson in 1862. This reading of Emerson brought about an important shift in the young thinker's way of setting up and posing the whole question of the relationship between fate and human freedom. Before reading Emerson, Nietzsche had conceived of fate as a force external to and opposed to the human will. For this "pre-Emersonian" Nietzsche fate is something which manifests itself through unpredictable and uncontrollable occurrences, which then determine, in some important way, the subsequent course of our lives. The Nietzsche of this period assumes that this external force coincides with the action of a superior being, that is to say, with the action of a God. In other words, the hypothesis that freedom and the human will have limitations becomes a tolerable hypothesis for the Nietzsche of this period only where the decision regarding the course our life is to take is delegated to God. On first reading Emerson at age 17, Nietzsche abandoned this conception of fate as an external force and came to conceive of it rather as an internal one: as the entirety of the pressures which limits the freedom of our thought and will. This reconception, furthermore, clearly involves an exclusion, henceforth, of the formerly entertained hypothesis of a God who governs and directs our lives in our stead.

It is in taking his cue from Emerson that the young Nietzsche comes to understand that, although there are indeed present in our lives such things as "immutable facts," we are free to the extent that we do not suffer passively the effects of these facts but rather take some active position with regard to and, where necessary, against them. In other words, one is free or not depending on the extent to which one becomes the agent of one's own actions. Moreover, reading Emerson's essay *Fate* enabled Nietzsche to understand that the feeling of freedom is nothing other than a feeling of power, of efficaciousness, and that in order to achieve this feeling one must learn to look upon necessity as an ally rather than opposing it head-on.

However, Nietzsche took a step beyond Emerson here and laid the foundations for an account of the will which was radically different from that of the older writer but which was to be fully developed only in his writings from *Human, All Too Human* on. Emerson had adhered to the hypothesis that there existed two different planes or realms of reality: the natural realm, which he saw as being subject to determinism, and the realm of thought, which he held to be free. The human individual, Emerson had claimed, partakes of both these realms. That is to say, he or she is, on the one hand, subject to the limitations imposed by existing natural circumstances while being, on the other hand, free either to take up some stance in opposition to these circumstances and thereby remove them, or, if they remain irremovable, at least to formulate plans which will preserve a certain latitude of action even in the face of them. Nietzsche, however, reacting to Emerson's position, extended, already in those essays of his adolescent years composed immediately after his first encounter with the older writer, the logic of causal determinism right into the interior of consciousness itself and advanced the hypothesis that human thinking and willing are quite as subject to these natural and material limitations as human acting is.

2.1.1. What Is Fate?

The problem of the relationship between fate and human freedom had, in fact, begun to occupy Nietzsche's mind and excite his interest very early in his life. Already at the age of 15, while a pupil at the prestigious grammar school Schulpforta, Nietzsche had invited his childhood friend and schoolmate Wilhelm Pinder to discuss with him a topic that he was to continue to consider, throughout his life, to be one of the most important: "On God's Freedom and Man's" (KSB 1: 56, n. 62). Nietzsche sent to his friend a series of key questions around which he intended them to structure their discussion, asking Pinder to send back to him his thoughts on each of the issues raised: "What is freedom? Who is free? What is free will?" (KSB 1: 56, n. 62). These questions must have remained a central concern for Nietzsche during the following years, because he tackled them once again in 1861, in an autobiographical essay entitled *The Course of My Life* (*Mein Lebenslauf*). In this short piece of writing Nietzsche examines the effects upon his own life of a dramatic event that had occurred during his early childhood. His father had died very young, when Nietzsche was only four years old, from an inflammation of the brain. Nietzsche observed that this event changed his and his family's life forever. Whereas previously the world that he, his sister, and his mother had lived in had been one of joyful serenity, the world they now came to know was a world pervaded by pain and by an anxious sense of precariousness. From that moment on they were constantly tormented by the apprehension that something terrible could befall them at any moment. Observing that the lives of even the happiest and most fortunate people can change in an instant through some unforeseen calamity, Nietzsche asks himself if there exists some divine plan that governs the course of events, or if all that happens does so just by chance. Being most likely not psychologically prepared yet to defend the hypothesis of a world without plan or purpose, Nietzsche opted for the former position, concluding that there surely must be some "higher being [*höheres Wesen*]" who governs the affairs of this world "in a manner calculated to imbue all that happens with sense and significance [*berechnend und bedeutungsvoll*]" (NL 1861 10[8], KGW I/2: 257). For the 17-year-old Nietzsche, then, all that befalls us can still be seen as part of a plan which, however hard to fathom, has been thought out by someone somewhere with a view to our ultimate good.

The following year, more precisely in April 1862, Nietzsche once again took up these questions of the presence of fate in the life of human beings and of the nature of human freedom, in two short pieces of writing entitled *Fate and History* and *Freedom of the Will and Fate*.[2] As a guide for his reflections on these matters Nietzsche used the theses proposed by Emerson in the essay that opens the collection *The Conduct of Life*, a piece likewise entitled *Fate*.[3] Nietzsche had purchased this volume following the suggestion of his schoolmate Gersdorff (see KGB II/4: 544, n. 569), but in all likelihood it had been from one of their Greek and Latin teachers at Schulpforta, Diederich Volkmann, that both young pupils had first heard of Emerson.[4] How great an influence the reading of Emerson exerted on these two essays of the young Nietzsche can be immediately recognized from the fact that, in both, Nietzsche tackles the very same questions that he had tackled in his efforts of the year before, only now in a radically different manner. Above all, we see removed from the equation here any notion of a transcendent and benevolent "higher being" who guides the lives of mortal men and women; the question of the relation between the individual and his or her destiny is now resolved in purely immanent terms. As Stack (1992) has remarked, reading Emerson played a decisive role in the mental evolution of the young Nietzsche and contributed very significantly to detaching him from that milieu of Christian faith and piety in which he had been born and raised. It was surely in part the influence of Emerson's extremely original and idiosyncratic approach to the Christian religion (see section 1.3) that allowed the young Nietzsche to arrive at the conclusion that "the totality of Christianity is grounded in presuppositions," that is, that dogmas like "the existence of God, immortality [and] Biblical authority" are in reality extremely open to critical question (FH, 154).[5] Nietzsche, indeed, came already at this date to repudiate Christianity not just as a doctrinal but also as a moral system. In other words, he began to question whether Christian morality really was, as it claimed to be, the only possible valid morality for human beings. He now considered the possibility that this morality had made its appearance merely "as a consequence of an era, a people, a direction of spirit" (FH, 155): in short, that it was really only one among very many possible moral systems—and one, moreover, whose day had already come and gone.

The influence exerted by the encounter with Emerson can also be seen in the fact that, in these essays of the year 1862, Nietzsche redefines his notion of fate to make of it no longer a power external to the human being but rather one internal to him or her. Emerson, in a highly original manner, had used the term "fate" to mean not just the combined action of unforeseen and uncontrollable external events such as natural catastrophes but also, and indeed above all, a certain internal necessity, which he also called "temperament."[6] With this word "temperament" Emerson referred to the combined whole formed by an individual's specific predispositions and personal behavioral tendencies, part of which is innate—that is, inherited from the individual's ancestors in the form of a sort of genetic kit—and part of which is acquired, for the most part unconsciously, through education, family environment, and, more generally speaking, life in society. Ultimately, we can say that what Emerson refers to with the word "temperament" corresponds to the modern concept of "personality," that is, to the totality of the behavioral and emotional characteristics which distinguish one individual from other individuals.[7] Emerson claims that our lives are influenced, far more than they are by external events such as earthquakes or other natural disasters, by our natural tendencies or predispositions. It is these latter that lead us to react to external stimuli in one way rather than another, to prefer certain activities, to indulge in certain states of mind, etc. If external events appear to escape our control, these inner tendencies do so even more, since they transcend even our powers of (self-)observation. Emerson notes that few people are truly aware of the extent to which their personality influences their ways of thinking and reacting, their desires and their feelings. In other words, where no external obstacles to their actions are evident, people delude themselves that they are free, without realizing that the plans and wishes that they formulate are not in fact free choices but are conditioned by forces lying outside of their control.

Emerson's treatment of this topic of "interior fate"—of the influence exerted on our lives by our innate temperament on the one hand and by the traits we acquire from our environment on the other—drew, in part, on the researches of the German physician Johann Gaspar Spurzheim (1776–1832), one of the founders of phrenology, and on those of the Belgian statistician Adolphe Quetelet (1796–1874), who had envisaged a comprehensive science of "social physics." At the time of Emerson's writing his essay *Fate* these two bodies of ideas were very much in fashion in New England, and he was personally conversant with both.[8]

The German physician Franz Joseph Gall (1758–1828) was the first to attempt to derive inferences regarding an individual's psychology from the observation of his or her physiognomy. His pupil Spurzheim concentrated his attention particularly on the brain, maintaining that each convolution of this organ was related to some specific psychical faculty and that, this being the case, whoever carried out a careful and thorough study of the shape and dimensions of any individual's brain would be able, with a reasonable degree of certainty, to infer therefrom the level of intelligence of the individual in question, his or her predispositions, idiosyncrasies, etc.[9]

Quetelet attempted to demonstrate, through a statistical study of crimes, suicides, and marriages in different historical epochs, that environmental factors also strongly influence human beings' moral disposition. Both Spurzheim's doctrine and Quetelet's studies represented significant assaults on the idea of the freedom of the human will. They thereby also placed in question the whole notion of human moral responsibility, since this concept is intimately linked to the former. Although he rejected Spurzheim's and Quetelet's often simplistic correlations between physiognomy and environment on the one hand and personality and behavior on the other, Emerson did draw upon their doctrines in order to stress that an individual's physical constitution and the circumstances under which he or she is born and raised represent "givens" that cannot be altered and which inevitably exert an important influence upon that individual's life.[10] Such an observation can easily give rise to pessimism and discouragement. And Emerson, indeed, seems initially prepared to run this risk. "Ask the digger in the ditch," he writes,

> to explain Newton's laws: the fine organs of his brains have been pinched by overwork and squalid poverty from father to son, for a hundred years. When each comes forth from his mother's womb, the gate of gifts closes behind him. Let him value his hands and feet, he has but one pair. So he has but one future, and that is already predetermined in his lobes, and described in that little fatty face, pig-eye, and squat form. All the privilege and all the legislation of the world cannot meddle or help to make a poet or a prince of him. (CL, 5–6; FL, 7)

In *Fate and History* and *Freedom of the Will and Fate* (1862) Nietzsche deploys arguments fundamentally similar to those proposed by Emerson, summing up the ideas already expounded by the American author and adding some new ones of his own.

More than on the influences exerted upon us by our own physical constitution, Nietzsche's attention in these essays is focused on those exerted upon an individual's personality, without this individual's necessarily being aware of it, by his or her sociocultural environment—that is to say, by the family and society in which the person is born and raised. The values and beliefs involuntarily internalized during childhood imprison even the adult mind within forms and structures that are very hard to transcend. Nietzsche observes, in particular, how difficult it is to objectively evaluate Christian doctrine if one has grown up embedded in this culture: "Confined as we are from our earliest days under the yoke of custom and prejudice and inhibited in the natural development of our spirit, determined in the formation of our temperament by the impressions of our childhood, we believe ourselves compelled to view it virtually as a transgression if we adopt a freer standpoint from which to make a judgment on religion and Christianity that is impartial and appropriate to our time" (FH, 154).

Believing himself to be merely paraphrasing Emerson, Nietzsche poses the question of whether the course of our life is not already, at least in large part, decided beforehand just by the fact of our having a certain specific personality:

> What determines our happiness in life? Do we have to thank events whose whirlpool carries us away? Or is not our temperament, as it were, the coloration of events? Do we not encounter everything in the mirror of our personality? And do not events provide, as it were, only the key

of our history while the strength and weakness with which it affects us depends merely on our temperament? Ask gifted doctors, Emerson says, how much temperament decides, and what, in general, it does not decide. (FH, 155; see CL, 5; FL, 6)

In fact, Nietzsche had somewhat misconstrued Emerson here. In the essay *Fate*, the elder author had only cited the positions of the "gifted doctors" Spurzheim and Quetelet with a view to making of them a polemical target. The views cited in no way represented Emerson's own actual point of view.[11] In contradistinction to Spurzheim's and Quetelet's, Emerson's vision is not at all a deterministic one. It is rather a vision which conceives of the human individual as essentially a free being and which thereby also maintains the notion of moral responsibility.

2.1.2. What Is Freedom?

In the second part of the essay *Fate* Emerson explains that, although it cannot be denied that humankind forms a part of Nature, it must also be conceded that belonging to the natural order is not the be-all and end-all of human existence; humankind is also endowed with a spiritual power that raises us above minerals, plants, and animals. This spiritual power consists in the power of thought and volition, which, according to Emerson, are unconditionally free. In other words, Emerson advances the hypothesis that Man belongs on the one hand to the realm of Nature and on the other to that of Mind and Spirit. He thereby rejects the thesis of Spurzheim, whereby thought is determined by the shape of the brain; instead, thought is unconditionally free, as is the will. As to the theses associated with Quetelet, whereby environment determines our vision of the world, Emerson maintained that, thanks to the fact of our possessing a free faculty of thought and a free will, we are capable of acquiring an awareness of the conditioning factors to which we are subjected and of taking a position countervalent to them, thus succeeding in the end in formulating our own autonomous vision of the world. The fact of possessing a faculty of thought and a free will allows one to take up a position vis-à-vis the circumstances in which one finds oneself and the physical constitution that has fallen to one's lot—in short, vis-à-vis the given facts of one's life—and to exploit these given facts to one's own advantage. "The water," writes Emerson, "drowns ship and sailor, like a grain of dust. But learn to swim, trim your bark, and the wave which drowned it will be cloven by it, and carry it, like its own foam, a plume and a power" (CL, 17; FL, 22). One cannot remove the "wave" in question here from the equation, nor can one hope to directly oppose and overcome its force. However, by adopting the right "disposition," one can use this unopposable force to one's own advantage. "Fate," concludes Emerson, "is a name for facts not yet passed under the fire of thought—for causes which are impenetrated" (CL, 17; FL, 22). As soon as one begins to see necessity as an ally, the very notion of "fate" as a hostile power dissolves. Indeed, in a certain sense, one's own power of action is redoubled.

What was the significance, then, of Emerson's placing such emphasis, in the first part of the essay *Fate*, on the many serious material limitations to which each individual is subject in his or her life? In making these remarks Emerson's intention was simply to provoke his readers to self-reflection: he aimed to instill in his readership a reverential perception of the "terror of life." He had complained at the beginning of the essay, "Our America has a bad name for superficialness" (CL, 2). Americans, argues Emerson, wrongly think that to affirm that one is free is tantamount to denying that one is subject to any limitation.[12] In his own view, however, to deny the presence in one's life of certain immutable facts is an extremely dangerous attitude which exposes one to failures and frustrations that might otherwise have been avoided. To identify and accept necessity is, for Emerson, the first and indispensable step toward a true development of one's own power. Indeed, it is only to the extent that one understands that certain "givens" of one's existence are unalterable that one will strive to draw benefit and advantage from these "givens." The fact of possessing a certain bodily structure, or the presence of certain specific external circumstances, are not factors that can be simply and entirely negated. In order to feel oneself free, then, one must formulate one's plans in a manner that uses necessity to one's own advantage rather than making the hopeless attempt to oppose this necessity head-on. This applies both to external necessity and to internal necessity. One must seek to take advantage of external circumstances, but one must also select for oneself an occupation in which one's physical constitution is put to optimal use. Emerson's vision here in many respects resembles that of Plato in his *Republic*, which envisages a polity in which every citizen is glad to perform the role and function for which Nature has prepared them. In a passage from the essay *Power* that Nietzsche noted down in his notebook from 1863 Emerson explains that the secret of successful people is precisely that they know how to set themselves in tune with Nature, that is to say, with necessity: "The mind that is parallel with the laws of Nature will be in the current of events, and strong with their strength" (NL 1863 15A[5], KGW I/3: 228; see CL, 30; FL, 37–38).[13]

2.1.3. *Quisque faber fortunae suae*

In the essay *Fate* Emerson declares, "A man's fortunes are the fruit of his character" (CL, 22; FL, 29). In writing this, Emerson meant to convey the idea that a man of character—that is to say, a man endowed with a clear intellect and a strong will—is not a slave to his temperament but rather the architect of his own fortunes. As we have seen, however, in the essay *Fate and History* Nietzsche failed to grasp the rather fine distinction between "temperament" and "character" and, as is evidenced by the passage from this essay which I cited earlier, believed that he was merely reiterating a position taken by Emerson when he affirmed that the good or bad fortune enjoyed by an individual is dictated by his or her temperament. Nietzsche does grasp, nonetheless, the central point of Emerson's argument, namely, that the extraordinary correspondence between an individual's personality and the events that befall him or her is not at all a matter of mere coincidence. People who tend to see necessity as an ally and use it to their own advantage will succeed in attaining their objectives, while people who are not able to provide themselves with such an advantageous interpretation of what confronts them as necessity and as immutable fact will succumb to the overwhelming power of forces external to them.

Ultimately the young Nietzsche drew two important conclusions from his reading of Emerson's writings during his years at Schulpforta. The first was that to conceive of freedom and necessity as notions opposed to one another was a misguided approach to this philosophical problem that could only be counterproductive. To be free does not mean to act in the absence of all necessity; it means to actively take up and use to one's own advantage some position vis-à-vis necessity, instead of vainly trying to oppose it head-on. Nietzsche sums up this first important lesson he learned from Emerson in the following terms: "Free will is nothing but the highest potency [*Potenz*] of Fate" (FH, 156).

The second important lesson that the young Nietzsche drew from Emerson's works was that there is no such thing as misfortune. For people who have a certain disposition of mind there are no negative circumstances; such a person will prove able to turn all circumstances to his or her advantage. Summing up a passage from Emerson, Nietzsche writes in *Fate and History*: "The good is only the most subtle evolution of evil" (FH, 156).[14]

Nietzsche makes mention of Emerson's highly original approach to the question of fate in a note from July 1863: "Emerson . . . His American way of looking at things: 'what is good remains, what is bad passes away'" (NL 1863 15[17], KGW I/3: 144). Slightly reformulated as "what is good remains, what is evil passes away" (NL 1863 15[17], KGW I/3: 145), this maxim recurs in a note from the summer of 1863, in which Nietzsche even announces a plan to write a piece of music with this title (see NL 1863 15[17], KGW I/3: 145). It is easy to imagine the surprise and enthusiasm he felt on reading these pages of Emerson's, which envisage an outcome of the conflict between fate and freedom that is completely different from that envisaged by the European literature of the Romantic period. The Romantic hero is typically a figure who struggles to overcome the limits imposed by Nature while knowing all along that this struggle must end in defeat. This is the case, for example, of Manfred, the hero of Byron's eponymous dramatic poem; of the brothers Von Moor, protagonists of Schiller's *Robbers*, and (to delve back into the prehistory of Romanticism proper) of Goethe's Prometheus.[15] For all these heroes' undoubted worth, they know they have no chance of emerging the victors from their struggles in any usual, tangible sense of this term. The only victory they can possibly gain is a moral one; as regards the material facts of the situation, they inevitably end up defeated. Nietzsche felt a profound fascination for all these figures, whom he called "superhuman."[16] He was fascinated by their superior qualities but also, and above all, by their extraordinary ability to bear even the greatest suffering: it is with their heads held high that all these individuals go to meet the tragic destiny to which their high aspirations inevitably condemn them. In other words, the European Romantic hero carries off a moral victory over Nature: he proves his moral worth by struggling against the limits imposed on him by Nature, even though he is aware that he can never be victorious in such a struggle. The American pioneer depicted by Emerson, by contrast, does not struggle against Nature but rather, as it were, conspires with it—both with the objective Nature around him and with that internal Nature that is his own temperament—so as to seek out in every situation whatever usefulness and benefit can be drawn from it. The upshot of this is that, while the European Romantic hero, despite all his many excellent qualities, ultimately founders and dies, the American hero, despite the many limitations (external and internal) to which he is subject, successfully achieves his goals.

2.1.4. "Consciousness" and "Will" Critically Examined

Already at this very early age of 17, however, Nietzsche was able to discern a set of problems here to which Emerson had given little or no consideration. Emerson states that one's destiny depends upon one's own power of interpretation. Individuals of clear intellect and strong will do not let themselves be discouraged by the fact of their being subjected to certain immutable facts or circumstances but rather always succeed in finding in these something that can serve their own personal ends. At this point, however, Nietzsche poses the question of whether this ability to interpret events in such a way as to discover one's own advantage in them is an ability that can be developed to any degree to which the interpreting individual cares to develop it. In other words, whereas Emerson establishes that "so far as a man thinks, he is free" (CL, 13; FL, 16), Nietzsche probes further and asks if the thinking man is free to think whatever he wants. He questions, that is to say, the transparency to itself of Man's own consciousness, anticipating later psychological thinking by suspecting that the mechanisms which allow us to take the decision to formulate plans compatible with necessity may be rooted in the unconscious and thus lie far beyond our control. The following passage from *Freedom of the Will and Fate* seems almost to be a critique of Emerson's position: "*Freedom of the will*, in itself nothing other than freedom of thought, is circumscribed in a similar way to freedom of thought" (FWF, 156, translation slightly emended).

Two years later, in 1864, Nietzsche explored this theme still further in the short essay *On Moods* (*Über Stimmungen*).[17] This essay is plainly a work deeply marked and formed by Emerson's *Essays: First and Second Series*, which Nietzsche must have read just a short time before writing it. His enthusiasm for *The Conduct of Life* had evidently prompted him to acquire, shortly afterward, a copy of the *Essays: First and Second Series*, which had been translated into German some years earlier.[18] In his essay of 1864 Nietzsche above all takes up the principal theme of Emerson's essay *Experience*, in which the American writer argues that it is impossible for any individual, however gifted, to attain to an entirely objective knowledge of reality. Our perception of the world, argues Emerson, is always and necessarily mediated through our specific psychophysical constitution: "Inevitably does the universe wear our color. . . . As I am, so I see; use what language we will, we can never say anything but what we are. . . . And we cannot say too little of our constitutional necessity of seeing things under private aspects, or saturated with our humors" (E II, 45–46; V, 330–331; Nietzsche underlines the words "necessity" and "private aspects" [*Privatanschauungen* in the German text]). Construing the physiological notion of "humors" in terms of the effects they produce—namely, the different "dispositions" or "tunings" of the mental and spiritual faculties that the predominance of different "corporeal fluids" is supposed, by the "theory of humors," to induce—Nietzsche observes that our vision of reality is always strongly conditioned by such "humors." He then takes up a notion proposed in *Circles*, another of Emerson's *Essays*. This is the notion that nothing in Nature—be it in the Nature that surrounds us or in our own internal nature—is firm or fixed and that, for this reason, no vision of reality can ever be considered final and definitive. Adopting this key contention of Emerson's, Nietzsche argues that, since our mind is in constant evolution, so too must our "mental dispositions" be subject to constant change. Anticipating, in a precocious flash of intuition, philosophical results that he would fully arrive at only a good few years later, he describes the internal world of each individual as a kind of civil war between different *Stimmungen*, with these latter acquiring, and losing, and reacquiring by turns the power of command over the individual's mental and spiritual faculties as a whole. This means, in turn, that our vision of the world will change depending on which *Stimmung* shall have attained to a position of predominance in us at any given time. Nietzsche then makes use of an observation found in yet another of Emerson's essays, *Spiritual*

Laws, in which he maintains, "A man is a method, a progressive arrangement; a selecting principle, gathering his like to him, wherever he goes. He takes only his own, out of the multiplicity that sweeps and circles round him" (E I, 117–118; V, 107; Nietzsche underlined this passage and marked it in the margin with several vertical lines; see Appendix Figure 9). Emerson continues, "Over all things that are agreeable to his nature and genius, the man has the highest right. Every where he may take what belongs to his spiritual estate, nor can he take any thing else though all doors were open" (E I, 118; V, 108; Nietzsche underlined "may take . . . he take" and added two vertical lines in the margin of this passage; see Appendix Figure 10).[19] In his short essay of 1864 Nietzsche takes this general observation of Emerson's regarding the curious correspondence between the form of our interior being and the external events that befall us and transforms it into a description of the process by which we perceive reality—or, in other words, of the process by which we turn the raw data of reality into "experience." He observes that, when confronted with anything new to us, we instinctively tend to accept those aspects, and only those aspects, of the new phenomenon which go to confirm the *Stimmung,* or "disposition of mind," to which our cognitive faculties have already been "tuned." "The soul," writes Nietzsche, "strives to attract what is like it, and the current mass of feelings squeezes like a lemon the new events that impinge upon the heart, but always in such a way that only a part of what is new fuses with what is old" (Moods, 6). In other words, from all the great variety of incrowding sense data, the individual instinctively selects and appropriates just those data alone that he or she can most rapidly and easily process. And these will tend to be the data which display an affinity with the current "disposition" or "attunement" of the individual's mental and spiritual faculties. "Anything the soul cannot reflect," however, "simply does not touch it" (Moods, 6). It follows from all this that each individual will tend to create "reality" in his or her own image and that the perception of this reality made to resemble him or her will, in turn, confirm and reinforce the interior "disposition of mind" that created it.

Nevertheless, Nietzsche observes, our interior state, upon which our representation of reality depends, seems to escape our conscious control. He appears here to exclude the possibility of what is usually called "the will"'s acting to settle the "civil war" he sees being fought between the various "mental dispositions." On the contrary, he suggests, an individual's "will" is itself something that depends upon and is defined by the outcome of this "civil war." In short, then, we may say that the young Nietzsche, while on the one hand accepting Emerson's definition of freedom as agency and concurring with the American philosopher's characterization of the feeling of freedom as a feeling of power (or, more precisely, as a feeling of the preponderance of our own power over the power of the external circumstances vying with it), is nonetheless, in 1864, already beginning to lay the foundations of that critique of the metaphysical notions of the freedom of thought and of the freedom of the will which he was to develop to its full logical conclusion only some 10 years later at the time he was writing *Human, All Too Human*. In the meantime, he had also come heavily under the influence of Schopenhauer.[20]

2.2. The Freedom of the Human Mind and Scientific Determinism

Under the influence of this first reading of the works of Schopenhauer Nietzsche came to adhere to a causal determinism which he was to persist in professing throughout all the rest of his life. Schopenhauer understood human action as the product of interaction between "representations" formed by the intellect and what he called "character." He conceived of character as innate and immutable—but not in its immediately experienceable, empirical form. In order to preserve, within the thoroughly causally deterministic vision of the world that he elaborated, the notion of human moral responsibility, Schopenhauer was obliged to hypothesize the presence, beyond the immediately experienceable "empirical character," of an "intelligible character" as the (as it were) "uncaused cause" of the former. Although standing outside of the causal nexus in the usual sense, this "intelligible character" performs the role of "first cause," that is, of a cause that is itself "free" in the sense of "unconditioned." With its juggling of radically different connotations of terms like "character" and "cause," the construction has much about it of a metaphysical sleight of hand. But it nonetheless serves Schopenhauer's purpose of reintroducing into his causally deterministic worldview the element of human freedom and the notion of moral responsibility inseparably connected with this freedom.

Nietzsche embraced this scenario of causal determinism that had been elaborated by Schopenhauer, but, rejecting the obviously metaphysical notion of an "intelligible character," he drew the conclusion that freedom, in the sense of a completely unconditioned action, simply did not exist. A consequence of this was that he had also to exclude the notion of moral responsibility. Parallel to this, however, Nietzsche redefined freedom as agency and worked out a compatibilist account of this set of philosophical problems whereby freedom and scientific determinism were conceived as being able to coexist with one another. If it is assumed that the notion of human freedom that Nietzsche defended was not freedom in that sense of a totally undetermined and unconditioned "first cause" that had been propounded by Schopenhauer but rather freedom in the sense of agency, the apparent incompatibility between, on the one hand, Nietzsche's profession of a belief in causal determinism and, on the other, the exhortations to the individual, repeated many times throughout his work, to "create" himself or herself is suddenly dissolved. If what Nietzsche means by human liberty is not metaphysical indeterminacy but agency, it is not just possible but even necessary that the free subject "create" himself or herself, in the sense (in Nietzsche's own later formulation) of "giving a style to one's own character." While being, then, of the "metaphysical" view that the human will and the human faculty of thought must somehow elude that causally deterministic logic to which the objects of the natural world remain necessarily subject, and while holding a conception of "character" which was very different from that developed by Nietzsche, Emerson must nonetheless be said to have drawn to the attention of the younger philosopher certain important new avenues of reflection regarding the possibility of transforming the structure of one's own personality and, so to speak, "creating oneself."

2.2.1. The Abolition of Moral Responsibility

In his essay *On the Freedom of the Will* ([1841] 2009) Schopenhauer states, endorsing a view of Kant's, that every object of experience as such is embedded in a net of causal relations that entirely determines it. He distinguishes three types of causes: mechanical causes, which determine physical changes in inanimate objects according to Newton's laws of motion; stimuli, which determine the behavior of organisms devoid of knowledge, such as plants; and motivation, which is causality filtered through a knowing mind. While animal behavior is characterized by immediate and uncontrolled reaction, moved by representations of immediately present objects, human beings act in accordance with abstract representations, formed through reasoning. In other words, human beings are capable of deliberation; that is, they can develop arguments and draw inferences to orient their actions. This, however, does not mean that human beings are free to choose between different courses of action. The intellect does no more than form ideas of possible motives for action, that is to say, possible aims or goals to be pursued. These ideas exert effects, in their turn, upon the character, and it is the character, reacting to these effects, that initiates actual action.

Schopenhauer defines character as the essence or the nature of every existing thing or, in other words, as its "inner moving force" or "internal mechanism." The human character, specifically, he sees as a mixture of "three basic incentives [of human action], namely, egoism [*Egoismus*], compassion [*Mitleid*], and malice [*Bosheit*]" (Atwell 1990, 38). This mixture, however, is different for each individual; indeed it is this that renders each individual unique. This is what distinguishes humankind from the animals: animals have only the character of their species.[21] This means that all the members of a particular animal species will react in the same way to the same stimulus. Since human character, however, is in each case individual character, each human being, when exposed to the same "motive force," will react in a unique individual way, slightly differently from every other human being.

But even if the way that each human being reacts to a stimulus will tend never to be entirely identical with the way another human being reacts to it, each human individual's way of reacting will tend nonetheless to remain "identical with itself," since character, according to Schopenhauer ([1841] 2009, 70), is innate and immutable: "Beneath the changeable mantle of his years, his relationships, even of his knowledge and outlook, there lurks, like a crab in its shell, the identical and intrinsic human being, wholly unalterable and always the same."

Schopenhauer's position can ultimately be defined as strictly determinist, inasmuch as he holds that if one knows every internal and external detail of the situation in which an individual is called upon to act, then one will be able to predict with absolute certainty the way the individual in question will behave in that situation. By the time he wrote *Human, All Too Human* Nietzsche had also come to share this position:

> If one were all-knowing, one would be able to calculate every individual action, likewise every advance in knowledge, every error, every piece of wickedness. The actor himself, to be sure, is fixed in the illusion of free will; if for one moment the wheel of the world were to stand still, and there were an all-knowing, calculating intelligence there to make use of this pause, it could narrate the future of every creature to the remotest ages and describe every track along which this wheel had yet to roll. The actor's deception regarding himself, the assumption of free-will, is itself part of the mechanism it would have to compute. (HH 106)

In this aphorism Nietzsche adopts as his own the hypothesis of an absolutely deterministic universe. His philosophical stance recalls that of the 18th-century French philosophes whose works counted among Nietzsche's main reading matter in this period—for example, that of Laplace, who had famously argued that, were there to exist an intellect knowing all there is to know about the world as it exists at this present moment, this intellect would, by this same token, also be able to predict with absolute precision the future of every being, regardless of whether it be inanimate or animate. As Nietzsche states, however, this gigantic "machine" of necessary causes determining necessary effects comprises, as one of its cogs, precisely humankind's belief that our "free will" lifts us safely beyond the sway of any such mechanistic necessity. He considers it, therefore, to be one of Schopenhauer's great merits and distinctions as a philosopher that he rejected this commonly held belief and insisted that the actions of an individual follow always from his or her character with absolute necessity and predictability: "The insight into the strict necessity of human actions is the boundary line which divides philosophical heads from the others" (AOM 33). Nietzsche criticizes Schopenhauer, however, for having failed to draw from this insight what is, in fact, the sole conclusion that it is possible to draw from it, namely, that people cannot be held morally responsible for their own actions. To avoid drawing this conclusion Schopenhauer has recourse to a frankly metaphysical notion: that of an "intelligible character." Schopenhauer, following Kant,[22] maintains that the character of an individual can be considered in each case from two different perspectives. If we direct our attention to "the common feature of the entire series of [an individual's] actions," what we are considering is the individual's "empirical character," which is, for its part, entirely causally determined (Atwell 1990, 39). But if, on the other hand, we direct our attention to the inward mechanism of these actions in the sense of their internal governing law, abstracting from the effects that these actions may produce in the empirical world, what we find ourselves considering in this case is the individual's "intelligible character." The intelligible character plays in Schopenhauer's philosophy, as it had in Kant's, the role of a *prima causa*, or "free cause," that escapes natural determinism. And to this "free cause" that is the "intelligible character" there can legitimately be imputed a responsibility for the individual's having the "empirical character" that he or she has. In the last analysis, Schopenhauer holds the individual to be responsible not for what he or she does but for what he or she is—that is to say, for his or her own "empirical character."

Nietzsche, however, dismisses this Kantian-Schopenhauerian notion of an "intelligible character" as nothing but a "fable" (HH 39).[23] He holds, even against his once-revered Schopenhauer, firmly to the view that from the premise of the absolutely necessary nature of all human actions it is possible to draw but one conclusion: that "Man can be made accountable for nothing, not for his nature, nor for his motives, nor for his actions, nor for the effects he produces" (HH 39). As Nietzsche was eventually explicitly to declare in *Beyond Good and Evil*, everything in Nature is just a link in a chain that can never be broken. Nothing is "causa sui" (BGE 21), that is to say, a "free cause" of its own self. And for this reason no one is ever morally responsible for the actions they perform, since at no time would they have been able to act in any other way than they did.

2.2.2. Do People Change?

In the period of *Human, All Too Human,* in addition to questioning Schopenhauer's metaphysical notion of an "intelligible character," Nietzsche also contested his former philosophical hero's assumption that character was something unalterable. Like Schopenhauer, Nietzsche conceived of character as the distinctive bundle of instincts that makes each individual unique.[24] Unlike Schopenhauer, however, he held character to be, in principle, thoroughly alterable. Indeed Nietzsche thought of instincts not as immutable properties but as interpretative patterns acquired through interaction with the external world. Since they are acquired, he reasoned, they can also be changed or replaced. However, certain of these habits are so deeply rooted in us that a very substantial period of time—a period much longer than the lifetime of the average human being—would be required to replace these old habits with other, new ones. It is thus that there arises the false impression that character is immutable.

That the character is unalterable is not in the strict sense true; this favorite proposition means no more than that, during the brief lifetime of a human being, the effective motives are unable to scratch deeply enough to erase the imprinted script of many millennia. If one imagines an 80,000-year-old person, however, one would have in him or her a character totally alterable, so that an abundance of different individuals would evolve out of him or her one after the other (HH 41).

It was, in fact, in Emerson's *Essays* that Nietzsche found the model for this notion of a character in constant evolution, so multifaceted as to give the impression of containing in itself, so to speak, a whole multiplicity of different characters. This is surprising, given that the notion of character that we find in Emerson is closer to Schopenhauer's conception than it is to Nietzsche's. Like Schopenhauer, Emerson considered each individual to be endowed with an original essence, or specific nature, by which he or she was distinguished from every other individual. In the essay *Fate* he wrote, quoting Schelling, "There is in every man a certain feeling, that he has been what he is from all eternity, and by no means became such in time" (CL, 7; FL, 8).[25] This individual nature, however, needs to be discovered and, as it were, "acquired" even by the individual who has been endowed with it. Emerson explains that, at every moment, an individual's character is the result of the interaction of two mutually opposed forces: one's inner urge to express one's own original nature and the resistance offered to this urge by one's environment, that is to say, by one's external circumstances. On the one hand, by reason of his or her own most intimate nature, each individual feels an urgent internal need to "become who he or she is," just as the seed of a rose tends to become a rose. In other words, each person tends, by nature, to realize all the potentialities inhering in his or her own individual nature. On the other hand, however, the pressure of external circumstances hinders and restricts such self-realization. For this reason, with a view to surviving in such an adverse external environment, individuals develop "reactive" attitudes that do not express their true nature. These attitudes, although initially of a certain utility, become, in the longer term, obstacles to the expression of the individual's true self. As Emerson puts it, "Every spirit makes its house; but afterwards the house confines the spirit" (CL, 5; FL, 6). However, each time the internal urge prevails over external pressures, one can say that one has removed some inauthentic feature of one's own character and drawn a little closer to the expression of one's own original, distinctive nature: "The changes which break up at short intervals the prosperity of men, are advertisements of a nature whose law is growth. Evermore it is the order of nature to grow, and every soul is by this intrinsic necessity quitting its whole system of things, its friends, and home, and laws, and faith, as the shellfish crawls out of its beautiful but stony case, because it no longer admits of its growth, and slowly forms a new house" (E I, 102; V, 94).

In contrast to Schopenhauer's crab, eternally imprisoned within its shell, Emerson's "crayfish" abandons, as it grows, the hard carapace that had contained it and goes in search of a more spacious domicile. Expressed without metaphor, individuals' innate urge to increase their own power—that is to say, to bring to realization all that is potential in their own nature—prompts them to develop and evolve, and thus to rid themselves, from time to time, of old habits and beliefs in order to form new ones. According to Emerson the frequency of these "self-renewals" is proportional to the internal force of the individual. In the case of the most vigorous natures, such "self-renewal" is something that goes on constantly and without interruption.

> In proportion to the vigor of the individual, these revolutions are frequent, until in some happier mind they are incessant, and all worldly relations hang very loosely about him, becoming, as it were, a transparent fluid membrane through which the living form is seen, and not as in most men an indurated heterogeneous fabric of many dates, and of no settled character, in which the man is imprisoned. Then there can be enlargement, and the man of to-day scarcely recognizes the man of yesterday. And such should be the outward biography of man in time, a putting off of dead circumstances day by day, as he renews his raiment day by day. (E I, 102–103; V, 94–95; Nietzsche underlined the passage "in some happier mind . . . membrane" and marked it in the margin with a spiral; he also underlined "a putting off of dead circumstances")

In short, the process of the development of the character in Emerson takes the form of an evolution. This means that there exists a telos toward which this process is directed, namely, the full unfolding of one's own essence. This essence, for Emerson, is present right from the moment of the birth of each individual even if it remains unknown to him or her up until the moment when he or she gains control of it and brings it to manifestation. However, given the great disproportion between the power that individuals in fact express and the power they might potentially free from within themselves, Emerson presents the process of disclosure of one's true self as infinite. Each time one thinks one has reached one's limits—that one has brought to expression all one's potentialities—one discovers new latent powers the existence of which one had not suspected: "A man's power is hooped in by a necessity, which, by many experiments, he touches on every side, until he learns its arc" (CL, 11; FL, 13). In other words, Emerson's "true Self" can be considered a sort of regulative ideal toward which one's efforts constantly tend but which is never fully brought to realization. As Conant (2001, 234) very clearly explains, one's true self can be thought of as "a series of attainable selves, each, once attained, leaning toward a further unattained yet attainable successor." [26]

The Emersonian model of a self in continuous development, aiming and straining always to achieve higher and higher degrees of power, exercised a great fascination on Nietzsche. From the period of *Human, All Too Human* onward, it was taken up by him as an essential point of reference for his elaboration of his own doctrine on the nature of human character, one decidedly alternative to Schopenhauer's. It was largely inspired by Emerson that Nietzsche began to envisage the "self" of each individual as being composed of "a multiplicity of individuals." This "multiplicity of individuals" consists in the many different configurations of drives that each person's "self," at different periods of his or her life or even at different moments, can take on.[27] Nietzsche's conception here, however, remains significantly different from that of Emerson. For Nietzsche, what animates these changes and pushes them on is not, as it is for the American philosopher, some metaphysical essence which is striving to emerge into the light; rather, the animating force here is conceived of by the younger thinker as the tendency of every living form to adapt itself to its environment, or rather to try to dominate its environment. In a note jotted down on the reverse side of the front cover of his copy of the *Essays*, Nietzsche wrote, "Suck all chance events, and all situations in which you happen to find yourself, *quite dry*—and then move on to others! It is not enough to be just *one* man—This would be to demand of you that you become restricted! Rather, pass from one over into the other! [*Saugt eure Lebenslagen und Zufälle aus—und geht dann in andere über! Es genügt nicht, Ein Mensch zu sein! Das hieße euch auffordern, beschränkt zu werden! Aber von Einem zum Andern!*]" (NL 1881 13[3], KSA 9: 618; see Appendix Figure 1).

Nietzsche moved away from Emerson's position in two other important respects: first, as regards the notion that the process of the formation of human character is a quasi-teleological one in the sense of tending essentially toward some preestablished end; second, as regarding the specific way in which this process unfolds.

Nietzsche, as we have said, does not share Emerson's metaphysical presuppositions, namely, that the human individual has a "true nature" which he should bring to light from beneath all the masks and subterfuges imposed by society.[28] In other words, for Nietzsche, the process of formation of one's character does not presuppose the eventual achievement of a "final state" which would coincide with drawing upon some preexisting metaphysical core of one's own personality. Nietzsche's position is rather that the process of development of our character is one that never ceases.[29] Second, the forms and modalities through which this process of formation of character is initiated and brought to realization are conceived of by Nietzsche in more complex terms than those in which Emerson had envisaged the process. Nietzsche supposes that there is formed in the first instance, at the level of an individual's basic drives, a certain ideal, or schema, of the person that he or she aspires to become. This "schema of how we should be" can be, and has been, defined as an "ideal self" or "aspirational self" (Constâncio, Branco, and Ryan 2015, 26).[30] Since Nietzsche recognizes the existence of no organizing and governing force within the human personality higher than the drives themselves, he is obliged to characterize this "aspirational self" as emerging directly out of the drives as an expression or creation of them. We find him writing in a note from 1880, "Ideals of this sort [i.e., ideals bearing upon the person that we want to become] are the anticipatory hopes of our drives, and nothing else. As surely as we have drives, they also lay out in our imagination a sort of schema of ourselves, a schema of how we should be in order to satisfy our drives—this is idealising!" (NL 1880 7[95], KSA 9: 336–337; see Constâncio 2012, 130). Nietzsche goes on to explain that the schema elaborated at the unconscious level of the drives then becomes translated into a conscious purpose. This, acting as a catalyst, then causes the drives to assume a certain configuration. In other words, as Constâncio observes, the schema outlining the person that we want to be—what we have called our "aspirational self"—is "not only the guideline, but the moving force itself" (NL 1881 11[18], KSA 9: 448; see Constâncio 2012, 133).[31] Once the "aspirational self" has been formed—a self which, at a certain point, takes the form of a goal consciously present to our mind (i.e. we consciously recognize this self as the self that we want to become)—those drives which had previously been inculcated in us by society begin to seem to us to be something alien to ourselves and lose the force that they had formerly enjoyed within the general structure of our personality.

Consequently, the patterns of behavior motivated by these latter drives are abandoned. The same thing happens with old behavior-patterns, habits and tastes
each time our aspirational self undergoes a change and we begin to feel a call
to become something different from that which we had felt ourselves called to
become before.

2.2.3. Are People Free to Change Themselves?

Since he rejected the notion of a "free will" in the sense of a will that remained
entirely causally isolated, along, necessarily, with the idea of moral responsibility
that has always been inseparably connected with this notion, Nietzsche—in
sharp contradistinction to Emerson—could not and did not believe that the individual could be held morally responsible either for carrying out this process of
the development of his or her character or for failing to do so. In *Twilight of the
Idols* he declared, "The individual is a piece of fate, from the front and from the
back, one more law, one more necessity for all that is coming and shall be" (TI,
Morality as Anti-Nature 6).

The distance that separates the positions of the two authors on this issue can
be clearly grasped if one examines and takes careful note of the underlinings
and marginal annotations that Nietzsche added to the following passage in the
copy of the German translation of Emerson's *Essays* that belonged to his personal library:

> I say, do not choose; but that is a figure of speech by which I would dis-
> tinguish what is commonly called choice among men, and which is a
> partial act, the choice of the hands, of the eyes, of the appetites, and not
> a whole act of the man. But that which I call right or goodness, is the
> choice of my constitution; and that which I call heaven, and inwardly
> aspire after, is the state or circumstance desirable to my constitution;
> and the action which I in all my years tend to do, is the work for my
> faculties. (E I, 114; V, 104; Nietzsche underlined the words "partial"
> and "the choice of my constitution" and wrote in the margin of this pas-
> sage, "Good [*Gut*]"; see Appendix Figure 7)

For Emerson, the admonishment "Do not choose" is a rhetorical figure, with
which he means to say, "See to it that your choice is not made in a superficial way,
as if you could do anything and be anything at all that you might wish to do or
be; let your choice rather be guided by your constitution; choose the occupation
and the role that are best adapted to your particular nature, because it is in this
way that you will optimize your results." In other words, Emerson appeals to the

(free) will of Man and to Man's intellect, which is equally free, in order that these human faculties preside over a choice that adapts itself to and goes along with necessity rather than attempting to oppose it.[32] For Nietzsche, however, there exists no such thing as a free choice in the sense of a choice effected by some disembodied mind; what "chooses" is always the organism in its entirety.

Likewise very worthy of attention is the annotation that Nietzsche added, in his personal copy, to the following passage in Emerson's essay *Character*: "Character repudiates intellect, yet excites it" (E II, 61; V, 348). Emerson is saying here that the choices of persons of character appear not to be completely "rational" choices but rather choices guided by instinct, that is to say, by that inspiration which we receive when we enter into contact with our "true self" (see section 3.4.2). Also in this case Emerson is drawing a distinction and an opposition between, on the one hand, that false freedom which consists in mere arbitrariness—that is, in the conviction that one is able to do or to become absolutely anything that one might arbitrarily wish to become—and, on the other, that true freedom which consists in an attunement with necessity and which leads one to follow that vocation, and only that vocation, to which one's constitution has predisposed one. At the foot of this page Nietzsche wrote, "Character = Organism [*Charakter = Organismus*]" (NL 13[18], KSA 9: 621; V 348). Nietzsche seems to suggest here that the word "character" can be replaced by the word "organism" in the passage in question. By transforming Emerson's phrase in this way Nietzsche reads in it a confirmation of his own meditations on the so-called freedom of the will. When an individual makes a decision, Nietzsche seems to be suggesting, it is not any discrete metaphysical faculty that might be called "the will" that is making this decision but rather the organism as a whole.

2.2.4. Freedom as Agency

The theory of the mutability of individual character that Nietzsche elaborated, drawing inspiration from Emerson, allowed him also to develop and maintain a theory of human freedom specifically as agency. In fact, it is only if there exists the possibility of the structure of one's own personality being modified—what Emerson calls "temperament"—that there also exists the possibility of the power of agency's being developed—what Emerson calls "character." As Katsafanas (2016, 171) has well observed, whoever claims to be the agent of his or her own actions needs, in order to do so validly, to fulfill two conditions: (1) he or she must be able to lay claim to a single unitary self; that is to say, he or she must be acting not under the sway of this or that passing impulse but rather motivated by some steady, willed deliberation; and (2) he or she must be acting on the basis of values that are genuinely his or her own. In support of his thesis to the effect that the unity of the self is a necessary but not in itself a sufficient condition for defining liberty as Nietzsche understands it, Katsafanas cites such figures as Achilles, Agamemnon, and the Pre-Socratic philosophers. These figures, he argues, while certainly possessing unitary selves—that is to say, being entirely capable of dominating their own impulses—were still not genuinely free agents inasmuch as they still adhered to the "morality of customs" (Katsafanas 2016, 170–171). I am inclined to concur with this argument that, in order for an individual to achieve freedom in the sense of true agency, it is necessary that both these conditions be fulfilled. Nevertheless, it should be observed that Nietzsche began to reflect on the idea of free will as agency not just after 1883, as Katsafanas claims, but already in the published works, and in the only posthumously published notes, of his middle period—at a time, that is to say, when he was vehemently denying the existence of free will in the sense of a will that was causally undetermined. In a note from the summer of 1879, for example, we read, "This . . . freedom of the will . . . consists in a *definiteness* and in a *strength* of wanting [*ist* Bestimmtheit *und* Stärke *des Wollens*] . . . and in a mastery or will to mastery, and in a sense of one's own self [*sowie Herrschaft oder Herrsucht und Selbstgefühl*]" (NL 1879 42[25], KSA 8: 600). Although Nietzsche denies that human willing can be free in the sense of being undetermined and unconditioned, he declares nonetheless that the freedom of the will can be defined in terms of "*definiteness* [Bestimmtheit]," that is to say, in terms of a strength or a force of specific willing, which arises, in its turn, out of a mastery over oneself. But one is "master of oneself" only in the moment in which the self in question has become unitary. We know that Nietzsche understood the self to consist in a "social structure of the drives and affects" (BGE 12) or, in other words, as a particular relation or configuration of the drives one to the other. It is, then, in and only in the moment when the drives which compose the self begin to work in synergy with one another under the governance and guidance of a single commanding drive that one can be said to have acquired a "mastery over oneself" and thus to be acting with "steady, willed deliberation" in the sense we have just described. In the case, on the other hand, where this unitary command is lacking, one cannot be said to have a "mastery over oneself" and must be recognized to be acting only under the sway of, and as the plaything of, one's ever-shifting impulses (see Richardson 2009, 133–135). In a note dating from the autumn of this same year of 1879 Nietzsche adds further information about what it means to possess a free will, or, as he prefers to characterize it, "strong will": "He has a *strong will*; his intellect, his judgment, and his imagination tend to remain constant and identical with themselves across different points in time [*sein Intellekt sein Urtheil und Phantasie ist sehr gleich in versch(iedenen) Zeiten*]; he tends to say the same things, or something close to the same . . .—All this has nothing to do with the 'free will': he is *independent* of others, and therefore *free* (in the sense of dependent on his own self) [*er ist* unabhängig *von Anderen, also* frei (*als abhängig von sich*)]. The unfree, weak individual [*Der Unfreie Schwache*] is not sufficiently dependent on his own self and only for this reason is he so extremely dependent on others" (NL 1879 47[1], KSA 8: 617).[33] Already in this note, then, there is present the idea that the so-called free will consists in two fundamental characteristics: self-mastery (i.e. the ability to act with willed deliberation) and the ability to take decisions guided by one's own values and not by values inculcated in one by others.

Besides the new lines of approach that Emerson suggested to Nietzsche as regards the theory of the mutability of the character, the American writer also provided decisive stimuli to the younger author's philosophical explorations of such topics as how to attain moral autonomy and how to master and control one's own natural drives. I devote the whole of chapter 3 to Emerson's contribution to Nietzsche's treatment of the first of these topics. We shall look just now, however, at the influence he exerted on Nietzsche as regards the second of them.

2.2.5. Tyranny and Mastery

The ability to control one's own behavior—that is to say, the ability to act with a steady, conscious deliberation—is the indispensable precondition for an individual's living in society and conforming to the rules that constitute it. The unity of the self, then, is a goal to which the modern human being has, in a sense, already attained by means of the "hard training" of historical socialization (Richardson 1997, 140).[34] Nevertheless, Nietzsche strongly contests the specific manner in which this unity has been achieved. The ascetic ideal that lies at the core of Socratico-Christian morality is one which characterizes our animal drives as "evil" and prescribes their repression and suppression. But a self which achieves its unity only at such a price—that of repressing all its natural instincts—is, Nietzsche argues, an impoverished self which no longer possesses any real energy and can, therefore, no longer even envisage any high goals or objectives for itself, let alone effectively pursue these goals and objectives, overcoming the obstacles to achieving them presented by its environment. In a note from 1888 Nietzsche observes that the natural human passions for "power, love, vengeance and possession" (NL 1888 14[163], KSA 13: 347) have always been considered dangerous, and therefore as something to be rooted out and eliminated, by Socratico-Christian morality. Nietzsche contests the logic of this operation, claiming it to be "madness [*Wahnsinn*]" (NL 1888 14[163], KSA 13: 347), and observes that the effect produced by it has been to render the modern human being passive, cowardly, and mediocre.[35] Nietzsche proposes a quite different solution to the problem of how to achieve a self that is unitary and at the same time strong, namely: "taking into service the great sources of strength, those impetuous torrents of the soul that are so often dangerous and overwhelming, and *economizing* them" (NL 1888 14[163], KSA 13: 347). In other words, Nietzsche's preferred vision of the unitary self is one in which the individual's natural impulses are "dominated," not in the sense of being repressed or suppressed but rather in the sense of their being placed in the service of and constrained to work in favor of the achievement of the individual's principal goal. As Reginster (2003, 76) writes, "The dominant drive achieves mastery over the dominated drives not when it represses them or diverts them from the pursuit of their own specific ends.... It achieves mastery, rather, when it manages to integrate the distinctive pursuits and activities of the dominated drives ... [into] the pursuit of its own specific end. The dominant drive, in other words, allows dominated drives expression, albeit within the constraints set by the pursuit of its own end." The mastering self, in contradistinction to the tyrannical self, will prove to be a truly powerful self inasmuch as it will succeed in availing itself of the energy of all its drives.

The thesis that I want to advance here is that the reading of Emerson was of decisive importance for Nietzsche in his elaborating of this distinction between tyranny and mastery. Emerson considered the presence of vigorously upsurging natural instincts in human beings to be a precious resource for humans. In the essay *Power*, collected in *The Conduct of Life*, Emerson celebrates the "plus men"—men characterized by "a surcharge of arterial blood" (CL, 36; FL, 47) and "coarse energy" (CL, 34; FL, 44)—because he considered such men to form the best "timber" for the construction of the "great man" (CL, 137; FL, 179). It is clear that such vigorously upsurging natural impulses can also have destructive effects. Emerson compares the animal drives of Man to such elemental forces as steam, fire, and electricity. Where these are not properly channeled, they can clearly be extremely dangerous. But it is equally clear that it would be very foolish to renounce the use of them for this reason because, where the correct relation to them is established, these things can become the most precious of resources: "All the elements whose aid man calls in will sometimes become his masters, especially those of most subtle force. Shall he then renounce steam, fire and electricity, or shall he learn to deal with them?" asks Emerson (CL, 68; FL, 47). His conclusion is: "All plus is good; only put it in the right place" (CL, 68; FL, 47). In other words, the human ideal that Emerson envisages is that of an individual endowed with great natural energies, but with these energies perfectly under control.

Nietzsche shares this ideal and describes great men as those who have learned to control their own natural "affects" and direct them into the service of their self-chosen ends and goals. "Greatness of character does not consist in not possessing these affects—on the contrary, one possesses them to the most terrifying degree—but in having them under control" (NL 1887-188 11[353],

KSA 13: 153–154).[36] "The 'great man' is great owing to the free play and scope of his desires and to the yet greater power that knows how to press these magnificent monsters into service" (GM II 3). Nietzsche first attempted to give concrete form to this ideal in the portrait he drew of Wagner in the fourth of his *Untimely Meditations, Wagner in Bayreuth*. There Nietzsche describes the great artist who had hitherto been his personal hero in the following terms: "Each of his drives strove without limit, each of his talents, joyful in its existence, wanted to tear itself free from the others and satisfy itself individually; the greater their abundance, the greater was the tumult and the greater the hostility when they crossed one another" (WB 3). Very soon after this, Nietzsche was to revise his judgment of Wagner, who becomes, in the philosopher's later work, a key example of a *décadent* (CW 5). The ideal thereby personified—that of a man endowed with a vigorous and impetuous nature who retains nonetheless a perfect mastery over his own self—was thus transferred by Nietzsche onto his character Zarathustra.[37]

Nietzsche's Zarathustra, indeed, is the exact personification of what Nietzsche understands by mastery: he is imagined as an individual endowed with a great wealth of natural drives but possessing, at the same time, a perfect control over them. In the following passage he teaches what he has learned through his own experience of life and, speaking (appropriately enough) to the animals that he has assembled around him, states that every instinct can be put to some profitable use and that especially in those instincts and drives that traditional morality has stigmatized as evil and wicked there is hidden an enormous creative potential:

> Oh my animals, this alone have I learned so far, that for mankind their most evil is necessary for their best—
> —that whatever is most evil is their best *power* and the hardest stone for the highest creator. (Z III, The Convalescent 2; see also Z IV, On the Higher Man, 5)[38]

As we have seen, it was only many years after having first raised it in his two schoolboy essays *Fate and History* and *Freedom of the Will and Fate* that Nietzsche found himself finally able to draw from his reading of Emerson the elements necessary to respond to the question How is one to become the agent of one's own actions, as opposed to the mere plaything of one's temperament? In the works of his maturity, as we will see in the next section, Nietzsche developed also the second of the intuitive impressions gleaned by him as an adolescent reader of Emerson's *Fate*: the intuition to the effect that the feeling of freedom coincides with a feeling of power, which, in its turn, can be acquired thanks to a different interpretation of the apparently given facts.

2.3. Feeling Oneself to Be Free

According to Robert Pippin (2009, 69), Nietzsche is not so much interested in discussing the issue of determinism and free will from a theoretical point of view as in looking at these questions from a psychological perspective. Pippin's assumption about Nietzsche's preference for a psychological rather than theoretical focus of inquiry is confirmed by the space which is occupied, respectively, by theoretical and by psychological discussions in the body of his work as a whole. A substantial proportion of Nietzsche's reflections on freedom have as their object, in fact, not freedom itself but rather the psychological feeling of freedom. Nietzsche inquires into the questions of what this feeling consists in, when it emerges, and who feels it. One exemplary description of this feeling is to be found in a note from 1885:

> That we are effective beings, forces, is our fundamental belief. Free means: "not pushed and shoved, without a feeling of compulsion."
>
> N.B. Where we encounter a resistance and have to give way to it, we feel unfree: where we don't give way to it but compel it to give way to us, we feel free. I.e., it is our feeling of having more force that we call "freedom of will," the consciousness of our force compelling in relation to a force which is compelled. (NL 1885 34[250], KSA 11: 505–506)

Nietzsche defines the feeling of freedom (1) negatively, as the absence of the feeling of constraint or constriction, and (2) positively, as the consciousness of the prevailing of one's own powers over the power being exerted over one by external circumstances. In confirmation of this position, in *Twilight of the Idols* Nietzsche describes the feeling of freedom as closely connected with the feeling of overcoming an external resistance: "How is freedom measured, in individuals as in nations? By the resistance which has to be overcome, by the effort it costs to stay aloft. One would have to seek the highest type of free man where the greatest resistance is constantly being overcome" (TI, Skirmishes 38). In the last analysis, the feeling of freedom is reducible to a feeling of power that arises when one is conscious of performing actions that are effective (i.e., that achieve the goals to which they are directed).

Nietzsche identified three main obstacles to the emergence in the individual of the feeling of being free: the doctrine of scientific determinism; the past or, in other words, the fact that "the will cannot will backward" (Z II, On Redemption); and the inevitable presence of pain and suffering in human existence. I will show here that his reading of Emerson was an important determining factor in Nietzsche's working out of strategies that would enable him to overcome these three obstacles. As we have already seen thanks to our analysis of the essay *Fate*, Emerson believed that our interpretation of the facts which we encounter is fundamental to determining our attitude in the face of them, and thus also, in the last analysis, in deciding whether we will be able to perform, vis-à-vis these facts, actions that are effective. In short, Emerson called Nietzsche's attention to the fact that it is our interpretation of the facts that determines how far it is possible for us to act in effective ways, to feel ourselves to be powerful, and thus to feel ourselves to be free.[39]

2.3.1. Does the Belief in Determinism Limit Our Freedom?

One of the beliefs which appear to act most strongly to restrict the individual's feeling of being free is the doctrine of fatalism, or the scientific restatement of this doctrine which goes under the name of "scientific determinism." In aphorism 363 of his *Opinions and Assorted Maxims* Nietzsche observes that it has indeed, historically, been suggested that these doctrines have had harmful effects upon the minds and spirits of human beings. Specifically, it has been claimed that they have tended to render people fearful and passively resigned or have even instilled in them a certain wantonness. In other words, by informing people that they are not free (in the sense of not being exempt from causal determination), such doctrines, it has been claimed, have tended to seriously undermine people's personal feelings of power and given rise in these people to the notion that their lives have been and are dominated by forces external to themselves. Nietzsche, however, opposed this conclusion, arguing that the consequences that ensue from a person's being exposed to a doctrine always depend on the person, never on the doctrine: "*The fatalist.* —You have to believe in fate—science can compel you. What then grows out of this belief in your case—cowardice, resignation or frankness and magnanimity—bears witness to the soil upon which that seedcorn has been scattered but not, however, to the seedcorn itself—for out of this anything and everything can grow" (AOM 363). In this aphorism Nietzsche maintains that the doctrine of determinism—in support of which science appears, indeed, in recent centuries to have provided much incontrovertible evidence—can produce, nonetheless, very different effects depending upon the person who is exposed to this doctrine. Nietzsche makes use here, in fact, of a line of argument that he encountered in his early youth when reading Emerson's essay *Fate*. As we have already noted, it was Emerson's contention in this essay that things alter their aspects and meanings depending upon how we interpret them, and that how we interpret them depends, in turn, on our own internal state of mind and being. This applies also to the doctrine of fatalism: "the weak and the lazy" (CL, 13; FL, 16) see fate as an adversarial, indeed invincible power that is bound to thwart all their plans. Thus, they take the existence of fate as an excuse for feeling themselves to be powerless and remain, for this reason, passive and inactive. By contrast, peoples of a wilder and more passionate national character, such as the Turks, the Arabs, and the Persians, tend to look upon fate as an ally and to construe the operation of fate in the world as a legitimation for still more audacious action on the part of mortal individuals. Their motto is "On two days, it steads not to run from thy grave, / The appointed, and the unappointed day; / On the first, neither balm nor physician can save, / Nor thee, on the second, the Universe slay" (CL, 3; FL, 3). In other words, Emerson observes that a person of strong character will tend to derive from the belief in fate, should he or she hold it, not a feeling of powerlessness but, on the contrary, a feeling of redoubled power.[40] Nietzsche takes up this theme again in the aphorism from *The Wanderer and His Shadow* entitled *Mohammedan Fatalism*. Still embracing Emerson's position, Nietzsche argues that these two different attitudes in the face of fate have their origins in two different cognitive frameworks. Whoever conceives of the individual will and fate as two distinct entities counterposed to one another will feel themselves quite unable to counter or oppose fate in any way. It will seem to them that, whatever efforts they might make to combat it, fate, in the end, will always be victorious over them "so that the most reasonable thing to do is to resign oneself or to live just as one pleases." The individual, however, who sees fate as an ally will tend to feel invincible (WS 61). Finally, then, taking up that theme of Emerson's that had so fascinated him in his youth, Nietzsche succeeded in establishing that it is not the facts themselves (in this case the doctrine of scientific determinism) but rather our interpretation of these facts that allows us, or alternatively does not allow us, to act effectively and to feel ourselves to be powerful or, in other words, free.

However, as we have seen, Nietzsche also takes his distance from Emerson in one important respect. Whereas Emerson holds that an individual can freely change his or her mindset—that is to say, freely adopt one attitude or another in the face of fate—Nietzsche holds that both an individual's cognitive framework and the attitude that he or she adopts in this situation are functions of his or her organism in its entirety. For Nietzsche, then, the individual is not free to choose how he or she will react to the idea of fate: "The follies of mankind are just as much a piece of fate as are its acts of intelligence: that fear in face of a belief in fate is also fate" (WS 61). For Nietzsche, then, it will be the strong individual, the individual endowed with a fortunate configuration of drives, who alone will be capable of interpreting the doctrine of scientific determinism to his or her own advantage, of altering his or her attitude toward the notion of the presence of immutable facts in his or her life and thus of producing efficacious actions—something that will, in turn, cause the individual in question to feel powerful and, finally, free or, in other words, to experience himself or herself as "a piece of fate" (WS 61), as an ally of necessity. The weak individual, on the other hand, endowed with a less fortunate configuration of drives, will, framing and interpreting necessity as an adversary, be prompted thereby to actions that oppose necessity head-on and which are bound, therefore, to be inefficacious, with the result that this type of individual will feel powerless, and therefore unfree.

If we consider Nietzsche's philosophical production in its entirety, we see that, in the course of time, he systematically developed this theme that he had originally taken over from Emerson. As regards the question of Fate and free will, Nietzsche examined, in essence, four basic cases: the "strong" individual claiming to possess free will; the "weak" individual claiming to possess free will; the "weak" individual endorsing fatalism; and the "strong" individual endorsing fatalism. We are using the terms "weak" and "strong" here in a psychophysiological sense: we define as a "strong" individual whoever possesses a strong faculty of willing, that is to say, whoever has achieved a perfect mastery of his or her drives and has succeeded in availing himself or herself of all the energy of these drives, without sacrificing any one of them (see section 2.2.5). The result will be an organism that is powerful and in good health. The "weak" individual, by contrast, is the individual who possesses a weak faculty of willing. His or her drives conflict with one another, with the result that the organism as a whole is weak and sick.[41]

The first case, then, is that of the strong type who believes himself or herself to be free, the exemplary incarnation of which is the "sovereign individual" whom Nietzsche describes in *On the Genealogy of Morality*. This "sovereign individual" is "a man with his own, independent, enduring will, whose prerogative it is to promise—and in him a proud consciousness quivering in every muscle of what he has finally achieved and incorporated, an actual awareness of power and freedom. . . . This master of the free will . . . how could he . . . not realize that he has necessarily been given mastery over circumstances, over nature, and over all creatures with a less enduring and reliable will?" (GM II 2). The "sovereign individual" is the evolved form of the individual raised within the "morality of custom." This "sovereign individual" is distinguished by his ability to promise: an ability which involves not just making commitments but also being able to abide by them. In other words, the ability to promise requires "a strong inhibitive power, to refrain from acting immediately upon one's drives" (Richardson 2009, 139). The difference between the individual who lives according to the "morality of customs" and the "sovereign individual" consists in this: that the latter makes use of his or her ability to hold back and control his or her drives not in order to be able better to obey some heteronomous moral system or to conform more closely to existing social norms but rather in order to carry out and bring to fruition his or her own individual desires and the things that he or she personally considers important. But what these two human types have in common, nonetheless, is a belief in freedom as a *prima causa* (first cause). In other words, both human types believe that they possess an "I" superordinated to the "self" qua set of relations among drives; they also both believe that it is the essential task of this superordinated "I" to discipline and order this "self" consisting in mutually contending drives and that the "I" is unconditionally free to decide how it will perform this task. "The notion of an 'I' is the idea the new ability [i.e., the ability to restrain our drives] has of itself. . . . The capacity takes a first-person point of view: it calls and thinks itself 'I.' It also thinks various things about itself, many of which are false. For example, it takes itself to be the essence or core of the organism, something different in kind from the drives, and so on" (Richardson 2009, 141).[42]

Nietzsche explains that, since the feeling of being free is born from the perception of one's own power, the doctrine of the freedom of the will also had its origins among the ruling classes: "Here an experience in the social-political domain has been falsely transferred to the farthest metaphysical domain: in the former the strong man is also the free man" (WS 9). The doctrine of the freedom of the will was, then, subsequently usurped by the weak in order to defend themselves against the aggressions of the strong. Christian priests give to all expressions of weakness—such as humility, meekness, benevolence, etc.—the name of "virtue." Then, claiming that the individual is free to determine his or her own behavior, they call those individuals "good" and "virtuous" who display these characteristics expressive of weakness, while calling the strong individual "wicked" because he or she displays the opposite characteristics. The Christian priest thus instantiates, for Nietzsche, the second of the cases examined above: namely, that of the weak individual professing the doctrine of the freedom of the will. Instilling in the strong individual a sense of guilt about his or her own behavior, the Christian priest wishes to make this strong type turn the energy of aggressiveness against himself or herself rather than against the world. In other words, it is the aim of the Christian priest to save himself and to destroy his enemy—or rather (given that the Christian priest does not in fact possess any means with which to prevail directly over this strong type of individual) that his enemy destroy himself or herself. In reality, says Nietzsche in *On the Genealogy of Morality*, "it is just as absurd to ask strength not to express itself as strength, not to be a desire to overthrow, crush, become master, to be a thirst for enemies, resistance and triumphs, as it is to ask weakness to express itself as strength" (GM I 13).

In this second case—that of the weak individual who professes the freedom of the will—one observes a desire to compensate for weakness by the use of cunning. But in the attitude that Nietzsche calls "Russian fatalism" (EH, Why I Am So Wise 6) the feeling of weakness is joined rather with a will to give in and give up. This attitude corresponds to the third of the cases mentioned above: that of the weak type who endorses the doctrine of fatalism. This "fatalism of the weak" is "the fatalism without revolt that you find when a military campaign becomes too difficult and the Russian soldier finally lies down in the snow" (EH, Why I Am So Wise 6). The organism has become so weak that it is no longer capable of reacting, and there reaches consciousness no feeling but that of being completely overwhelmed by external forces.

As we have seen, this is not the only attitude that it is possible to adopt with regard to the doctrine of fatalism. There is also the fourth case: that of the strong type who endorses the fatalistic view. What the strong individual draws from this doctrine is the conviction of being inevitably destined to succeed. This human type possesses the ability to settle, automatically, into a mental disposition such that he or she can always extract some advantage from necessity. In other words, this type of individual no longer feels dominated by Fate but rather to be himself or herself a "piece of Fate." As Nietzsche was to specify in the works that followed *Zarathustra*, strong individuals who endorse fatalism are obviously themselves aware that their drawing of their own advantage from necessity is no free choice on their part but rather simply the consequence of their internal drives' being as marvelously well-organized as they are. This does not, however, mean that the strong individuals cease to take any personal credit for all that they achieve thereby; they continue, essentially, to do so, merely shifting the praise due for these achievements away from the "I" conceived in the narrow traditional sense of an acting consciousness over toward their "nature" in the sense of their organism in its entirety. Nietzsche writes, indeed, of himself in these terms in *Ecce Homo*, declaring, "I took myself in hand, I made myself healthy again: this is possible—as any physiologist would admit—as long as you are basically healthy. Something with a typically morbid nature cannot become healthy, much less make itself healthy; on the other hand, for something that is typically healthy sickness can actually be an energetic stimulus to life, to being more alive" (EH, Why I Am So Wise 2).

2.3.2. Redeeming the Past

There appears, then, to remain in the path of that strong individual who proves able to turn every circumstance to his or her own advantage just one single obstacle that limits his or her feeling of efficaciousness and thus of power. This, admittedly, seems prima facie to be an obstacle that is difficult, indeed quite impossible to surmount: it is the past. In the face of that which has already occurred even the strong individual must feel powerless, that is to say unfree, because nothing this individual can do in the present moment can ever possibly change or modify what has already transpired:

> "It was": thus is called the will's gnashing of teeth and loneliest misery. Impotent against that which has been—it is an angry spectator of everything past.
> The will cannot will backward; that it cannot break time and time's greed—that is the will's loneliest misery. . . .
> That time does not run backward, that is its wrath. "That which was"—thus the stone is called, which it cannot roll aside. (Z II, On Redemption)

The natural resentment of the individual human being toward his or her unalterable past seems only to be accentuated by that peculiar hypothesis which Nietzsche advances with his so-called doctrine of eternal return, namely, that the universe is so constructed that we must necessarily relive the lives we have lived, unaltered in any detail, again and again throughout eternity. It is not just by chance that Nietzsche chooses to call the prospect he conjures up here "the heaviest weight" (GS 341).

As Paolo D'Iorio (2000) has emphasized, this notion of "the eternal return of the same" is not an invention of Nietzsche's. It was a common *topos* of pessimistic literature which had traditionally been employed in order to show that human life is senseless and an intolerable burden on those who have to live it. Nietzsche had already encountered this notion in the writings of many authors of the 18th and earlier 19th century, for example in the work of the deeply pessimistic Italian poet Leopardi ([1834] 1983, 479) and in the famous journal of the Goncourt brothers (de Goncourt 1887, 193). But there can be no doubt that the formulation that must have made the strongest impression on him was that which is to be found in Schopenhauer's ([1819] 1969) *The World as Will and Representation*. Schopenhauer claims here that, at the end of his life, "no man, if he be sincere and at the same time in possession of his faculties, will ever wish to go through it again." He states resolutely, "If we knocked on the graves and asked the dead whether they would like to rise again, they would shake their heads" (I 59, 324). This argument of Schopenhauer's was taken up a little later by Eduard von Hartmann, his disciple and popularizer. Hartmann imagines a man who has arrived at the term of his natural life being asked by Death if he wishes to live this life over again. "The span of your life is expired," Hartmann has Death say to the man. "The time has come when you must become the prey of nothingness. Yet, it is up to you to choose if you wish to start again—in the same conditions, with full forgetting of the past—your life that is now over. Now choose!" Hartmann specifies that the man whom he envisages being addressed by Death in this scene is a man who has been neither especially fortunate nor especially unfortunate in life; he has benefited from a normal education and has enjoyed a social status such as not to have had to suffer any special material privations; he "is not exhausted, has not become blasé through excessive pleasures, and is not oppressed by any exceptional personal misfortunes." Hartmann (1869, 534) concludes nonetheless, "I doubt that our man would prefer to begin again the play of the life that has preceded this hour, instead of entering into nothingness." In aphorism 341 of *Gay Science* Nietzsche imagines not Death himself but a certain "demon" who one day addresses us and outlines for us the following possibility: "This life as you now live it and have lived it you will have to live once again and innumerable times again." At this point Nietzsche appeals to his reader, asking, "Would you not throw yourself down and gnash your teeth and curse the demon who spoke thus? . . . Or how well disposed would you have to become to yourself and to life to long for nothing more fervently than for this ultimate eternal confirmation and seal?" (GS 341). The entirely novel notion that is introduced by Nietzsche here is that despair is not, in fact, the sole possible reaction to the prospect of having to live the very same life as one has already lived, again and again throughout all eternity. Nietzsche imagines a type of human being who would be capable of reacting rather with a feeling of joy at this prospect. Who is this human type? To identify the type in question we must turn once again to the *Essays* of Emerson, in one of his several readings and rereadings of which Nietzsche was, in fact, engaged in this summer of 1881 during which he noted down the first outlines of his idea of the "eternal return of the same."[43]

A passage from Emerson's *Spiritual Laws* strongly recalls, both in its form and in its substance, this key aphorism 341 of *The Gay Science*. It is important, if we are to grasp all the nuances of the influence that this passage exerted on Nietzsche, to look at it in the form in which Nietzsche would actually have read it, namely, Fabricius's German translation of 1858: "Der Maßstab, den du selbst an dein Thun und Sein legst, wird sich immer daraus ersehen lassen, ob du dies Thun und Sein gern umgehen möchtest und deinen Namen verleugnen, oder ob du dein Werk an der concaven Sphäre des Himmels sichtbar werden läßt, wo es eins ist mit dem Umlauf der Sterne" (V 112–113). Literally transcribed back into English: "It will always be possible to gauge the measure that you yourself apply to your own doing and being by whether you aspire to avoid this doing and being and deny your own name, or whether, alternatively, you strive to make your work resplendent upon the concave sphere of the heavens, where it will become one with the revolution of the stars."[44] In this passage Emerson—at least in Fabricius's German rendering of him—maintains that the value that one ascribes to oneself and to what one does can be gauged by whether one hides oneself and one's works from others and seems ashamed of them or whether, on the contrary, one wishes all the world to see these works. Nietzsche heavily underlined this whole passage and wrote in the margin, in large letters, "Ecce Homo" (V, 113; see Appendix Figure 11; see Baumgarten 1956, 12).[45] Combining these suggestions originating with Emerson with the framing of the problem of the value of life envisaged by Schopenhauer and Hartmann, Nietzsche arrived at the conclusion that an individual's reaction in the face of the notion of the "eternal return of the same" can act as a moral litmus test distinguishing and separating the strong individual from the weak one.

Weak individuals, who find no value in themselves and in the life they are presently living, remain impotent in the face of the past, so that the idea of this past's "eternal return" is experienced by these individuals with despair, as the greatest possible accentuation of their powerlessness and of the defeat of their will. Strong individuals, by contrast, rejoice at the thought of the "eternal return of the same" because it is the instrument which allows them to "redeem" their own feeling of powerlessness in the face of that which is past and done. In that representation of time as something circular which the notion of the "eternal return" suggests, every event is intricately interwoven with every other in such a way that in order to affirm the present moment it is necessary to affirm at the same time the entirety of the past. In other words, the individual recognizes that all that which has occurred in the past has been necessary in order to lead him or her to "becoming what he or she is." "All 'it was' is a fragment, a riddle, a grisly accident—until the creating will says to it: 'But I will it thus! I shall will it thus!'" (Z II, On Redemption). Strong individuals, who ascribe value to what they are in the present moment and recognize themselves in their own actions, stamp, by envisaging the past to be inevitably connected and united to this present moment, the seal of their "creating will" on all that which has already happened or been done. These strong individuals thus attain to a feeling of freedom—that is to say, a feeling of the preponderance of the force of their will over the force of all external circumstances—in the highest possible measure. This is why the strong individual is able to respond to the demon with words that could not be further from desperation or despair: "You are a god, and never have I heard anything more divine" (GS 341).

2.3.3. Redeeming Suffering

The inevitable presence of suffering in human life—even in the apparently most leisured and pleasurable of human existences—tends to impose great frustration on the individual will and thus greatly to restrict the individual's sense of his or her power and freedom. What is needed in order to restore these lost feelings of power and freedom is not only that this suffering be made acceptable but that it be embraced and affirmed as something one positively wanted to occur. It is only by saying to every suffering "But I will it thus! I shall will it thus!" (Z II, On

Redemption) that one can restore the feeling that one's own power is preponderant over the power of external circumstances. This transvaluation of suffering
is, according to Reginster (2006, 185), precisely the ultimate aim of Nietzsche's
philosophy.[46]

In *On the Genealogy of Morality* Nietzsche goes so far as to maintain that what
makes Man flee suffering is not anything in suffering per se but rather only Man's
inability to give a sense and a purpose to it: "Man . . . does not negate suffering
in itself: he wills it, he even seeks it out, provided he is shown a meaning for it, a
purpose of suffering. The meaninglessness of suffering, not the suffering, was the
curse that has so far blanketed mankind" (GM III 28).

To redeem suffering does not mean to transform it into joy but rather to situate it in some longer-term perspective within which it acquires significance. We
can identify just what this perspective is by examining a note which Nietzsche
jotted down on the title page of his German copy of Emerson's *Essays*:

> The capacity for pain is an outstanding sustainer [*Erhalter*] of things,
> a kind of assurance of life: *this latter, indeed, is the thing that pain has
> sustained* [dies ist es, was der Schmerz erhalten hat]: pain is—to say
> the very least that might be said—as useful as joy. I laugh at the enu-
> meration of pains and afflictions through which pessimism aspires to
> prove itself—Hamlet and Schopenhauer and Voltaire and Leopardi
> and Byron. "If this is the only way that it can be sustained, then life is
> something that ought not to be!" you say. I laugh at this "ought" and
> turn rather toward life, to help bring it about that, out of pain, there
> grows as rich a life as possible—security, prudence, patience, wisdom,
> variety [*Abwechslung*], all subtle nuances of bright and dark, bitter
> and sweet—for all these things we are indebted to pain, and an en-
> tire canon of beauty, sublimity [*Erhebung*], divinity is possible only in
> a world of deeper and more variable and more diversified pain. That
> which prompts you thus to stand in judgment over life cannot be justice
> [*Gerechtigkeit*]—because justice would know that pain and evil—My
> friends! We must increase the world's pain if we want to increase the
> world's pleasure [*Lust*] and wisdom. (NL 1881 13[4], KSA 9: 618–619)

The argument by means of which Nietzsche undertakes to transform the
usual[47] human attitude toward suffering—namely, repulsion—is principally[48]
that which points up suffering's usefulness in forming the individual character.
Suffering—or rather the struggle that one must engage in order to overcome
the events or circumstances that involve it—represents a precious opportunity
for growth. Every type of suffering—be it the physical suffering caused by an
illness or a mutilation, or the psychological suffering resulting from the loss of

a loved one or from frustration or disappointment—triggers a reaction, aimed at overcoming the suffering in question, which tends in turn to awaken hitherto dormant energies and to cause new skills and abilities to develop. Moreover, by confronting painful and adverse circumstances an individual can acquire such important virtues as prudence, patience, and wisdom. History shows that all great men have passed through periods of great suffering; without the experience of such periods, then, much "beauty, sublimity and divinity" would never have come to be. This being the case, the condition of the person who has encountered and overcome situations of pain and suffering is greatly to be preferred to that of someone who has known no adverse circumstances at all.

The fact that Nietzsche noted down these thoughts specifically on the title page of his copy of the *Essays* shows how decisive a role the reading of Emerson played in the process of their maturation. It is in fact Emerson who first suggests to Nietzsche the above-mentioned motivations for carrying out a "transvaluation" of the experience of pain and suffering. First of all, Emerson insists that encountering adversity (1) prompts one to draw on resources that might otherwise have remained dormant. In a passage from the essay *Compensation* heavily underlined by Nietzsche Emerson declares, "Our strength grows out of our weakness. Not until we are pricked and stung and sorely shot at, awakens the indignation which arms itself with secret forces" (E I, 97; V, 89). Second, Emerson maintains that (2) one becomes aware of one's own strength only in combating adversity and overcoming it. In other words, overcoming adversity reinforces one's faith in oneself. In the essay *Power*, for example, Emerson declares, "The rancor of the disease attests the strength of the constitution" (CL, 33; FL, 43). Nietzsche takes up this same theme again in *The Gay Science*, declaring, "The poison from which the weaker nature perishes strengthens the strong man—and he does not call it poison" (GS 19).[49] By virtue primarily of these two arguments Emerson concludes in favor of the usefulness of suffering and of adversity in the formation of human character. He writes, "Every evil to which we do not succumb is a benefactor" (E I, 97; V, 89, heavily underlined and marked in the margin by Nietzsche).[50] It is impossible not to recognize in this observation of Emerson's a clear prefiguration of what has become one of Nietzsche's best-known dicta: the aphorism from *Twilight of the Idols* that runs "What doesn't kill me makes me stronger" (TI, Arrows and Epigrams 8). Obviously, as is emphasized by Katsafanas, the modification of our feelings with regard to certain specific experiences, such as the experience of pain and suffering, by means of some conscious process of thinking about them (i.e., by means of some different interpretation of these experiences which reconstrues them as useful to the individual in the long term) is not something that can occur in an instant. "I cannot simply decide, in a moment of choice, that I will henceforth experience suffering as alluring" (Katsafanas 2016, 157). Rather, as Nietzsche himself writes in *Daybreak* 103, such a modification of our feelings can only be the result of a long training and practice: "We have to learn to think differently—in order at last, perhaps very late on, to attain even more: to feel differently" (D 103; see also GS 58).

2.3.4. The Principle of Compensation and the "Gay Science"

The argument that pain and suffering are useful in forming the character is by no means the only argument that Emerson employs in trying to change the individual's attitude in the face of pain from one of repulsion to one of joyous acceptance. In the essay *Compensation* he also introduces an extremely powerful metaphysical argument. He goes so far as to hypothesize the existence of a moral principle, which he calls "the law of compensation." This law, he claims, governs the entire universe and infallibly compensates for every suffering and makes good every wrong. He elaborates this doctrine on the basis of Goethe's theory of the polarity of Nature: "Polarity, or action and reaction, we meet in every part of nature; in darkness and light; in heat and cold; in the ebb and flow of waters" (E I, 80; V, 73). According to Goethe, every natural phenomenon is but the half of a whole and, as such, heralds and invites its opposite. Thus, "inspiration already presupposes expiration . . . every systole its diastole. It is the universal formula of life which manifests itself in this as in all other cases. When darkness is presented to the eye it demands brightness, and vice versa: it shows its vital energy, its fitness to receive the impression of the object, precisely by spontaneously tending to an opposite state" (Goethe [1810] 1840, 15). Emerson combines the ideas which Goethe suggests to him here with other ideas which he derived from the sacred texts of the Oriental world, of which Emerson was a passionate reader. He was particularly inspired by the account of universal "cause and effect" which he found in these sacred books of the East and which stated that every single action that we perform represents a "cause" introduced into the entirety of the cosmos and that, sooner or later, some "effect" will and must necessarily ensue from every such "cause." The doctrine of "cause and effect" which Emerson encountered in these books, indeed, went so far as to teach that the following of effect upon cause was not even, strictly speaking, a "following" and that the latter was linked inevitably with the former because every cause's effect comes into existence already with and through it—that is to say, the effect, or effects, of every cause are always already in existence, just not yet perceptible to human beings.[51] Drawing on these two sources, Emerson hypothesized the existence of a moral principle that governs the entire universe and compensates for each negative fact through the emergence of a positive one: "For every thing you have missed, you have gained something else" (E I, 81; V, 74). Ultimately, Emerson's "law of compensation" appears to take the place of divine justice, with the difference that, whereas within the Christian perspective people will be punished or rewarded for their actions only after death, the law of compensation works with inexorable precision in the here and now. Emerson writes, "The dice of God are always loaded. The world looks like a multiplication-table or a mathematical equation, which, turn it how you will, balances itself . . . every crime is punished, every virtue rewarded, every wrong redressed, in silence and certainty" (E I, 84–85; V, 77). He insists that, if we only observe attentively enough the way things go in the world of our experience, we can acquire the certainty that there does indeed exist a positive force that directs the course of events toward the better. For this reason, we can and must be confident that everything that happens ultimately for our good: "The whole course of things goes to teach us faith. We need only obey. There is guidance for each of us, and by lowly listening we shall hear the right word. . . . Place yourself in the middle of the stream of power and wisdom which flows into you as life, place yourself in the full centre of that flood, then you are without effort impelled to truth, to right, and a perfect contentment" (E I, 113–114; V, 103). "All wrong [*Alles falsch*]" (see Appendix Figure 6), wrote Nietzsche in the margin of this passage in his personal copy of Emerson's *Essays*. In Nietzsche's view, the "law of compensation" was a metaphysical idea that Emerson owed to the harmful influence of German philosophy. In the note from the autumn of 1881 in which Nietzsche described Emerson as "the thinker richest in ideas of this our present century . . . but dimmed and obscured by German philosophy," he added, "Three errors 1) Compensation—" (NL 1881 12[151], KSA 9: 602).[52] We do not know what the other two errors were that Nietzsche imputed to Emerson, but it is clear that the notion of a cosmos morally regulated and oriented toward the good is not one that could possibly have met with Nietzsche's approval. For Nietzsche, the world is chaos: "Chaos sive natura: the world is not at all divine—even by human standards it is not rational, merciful, or just. We know it: the world we live in is ungodly, immoral, 'inhuman'" (GS 346). As Nietzsche sees it, if it does indeed prove possible in our lives to "make a virtue of necessity," or to transform a misfortune into a benefit, this is not due to some "compensating" metaphysical principle that is objectively operative in the universe but rather to the interpretative and reinterpretative capacities that characterize the strong individual. In aphorism 277 of *The Gay Science*, entitled "Personal Providence," he writes:

> There is a certain high point in life [when] the thought of a personal providence confronts us with the most penetrating force . . . now that we so palpably see how everything that befalls us continually turns out for the best. Every day and every hour life seems to want nothing else

than to prove this proposition again and again; be it what it may—bad or good weather, the loss of a friend, a sickness, slander, the absence of a letter, the spraining of an ankle, a glance into a shop, a counter-argument, the opening of a book, a dream, fraud—it shows itself immediately or very soon to be something that "was not allowed to be lacking"—it is full of deep meaning and use precisely for us! (GS 277)

But, taking his distance here from Emerson, Nietzsche goes on immediately to explain that the impression that all events turn to our advantage, far from demonstrating that the gods are interested in what becomes of us, or that the universe is governed by some moral law, is merely a sign that one's own "practical and theoretical skill in interpreting and arranging events has now reached its apex" (GS 277).[53]

Emerson's "law of compensation," indeed, has been criticized not only by Nietzsche but by many other scholars as the naive worldview of an incurable idealist or, even worse, as a deliberate closing of one's eyes in the face of social evil. Particularly representative is Santayana's ([1900] 1962, 36) judgment here:

> There is evil, of course, he tells us. Experience is sad. . . . But, ah! the laws of the universe are sacred and beneficent. . . . All things, then, are in their right places and the universe is perfect above our querulous tears. Perfect? We may ask. But perfect from what point of view? In reference to what ideal? To its own? To that of a man who, renouncing himself and all naturally dear to him, ignoring the injustice, suffering, and impotence in the world, allows his will and his conscience to be hypnotized by the spectacle of a necessary evolution, and lulled into cruelty by the pomp and music of a tragic show? In that case the evil is not explained, it is forgotten; it is not cured, but condoned. We have surrendered the categories of the better and the worse, the deepest foundation of life and reason; we have become mystics on the one subject on which, above all others, we ought to be men.

Nevertheless, a more attentive analysis of the essay *Compensation* reveals that Emerson's view is not, in fact, that certain miraculous, quasi-"providential" events intervene in order to really materially "compensate" us for the harms and losses that we suffer in our lives. On closer examination Emerson turns out rather to hold a view—one which he reiterates several times in this essay—that is very close to Nietzsche's after all, namely, that this "compensation" is achieved thanks to our capacity to interpret all that befalls us in a way that works ultimately to our own advantage, "tuning ourselves in," as it were, to the perhaps not immediately perceptible positive aspect of each event. Emerson writes:

> A fever, a mutilation, a cruel disappointment, a loss of wealth, a loss of friends seems at the moment unpaid loss, and unpayable. But the sure years reveal the deep remedial force that underlies all facts. The death of a dear friend, wife, brother, lover, which seemed nothing but privation, somewhat later assumes the aspect of a guide or genius; for it commonly operates revolutions in our way of life, terminates an epoch of infancy or of youth which was waiting to be closed, breaks up a wonted occupation, or a household, or style of living, and allows the formation of new ones more friendly to the growth of character. (E I, 104; V 96. Nietzsche added, next to the first sentence of this passage, three heavy vertical lines in the margin; he also underlined the words "guide," "genius," "waited to be closed," and "more friendly to the growth of character." In the margin beside this last expression he also added three vertical lines.)

An apparent misfortune, claims Emerson, can open up new life-prospects and, in the long term, reveal itself to be a positive event if and only if one makes of it a "guide or genius" for one's own subsequent action, or, in other words, if one makes the effort to seek out the positive things that might be derived from such seeming disasters. We may advance the hypothesis, then, that the "principle of compensation" was formulated by Emerson as a rhetorical strategy to increase the optimism of his philosophical audience as regards the possibility of being able to overcome adversity.

Such a hypothesis seems confirmed also by a journal entry from July 6, 1841, in which Emerson writes that, whenever negative thoughts insinuate themselves into his mind, he reminds himself that he is "a professor of the Joyous Science, a detector and delineator of occult harmonies and unpublished beauties, a herald of civility, nobility, learning, and wisdom; an affirmer of the One Law, yet as one who should affirm it in music or dancing" (JMN 8: 8).[54] Here Emerson establishes a functional equivalence between the One Law and the Joyous Science. The former, as we have seen, is the supposed cosmic law of cause and effect, the modern version of which is represented by Emerson's "principle of compensation"; the latter is an interpretative strategy inspired by the so-called *gaya scienza* of the Provençal poets, which Emerson presents to his readers also in the essay *Poetry and Imagination* that opens the collection *Letters and Social Aims*.[55] Here, he identifies "the Joyous Science" with the wisdom of the poet, or with the poet's specific way of looking at the world. Whereas the scientist, using his intellect, sees and forms a judgment about each fact in and for itself, the poet, by availing himself rather of his faculty of poetic imagination, is able to perceive the infinite number of links and connections that exist between all things. This means that the poet frames each fact in a perspective much broader than that of the scientist: a perspective within which negative facts such as the loss of a loved one or some other grave misfortune can be reinterpreted and subjected to, as it were, a transvaluation. This is why Emerson says, "Poetry is the 'gai science' [*Poesie ist die "heitere Wissenschaft"* in the German text]. The trait and test of the poet is that he builds, adds, and affirms. The critic destroys: the poet says nothing but what helps somebody; let others be distracted with cares, he is exempt. All their pleasures are tinged with pain. All his pains are edged with pleasure" (LSA, 19; NE, 36). When, in the journal entry mentioned above—worked, in subsequent years, in various more or less modified forms into several of his public lectures and published works—Emerson reminds himself that he is a "professor of the Joyous Science," he is appealing to the human capacity to see apparently tragic events in a different light with a view to bringing about the emergence from these events of their possible positive implications. By concentrating in this way on the positive things that can be drawn out of every set of circumstances, instead of merely sitting back and lamenting all that is negative, one will succeed in carrying out efficacious actions which will then give a positive orientation to the general course of one's life.

Nietzsche, since he did not have access to the *Journals* of Emerson, nor to any of the texts in which Emerson reutilized the above-mentioned brief passage, could, of course, not have been aware of this fact that Emerson envisaged an equivalence between the "principle of compensation" and the "gay science." If he had, *per impossibile*, been aware of this, he would certainly have judged the former of these two notions very differently, given the very positive reception he gave to the second. In a letter to his friend Rohde Nietzsche claimed that his sole inspiration for the use of the term "gay science [*fröhliche Wissenschaft*]" was the *gai saber* of the troubadours (KSB 6: 292, n. 345). Nietzsche certainly learned a lot about the troubadours from a tourists' guide to southern France authored by Theodor Gsell-Fels (1878).[56] Gsell-Fels describes how, in Provence during the early Middle Ages, poetry was an activity engaged in not just by a few select individuals but by the entire population. It was invariably accompanied by music, hence the common designation of poems as *canzoni*. These *canzoni* dealt with a whole range of themes and topics, sometimes taking the form of denunciations of social and political injustices and satirical critiques of the vices endemic within the medieval Church (13).[57] During the 1880s Nietzsche was also an assiduous and enthusiastic reader of Stendhal, whose writings would have confirmed for him that medieval Provençal culture was characterized by "the absence of any religion or sad legislation [*l'absence de toute religion ou législation triste*]" (Stendhal 1876, 165–166; see D'Iorio 2013). Nietzsche's hope was that this way of living—which had first proven itself to be possible in the brief efflorescence of Provençal culture during the early Middle Ages—could be brought back to life once again: "Perhaps laughter will then have formed an alliance with wisdom; perhaps only 'gay science' will remain. At present, things are still quite different, at present, the comedy of existence has not yet 'become conscious' of itself; at present, we still live in the age of tragedy, in the age of moralities and religions" (GS 1).

However, the fact that Nietzsche must very definitely have had in mind the "gay science" of the troubadours, as described in Gsell-Fels's book and in Stendhal's, when he was composing his own work of this name in the period 1881–1882 far from excludes the possibility that a decisive influence was also exerted on him by the specific notion of *la gaya scienza* that was to be found in Emerson. This notion, as we have seen, also drew his inspiration from the meaning of the term once current in Provençal culture (to which, indeed, the whole second part of *Poetry and Imagination* is devoted)[58] but conceived, in the last analysis, of "the Joyful Wisdom" as the use of one's own artistic powers not to create works of art but rather to transform one's own reality.

In the essay *Art*, which counts among those collected in the *Essays: First and Second Series*, Emerson maintains that the fine arts are, in fact, an inadequate outlet for the creative powers and energies of Man, which are, he says, more appropriately employed in the (re-)creation of himself and of his own reality. The role of works of art is simply that of training the senses to appreciate beauty and to awaken in Man an artistic instinct which must, then, be applied elsewhere than just in the arts.[59] In a passage heavily underlined by Nietzsche in his personal copy of the *Essays*, Emerson deplores the fact that this artistic instinct, in his own day, is being used in order to create imaginary worlds to which people flee when they find themselves disappointed by the worlds they really live in:

> The artist, and the connoisseur, now seek in art the exhibition of their talent, or an asylum from the evils of life. Men are not well pleased with the figure they make in their own imaginations, and they flee to art, and convey their better sense in an oratorio, a statue, or a picture. . . . They reject life as prosaic and create a death which they call poetic. They despatch the day's weary chores and fly to voluptuous reveries. They eat and drink, that they may afterwards execute the ideal. (E I, 301–302; V, 267–268. Nietzsche underlined the part of this latter passage that begins with "asylum" and wrote, in the margin, a large "Yes [Ja]!" as a sign of his approval. He also underlined "they make in their own imaginations" and "convey their better sense in an oratorio, a statue, or a picture." The phrase "They reject life as prosaic and create a death which they call poetic" is marked in the margin with a vertical line.)

"Would it not be better," Emerson asks himself, "to serve the ideal in eating and drinking, in drawing the breath, and in the functions of life?" (E I, 302; V, 268; Nietzsche heavily underlined this passage from "to serve" on). Emerson, in other words, hopes that Man's creative powers can be employed to transform himself and his own life. This passage too was heavily underlined and marked in the margin by Nietzsche, who must have agreed thoroughly with the American writer in this regard. In his middle period Nietzsche became extremely critical of the arts and of those who practiced them. Wagner's art, that Nietzsche, in his youth, had believed provided necessary moments of solace for individuals committed to the struggle to reform culture, had, by the period of *The Gay Science*, come to be condemned by him as a kind of narcotic for weak individuals. In this latter work Nietzsche writes that the art of Romanticism "tries to intoxicate its audience and drive it to the height of a moment of strong and elevated feelings" (GS 86). This audience is composed of "everyday souls who, in the evening, look not like victors on triumphal chariots, but rather like tired mules who have been whipped somewhat too often by life" (GS 86). The role of Romantic art, then, is to allow weak individuals to experience those courageous thoughts and strong passions that they are not in fact, in their own lives, capable of experiencing. It is, in other words, indeed the case that art here serves the purpose of replacing real life and diverting Man's energy and attention from it. Nietzsche tended now to place the artist in the same class as the priest or the metaphysician, namely, the class of those who aspire to create an unreal world so as to distract human beings' attention from the real world and make existence in this real world bearable for them. But by doing so, they succeeded only in devaluing this world: "Poets . . . deliberately set out to discredit that which is usually called reality and transform it into the uncertain, apparent, spurious, sinful, suffering, deceptive" (AOM 32), wrote Nietzsche in the *Assorted Opinions and Maxims* that went to form the first part of the second volume of *Human, All Too Human*.[60] It was probably also thanks to his readings in Emerson that Nietzsche, in the period of *The Gay Science*, reevaluated the role of art in human existence and gave expression to a revised judgment of the poets. This is because, with the term "art," he, like Emerson, no longer refers to "les beaux-arts" but rather, now, to the creative power that every human being possesses and which they must use to transform the reality in which they live.

In his *Attempt at Self-Criticism* (1886) Nietzsche explains very clearly what gay science signifies for him: "to look at science from the perspective of the artist" and "to look at art from the perspective of life" (BT, An Attempt at Self-Criticism 2). "To look at science from the perspective of the artist" means to make use of the resources that science has put at our disposal in order to create in the way that artists create. And "to look at art from the perspective of life" means that this artist-like power must not be employed as artists have tended to employ it—namely, in order to create illusory worlds—but rather to transform ourselves and the reality in which we live.[61] Nietzsche's "transvaluation," then, consists precisely in this: interpreting things differently, giving them new names, in such a way as to create, over time, new things or, in other words, new values and styles of life (see GS 58).

2.3.5. Amor fati

In the last analysis, then, we can say that the mature Nietzsche—that is to say, the Nietzsche of *The Gay Science* and *Thus Spoke Zarathustra*—looks back and reflects more deeply on those questions and considerations drawn from Emerson which had first caused to stir in him, during his adolescence, his philosophical vocation. As we have seen, in the essays *Fate and History* and *Freedom of the Will and Fate* Nietzsche had drawn two important conclusions from his reading of Emerson: (1) that the battle against fate can be won only by making ourselves "allies of necessity," that is to say, by interpreting all those events in life that we cannot change in such a way that they are seen to have occurred ultimately to our advantage and benefit, and (2) that, for this reason, there is no such thing as "misfortune" for the man of strong will; he will be able to transmute every event, however apparently unfortunate, into a benefit and an advantage.

Deepening and developing these philosophical considerations first suggested to him as a schoolboy, the adult Nietzsche arrives at the conclusion that the strong-willed individual, by reinterpreting the given facts, is capable of altering his or her own attitude toward these facts and thus of acting in an effective way. This gives rise to the feeling that the force of one's own will is preponderant vis-à-vis the force of environing circumstances, that is to say, that one is capable of overcoming all resistance to this will by the world around one. The feeling of personal freedom that arises in this way coincides with the feeling of being "an ally of necessity" or, as Nietzsche writes, "a piece of fate [*ein Stück Fatum*]" (WS 61).

The teaching that Nietzsche draws from Emerson regarding how to emerge victorious in the struggle against fate has taken the form, by the period of *The Gay Science*, of the following proposition: "I want to learn more and more how to see what is necessary in things as what is beautiful in them—thus I will be one of those who make things beautiful. *Amor fati*: let that be my love from now on! I do not want to wage war against ugliness. I do not want to accuse; I do not even want to accuse the accusers. Let looking away be my only negation! And, all in all and on the whole: some day I want only to be a Yes-sayer!" (GS 276). The passage from Emerson's *Essays* which Nietzsche placed as an epigraph at the head of the first edition of *The Gay Science* expresses this same notion: "To the poet, to the philosopher, to the saint, all things are friendly and sacred, all events profitable, all days holy, all men divine" (E I, 11; V, 9. Nietzsche marked the passage in the margin and also enclosed it in handwritten brackets; see Appendix Figure 3. However, when adopting this passage as an epigraph for his book, he pointedly omitted the words "to the saint"; see KSA 3.343).[62] But, as Cavell has rightly pointed out, no sane person could honestly affirm that all the things and people they encounter are excellent, benevolent, and perfect just as they are. Clearly, such a judgment needs to be understood as the result of an "interpretative choice" (Cavell 1979, 133). The choice in question is a choice to focus on the positive elements contained in every situation, event, or encounter, rather than on the negative elements, in such a way as to transform our own attitude to the situations, events, and encounters in question so as to produce effective actions on our own part.[63]

This attitude of *amor fati* is given personification by Nietzsche in the character of the eponymous hero of the book he considered to be the magnum opus among his published works. The name alone, "Zarathustra," being etymologically interpretable as "'golden star' [*Gold-Stern*],"[64] already proclaims its bearer's essential nature: just as the sun descending into the sea tinges everything with its own golden light, making it beautiful and precious (see Z, Prologue 1), thus does Zarathustra know how to see "what is necessary in things as what is beautiful in them" and thus to render everything beauteous. The inspiration for this image of a golden medium by which all that is rendered beautiful was certainly drawn by Nietzsche from Emerson. In a note written on the flip side of the title page of his copy of Emerson's *Essays* Nietzsche observed, "Be a plate of gold—then things will inscribe themselves upon you in a golden script" (NL 1881 13[6], KSA 9: 619). He is paraphrasing here the following statement of Emerson's: "We are the photometers, we are the irritable gold-leaf [*Blattgold* in the German translation] and tinfoil that measure the accumulations of the subtle element" (E I, 135; V, 123). If one is "made of gold," all the events that will come to imprint themselves on one will be as precious and beautiful as gold. Zarathustra, the "golden star," says of himself:

> I have become a blesser and a Yes-sayer, and for this I wrestled long and was a wrestler, in order to free my hands one day for blessing.
> But this is my blessing: to stand over each thing as its own sky, as its round roof, its azure bell and eternal security—and blessed is he who blesses so! (Z III, Before Sunrise)

Also in this case Nietzsche is stealing a beautiful image from Emerson, who had written that, from childhood on, our horizon is so limited that we suffer from the illusion of enjoying a prospect over the whole world. This illusion gave us a sense of security and made us feel protected:

In childhood, we fancied ourselves walled in by the horizon, as by a glass bell, and doubted not, by distant travel, we should reach the baths of the descending sun and stars. On experiment, the horizon flies before us, and leaves us on an endless common, sheltered by no glass bell. Yet 'tis strange how tenaciously we cling to that bell-astronomy, of a protecting domestic horizon. I find the same illusion in the search after happiness, which I observe, every summer, recommenced in this neighborhood, soon after the pairing of the birds. (CL, 142; FL, 185–186)

According to Nietzsche, this sense of protectedness can be reconquered if we become reconciled with necessity. Those individuals who welcome each event with the conviction that they can derive from it some benefit or advantage will never feel themselves threatened by anything that befalls them.[65]

Thus Spoke Zarathustra is so thoroughly pervaded with images drawn from Emerson's *Essays* that Gersdorff, after having read it, wrote to Nietzsche, "Now I am experiencing at first hand how one does not possess [some authors], but is rather possessed [by them]" (KGB III/2: 385, n. 201). Above all, these images describe the ability to "make a virtue of necessity," which, according to Emerson, distinguishes the strong individual. Zarathustra is distinguished in just this way, having learned to "run over and past the mud," to dance "as if on cleanswept ice" (Z IV, On the Higher Man 17), to use the destructive power of lightning for his own purposes (Z IV, On the Higher Man 7), to "drink from all glasses," and to "wash himself even with dirty water" when clean water is not available (Z II, On Human Prudence).[66] Zarathustra is a "wise man," indeed, but he is so specifically in the sense in which Emerson construes the notion of "wisdom." That is to say, he has the capacity to find enjoyment in what is, without tormenting himself with thoughts of what is not. As Emerson writes:

The whole frame of things preaches indifference. Do not craze yourself with thinking but go about your business anywhere. Life is not intellectual or critical, but sturdy. Its chief good is for well-mixed people who can enjoy what they find, without question. . . . Under the oldest, mouldiest conventions a man of native force prospers just as well as in the newest world, and that by skill of handling and treatment. He can take hold anywhere. . . . To finish the moment, to find the journey's end in every step of the road, to live the greatest number of good hours, this is wisdom. (E II, 35; V, 315; Nietzsche added a vertical line in the margin to this last sentence)[67]

Summing up, then, we may say that it is Emerson's specific construal of gay science—namely, as a strategy for appreciating and loving reality rather than fleeing from it—that makes it possible for the mature Nietzsche to work out his own notion of *amor fati*, a notion with which he finally responded to the question that had been tormenting him for twenty years: How can the individual emerge victorious from the struggle with fate? The struggle with fate is won by changing the mental and emotional attitude we adopt in the face of necessity: specifically, by "attuning ourselves" to necessity and thus enabling ourselves to perform actually efficacious actions which make us feel that the force of our will is a force preponderant over the force of the adverse circumstances which surround and exert their pressure upon us. Emerson writes that whoever attunes their own action to necessity has "the consciousness of being an agent and playfellow of the original laws of the world" (E II, 55; V, 339; Nietzsche marked this passage with lines in the margin). As a personification of Emersonian wisdom, Zarathustra does not feel himself to be a puppet either in the hands of a Christian God or of an inscrutable pre-Christian Moira; rather, he feels himself to be someone who is seated with the gods themselves at that "gaming table" that is the earth and who is rolling dice with them there (Z III, The Seven Seals 3; see Vivarelli 1992, 261–262).

2.4. Conclusion

In the last analysis, then, Nietzsche's and Emerson's theoretical views are completely opposed to one another.

First, Emerson's conception of character is a metaphysical one. For Emerson each individual is born into the world with a unique and unrepeatable nature of his or her own—even if these our unique natures come often to be obscured by traits which we have acquired in response to external pressures emanating from the society around us. From Emerson's point of view, to bring one's character to maturity means to free oneself from the traits through which this propensity to social conformism manifests itself, and to "be oneself," that is to say, reveal one's own individual essence.

Second, Emerson's conception of free will is also a metaphysical one. He conceives of the human will as unconditionally free because he assumes that thought does not at all belong to the same ontological realm as matter. The individual, although he or she is not free to choose his or her own nature, is nonetheless free to choose whether to develop his or her potential or, alternatively, to leave it undeveloped. In this way Emerson was also able to preserve the notion of moral responsibility.

For Nietzsche, by contrast, although each of us is born into the world with a particular personality, this personality is, in principle, susceptible of being altered in every single one of its various component aspects and elements. In other

words, Nietzsche's conception of character is a non- and indeed antimetaphysical
one. There is, for Nietzsche, no such thing as an individual nature qua metaphysical entity. However, since changes in a person's character are a function of his
or her reactions to changing circumstances, and since within the limited period
of an individual life it is only possible to pass through a limited number of such
changes in conditions and situations, the number of changes undergone by a
specific individual's character will likewise be limited.

Second, Nietzsche's conception of free will is likewise a non- and indeed
antimetaphysical one. For Nietzsche, that individual is free who acts with
deliberation and in a way that expresses values which he or she has decided
upon autonomously. He insists, however, that there exist no metaphysical
faculties, such as "the will" or "the intellect," which can be said to govern and
control our drives and thus to bring about the changes in our character. On
Nietzsche's view, the intentions which orient our actions and the conscious
thoughts which mold and shape our drives are not agencies superior to these
drives themselves. Rather, the "schemata" for the changes that we undergo are
"drawn up," as it were, at the subconscious level of our own drives. A "schema"
of this sort works upon our drives as their organizing and disciplining principle. Thus, in sharp contrast to Emerson, Nietzsche is not willing to recognize
any moral responsibility on the individual's part either for a decision taken to
perfect himself or herself or for a decision taken not to do so; nor does he recognize any moral responsibility in an individual's choice either to "attune" his
or her life-plans to necessity or to neglect or refuse to do this and to confront
necessity "head-on."

Both Emerson and Nietzsche, however, are more interested in discussing the
problem of human freedom from a psychological point of view than they are
interested in discussing it from a theoretical one. On this level the divergences
between the two thinkers are nowhere near so great. For both philosophers, to
feel free is not to feel unconditioned or undetermined but rather to feel powerful. In other words, the feeling of freedom coincides with a feeling of personal
attainment and achievement.

Nevertheless, also on this level there are differences between the positions
of the two philosophers. Emerson's claim is that whoever views themselves as
free will thereby become powerful. Or, in other words, believing that one has
the freedom to transform one's own circumstances will allow one to achieve
the greatest possible expression of one's own nature. For Nietzsche, it is rather
the contrary to this that is the case: it is the powerful individual who feels
himself or herself to be free; that is to say, it is the powerful individual who
feels the force of his or her will to be prevalent over the force of resistance that
proceeds from the adverse circumstances that he or she encounters. As soon
as one finds oneself capable of interpreting necessity to one's own advantage,

the fact of not being "free" in the sense of absolutely materially undetermined and unconditioned—or of not being, in other words, a metaphysical causa sui—no longer diminishes in the least one's feeling of personal attainment and achievement. Therefore, it does not, in the last analysis, diminish in the least one's feeling of freedom.

Self-Reliance as Moral Autonomy and Original Self-Expression

3.1. Overcoming Morality

3.1.1. Why Nietzsche Is an Immoralist

In *Ecce Homo* Nietzsche calls himself an "immoralist" or, to be more precise "the first immoralist" in human history (EH, Why I Write Such Good Books, The Untimely Ones 2), as if to suggest that, following his example, other such "immoralists" will soon emerge. However, it cannot be said of Nietzsche that he rejects morality tout court. Rather, he rejects a certain type of morality: one which succeeded so well, for such a long time, in imposing itself as the dominant type that the impression arose, in the minds of many, that there could not possibly exist any other type: "Morality in Europe today is herd animal morality—in other words, as we understand it, merely one type of human morality beside which, before which, and after which many other types, above all higher moralities, are, or ought to be, possible. But this morality resists such a 'possibility,' such an 'ought' with all its power: it says stubbornly and inexorably, 'I am morality itself, and nothing besides is morality'" (BGE 202). Nietzsche coined this term "herd animal morality" in his book *Daybreak* after having read a work entitled *The Origin of the Moral Sensations* (Der Ursprung der moralischen Empfindungen, 1877) authored by his personal friend Paul Rée. As Robin Small (2003, xxxv) has observed, it is the main argument of Rée's book that is summed up and presented by Nietzsche in aphorism 40 of that book of Nietzsche's own that immediately preceded *Daybreak*, that third part of *Human, All Too Human* published in 1880 as *The Wanderer and His Shadow*:

> The same actions that within primitive society were first performed with a view to common utility have later been performed by other generations from other motives: out of fear or reverence of those who demanded and recommended them, or out of habit, because one had

seen them done all around one from childhood on, or out of benevolence, because their performance generally produced joy and ap-
proving faces, or out of vanity, because they were commended. Such
actions . . . are called moral actions. (WS 40)

This type of morality was to be defined by Nietzsche as the "morality of customs," since certain actions are here declared to be "moral" simply out of habit,
with not even the question of their usefulness being posed by anyone any longer.
Nietzsche's project, then, initiated in the works of the so-called middle period,
such as *Human, All Too Human* and *Daybreak*, and pursued in such late works
as *On the Genealogy of Morality* and *Beyond Good and Evil*, is precisely that of
shedding light on this usefulness. Put more plainly, what Nietzsche wants to do
is shed light on the specific conditions of existence which that type of morality,
which, as we have said, tends today to be looked on as the sole possible morality,
or as "morality" per se, in fact came into existence in order to satisfy. In aphorism
103 of *Daybreak* Nietzsche makes it clear that what he contests is not so much
the values that are affirmed by this morality as the fact that these values do not
arise out of a personal moral search carried out by each individual for himself or
herself: "I deny morality as I deny alchemy, that is, I deny their premises. . . . It
goes without saying that I do not deny—unless I am a fool—that many actions
called immoral ought to be avoided and resisted, or that many called moral ought
to be done and encouraged—but I think the one should be encouraged and the
other avoided for other reasons than hitherto" (D 103). What Nietzsche hopes
for is that the individual become creator of his or her own values—that is to say,
that he or she act no longer simply with a view to adapting to and conforming
with the "herd" but rather on the basis, in each case, of personal, individual deliberation. Since, however, from the perspective of traditional morality " 'autonomous' and 'moral' [*sittlich*, i.e., subject to the morality of customs] are mutually
exclusive terms" (GM II 2, translation revised), whoever pursues such an aim
will necessarily be accused of "immoralism."

In the last analysis, then, the ethical model proposed by Nietzsche consists
in a "journey of individualization," a journey through which one attains to full
maturity as an individual. Nietzsche famously makes repeated use in his writing
of the striking expression "Become what one is." But since, as we have seen in
chapter Two, "character" is, for Nietzsche, no metaphysical essence within each
individual that needs to be "brought to light," we must assume that what he
meant by this famous phrase was nothing more nor less than "Live according to
one's own self-chosen or self-created values." Nietzsche appears to confirm just
this interpretation of his thought at GS 335: "We . . . want to become who we
are—human beings who are new, unique, incomparable, who give themselves
laws, who create themselves!" To become an individual, or to "become what one

is," means to conquer moral autonomy and, in and through one's own actions, express one's own self.[1]

3.1.2. Nietzsche's (Im)moral Proposals

How, then, is one to overcome this "morality of custom" and become a true individual? Toward the end of his active life, in 1886, Nietzsche provided several of the works of his middle period with new prefaces. In the new preface written at this time for 1881's *Daybreak* he describes the overcoming of Socratico-Christian morality as a historical enterprise which originated in what was itself inarguably a moral impulse: the impulse toward truthfulness. It was the Christian virtue of moral honesty (*Ehrlichkeit*),[2] argues Nietzsche, that gradually led "free spirits" to put radically into question just that traditional morality out of which the virtue of *Ehrlichkeit* had emerged. It is a case of "morality's self-abolition [*Selbstaufhebung der Moral*]" (D Preface 4, translation emended), of the "self-overcoming of morality from out of truthfulness" or of the "self-overcoming of moralists into their opposite" (EH, Destiny 3). In other words, "free spirits," prompted by an impulse to discover and speak the truth, inquire into the origin of moral values. And the result—we might say, as it were, the unintended result—of this inquiry is that these once sacrosanct values lose their normative force. "Your knowledge of the way in which moral judgments have originated would spoil these grand words for you" (GS 335), writes Nietzsche in *The Gay Science*, emphasizing that intention of psychological critique that underlies his moral and ethical project.[3]

It is not enough, if we decide we want to become true individuals, to call into question the values which have guided our lives prior to the point of this decision. If we are really to achieve this goal we need also to create, and allow to ripen within us, values of our own. But here a serious problem arises: from where, exactly, do these values that we autonomously adopt derive their normative force? Katsafanas orients his reflections on this topic in terms of the ideas advanced, respectively, by Kant and Hegel, who in fact take up diametrically opposite stances on this question. For Kant, precisely the fact that we have chosen certain values autonomously guarantees that we will respect them. For Hegel, by contrast, the fact that the values we adopt have been autonomously chosen by us makes them appear to us to be easily transgressible: since it is we who have endowed such values with the authority they enjoy, we remain capable of revoking this authority at any moment (see Katsafanas 2013, 22). I am inclined to agree with Katsafanas when he writes that, according to Nietzsche, if we are to avoid the danger of nihilism—that is to say, in order to be able to consider our own projects as projects imbued with sense and meaning—it is necessary that the values we adopt possess normative force (see 23). We must ask ourselves, however, if "possess normative force" means, for Nietzsche, "to be valid in an absolute sense" or simply "to be absolutely valid for us." As we have noted, Nietzsche rejects universalism. "To become what one is" means, for him, precisely to discover or create one's own values, as opposed to values which claim to function equally well for all and sundry. Zarathustra says, "But he will have discovered himself who speaks: 'this is my good and evil.' With this he has silenced the mole and dwarf who says: 'Good for all, evil for all'" (Z III, On the Spirit of Gravity). But according to Katsafanas (2013, 218), Nietzsche likewise rejects moral relativism, a stance whereby the truth of all normative claims would be relative to the traditions, practices, or beliefs of a group of individuals. Katsafanas considers Nietzsche to be a proponent rather of a "parametric universalism": "[Nietzsche] holds that there is a universally valid normative standard but argues that the particular results generated by this standard vary across different types of individuals" (218). Katsafanas believes that he can identify this universal standard of Nietzsche's in the notion "will to power"; this notion, he argues, possesses normative force and value inasmuch as it inheres in the very structure of all action (159). The will to power does not tell us what to do but rather how to do it, namely, by maximizing the encountering and overcoming of resistances. According to Katsafanas, for Nietzsche the will to power is not a foundational principle from which normative claims can be derived but rather solely a "principle of revaluation," that is to say, a "standard in terms of which we are to assess all other values" (189). "If a value conflicts with power, it is to be rejected; if it harmonizes with power, it is to be accepted" (149). I am inclined to concur with Katsafanas that Nietzsche can be defined as a proponent of "parametric universalism," but I must disagree with him (1) as regards his definition of will to power and (2) as regards his claim that we must consider this will to power to be, throughout the whole course of Nietzsche's philosophical development, the parameter by which "the value of values" is judged.

Swanton (2015, 158) likewise seems inclined to make of Nietzsche a "parametric universalist." On Swanton's account, however, Nietzsche's ethical model includes a recognition of various different "universal virtues," which he then sees as producing different results depending upon the specific human type that applies them. According to Swanton "forgetfulness, justice, and wisdom," etc. are, for Nietzsche, "basic virtues" (i.e., universal virtues). These, nonetheless, "should be differentiated according to such factors as strength, roles such as leadership, and even the narrative particularities of individuals' lives" (159). This does not mean that "a virtue in the 'higher man' is a vice in the 'herd'" (159). It means rather that virtues, which are virtues for all, "will take different forms in different types of human being" (174). For example, wisdom, which Nietzsche presents as a universal virtue and describes in considerable detail (see Swanton 2015, 170–171), produces different forms of behavior depending on the specific human type that applies it.[4] Swanton calls this a "pluralist" account. It presents the advantage of allowing the philosopher to make statements such as (1) something can be good for one type of human being but bad for another and (2) conflicting judgments can, if formulated respectively by different types of human beings, both be true, without this philosopher being thereby forced into a position of moral relativism, that is to say, into the contention that there exist no universal values.

Swanton does not say so explicitly, but she too appears to hold that these "basic" or "universal" virtues do not, for Nietzsche, concern the goals and objectives that we set ourselves, but rather the manner in which we formulate and pursue these goals and objectives. Indeed, in the last analysis the majority of Nietzsche scholars agree that Nietzsche's ethical model comprises and concerns solely those virtues that Harcourt (2015) calls "executive virtues" or "formal excellences": virtues that allow one to perform the virtues proper and peculiar to one's own self.[5]

Swanton (2015, 119) too assumes that, for Nietzsche, the will to power is the criterion by which there is judged and assessed "the value of (specific sets of) values"; in other words, it is by reference to the will to power that a type of behavior is defined as a "vice" or a "virtue." Swanton distinguishes here between "distorted or undistorted" forms of will to power (120): from the former there originate the vices, from the latter the virtues.[6] For example, Swanton claims that, for Nietzsche, pity is a vice because it expresses distorted will to power; what moves one, in the form of the impulse of pity, to concern oneself with the fate of others is in fact, in Nietzsche's view, the desire to flee one's own self—that is to say, self-hatred. But Nietzsche's model of morality, claims Swanton, also comprises a genuine virtuous altruism which takes the form of "a self-love which overflows to others with whom one has a bond" (124–125). In the last analysis, then, Swanton appears to see as coinciding with one another the will to power—or, put more precisely, the undistorted forms of will to power—and what she calls "self-love." This is defined as the attitude of affirming one's own life, not, however, in the sense merely of this life's passive acceptance but in the sense of an active striving directed toward self-realization or self-actualization (118). Wherever, Swanton argues, a specific value expresses self-affirmation in this sense and the desire to acquire a greater degree of power, it is judged by Nietzsche in a positive sense; wherever, on the other hand, it expresses self-negation and a refusal of life, it is judged by him to be something negative.

My own position preserves a fair proportion of both Katsafanas's (2013) and Swanton's (2015) arguments, mediating between and integrating the two approaches while also adding certain new elements which come to light when we retrace the history of Nietzsche's reading of Emerson. In order properly to expound my position it is necessary to take up once again the question of the normative value of those values which we ourselves autonomously choose as our own. Nietzsche criticizes the individual who adheres to the "morality of customs" because this individual accepts and adopts values without inquiring into their origin and without asking himself or herself whether these values are such as are likely to work well also for him or her as an individual human being. Useful in order to better understand just what Nietzsche means here are some notes from quite late in his philosophical career. In a note from 1884, for example, he states, "Value judgments [*Werthschätzungen*] originate from what we consider to be our own conditions of existence" (NL 1884 25[397], KSA 11: 116). All judgments of value, he insists, are born out of the perception of such conditions of existence. He goes on to say, "If these [conditions of existence] change, or our belief about them changes, then our judgments change as well" (NL 1884 25[397], KSA 11: 116). The "if" here is very important: our value judgments will indeed change if they arise from the perception of altered conditions of existence; but if, on the other hand, these values arise from the instinct to follow the herd, they will tend to remain the same. Nietzsche advanced the hypothesis that there are periods in which social cohesion is more important than anything else, for example, when one population is struggling against a population external to it. In periods in which the broader social or historical situation is more "relaxed," this need for uniformity is eased and relaxed as well, and certain people begin to be able to ask themselves questions regarding what conditions of existence would be optimal for them as individuals. In a note from a slightly earlier period, 1881, Nietzsche writes, "Once the moment of greatest danger for all is past, individual trees can begin to grow up with their conditions of existence [*Existenzbedingungen*])" (NL 1881 11[59], KSA 9: 463). In other words, only at this moment do the conditions obtain that are required for the birth of an individual morality. "Individual morality . . . a being is there which seeks after its own conditions of existence" (NL 1881 11[46], KSA 9: 459). The values that such a being will choose, once he or she has become aware of what these "own conditions of existence" are, will then possess normative value for him or her (but only for him or her). The individual will not be able to revoke the validity of these values because he or she will not have chosen them merely arbitrarily. The values in question will lose their normative force and will be replaced by others only if and when the "conditions of existence" of the individual in question change. To act differently—that is to say, to act on the basis of values which are not rooted in one's own conditions of existence—means not to act as an individual, not to possess an individual morality. Let us note, moreover, that this type of action—that is, a deliberated action which proceeds from values autonomously "chosen"—corresponds to the notion of freedom as agency presented in chapter 2. For this reason, we can state that Nietzsche's moral project aims at the formation of a free individual.

Let us look now at the problem of the universality of values. I am inclined to agree with Swanton regarding the fact that, for Nietzsche, all the virtues originate in the acceptance of oneself and in the wish to actualize all one's own potential. I propose, however, that this attitude be called an attitude not of "self-love" but rather of "self-reliance." This latter notion, of course, comes from Emerson and sums up, indeed, the American writer's entire ethical project. Emerson's notion of "self-reliance" has many facets, but these facets certainly not only include all the characteristics that Swanton recognizes in the notion "self-love" but also, in addition, certain other characteristics that are of central importance for understanding the ethical project advanced by Nietzsche. As we shall demonstrate, self-reliance is the common thread which ties together Nietzsche's various reflections regarding the process of individualization.

Let us move on now to clarify the definition of the will to power and the role that Nietzsche assigns to it. In BGE 259 Nietzsche states that every living thing aspires "to grow, spread, grab, win dominance" and that this is the case because every living thing consists in will to power. This expression "will to power," then, as Müller-Lauter (1998) has correctly pointed out, does not, for Nietzsche, describe some spiritual force which informs both Nature and Man, as might be said, for example, of "will" as it is defined in the philosophy of Schopenhauer; rather, Nietzsche's "will to power" is conceived of as the very structure of all that exists. To claim this is tantamount to claiming that reality is a multiplicity organized specifically in the form of relations of domination and subordination.[7] To say that human subjectivity itself consists, in its very structure and substance, in will to power means not only recognizing that this subjectivity aspires to assert itself against external resistances and against other wills to power but that even the interiority of such a subjectivity displays no real unity or unicity but rather itself takes, in its turn, the form of a multiplicity of drives organized as relations of domination and subordination.[8]

Now this notion of will to power becomes a central one for Nietzsche only in a relatively late period of his philosophical development, let us say after 1883. It can, then, hardly be called upon to explain the philosophy he expounded in the works of his youth and of his so-called middle period. I would argue, in fact, that one is much better advised to employ the notion of self-reliance, rather than that of will to power, to discuss the ethical model that Nietzsche developed in these last-mentioned works. Self-reliance, understood as an aspiration to assert and to develop oneself as a unique and original individual, defines itself in clear opposition (as does also "will to power" as Nietzsche understood it) both to the mere instinct of self-preservation and to the natural desire to experience pleasure and avoid pain.

I shall moreover assume, concurring here with the majority of Nietzsche scholars, that this ethical model of Nietzsche's concerns not the question of "what to do" but rather that of "how to do it," or, in other words, not the content but rather the form of the values in question. More precisely, I assume that the response Nietzsche gives to this question "How to do it?" is "Do it as an individual." In other words, I hold that the ethical model proposed by Nietzsche describes the conditions that values must fulfill if they are truly to be said to be "one's own values." To say that values are "our own values" is tantamount to saying that in our actions we express our own selves. In GS 290, when he speaks of "giving style to one's character," Nietzsche defines this as "the one thing needful" ("One thing is needful. —To 'give style' to one's character").[9] In this chapter I will argue that, following Emerson, Nietzsche considers every value to be acceptable provided that it proceeds out of the consciousness of one's own conditions of existence and out of the will to assert and to develop oneself—or, in other words, proceeds out of "self-reliance."

3.1.3. The Nietzschean Typology

The virtue ethics propounded by Nietzsche can be defined, as Brobjer (1995) suggests, as a "character ethics" inasmuch as Nietzsche chooses not to expound his own conception of morality directly, by offering a list of abstract precepts, but rather proceeds indirectly, by pointing up concrete personalities who incarnate the teaching that he wishes to convey. In this regard, Nietzsche's virtue ethics recall the ethics of ancient Greece: whereas modern ethics abstracts and generalizes with the aim of classifying actions into "right" and "wrong," ancient Greek ethics tended to focus on the individual person and on the teaching which was imparted through the example of such a person. In his essay on philosophy in the "tragic"—Pre-Socratic—age of the Greeks, for example, Nietzsche makes the observation, "For us [modern men], even the most personal is sublimated back into an abstraction; for them [the ancient Greeks], the greatest abstraction kept running back into a person" (PTAG 3). Nietzsche probably had in mind here the *Parallel Lives* (23 vols.) of Plutarch, in which Plutarch sums up the fundamental characteristics of each epoch prior to his own in the form of portraits of personalities whom he considered to be representative examples of these epochs. He was, however, also surely thinking of the modern exponents of an art very similar to Plutarch's: Carlyle and Emerson. It should be noted, however, that, in contradistinction to Plutarch in the Classical era and even to Carlyle in the modern one, Emerson did not make use of this method of portraying exemplary individuals in order to practice historiography. Rather, what Emerson was concerned to personify in what he called his "representative men" was virtue, that quality which these outstanding individuals had borne and developed to the level of excellence. On examination, in fact, the virtues that these outstanding individuals of Emerson's display in exemplary form are all just facets of the one central virtue that Emerson calls "self-reliance." In other words, Emerson concentrated not on the specific results that these men achieved through their expression of their own selves but on the question of how they achieved these results. The collection of portraits of such outstanding individuals that Emerson presents in the book of his which bore, in fact, the name *Representative Men* thus takes on, in the last analysis, the function of a sort of breviary of the process of individualization, one which offers itself to every individual to learn from and be guided by.

Drawing inspiration from Emerson, Nietzsche envisages as bearers and personifications of his ethical program three principal imaginary figures: the "Schopenhauer as educator," who is the protagonist of the third of the *Untimely Meditations*; the "free spirit," who takes on this role in *Human, All Too Human* and *Daybreak*; and Zarathustra, who personifies Nietzsche's mature philosophical vision.[10] Nietzsche conceived these three figures at just those three moments in his life at which Emerson was most present to his mind: the period of the *Untimely Meditations*, that of *Human, All too Human*, and that of the conception of *Zarathustra* (1881–1883). The thesis I want to advance is that these three figures embody three different manifestations of Emersonian self-reliance, respectively: (1) nonconformism, that is, a respect and admiration for one's own distinctive individuality and a desire to defend this individuality against all external intrusions and to develop it to the fullest possible extent; (2) skepticism, an openness to multiple points of view, proceeding from respect and admiration for the individuality of others in this individuality's distinctness and difference from our own; (3) original expression of the self and active affirmation of one's own values, proceeding from a state of imperturbability and god-like indifference.

3.2. Self-Reverence as Recognition and Defense of One's Own Individuality

3.2.1. On Envy

Before proceeding to the analysis of these three figures it will be worthwhile considering Emerson's contribution to the maturation of Nietzsche's philosophical position on the emotion of envy. This emotion takes on a paradigmatic significance for Nietzsche because it manifests, in exemplary manner, the absence of self-reliance, that is, the absence of reverence for one's own distinctive individuality and of the desire to develop it.

Nietzsche uses, for the first time, considerations drawn from Emerson in order to develop some reflections of his own on the emotion of envy in a short essay from 1863 entitled *Can the Envious Man Be Really Happy?* (NL 1863 15[42], KGW I/3: 193). At this time, Emerson was at the very top of the list of Nietzsche's favorite authors (see NL 1863–1864 16[23], KGW I/3: 299). It is not surprising, then, that this essay is in very large part a reformulation of certain theses expounded by Emerson in *The Conduct of Life*, specifically in the essays *Beauty* and *Power*.[11]

Nietzsche bases his argument here on the etymology of the word "envy," derived from the Latin verb *invidere*, "to look askance at." Envy, Nietzsche contends in this essay, is indeed a "looking askance" or rather a "looking askew"; the envious individual is afflicted with a distorted way of looking at things, which results in a distortion or defect of the understanding. The envious individual fails to see, and thus to understand, that a person's success in life is linked to many things that chronologically precede this success, such as hard work, sacrifice, exclusive dedication to a goal, and resilience, and indeed also to many things that chronologically succeed it, such as responsibilities and the expectations of others. Viewing success as an isolated fact which neither requires effort to achieve nor imposes obligations once achieved, the envious individual calls it a "gift of fortune" and desires it for himself or herself: "Fortuitous events, gifts of fortune . . . stand out at first sight like mountain peaks. . . .The envious man . . . like any selfish and short-sighted person, sees these mountain peaks jut out from the clouds and believe that they float isolated in the air, while the man who looks more deeply intuits a hidden connection between them and recognizes them to be in fact the tips of a continuous mountain range" (NL 1863 15[42], KGW I/3: 194). In order to develop this line of meditation Nietzsche makes use of Emerson's essay *Power*. In this essay, which immediately follows the essay *Fate* in Emerson's collection *The Conduct of Life*, the American argues that the success of great individuals is due to their accepting and honoring the principle of cause and effect. Nietzsche entered in his 1863 notebook the following excerpt from this essay: "All successful people have agreed on one thing,—they were causationists [*Causalisten*]" (NL 1863 15A[5], KGW I/3: 228; see CL, 28–29; FL, 37–38). Emerson goes on, in this essay, to explain, "They believed that things went not by luck, but by law; that there was not a weak or cracked link in the chain that joins the first and last of things. A belief in causality, or strict connection between every pulse-beat and the principle of being, and, in consequence, belief in compensation, or that nothing is got for nothing, —characterizes all valuable minds, and must control every effort that is made by an industrious one" (CL, 28–29; FL, 37–38). In other words, according to Emerson all great individuals display an absolute concentration on their own particular task and a great dedication to it, and this as a consequence of the acceptance of the principle that everything has its price.[12] In Emerson's vision of the world chance does not exist; every real benefit and advantage has somehow been earned, and if certain benefits and advantages seem to be unearned, this is only because they are merely apparent, and not real, benefits and advantages. In that one of the *Essays* that is dedicated to the principle of compensation Emerson explains, "In labour as in life there can be no cheating. The thief steals from himself. The swindler swindles himself" (E I, 94; V, 86). In other words, the real reward for one's own labor consists in the knowledge or the skills that one will have acquired simply by performing it, and not so much in the fame or wealth that one might also acquire thereby, these latter being merely secondary and inessential consequences. This is why the person who "cheats" obtains nothing thereby.

The young Nietzsche continues his essay by arguing that an asset that has not been worked for will not just fail to enrich but will actually damage the individual who acquires it. He arrives at this conclusion by applying to the sphere of ethics a claim that Emerson had advanced for the sphere of aesthetics in his essay *Beauty*. Emerson contends in this essay that beauty depends upon an excellence of structure, that is to say, upon the perfection of each thing's own specific nature. The adding of external ornament to a thing, far from augmenting its beauty, obscures the original purity of its form and, as it were, "weighs down" this form. Beauty can be increased only through a "real enhancement of capacity [*Vermehrung der Tüchtigkeit*]" (NL 1863 15[36], KGW I/3: 181; see CL, 154; FL, 201).[13] Transposing this argument into the ethical sphere, Nietzsche contends that the sole true asset for an individual must consist in the perfecting of his or her own self, that is to say, in the real development of all his or her inherent capacities. "Since all beauty," he argues, "must be organic, since external beautification is only deformation, then even happiness [*Glück*] and honour must grow out of the very same stock and trunk as they later adorn" (NL 1863 15[42], KGW I/3: 194; see CL, 155; FL, 201). Still following the pattern of argument outlined by Emerson, Nietzsche maintains that acquiring an asset not due to oneself but to another will not only bring no advantage to the individual who thus acquires it but can even prove harmful: "Let us even assume that destiny might give to an envious person all that he had craved for: this gift would cling to him as an inorganic growth [*unorganischer Anwuchs*], sapping his strength, corrupting his will and deceiving him anew with further sparkling illusions [*Trugbilder*], toward which his endlessly craving soul would now turn. What he so eagerly diverted from others falls now upon his own head with a weight that crushes him" (NL 1863 15[42], KGW I/3: 194). Thus, just as external ornament will tend to diminish a thing's beauty by obscuring its original form, any benefit or advantage that an individual acquires without having earned it will do, in the end, nothing but oppress and harm this individual. What is more, by enviously desiring something that is not suitable to one's own nature, one forfeits the chance of finding something which might make the most of this nature and thereby secure one's happiness. Nietzsche argues in his essay of 1863, "It is thus a defect in one's own inward knowledge to wish oneself into the outward circumstances of others, in the belief that one will grow more happily in this new soil" (NL 1863 15[42], KGW I/3: 195). Making good use, then, of his readings in Emerson, the young Nietzsche focuses on the danger posed by envy for the individual who feels this emotion. This emotion is dangerous for the person feeling it inasmuch as it distracts and removes him or her from self-perfection, the sole true source of happiness. Nietzsche already implicitly identifies happiness here with the feeling of an increase in one's own power (and not, as might seem more natural in such a young writer, with the mere enjoyment of pleasure), thus anticipating an important theme of his mature works.

And indeed, the theme of envy was itself to become a topic of central importance in the works of Nietzsche's middle period. If the important role that the reading of La Rochefoucauld played in drawing Nietzsche's thoughts in this direction has already been noted by Shapiro (1983), the much more important role played by Emerson in this regard has hitherto not been mentioned at all. In a passage of the essay *Self-Reliance* Emerson declares that to be envious of someone—that is to say, to want to be what that person is in every detail—is tantamount to committing suicide. In other words, to desire to be someone else signifies killing one's own self as a unique and unrepeatable individual. The actual passage from Emerson runs, "There is a time in every man's education when he arrives at the conviction that envy is ignorance, that imitation is suicide . . . that though the wide universe is full of good, no kernel of nourishing corn can come to him but through his toil bestowed on that plot of ground which is given to him to till" (E I, 38). Nietzsche copied this passage into the notebook that he filled with excerpts from the *Essays* in 1882. The text actually entered in Nietzsche's notebook runs, however (when translated back into English from the German), "There is a time in every man's development in which he arrives at the conviction that envy is only ignorance, imitation is assassination; that though the wide universe is full of good, no kernel of corn can come to him but through his toil bestowed on that plot of ground" (NL 1882 17[22], KSA 9: 669; see V, 33). The deviations from Emerson's original text are partly the fault of Fabricius, the 1858 German translator of Emerson's *Essays*, who mistranslates "suicide" as *Meuchelmord*. This is not only linguistically inaccurate (suicide is "self-killing"; *Meuchelmord* is very decidedly the killing of another person); the linguistic inaccuracy in fact obscures Emerson's whole point: those who imitate someone else do not "kill" the person they imitate but rather "kill themselves" (i.e., kill their own unique individuality). This idea is entirely lost in Fabricius's translation, and thereby also in Nietzsche's 1882 note. By the way, Fabricius also misunderstands and mistranslates the words of Emerson's that follow "imitation is suicide," namely, "that he must take himself for better or worse as his portion." He translates them as "wo er sich selbst für besser und für schlimmer halten muss, als wirklich auf sein Teil gekommen ist"—a complete misunderstanding of Emerson's meaning. Nietzsche omits these words completely from his own note of 1882.[14] In any case, the extract that Nietzsche makes from the German edition nonetheless preserves the basic idea of Emerson's passage, an idea that Nietzsche had already placed at the center of his schoolboy essay of 1863, namely, that envy is the product of a defect of consciousness, that is to say, of an ignorance on the part of the individual of what is his or her own true good. This true good does not consist in the ephemeral enjoyment of pleasures but rather in the development and the expression of the self. To avoid the hard work and the other inconveniences that are necessarily involved in the project of bringing one's own individuality to full realization and to choose instead to imitate or emulate some already successful person—this means to deprive oneself forever of the possibility of achieving happiness, which consists precisely in the feeling of the augmentation of one's power.

In another excerpt made in 1882, this time from Emerson's essay *History*, Nietzsche once again associates envy with a defect of consciousness. On this occasion, however, he uses a metaphor drawn from the realm of optics. Nietzsche's note runs, "It must be impossible for my eyes to look at this and that with squint-eyed glances [*mit schielenden Blicken*]: I always have to turn my head—this is noble" (NL 1882 17[14], KSA 9: 667). In the passage that Nietzsche is summing up, in very abbreviated manner, Emerson had in fact set off against one another the "incorrupt, sharply defined and symmetrical features" that had inspired the statues of "Hercules, Phoebus, and Jove" and "the forms abounding in the streets of modern cities." While the faces of modern men and women are "a confused blur of features," the ancient Greeks' eye sockets were so formed that "it would be impossible for such eyes to squint and take furtive glances on this side and on that, but they must turn the whole head" (E I, 20; V, 18; in his personal copy Nietzsche underlined "eye-sockets were so formed," "impossible," and "take furtive glances on this side and on that"; he also added three vertical lines in the margin to the whole passage, as well as the number "16"). Clearly, for Emerson these aesthetic considerations have an ethical implication: he assumes, in fact, that people's physiognomies are manifestations of their psychological states. This connection is made still more explicit by Nietzsche, who, following Emerson, imagines two types of individual, with two quite distinct physiognomies, as representatives of two opposed ethical ideals. On the one hand we have the individual who identifies happiness with self-realization or (given that this is a regulative ideal) with the feeling of the augmentation of one's own power. This individual devotes himself or herself to his or her own goals and objectives and can therefore be said to "look straight ahead," far into his or her own future. This individual's soul is serene because it is satisfied and, for this reason, the person's posture is composed and stately. Nietzsche describes this physiognomic type in the rhyme *Without Envy*: "His gaze is envyless: and him you praise? / No thirst for your esteem perturbs his gaze; / he has the eagle's vision for the long view, / it's stars he sees, just stars—he looks beyond you!" (GS Joke, Cunning and Revenge 40). On the other hand we have the individual who identifies happiness with the enjoyment of pleasure and the absence of pain. The happiness that this individual seeks is a small happiness and one, therefore, that must not cost him or her too much effort. The pleasures that cost little effort, however—that is to say, all those pleasures that do not arise from the work of self-perfection—are necessarily fugacious. The result is that this type of individual will be the victim of constant dissatisfaction and a continuous sensation of anxiety. The lineaments of his or her face will be contorted, and his or her hungry, dissatisfied gaze will turn nervously from left to right and back again, squinting toward the happiness of others. Such a human type is the central figure in Zarathustra's parable "The Virtue That Makes Small": "To modestly embrace a small happiness—that they call 'resignation' and already they are squinting around modestly for a new small happiness" (Z III, The Virtue That Makes Small).[15]

Nietzsche deals with envy also in another of the parables related in Zarathustra, "On the Tree on the Mountain," which, as Shapiro (1983, 4) observes, "may appear somewhat puzzling until it is realized that envy is the crucial notion around which this particular slice of the drama revolves." Indeed, since the word "envy" never actually appears in this particular parable of Zarathustra's, it is only where we understand Nietzsche's concept of envy in the light specifically of his reading of Emerson that we can recognize this emotion to be in fact the central topic addressed here. Shortly after his arrival in "the town called The Motley Cow" Zarathustra realizes that one of the young men of this town is deliberately avoiding him. Zarathustra confronts him about this, and, bursting into tears, he confesses to Zarathustra, "I no longer trust myself since aspiring to the heights. . . . How ashamed I am of my climbing and stumbling! How I mock my violent panting! How I hate the flying one!" (Z I, On the Tree on the Mountain). The young man no longer has faith in himself or in the possibility of bringing his true self to realization; he lacks, in other words, self-reliance. We understand, then, that the emotion that leads him to avoid Zarathustra is envy. Zarathustra's presence "would remind him of his distress at not having the thing that he lacks or at not being the person he is not" (Shapiro 1983, 5). Zarathustra embraces the young man and comforts him with these words: "Do not throw away the hero in your soul! Hold holy your highest hope!" (Shapiro 1983, 30). It is interesting to note that in this parable Nietzsche does not establish, as he had previously done, a dichotomy between two distinct human types, ascribing the vice of envy to only one of these two. Rather, it emerges here that this vice of envy can arise even in the subject who aspires to become a true individual wherever he or she fails to keep faith with himself or herself and with his or her own potentialities.

In short, drawing various impulses and inspirations from the essays of Emerson at various points in his life, Nietzsche carries out a complex examination of the feeling of envy and recognizes it to be the first and most evident symptom of a lack of self-reliance, that is, of ignorance of the value of one's own distinct individuality and/or lack of faith in the possibility of developing it.

3.2.2. Social Conformism as Loss of Self

The figure of "Schopenhauer as educator," protagonist of the third of the *Untimely Meditations*, represents the first stage in Nietzsche's journey of individualization. The thesis that I want to advance and defend here is that the virtues incarnated by this idealized figure correspond to the first and most fundamental manifestation of Emerson's "self-reliance": the desire to express oneself and to defend one's own distinct individuality against any external interference. We see how present Emerson was to Nietzsche's mind in this period of the writing of the *Untimely Meditations* from a letter to Gersdorff from September 1874. Nietzsche tells of having spent the summer in Bergün, revising the text of the third of the *Meditations*, to which, he reported, he had had to make significant alterations. He also mentions how, on his way back home, his suitcase had been stolen at Würzburg railway station, "together with the excellent Emerson that I had had with me in Bergün" (KSB 4: 258, n. 390). Nietzsche was most likely referring here to the volume containing the *Essays: First and Second Series*, which is in fact cited at two points in the third *Untimely Meditation*.

Nietzsche's overriding preoccupation in this third *Untimely Meditation* is the alienation produced by human life in society. The essay opens with the description of a social and cultural scenario dominated by a bleak conformism in which people are afraid to express judgments of their own and simply borrow their opinions one from the other. These people are either completely unaware of having any distinct individuality or, if they are aware of it, are also ashamed of it and seek to keep this individuality disguised. Living rather as a flock of sheep than as individuals, they willingly degrade themselves to "factory products" and "pseudo-men" (SE 1). In other words, they deny to their own selves the dignity of human beings. But in order to recover this dignity, claims Nietzsche, one need do no more than simply follow the voice of one's own conscience and live as an individual: "The man who does not wish to belong to the mass needs only to cease taking himself easily; let him follow his conscience, which calls to him: 'Be your self! All you are now doing, thinking, desiring, is not you yourself!'" (SE 1).[16]

Here, Nietzsche appears to assume (1) that the subject possesses a well-defined identity of his or her own which tends to become lost as we enter into life in society, and that (2) by exerting a certain effort of will one can repulse and beat back these impinging forces of social conditioning and attain once again one's "true nature." As we have seen in the previous chapter, from *Human, All Too Human* onward Nietzsche subjects both these assumptions to a rigorous philosophical critique, rejecting (1) the metaphysical notion that human individuals have some "original nature" that they might, through effort, rediscover and recover (2) the equally metaphysical notion of a "free will" in the sense of a will completely materially unconditioned. The position taken by Nietzsche in the third of the *Untimely Meditations* becomes comprehensible only if we take into account the influence exerted on him in this period by Emerson's essay *Self-Reliance*.

In this essay Emerson accuses society of robbing its members of their own individuality and thus of insulting their dignity as human beings. Self-reliance—that is to say, the awareness of the value of one's own distinctive individuality and the desire to develop it—manifests as the adoption of a stance of opposition to society and a refusal to conform to society's habits and customs. "Society everywhere is in conspiracy against the manhood of every one of its members. . . . The virtue in most request is conformity. Self-reliance is its aversion, . . . Whoso would be a man, must be a nonconformist" (E I, 41; V, 36). Emerson too, then, assumes that each of us has a true or "aboriginal Self" (E I, 52; V, 47) that is the depository of a "primary wisdom" (E I, 52; V, 47) which manifests in the form of "Spontaneity or Instinct": it is "Intuition, whilst all later teachings are tuitions" (E I, 52; V, 47). Society, Emerson argues, successively imposes upon the individual habits and customs which displace and replace the individual's "inner voice," telling him or her what to think or how to behave. To be self-reliant means to value the persisting spontaneous intuitions of the "inner voice" more highly than the outward voice of dominant social opinions.[17] As Kateb has emphasized, this "self-reliance" of Emerson's must not be confused with arrogance or with a desire for self-aggrandizement. It must instead be understood as a defense of human dignity. To be "self-reliant," means to think for oneself and to live according to one's own law, respecting and indeed emphasizing the difference between oneself and others (Kateb 2002, 32).

The role that Nietzsche assigns to the figure of "Schopenhauer as educator" is precisely that of reminding us how each human being can and should live, namely, as an individual. As I shall explain in more detail in chapter 5, Nietzsche, following Emerson, assigns to the "great man" the function of stimulating the so-called common man to live to the very limit of his individual possibilities. The "great man" ignites in the souls of all those who observe him the desire to emulate him—that is to say, to perfect themselves until they have raised themselves to his level. In this case, the level that one is stimulated to attain by observing the figure "Schopenhauer as educator" is that of the human dignity that is acquired through an original expression of one's own self: "Artists alone hate this sluggish promenading in borrowed fashions and appropriated opinions and they reveal everyone's secret bad conscience, the law that every man is a unique miracle; they dare to show us man as he is, uniquely himself to every last movement of his muscles, more, that in being so strictly consistent in uniqueness he is beautiful, and worth regarding, and in no way tedious" (SE 1). Artists, by expressing themselves in an original manner, remind other people of the fact that they themselves each have a unique and unrepeatable individuality and that their value as human beings depends precisely upon the degree to which they succeed in bringing this individuality to expression (SE 1). In this part of the essay Nietzsche is indeed speaking of artists. It is not easy, then, to see how what he says here relates to Schopenhauer, who is a philosopher. To grasp the meaning of this passage we must bear in mind that, in this phase of his intellectual development, Nietzsche conceived of philosophy as, like the arts, a form of "free lie" or falsehood freely consented to—that is to say, as a vision of the world that does not purport to be scientifically credible but aims rather at inspiring and setting directions for human action. Such a conscious and admitted falsehood, it follows, can be judged only on the basis of its beauty and of the moral force this beauty inspires. Nietzsche considers Schopenhauer's system to be a splendid example of *Begriffsdichtung*, "conceptual poetry" (KSB 2: 269, n. 568; see Gerratana 1988, 410), through which Schopenhauer succeeded in expressing himself and his own original thought.[18]

Schopenhauer, argues Nietzsche here, is an "educator" not so much by virtue of what he says in his books—because Nietzsche, in fact, was already at this time no longer in agreement with much of what was said there—as by virtue of the way he had lived his life. Expressing his own personal vision of things without fearing to contradict the dominant opinion, Schopenhauer could be said to have brought his own self to expression in an entirely original way or, in other words, to have truly lived as an individual. In doing this, Schopenhauer had imparted to the world a moral teaching of inestimable value—one which concerns all human beings and will never fall out of fashion.

In conclusion, we can state that the figure of "Schopenhauer as educator," in whom Nietzsche incarnated the philosopher as he personally understood him, in fact more closely resembles the "self-reliant" individual of Emerson than he does the Schopenhauerian "genius." This "genius" is conceived of as an individual who, by mastering a whole sequence of ascetic attitudes and practices, has succeeded in blotting out in himself or herself all desire, the cause of every type of human suffering. Thanks to superior powers of intuition, this "genius" realizes that his or her individuality itself is nothing but an illusion and recognizes that, in reality, he or she is one with all other human beings and form a single entity with them. While the Schopenhauerian "genius" personifies the moral ideal of a liberation from desire and from individuality, Emerson's "self-reliant" thinker, by contrast, personifies that of a liberation achieved through desire and through an emphasizing of one's own distinctive individuality.[19] "Desire," needless to say, is understood by Emerson to mean not the pursuit of pleasure but rather the aspiration to live to the very limit of one's own possibilities and potentialities. As Aaron (1962, 92–93) has observed, in a society dominated by crude materialism, in which people had "appetites but no passions" (Thoreau, quoted in Aaron, 86), Emerson wanted to shake the "cowed" and the "trustless" out of their lethargy, and to contrast, with the average "mediocrity of desires," a great ideal.[20] This ideal is that of the full actualization of the self. "We but half express ourselves and are ashamed of that divine idea which each of us represents" (E I, 38; V, 34), says Emerson in a passage from the essay *Self-Reliance* that Nietzsche enters, in 1882, into his notebook of excerpts.[21]

The "Schopenhauer as educator" of the third *Untimely Meditation* does not teach, by his example, to snuff out the will to live and to free oneself from individuality. Rather, what his example teaches is to free oneself from the conditioning imposed by society and to listen solely to the voice of one's own conscience, or, in other words, to live an authentic life.[22] We can, then, conclude that, through this figure, Nietzsche wanted to represent the first and most important aspect of Emersonian self-reliance and the first step on the journey to becoming an individual, namely, the awareness of the value of one's own distinctive individuality and the desire to develop it.

3.2.3. The Conflict between the Free Thinker and the Institutions

In this figure of "Schopenhauer as educator" there comes to light not only the first step in this journey toward the actualization of individuality but also the reason why many choose not to set out on this path at all. To lend one's ear solely to the inner voice of one's own conscience and to refuse to conform either to dominant opinion or to the habits and customs of society will necessarily lead one into collision with society. Nietzsche compares the "self-reliant" thinker personified in the figure of "Schopenhauer as educator" to a "terrible explosive that is a danger to everything" (EH, Why I Write Such Good Books, The Untimely Ones 3). In the third *Untimely Meditation* Nietzsche illustrates this idea by citing a passage from Emerson's essay *Circles*:

"Beware," says Emerson "when the great God lets loose a thinker on this planet. Then all things are at risk. It is as when a conflagration has broken out in a great city, and no man knows what is safe, or where it will end. There is not a piece of science but its flank may be turned to-morrow; there is not any literary reputation, not the so-called eternal names of fame, that may not be revised and condemned; the things which are dear to men at this hour are so on account of the ideas which have emerged on their mental horizon, and which cause the present order of things, as a tree bears its apples. A new degree of culture would instantly revolutionize the entire system of human pursuits." (SE 8; see E I, 256; V, 226–227).

In *Circles* as well as in other essays Emerson confronts the problem of the inev-itable conflict which arises between the self-reliant thinker, who feels the need to rethink for his or her own self everything that is usually taken for granted, and the institutions, which for their part are founded upon the single value of sta-bility.[23] Those persons, then, who want to be their own self, Emerson maintains, must be prepared to fight to do so: "Heroism is an obedience to a secret impulse of an individual's character. . . . Self-trust is the essence of heroism. It is the state of the soul at war, and its ultimate objects are the last defiance of falsehood and wrong, and the power to bear all that can be inflicted by evil agents" (E I, 208; V, 185; Nietzsche marked the passage in the margin).

Drawing on these essays of Emerson's, Nietzsche portrays the true philos-opher as a militant philosopher: as Nietzsche writes, this philosopher is con-stitutively "untimely," that is to say, someone "acting counter to our time and thereby acting on our time and, let us hope, for the benefit of a time to come" (SE Foreword).

According to the conceptions dominant in the first half of the 19th century the "great man" was looked on as an expression of the Spirit of the Age: a mental and spiritual guide for the epoch in which he made his appearance. In his *Lectures on the Philosophy of History* Hegel ([1837] 1975, 83) spoke of "world-historical individuals" who "desired and brought to being not any object of their own imagination or opinion but rather a just and necessary reality: those who know, having had their own inward revelation of it, what is henceforth the bent of Time and of Necessity." Since the discoveries and the enterprises of the "great man" work to the advantage of humankind as a whole, this great man is praised with gratitude or, as in the case of the attitude promoted by Carlyle, made a veritable object of veneration. The philosophies developed by Emerson and Nietzsche run counter to this idea, since they look on society as a "mass society" or, in other words, as a bearer of values quite opposed to those of the individual.

There are two main reasons the original thinker tends to be marginalized. First is fear. This individual's values tend to be situated at points diametrically opposed to the values dominant in society. This means that the masses see the original thinker as a threat to their very survival. The second reason is incomprehension. The original thinker's ideas are so innovative that those around him or her, still dominated by old conceptual schemes and values, are not able to understand him or her.

It is Emerson who makes Nietzsche aware of the inevitable destiny that will befall anyone who truly decides to live as an individual. A passage from Emerson's *History*, which Nietzsche summed up in a notebook from 1882, gives a striking account of the first reason why "mass society" tends to marginalize the independent thinker. In this passage Emerson narrates the story of Prometheus, who stole fire from the gods to give to humans in order to free them from the gods' authority. Zeus, fearful of losing his position of supremacy, punishes Prometheus for his attempt at emancipation and chains him to the rock of the Caucasus. Emerson concludes, "The *Prometheus Vinctus* is the romance of scepticism" (E I, 25–26; V, 17).[24] In other words, the experience of Prometheus can be extended to whoever, like him, dares to challenge authority and try to emancipate himself or herself.[25] Just like Zeus, mass society, preoccupied by caring for its own survival, tries to marginalize and render powerless the self-reliant thinker who refuses to submit to its authority.

In a passage from the essay *Self-Reliance* which Nietzsche copied into his notebook for the summer of 1878,[26] Emerson draws attention to the second reason the original thinker tends not to be accepted by society: incomprehension. "To be great is to be misunderstood" (NL 1878 30[104], KSA 8: 540; see E I, 47; V 42–43), wrote Emerson. In his notebook of excerpts from 1882 Nietzsche also copied down another passage of the same tenor: "When the Gods come among men, they are not known. Jesus was not; Socrates and Shakespeare were not" (E I, 26; V, 42–43).[27] It is only by bearing in mind the equivalence Emerson established between originality and incomprehension that we can correctly interpret such apparently paradoxical statements as Nietzsche's in *The Gay Science*, where he asks, "Have we ever complained about being misunderstood, misjudged, misidentified, defamed, misheard and ignored?" and then goes on, in a proud and arrogant tone, to say, "This is precisely our lot . . . and also our distinction; we wouldn't honour ourselves enough if we wanted it otherwise" (GS 371).[28] In Emerson's *Essays* Nietzsche discovered a criterion by which to carry out a transvaluation of the apparently positive value of social recognition and appreciation. On Emerson's valuation, adopted by Nietzsche, the appreciation of society is no longer a source of pride because it is a sign of one's own conformism. Social marginalization, conversely, ceases, for both thinkers, to be a negative thing and becomes something positive, since to suffer it shows that one has raised oneself high above the ideals of the present age.[29]

In the last analysis, then, through reading Emerson Nietzsche becomes aware that the person who attempts to live as an individual is placed thereby in the very midst of a battle for culture, in which to meet opposition from others will be, at every moment, the greatest victory because it will show this person that he or she is on the right road.

3.2.4. On Vanity

If envy is counted, in Nietzsche's ethics, among the vices inasmuch as it signifies a lack of reverence for one's own distinctive individuality and a lack of faith in one's ability to develop it, the same goes for vanity. Vain individuals look outside themselves for confirmations of their own value because they lack all sources of self-certainty and security within themselves. Such individuals are thereby led to modify their own thought and behavior in order to satisfy other people's expectations of them, thus losing, as a consequence, their own self. That figure of "Schopenhauer as educator," then, who forms the subject of the third *Untimely Meditation* is necessarily characterized by Nietzsche—since he must stand as an example and model of self-reliance—as completely indifferent to the praise or blame of others. He is shown to be able to put up with the incomprehension and condemnation with which society rewards his genius as well as the utterly isolated position in which he is forced to live within this society. "Schopenhauer never wants to cut a figure," states Nietzsche; "he writes for himself" (SE 2). As Nietzsche was to acknowledge in *Assorted Opinions and Maxims,* "writing for oneself alone" has been the distinctive characteristic of every true thinker (AOM 167).[30] Nietzsche had found the Latin expression *sibi scribere* in a book by Valentin Rose (1863, 717), who claimed that he had intentionally adopted an awkward style to protect his books from readers who would be bothersome to him. But this same idea is expressed also by Emerson, in a passage from the *Essays* which Nietzsche takes note of as early as the winter of 1867–1868: "Emerson, p. 114. He who writes for himself writes for an immortal public" (NL 1867–1868 58[60], KGW I/4: 501).[31] Following Saint Augustine,[32] Emerson distinguishes between a social self and a true self. The social self is the image of us that is created by society, a sort of mask which we put on and which corresponds to our social role. Emerson considers an attachment to one's own social image, which manifests itself as a seeking after others' approval, to be a distorted form of self-love. An authentic, undistorted self-love instead leads one to pursue, with great abnegation, one's own vocation and to put up with the violent censure that society reserves especially for those thinkers who show themselves to be averse to it. "Abnegation," indeed, means renunciation of the self. But what is renounced here is only that "social self" that is one's social image, since it is only thus that the way is opened for the development of one's own distinctive individuality. As is taught not only by Neo-Platonism but also by the great works of the Vedic tradition—of which Emerson was a passionate reader—it is only "the man who renounces himself [that] comes to himself" (NAL, 78; see Versluis 1993, 67). In other words, the more one succeeds in setting aside one's "ego" (meaning the desire to be recognized and appreciated), the more one brings to realization one's true self. This is the reason Emerson warns against listening to one's own contemporaries and advises seeking examples to emulate among the great men of history or even in Nature. Each living being, indeed, gives us an insight into that effort of self-transcendence—that is to say, into the movement toward a higher phase of one's own development—which pervades all Nature. Nietzsche sums up a passage from Emerson's essay *History* which is particularly eloquent in this regard in his notebook of excerpts from the year 1882: "I hear well the world's praises, but they are not for me: my ears hear in them only the much sweeter sounding praise of the character I pursue, and that I hear in every word, in every fact—in running river and undulating grain" (NL 1882 17[2], KSA 9: 666).[33]

We find further evidence of Nietzsche's having looked on abnegation as a manifestation of Emersonian self-reliance and as an extremely important element in the process of the realization of one's own true individuality in the following passage from the third of the *Untimely Meditations*: "There is in the world only one way, on which nobody can go, except you. Where does it lead? Do not ask, go along with it. Who was it who said: 'a man never rises higher than when he does not know where his way can still lead him'?" (SE 1). These are the words of Oliver Cromwell, quoted by Emerson in his essay *Circles*.[34] But it is, in the last analysis, to the English poet Coleridge that Emerson is indebted for the substantive content of this claim, since it is from Coleridge that he draws the phrase that directly precedes it in his essay: "Nothing great was ever achieved without enthusiasm." To which Emerson adds, "The way of life is wonderful. It is by abandonment [*völliges Dahingeben* in the German text]" (E I, 265; V, 236; Nietzsche underlined "wonderful" and abandonment"). By "enthusiasm" Coleridge means the transcendence of one's own particular self and the elevation of the spirit to the intuition of universal principles. The abandonment to which Emerson refers, then, has nothing to do with the animal joy of giving vent to one's instincts or with the general blurring of the mind of the person who sacrifices reasoning to passion. On the contrary, Emerson is referring to the need, if one wishes to achieve great results, to transcend the ego and all its needs and to concentrate instead on one's own task. By clarifying the specific source Nietzsche draws on in the passage mentioned above it is possible to grasp the meaning of a statement that would otherwise have remained obscure and subject to misunderstanding. Nietzsche is not singing the praises of irrationalism but, consistently with everything else he argues in this third of the *Untimely Meditations*, is listing the fundamental components of the process of the bringing to realization of true individuality. That abnegation is one of these, and that Nietzsche means by "abnegation" precisely a setting aside of all attachment to our "social image," is confirmed by a note of Nietzsche's from 1883: "Zarathustra—I have unlearnt sympathy with myself. To forget the ego. Emerson p. 237" (NL 1883 15[27], KSA 10: 486). On page 237 of (Nietzsche's German copy of) the *Essays* we do, in fact, find the very quotation from Oliver Cromwell that Nietzsche uses in the third of the *Untimely Meditations*.

Abnegation corresponds to that control over one's own drives which, as we saw in section 2.2.4, distinguishes the unitary from the nonunitary self. In this condition of attained self-control, one is able to act with deliberation and to hold back one's instinctive reactions. Abnegation thus represents one of the component elements of the ascetic ideal. It is the result, in other words, of a systematic training of the animal "Man" in whom a certain morality is inculcated with a view to making him able to abide by the rules of society. Nietzsche clearly hopes to see the ability that has been acquired in this way placed in the service of a new goal: that of living as a true individual.

3.3. Putting Oneself in Question

The second stage on the journey toward true individuality is personified in the figure of the free spirit, the protagonist of Nietzsche's philosophy of the Middle Period. Contrary to the view expressed by Andler (1920, 247) and other exegetes, Nietzsche did not in fact distance himself from Emerson during this period of his philosophical development. On the contrary, further reading of Emerson formed a fundamental part of that therapy to cure his youthful Romanticism that Nietzsche prescribed for himself after 1876.[35] Both in the published works and in the only posthumously published notes of this middle period we find countless implicit quotations from as well as many explicit references to Emerson's various essay collections.[36] The thesis that I want to demonstrate next is that Nietzsche's "free spirit" is the incarnation of "self-reliance" in yet one more of the several senses in which Nietzsche adopts and uses this term of Emerson's. If the figure of "Schopenhauer as educator" personifies self-reliance in the sense of a reverence for one's own distinctive individuality and a desire to defend and develop it, the "free spirit" personifies self-reliance as a capacity to come face to face with other individuals and to allow one's own self to be placed into question by this face-to-face encounter.

3.3.1. Who Is Nietzsche's "Free Spirit"?

In *Human, All Too Human* Nietzsche portrays the free spirit as someone "who thinks differently from what, on the basis of his origin, environment, class and profession, or on the basis of the dominant views of the age, would have been expected of him" (HH 225). The free spirit's thinking and behavior, insofar as they deviate from the dominant codes and structures, "shock and offend" (HH 225). Therefore, the free spirit is constantly feared and opposed by the masses, or "fettered spirits" (HH 225), who prefer to cling to tradition. Thus far, the free spirit is merely the inheritor of characteristics already displayed by the figure of "Schopenhauer as educator." He or she is certainly, at the very least, a non-conformist who takes a position against the morality of custom and demands the right to live according to his or her own law (see also D 104; GS 116). Nevertheless, we must assume that this is not the distinctive characteristic of the free spirit. In the closing lines of HH 225 Nietzsche suggests a further trait: "As a rule . . . [the free spirit] will . . . have truth on his side, or at least the spirit of inquiry after truth. . . . The rest [the fettered spirits] demand faith." Also, in an aphorism which he placed later in the same book, Nietzsche describes the free spirit as someone who is dominated by the "pathos of seeking the truth" (HH 633), while the "fettered spirits," by contrast, are dominated by the "pathos of possessing the truth" (HH 633), that is to say, by the need to believe. We may suppose, then, that the distinctive characteristic of the free spirit is the pathos of seeking the truth, or the drive toward truth.

Nevertheless, as Acampora (2015) emphasizes, the so-called free thinkers—whose most iconic representative is, according to Nietzsche, Giordano Bruno (BGE 25)—are also dominated by this same drive. But in contrast to these "free thinkers," who are disposed to pursue their truth to the point of martyrdom, the free spirit is not inseparably attached to his or her own truth but is rather ready at any time to revise his or her opinion. Indeed, the free spirit considers knowing how to change his or her opinion to be a "rare and high distinction" that he or she enjoys (D 56). In the last analysis we must conclude that the distinguishing characteristic of the free spirit is "the freedom from unconditionality" (Acampora 2015, 192) or, in other words, the attitude of pursuing truth without attachment to the particular truth that might happen at any moment to be one's own. If we assume this "freedom from unconditionality" to be indeed the distinguishing characteristic of the free spirit, we understand also why Nietzsche describes the free spirit as a "wanderer"; it does, in fact, become the eponymous protagonist of the second section of the second volume of *Human, All Too Human*:

> *The Wanderer.* —He who has attained to only some degree of freedom
> of mind cannot feel other than a wanderer on the earth—though not

as a traveller to a final destination: for this destination does not exist. But he will watch and observe and keep his eyes open to see what is really going on in the world; for this reason he may not let his heart adhere too firmly to any individual thing; within him too there must be something wandering that takes pleasure in change and transience. (HH 638)

In this aphorism Nietzsche identifies "freedom of mind" with the awareness that truth understood as a stable and definitive possession (the "final desti-nation" of the journey of knowledge) simply does not exist. The free spirit conceives of knowledge as a collecting of many different perspectives on things, none of which is to be promoted to the status of an "absolute" perspec-tive ("he may not let his heart adhere too firmly to any individual thing"). The fact that there is foreseen for this process no final, definitive moment of con-clusion does not discourage the free spirit; on the contrary, this fact is a source of joy for the free spirit, since, as Nietzsche writes, "within him too there must be something wandering that takes pleasure in change and transience." In AOM 211 Nietzsche takes up once again this last observation and explains that, in contrast to those "fettered spirits" who are "firm-rooted intellects," the free spirits can also be defined as "free ranging spirits" because they feel "the tug toward freedom as the strongest drive" of their being. Their ideal mode of life is defined by Nietzsche as "spiritual nomadism [*geistigen Nomadenthum*]." In order to fully understand what Nietzsche means by this expression, and thus also fully understand the nature of the free spirit, it is necessary to an-alyze that passage from Emerson's essay *History* from which this image is, in fact, drawn. Emerson describes in this passage the conflict which has always historically recurred between nomadic and sedentary peoples. Whereas some peoples, those whose means of livelihood and survival were based on agricul-ture and the breeding of livestock, needed to settle down in a single region or territory if they were to prosper, others, those who survived by sacking and looting the lands they crossed, needed to be constantly moving from place to place. These two types of population groups ended up, naturally, coming into conflict with one another, since their lifestyles were mutually irreconcilable. The nomadic groups swooped down, periodically, on the settlements estab-lished by the sedentary groups, throwing everything into chaos and leaving a legacy of despair and anger.

Emerson observes that something analogous still transpires in the modern world, albeit on a more spiritual plane, inasmuch as "sedentary" and "nomadic" tendencies are still today to be found within the soul of modern humankind. Whereas some individuals tend to want to establish firm beliefs around which to consolidate their lives, others are more inclined to practice thought as a constant "wandering":

The intellectual nomadism [*geistige Nomadenthum* in the German text] is the faculty of objectiveness [*die Gabe der Objektivität* in the German text][37] or of eyes which everywhere feed themselves [*oder die Gabe überall Augenweide zu finden* in the German text]. Who hath such eyes, everywhere falls into easy relation with his fellow-men [*Wem dies gegeben ist, der is überall zu Hause* in the German text]. Every man, every thing is a prize, a study, a property to him, and this love [*und die Liebe, die ihn so für Alles gleich beseelt* in the German text] smooths his brow, joins him to men and makes him beautiful and beloved in their sight. (E I, 19; V, 17; Nietzsche underlined the phrase "die Gabe überall Augenweide zu finden" and enclosed it in parentheses and added two vertical lines in the margin, one straight and one a spiral; see Appendix Figure 4)[38]

How is it that Emerson's "intellectual nomad" is constantly changing his own vision of the world and the things around him? We find the answer to this question in the essay *Circles*, where Emerson celebrates Nature as a constant becoming: one form passes continuously into another, and none remains identical with itself. The spirit of humankind does the same: it grows and changes, so that what had appeared true to it just yesterday may no longer seem so tomorrow. Those who aspire to be honest with themselves are obliged to admit that every truth which they have arduously formed for themselves and every value in which they believe might well collapse from one day to the next in the light of some new experience: "Our life is an apprenticeship to the truth, that around every circle another can be drawn; that there is no end in nature, but every end is a beginning; that there is always another dawn risen on mid-noon, and under every deep a lower deep opens" (E I, 249; V, 220–221; Nietzsche underlined the phrase "there is no end in Nature, but every end is a beginning"). It is the attitude that consists in searching for definitive truths and absolute values that leads to error, madness, and sickness, writes Emerson. "No truth [is] so sublime but it may be trivial to-morrow in the light of new thoughts. People wish to be settled: only as far as they are unsettled, is there any hope for them" (E I, 264; V, 236). For this reason it will be the thinker possessed of integrity, the thinker who is genuinely pursuing truth, who will always prefer "the truth to his past apprehension of truth" (E I, 255; V, 227). This thinker, in other words, is not emotionally bound to his or her own truth but is always ready to place that truth in question. This connection that Emerson draws between love of the truth and "intellectual nomadism" is evident also in the following passage from the essay *Intellect*, in which he opposes to and contrasts with one another the minds in which there prevails "the love of repose" and those in which there prevails "the love of truth":

He in whom the love of repose predominates, will accept the first creed, the first philosophy, the first political party he meets, —most likely his

father's. He gets rest, commodity, and reputation;[39] but he shuts the
door of truth. He in whom the love of truth predominates will keep
himself aloof from all moorings and afloat. He will abstain from dogmatism, and recognize all the opposite negations between which, as walls,
his being is swung. He submits to the inconvenience of suspect and imperfect opinion, but he is a candidate for truth, as the other is not, and
respects the highest law of his being. (E I, 282–283; V, 251; Nietzsche
underlined "love of repose" and marked the passage "He in whom the
love of truth . . . being" with a vertical line, next to which he added the
note "bravo!"; see Appendix Figure 24)[40]

Taking up Emerson's argument as his own, Nietzsche sets up an opposition between, on the one hand, the "free spirit" who, just because there predominates
in him or her the "spirit of inquiry after truth," "demands reasons" —that
is to say, weighs up the reasons for and against everything that he or she
believes—and, on the other hand, the "fettered spirit" who, on the contrary,
merely "demands faith" (HH 225). As Nietzsche explains in the *Antichrist*,
"Faith means not wanting to know what is true" (A 52). For this reason the
"fettered spirit," adds Nietzsche at HH 226, tends to cling to the very first belief
that he or she happens to encounter, which is in most cases that which his or
her culture has handed down: the "fettered spirit" "takes up his position, not
for reasons, but out of habit. He is a Christian, for example, not because he
has knowledge of the various religions and has chosen between them. . . . He
encountered Christianity . . . and adopted [it] without reasons, as a man born
in wine-producing country becomes a wine drinker."

Having identified these important sources of Nietzsche's, we can now understand that the "freedom from unconditionality" that characterizes his free spirit
is a consequence of the drive toward truth. The virtue of truthfulness, taken to
its ultimate consequences, leads finally to a realization that "truth" in the sense
in which it has traditionally been understood—that is to say, truth conceived of
as something that can be stably and definitively "possessed" —simply does not
exist. Nietzsche's "free spirit" figure, then, is the personification of the awareness
that (1) every opinion is necessarily subjective and partial, and (2) no vision of
the world and what is in it is eternally valid. This awareness carries the free spirit
into an existence of "intellectual nomadism,"[41] which consists in a constant availa-
bility and openness for the revision and the bringing "up to date" of his or her own
opinions and indeed in a positive pleasure in this process of constant revision.

3.3.2. Coming Face to Face with Others

What is it that leads the individual whom Nietzsche calls the "free spirit" to alter
his or her opinions? The fact that there changes, with growing experience of life,

his or her way of seeing things and his or her feelings about the things that he or she sees (see GS 307). But this mental growth can occur only in and through encounter and confrontation with that which is other than oneself. In the passage cited above from the essay *History* Emerson says that the "intellectual nomad" has no need to settle on any fixed domicile because he feels himself to be at home wherever he goes. The metaphorical form of expression aside, this means that the "intellectual nomad" loves to encounter and confront people different from himself, to experience new ways of life and to make these new ways of life, if only for a time, his own. The "nomad" is distinguished by the ease with which he is able to identify and empathize with people belonging to different peoples and cultures, while never allowing any one of these different visions of the world with which he empathizes to pervade him and take him over to the point of becoming his definitive vision. He seeks encounter and confrontation with that which is "other" than himself in order to take possession of this "other," or, in other words, to integrate it into his own personal vision. This aspect emerges particularly clearly in the brief summary of the above-cited Emerson passage that Nietzsche copied into his 1882 notebook of excerpts: "Intellectual nomadism is the gift of objectivity or the gift to find everywhere a feast for the eyes. Every human being, every individual thing, is my discovery, my possession: the love which is inspired in him for everything smoothes his forehead" (NL 1882 17[13], KSA 9: 667).

According to Kateb (2002, 4), Emerson's "self-reliance" is principally an intellectual method which consists in receiving and weighing up the greatest possible number of points of view upon a single object so as to form a new and original way of seeing it. Without receptivity or responsiveness to individualities different from one's own, the determination to express one's own point of view—a positive thing, certainly, in itself—is at risk of degenerating into blind arrogance.[42] Moreover, according to Emerson, the more different from ourselves are the people we engage with, the richer and broader our vision of things will be. This is the reason whoever aspires to truth "seeks those [minds] of different quality from his own, and such as are good of their kind; that is, he seeks other men, and the otherest" (RM, 4; see Kateb 2006, 197; as we shall see in chapter 4, it is for this reason that one's adversaries are to be considered one's best friends). How, according to Emerson, does this receptivity to the opinions of others develop? Through empathetic identification. And this empathetic identification, in turn, occurs when the individual attains to a sense of the contingency of his or her own individuality. Kateb (1992, 265) describes it as the sense that "it is a matter of chance that any person has been born and then been raised in one way rather than another. . . . The same biological being that I am could have been culturally situated in an indefinitely great number of places and acquired a different personality and outward life in each case." These individual, in other words, experience what Kateb calls a "democratic ecstasy" (244), during which they feel other people to be actualizations of possibilities which they themselves never brought to realization, although they potentially might have done so. As Emerson writes, "I am certified of a common nature; and so these other souls, these separated selves, draw me as nothing else can" (E I, 229; V, 203–204; Nietzsche marked this passage with two vertical lines in the margin). Nietzsche wrote in the margin of this passage, "Why is it that it is natures opposed to mine that exert the strongest attraction upon me? [*Warum ziehn die entgegengesetzten Naturen mich am heftigsten an?*] They make me feel the necessity of becoming complete [*Sie lassen mich das Voll-werden-müssen fühlen*]; they belong within me [*sie gehören in mich hinein*]" (NL 1881 13[13], KSA 9: 620; V, 203; see Appendix Figure 21). Clearly, Nietzsche does not accept Emerson's mysticism here and translates it into psychological terms. He observes that the thinker who seeks truth does not fear but is, on the contrary, attracted by those who think differently from him or her, because being confronted by different views gives the thinker the chance to expand his or her point of view.[43] As Nietzsche was to explain at GM III 12, to "put oneself in the shoes" of different individuals and to make their point of view one's own constitutes a valuable education in objectivity, or a "propaedeutic" of seeing:

> One knows how to employ a variety of perspectives and affective interpretations in the service of knowledge.... To see differently, and to want to see differently ... is no small discipline and preparation of the intellect for its future "objectivity"—the latter understood not as "contemplation [*Anschauung*] without interest" (which is, as such, a non-concept and an absurdity), but as having in our power the ability to engage and disengage our "pros" and "cons": we can use the difference in perspectives and affective interpretations for knowledge.

In other words, it is the confrontation with the "other" that provides one with the opportunity to broaden one's own view of things. The greater the number of people whose viewpoints we welcome and draw into account, and the greater the difference is between these viewpoints and our own, the greater will be our knowledge of the world and all that makes it up or, in other words, the closer we will come to "objectivity." This is why, as Emerson writes in the passage cited above, "intellectual nomadism is the faculty of objectiveness."

Reading Nietzsche specifically in the light of his own reading of Emerson makes it possible to propose an interpretation of that famous critique of traditional notions of "objective knowledge" that Nietzsche develops in the third of the three essays that make up *On the Genealogy of Morality* which differs significantly from the interpretation of this passage recently proposed by Jensen (2010). The passage in question runs as follows: "There is only a perspectival seeing, only a perspectival 'knowing,' and the more affects we are able to put into words about a thing, the more eyes, various eyes we are able to use for the same thing, the more complete will be our 'concept' of the thing, our 'objectivity'" (GM III 13). Jensen is certainly right in his observation that, in this passage, Nietzsche is refusing the notion of "objectivity" both (1) in the sense of "subject-free observation" and (2) in the sense of a universally accepted description. Nevertheless, I must take issue with Jensen's interpretation of the specific notion of objectivity with which Nietzsche wished to replace these more traditional notions that he rejected. According to Jensen (2013, 127), in this famous passage from the third essay of the *Genealogy*, Nietzsche wanted to redefine objectivity in terms of an "intersubjective agreement about judgments from within a specific type." By "type" Jensen means "psychological type," that is to say, a particular configuration of drives that various different individuals have in common. For Jensen, agreement within a type is possible because "the distortive character of the affective component of judgments is neutralized among those judges who share a similar set of affects" (127).[44] According to Jensen, then, when Nietzsche writes "the more eyes . . . we are able to use for the same thing, the more complete will be our 'concept' of the thing, our 'objectivity,'" he means "eyes" belonging to different individuals but individuals of the same psychological "type" (GM III 13; see Jensen 2013, 129).[45] However, if we consider this passage from the third essay of the *Genealogy* (GM III 12) in the light of Nietzsche's reading of Emerson, it clearly emerges that the "more eyes" with which, according to Nietzsche, we need to look at a thing if we are to secure the most complete possible view and understanding of it are, in fact, "eyes" internal to each individual himself or herself. It seems to me that we must conclude, then, that the (nontraditional) objectivity evoked by Nietzsche at GM III 12 does not, as Jensen claims it does, correspond to an intersubjective agreement between different individuals but rather to an agreement internal to each individual, that is, to a particular configuration of this individual's drives which leads him or her to construct a unitary view or vision of a thing (or of a state of affairs) after having considered this thing from a whole range of different points of view.

3.3.3. The Skepticism of Strength

At this point we may ask ourselves just what it is that makes possible the "intellectual nomadism" that Nietzsche personifies through the figure of the "free spirit" as "wanderer." Reginster manages to give an answer to this question by analyzing that figure who represents the very contrary of the "free spirit," namely, the "fettered spirit." According to Reginster, Nietzsche sometimes refers to the "fettered spirit" as the "man of faith [*der Mensch des Glaubens, or der Gläubige*]"

(A 54), sometimes as "the believer" (HH 225), sometimes as the "man of conviction [*der Mensch der Überzeugung*]" (HH 629), and, finally, sometimes as
"the dogmatist" (BGE 43). All these expressions, claims Reginster (2003, 52),
refer to a single psychological type: the fanatic. The fanatic is distinguished by
his or her need to believe that he or she is in possession of "the unconditional
truth." He or she needs "a faith, a support, a backbone, something to fall back
on" (GS 347). Being the antithesis of the fanatic, the free spirit is distinguished
by the absence of any need for a "support" of this kind. In other words, whereas
the "fettered spirit" is a weak personality, the free spirit is decidedly a strong one.

The tendency to "intellectual nomadism" that Nietzsche identifies as characteristic of the free spirit was to be designated in the following works by the term
"skepticism." Skepticism (or at least a certain type of skepticism) is considered by
Nietzsche to be a manifestation of "strength and super-strength of spirit" (A 54).
It consists in the capacity to keep in mind and under conscious consideration a
whole wide range of viewpoints before formulating one's own. Fanaticism, by
contrast, is born of weakness: "How much one needs a faith in order to flourish,
how much that is 'firm' and that one does not want to be shaken because one
clings to it, that is a measure of the degree of one's strength (or, to put it more
clearly, of one's weakness)" (GS 347). As we saw in section 2.2.5, for Nietzsche
the "strong" self is the self that is both internally rich and integrated, that is to
say, the self in which a multiplicity of elements has been directed and configured
in such a way as to form a unity. The "weak" self, by contrast, is the self which
has had, in order to achieve its unity, to eliminate or forgo much of its internal
richness. The unitary, or strong, self thus possesses a capacity for internal coordination (also called a "will") such that it is able to welcome into itself a large
number of different visions of the world without thereby forfeiting the ability
to formulate a vision that is specifically its own. In the case of this strong self,
worldviews different from its own serve to enrich it and provide it with the material it needs to construct a new vision of the world still broader than the one it
already possesses.[46] In the case of the weak self, however, the mere consideration
of visions of the world that differ from its own tends to have a disorienting effect,
that is to say, to place in jeopardy this same project of the self's conceiving and
constructing a worldview of its own. This type of human being needs necessarily
to eliminate from his or her cognitive horizon all viewpoints and perspectives
diverging from his or her own, with this "own perspective" thereby becoming
absolutized into absolute and unconditional truth (see GS 347, 335; HH 228).
Reginster (2003, 75) writes:

> The fanatic typically shows a great resistance to the consideration of
> points of view other than that to which he has chosen to subscribe.
> However, it is not as if he at first gives them serious consideration, then

rejects them; he rather refuses to give them serious, honest consideration in the first place. He "clings" to his one point of view and summarily dismisses the others. His need for "something firm" makes him intolerant of uncertainty, ambiguity and variability, and induces him to believe that, with a certain view of the world and the good, he is "in possession of the unqualified truth."

The "free spirit," conceived of as the type of the "strong individual," is not contrasted by Nietzsche just to the type of the "fanatic" but also to that of the "nihilist," who in fact represents another variant on the type of the "weak self." Whereas the self of the "fanatic" achieves a certain unity and integrity only through absolutizing a single point of view among many and assuming it to represent "unconditional truth," the self of the "nihilist" proves unable to achieve unity or integrity at all and disintegrates under the pressure of the awareness of the vast multiplicity of possible perspectives.

In the philosophy of his middle period Nietzsche picks out and assigns to the skeptic qua "spiritual nomad" or "wanderer" a certain dark counterpart. This dark counterpart Nietzsche calls "the shadow." The "wanderer" represents the "strong self" that is able to contain within itself a multiplicity of perspectives without falling apart, or, in other words, the individual who is capable of sifting through an enormous quantity of arguments and considerations "for" and "against" before formulating his or her own judgment.[47] The "shadow," on the other hand, who accompanies the "wanderer" wherever that figure goes, embodies the other possible reaction that we have mentioned to a dawning awareness that no perspective on the world is universally valid or definitive. It personifies, in other words, the "weak self" that does not succeed in dominating the multiplicity of possible interpretations and thus does not succeed either in forming its own perspective and point of view. The shadow says, "All is the same, nothing is worth it, searching does not help" (Z IV, The Cry of Distress). It personifies skepticism, as indeed does the "wanderer," but a skepticism very different from that personified by the latter: a skepticism that Nietzsche calls "the scepticism of weakness [*Skepsis der Schwäche*]" (NL 1883–1884, 24[30], KSA 10: 662; see also Sommer 2006, 263). This "scepticism of weakness" corresponds to nihilism. In a "weak" type who endorses skepticism, thinking is paralyzed, since all perspectives are seen as equally devoid of value.

What distinguishes "the scepticism of strength" from "the scepticism of weakness" (which Nietzsche also calls "the lethargy of despair [*Trägheit der Verzweiflung* in the original German]"; NL 1880 6[356], KSA 9: 287) is an experimental attitude, the courage to attempt an interpretation even while being aware that all perspectives are inevitably subjective and partial. Such an experimental attitude resembles the one adopted in what is called a "lucid dream": a dream dreamed in full awareness that one is dreaming. After the death of God, explains Nietzsche, the man who does not want to fall into nihilism should "go on dreaming," even though he is aware that he is indeed in a dream (GS 54). In other words, the individual should go on affirming his or her views and values in full consciousness of their merely relative, transient, and ultimately "human all too human" character.

The distinction between these two types of skepticism—one an expression of strength, the other an expression of weakness—is reiterated by Nietzsche in more systematic manner in the section of *Beyond Good and Evil* devoted to the theme *We Scholars*. In this section of the book Nietzsche criticizes above all "the average man of science" (BGE 206) and the manner in which he pursues "objectivity," "objectivity" being (mis)conceived by "the man of science" as the absence of all personal opinions. Nietzsche praises, indeed, the virtues of industriousness and patience (BGE 206) that this "average man of science" still displays, but he also warns against the excessive praise that he feels is accorded by the culture of his day to the "desubjectivization and depersonification of mind" of this "man of science" (BGE 207, translation slightly amended). This "man of science," indeed, having been educated and trained to aspire to the ideal of "objectivity" in the sense of complete impersonality, has become incapable, Nietzsche argues, of expressing personal opinions and thereby also incapable of creating new values. The real philosopher is presented, in contrast to this "man of science," as a skeptic. But what kind of skeptic? In fact, Nietzsche raises fundamental objections against what is normally understood by the term "skepticism": a "noble abstinence" from the expression of any personal opinion (BGE 208). This type of skepticism, states Nietzsche, "is the most spiritual expression of a certain complex physiological condition which in layman's terms is called weak nerves or a sickly constitution. . . . What is most profoundly sick and degenerate about such hybrids is the will" (BGE 208). This type of skepticism, which is born from a "paralysis of the will" (BGE 208), is the expression of a weak self, not so different in the final analysis from the expression of this same weak self that we see in the case of the "man of science." The subject does not succeed in governing and coordinating the broad range of different viewpoints to which he or she has been exposed so as to make of them, and thus of himself or herself, a coherent cognitive unity, and the result of this is a weak will and the inability to affirm any vision of things as specifically one's own.

The skepticism that Nietzsche hopes and wishes to see arise—as a remedy against both the "depersonification of spirit" typical of the "man of science" and the "bad skepticism" which views all individual opinions as indifferent— is a "scepticism of bold masculinity" (BGE 209). Nietzsche's characterization of this skepticism may at first appear extremely enigmatic: "This scepticism despises and nevertheless appropriates; it undermines and takes possession;

it does not believe but does not die on this account" (BGE 209). What does this mean? A clarification of this passage is to be found at BGE 205: the real philosopher has the right/duty to call into question all established truths and all received opinions, but, at the same time, this philosopher also has the right/ duty to formulate his or her own vision of things—that is to say, to advance an interpretation of his or her own, even while being aware of the necessarily limited and partial status of any such interpretation. In short, the true philosopher cannot be placed in the general category of the "skeptic" but must rather be characterized specifically as someone who embraces the "scepticism of strength." It was this way of practicing philosophy that Nietzsche was referring to when he used the expression "live dangerously" (BGE 205). Whereas the person who pursues "objectivity" in the "bad" senses that we described above—or who lives, in other words, under the sheltering shadow of the ideal that "truth" must be something eternal and incontrovertible—is seeking, above all, safety and security, the real philosopher, the "sceptic out of strength," is someone who risks advancing an interpretation of the world even while knowing that this interpretation will surely be called into question by others, or even by his or her own self, at some point in the near or distant future: "The real philosopher . . . feels the weight and duty of a hundred experiments. . . . He constantly puts himself at risk" (BGE 205).

This attitude of constant experimentation is precisely the attitude that Emerson holds to be the appropriate one for the "self-reliant" thinker who has come to an awareness of the inevitable partiality of every perspective and point of view. In the essay *Circles*, after having declared that the true thinker is always ready to revise and re-revise his or her vision of things, he further declares his own identification with this type of thinker[48] and writes of himself, "I am only an experimenter. Do not set the least value on what I do, or the least discredit on what I do not, as if I pretended to settle any thing as true or false. I unsettle all things. No facts are to me sacred; none are profane; I simply experiment, an endless seeker, with no Past at my back" (E I, 262; V, 234; Nietzsche underlined this last phrase). In the margin of the page Nietzsche scribbled the note "Really [*Ja*]??" (see Appendix Figure 23), probably indicating that he found this intellectual self-portrait of Emerson's to be quite at odds with the peremptory tone of many of the American writer's statements. Nietzsche takes up once again the key motifs of this self-portrait of Emerson as an "experimenter" in a note which he jotted down on the endpapers of his copy of the *Essays*: "Beyond love and hate, and good and evil, a cheater with a clear conscience, cruel to the point of self-mutilation, undetected and in plain sight, an experimenter [*ein Versucher*], who lives on the blood of other souls, who loves virtue as an experiment, as he loves vice" (NL 1881 13[21], KSA 9: 622). Very probably, rather than sketching a portrait of Emerson, Nietzsche is sketching here the portrait of his "ideal philosopher," who, as we have seen, is necessarily an "experimenter," that is, a "sceptic out of strength."[49]

Further proof of how important a role the reading of Emerson played in helping Nietzsche to grasp and to focus on that "experimental" character that must form part of the nature of every true philosopher is the marginal note that Nietzsche made to a passage in the essay *History* in his personal (German) copy of Emerson's *Essays*. In this passage Emerson recounts the ancient legend of the Sphinx. In Greek mythology the Sphinx was a lion with the face of a woman and the wings of a bird that had been set by the goddess Hera upon Mount Fagas at the entrance to the city of Thebes. This being posed a riddle to everyone who approached the city and devoured whoever failed to solve it. It was Oedipus, the city's future king, who proved finally able to solve this riddle, and the Sphinx, defeated, cast herself to her death from the high rock. Emerson used this myth to express the idea that history poses a riddle to us much like the riddle posed to travelers by the Sphinx. If one proves unable to solve this riddle—that is to say, proves unable to establish a connection between what one reads in history books and one's own life—then one will be devoured by history as travelers to Thebes were devoured by the Sphinx. If, however, one proves able to solve it, then one will dominate history. "As near and proper to us is also that old fable of the Sphinx, who was said to sit in the road side and put riddles to every passenger. If the man could not answer she swallowed him alive" (E I, 27; V, 25; Nietzsche marked this whole passage with a thick vertical line in the margin and underlined the words "If the man could not answer").

In the margin next to this passage, Nietzsche wrote the following reflection: "To give an answer at all when such a riddle is posed to one—this is already to do a very great thing; and merely to believe that one has solved such a riddle—this too is already to do a very great thing. That someone proves bold enough to give any answer at all to the riddle that is life—this alone is enough to send the Sphinx plunging from the rock (ego)" (NL 1881 13[9], KSA 9: 620; V, 25).[50] Nietzsche, clearly, is conferring upon this passage from Emerson a sense that Emerson himself had not envisaged for it. His reflection here seems to allude to the fact that every honest thinker knows all too well that the riddle that life, like the Sphinx, poses to us is a riddle that can never be solved once and for all. In other words, thinkers who are honest with themselves will have no illusions regarding the absolute validity of their own interpretations and will know them to be in every case necessarily partial and historically limited. For all that, though, contends Nietzsche, it is only the thinkers who—in full awareness of the partial and limited character of any and every interpretation they might possibly propose—have the strength and boldness to propose an interpretation nonetheless who can save themselves from the abyss of nihilism. It is precisely, in other words, this boldness that distinguishes and sets off from the nihilist the person who is a "sceptic out of strength."[51]

3.3.4. Self-Reliance as Receptivity or Responsiveness to Others' Opinions

Let us conclude by observing that, first in the figure of the "free spirit" in his aspect of "wanderer" and then in the figure of the philosopher as a "sceptic out of strength," Nietzsche embodies the second fundamental aspect of the Emersonian virtue of self-reliance: an openness toward the "other" as an individual different from myself. The encounter and engagement with the "other than oneself" is the necessary complement to the attitude that Nietzsche had earlier embodied in the figure of "Schopenhauer as educator": an attitude of reverence toward one's own self and a desire to develop one's own potential. Without an openness toward the "other" and a certain confrontation with the experience of this "other," the mere expression of the self will prove in the end to be something poor and sterile. Clearly, however, whereas for Emerson this confrontation with the "other" is a choice, for Nietzsche it is a consequence of the possession of a unitary (and thereby of a strong) self. Only this type of self will be capable of encountering and engaging with views and opinions different from its own without falling to pieces. These two figures, that of "Schopenhauer as educator" and that of the "free spirit," along with the specific virtues they represent, thus complete the first phase of that process of achieving true individuality which will be carried to consummation by the figure of Zarathustra.

3.4. Creating New Values

Nietzsche conceives of Zarathustra as the embodiment of the final stage in the process of bringing individuality to full expression. Zarathustra represents the individual who has overcome traditional morality and has acquired moral autonomy, or, in other words, the individual who no longer acknowledges himself to be subject to any judgment or authority. The only values by which such an individual lives are those he has created for himself. On the one hand, then, the figure of Zarathustra displays traits continuous with those displayed by the figures of "Schopenhauer as educator" and the "free spirit," inasmuch as this figure too certainly possesses the virtues embodied by these latter. On the other hand, however, Zarathustra also displays certain virtues that these figures lack, so that he represents, in fact, a new and higher phase in the journey toward the full realization of individuality. Both the figure of "Schopenhauer as educator" and that of the "free spirit" can be defined as figures embodying negative liberty (i.e., liberty as "freedom from . . ."). In other words, through these two figures Nietzsche underlines the necessity of taking one's distance from everything which limits one's expression of oneself as an individual. But even though this is a necessary stage in the journey toward becoming an individual in the fullest sense, it is not sufficient to carry one all the way to this goal. In the stage of negative liberty the individual does not yet dispose of liberty in the real sense, since his or her actions ensue from opposition to something other than himself or herself. In other words, such individuals are not yet truly acting but rather, properly speaking, only reacting. Although they no longer attempt to make their actions conform to the traditional codes of moral judgments and values or to the standards imposed by society, these codes and standards remain nonetheless decidedly present to their mind. Moreover, in the struggle against the obstacles that limit the expression of the true self there will inevitably emerge certain feelings and attitudes which are also "reactive" in the sense just alluded to, such as rage, disgust, or resentment—feelings and attitudes which deprive the individual of precious inner resources. If, then, one is really to succeed in bringing to expression all one's potential, one must somehow succeed in freeing oneself also from these reactive feelings and attitudes. This, Nietzsche believes, is achieved in the figure of Zarathustra. Zarathustra represents a figure embodying positive liberty (liberty as "freedom to . . ." or "freedom for . . .") inasmuch as, after having overcome all that which had formerly limited and restricted him, he has now also overcome the resentment and the feeling of guilt that had arisen in him during the earlier phases of his journey toward realizing individuality. Zarathustra is now the possessor of all his inherent powers and uses every word he speaks and every gesture he makes to give positive expression to his own real self.

Zarathustra, we will argue, personifies Emersonian "self-reliance" in one last and supremely important sense of the term: that of spontaneous and original self-expression. At its highest level of development, Emerson's "self-reliance" does not take the form of opposition to, but rather that of utter disregard for, all that is contrary to one's own nature. It is only after having attained this divine state of indifference that one can completely and authentically express all one's potential.

3.4.1. Negative Liberty and Positive Liberty

The figure of Zarathustra is introduced, in the Prologue of the work that bears his name, by an old man who, observing him descend from his mountain, exclaims with astonishment and admiration:

> This wanderer is no stranger to me: many years ago he passed by here. Zarathustra he was called; but he is transformed. . . .
> Yes, I recognize Zarathustra. His eyes are pure, and no disgust is visible around his mouth. Does he not stride like a dancer?
> Zarathustra is transformed, Zarathustra has become a child, an awakened one is Zarathustra (Z Prologue 2).

The old man, by stating that he had formerly encountered Zarathustra in the form of a "wanderer" and declaring that he now beholds him changed and transformed, emphasizes the distance that separates these two figures—the "wanderer" of Nietzsche's philosophy of the "free spirit" and Zarathustra, the eponymous protagonist of Nietzsche's new work—despite the many traits they share. The old man also clearly enumerates the signs by which this difference between the two figures manifests itself. In Zarathustra there is no longer visible any sign of anger, contempt, or "heaviness." His gaze is clear, the features of his face relaxed, and his gait light and nimble. Like the "wanderer," Zarathustra no longer believes in truth as something that can be eternally and definitively possessed. "Make no mistake about it: great spirits are sceptics. Zarathustra is a sceptic" (A 54). Consequently, also like the "wanderer," Zarathustra is characterized by a distancing of himself from traditional morality, from metaphysics, and from religion. In sharp contrast to the "wanderer," however, Zarathustra no longer struggles, negates, or accuses. He has the innocence and lightheartedness of a child.

In the parable *On the Three Metamorphoses*, in which Nietzsche describes the three stages of the process of overcoming morality, it is the image of the child that is used to illustrate the last and highest stage—that is to say, the moment of the creation of new values. The first stage in this process of moral evolution is the stage of "morality of customs." In this stage, says Nietzsche, individuals take upon themselves, like a camel, the burden that consists in the truths and values in which they have been raised and educated. But in the second stage individuals take their stand against them. With a roar like a lion's, these individuals utter their "no" to all that which they had hitherto passively accepted. In other words, the lion represents the phase of negative liberty: individuals who claim their right to moral autonomy. But even the lion, says Nietzsche, is not yet able to create its own values. In order to do this, the lion must transform itself, in its turn, into a child.[52] What exactly is this "childlike" state? That is to say, what exactly is this state in which one becomes capable of creating new values?

The answer to this question is to be found, once again, in the pages of Emerson's *Essays*. In the essay *Self-Reliance* the American author describes a path of development that passes through a phase of negative liberty so as to arrive ultimately at a state of positive liberty, a state of freedom in the true and proper sense. After having shown that one can hope to obtain great results only by authentically expressing one's own true self, and that to pursue such an aim will mean necessarily coming into conflict with society and with tradition, Emerson goes on to point out that it is also crucially important to cleanse one's soul of all the negative emotions and attitudes that this conflict will inevitably have given rise to. The virtue that Emerson evokes here is magnanimity. This virtue has nothing to do with Christian compassion. What Emerson means by it is rather (as, indeed, accords with the word's etymology: *magna anima* = possessing a great soul) a raising of oneself onto a super-personal level on which the personal ego ceases to have any importance. Once the needs of the ego—such as the need for moral support and approval—have been eliminated, one no longer feels any resentment toward those who fail or refuse to satisfy these needs, and one becomes able to concentrate completely upon one's own life aim. Nietzsche copied into his notebook these lines from Emerson: "When the poor and the ignorant join in the agitation, when the unintelligent animal mass [*thierische Masse* in the German text] contorts its face and snarls—then magnanimity [*größer Seele* in the German text] is needed to shove it aside, in godly fashion and as if it were a trifle. NB" (NL 1882 17[28], KSA 9: 670; see V 41).[53] This is exactly the advice given by Zarathustra to the "foaming fool" whom he meets when he goes down into the "big city." This "foaming fool," full of disgust and rage, spends all his time blaming society as a mere mass of "mud" where all great thoughts and aspirations inevitably die. Though sharing his view, Zarathustra wants to preserve his energies for pursuing his goal. Thus, he does not abandon himself to resentment but says to the fool, "Where one can no longer love, there one should—pass by!" (Z III, On Passing By).[54]

To those who want to be entirely themselves Emerson offers as an example the ways of children. Children are free in the truest and highest sense: they conform to no one's laws, but to do this they do not need to violently distance themselves from those around them. Their freedom consists simply in their seeing, and being aware of, nothing except what they themselves are doing at any given time; they are completely concentrated upon their own selves. Nietzsche, in one of his notebooks, sums up this thought of Emerson's as follows:

> The divided, suspicious mind, the high craftiness [*Kunstfertigkeit*] which computes what strength and means could stand opposed to our purpose: children do not have it. As one looks in a child's face, one is disconcerted [*so wird man verlegen*]. They conform to nobody: all conform to them; they never worry about the consequences [of their own behavior], or the interests of others [*Interessen Anderer*]: they give an independent [*eigenmächtiges*], genuine [*unverfälschtes*] verdict. They do not seek to please you: you must court them. (NL 1882 17[24], KSA 9: 669; see E I, 39–40; V, 35)[55]

Emerson exhorts individuals to reestablish within themselves—through the exercise of magnanimity—this state of "naive inconsiderateness" which comes naturally to children. Nietzsche sums up this thought in his own notebook: "To effect one's perceptions again and again from the same unbribable, unaffrighted standpoint of innocence [*Unschuld*]—this is formidable [*furchterregend*]: one cannot help but feel the power of such immortal youth [*die Macht solcher unsterblichen Jugend wird gefühlt*]" (NL 1882 17[25], KSA 9: 669).[56] What Nietzsche learns through his reading of Emerson is that it is only the person who has become completely concentrated upon himself or herself, and who no longer negates, accuses, or struggles, who is in a position to create values that do not emerge out of a reactive opposition to anything but rather solely out of the drive toward full self-expression. It is also only in the light of this reading of Emerson that it becomes clear why Nietzsche's Zarathustra, to whom there has been confided the task of the "transvaluation of all values," is not in the least bit affected by any sense of guilt. His action of destruction, in fact, is not born out of any polemical intention but is simply the unintended consequence of a movement of self-expression. Emerson maintains that the person who has finally begun to live as a true individual—that is, to live in a way that is autonomous and original—cannot help but judge each thing he or she encounters in a way that is new and uniquely personal. The undermining of the status quo ante is an unintended effect of the positive expression of the self. Such an individual, therefore, destroys centuries of tradition and the most revered institutions with the lightheartedness of a child at play: "The great will not condescend to take any thing seriously; all must be as gay as the song of a canary, though it were the building of cities or the eradication of old and foolish churches and nations, which have cumbered the earth long thousands of years," writes Emerson. "Simple hearts put all the history and customs of this world behind them, and play their own play in innocent defiance of the Blue-Laws of the world" (E I, 212; V, 189).[57] Nietzsche takes up this sugges- tion and describes the individual who "transvalues all values" as like a child who "plays naively, i.e. not deliberately but from overflowing abundance and power, with everything that has hitherto been called holy, good, untouchable, divine" (GS 382). The lack of reverence of the autonomous individual for all that which was, for a long time, called sacred; his or her enormous destructive force and drive—these things are not, in such an individual's case, born from aggressiveness or from hatred. It is simply that such an individual is totally concentrated upon his or her own self, and by expressing this self he or she revolutionizes the world.[58]

3.4.2. Virtue as Spontaneity

Among the characteristics that must be possessed by the creator of new values we must count not only this "naive inconsiderateness" typical of children, which can be summed up as (1) a propensity not to comply with or conform to commands issued by others or models handed down from the past and (2) an absence of contentiousness, anger, and guilt, that is, of attitudes which still show traces of forms of conditioning. The action of creating new values is also, and above all, described by Nietzsche as a spontaneous action, in the sense that it transcends any command that one might have to give to oneself. For a still clearer illustration of just what Nietzsche meant us to understand by this notion of spontaneity it is useful to consider a private jotting from 1883 in which he provides some additional information concerning the process of the overcoming of morality which is described through imagery alone in the parable *On the Three Metamorphoses*. Nietzsche observes here that the first stage of morality corresponds to the command "you must" or, in other words, to an "unconditional obedience" to a moral code imposed by an authority external to the individual. The second stage of moral development, by contrast, corresponds to "I want" or, in other words, to the individual's demand for moral autonomy. There exists, however, yet a further stage, one in which the individual says simply "I am." In other words, individuals in this final stage are neither commanded by others nor do they give commands to themselves, but rather simply express themselves for what and how they are (NL 1884 25[351], KSA 11: 105). We may observe that in the first two stages of moral development as described by Nietzsche, virtue is an act of obedience: in the first stage obedience to what others command one to do; in the second stage to what one commands oneself to do. In the third stage, however, virtue is an expressive, creative act: the spontaneous behavior that flows from a perfected nature. It is not by chance that Nietzsche considers the ancient Greek gods to be representative of this third stage.

In the parable *On the Sublime* we find further information concerning spontaneity as the distinctive sign of the person who possesses virtue as opposed to the person who laboriously pursues it. In this parable Zarathustra mocks that human type whom he refers to as "the sublime ones," or the ascetics of the spirit, who represent those who strain effortfully to be virtuous by imposing a violent constriction upon their own natures. "I saw a sublime one today," says Zarathustra, "adorned with ugly truths, his hunter's spoils, and rich in tattered clothing." Zarathustra goes on to deplore that "he [has] not yet learned laughing and beauty. . . . There is still contempt in his eyes, and nausea lingers on his lips" (Z II, On the Sublime Ones). The face of those who attempt to dominate their own instincts will be deformed by the terrible effort, as well as by anger, and they will have an ugly appearance. But those who possess virtue will be distinguished by grace and beauty. Their exterior physiognomy will reflect a state of mind that is serene and relaxed because there is no interior conflict. "When power becomes gracious and descends into view," says Zarathustra, "beauty I call such descending" (Z II, On the Sublime Ones). Nietzsche's use of this terminology immediately suggests that he is making an implicit allusion to Schiller.[59]

Schiller claims that the self of each individual is characterized by, on the one hand, a rational component (which he calls a "rational nature") which manifests in the faculty of judgment and, on the other, a sensible component (which he calls a "sensible nature") which manifests in the faculties of perception and emotion. In the case where an individual's self is dominated by its sensible component, the actions of the individual in question will be actions governed by his or her impulses, that is, by factors over which he or she has no (or insufficient) control. If, on the other hand, the self is dominated by its rational component, the actions of the individual in question will be actions governed by processes of conscious deliberation. A critic of Kant's conception of the categorical moral imperative, Schiller argued that true virtue is attainable only when reason and sensibility cease to struggle against one another and the rational moral drive, which Schiller also called the "forming drive [*Formtrieb*]," no longer needs to exercise coercion upon the sensual one, also called by Schiller the "material drive [*Stofftrieb*]" (see Townsend 2010, 282, translation emended). In the virtuous individual, whom Schiller called "the beautiful soul," the forming drive and the material drive are joined and reconciled with one another in what Schiller called the "play drive [*Spieltrieb*]." "A harmonious individual would have affects that incline her to pursue the very same ends that rational thought inclines her to pursue" (Katsafanas 2016, 183). Whereas, then, the person who is still effortfully striving after virtue is distinguished by the quality of sublimity or dignity (*Würde*), the person who actually possesses virtue (i.e., the "beautiful soul") is distinguished rather by the quality of grace (*Anmuth*).

Katsafanas (2016, 185) observes that for Nietzsche no less than for Schiller the unity of the self is obtained only where there has ceased to be any conflict between reason and sensibility or (to use the rather more modern terminology adopted by Nietzsche, who was writing almost a hundred years after Schiller) between conscious thought and the drives.[60] Nietzsche's position also coincides with that of Schiller as regards the claim that the unity of the self cannot be achieved via one part of this self's dominance over the other part (Katsafanas 2016, 184). Nevertheless, we need to insist that the ethical ideal embodied by Schiller in the "beautiful soul" is completely different from Nietzsche's ethical ideal. Schiller's "beautiful soul" is an individual who has so completely interiorized the code of moral action that he or she acts morally not against but rather by instinct. It is clear, then, that Nietzsche could not possibly have shared Schiller's notion of virtue as an interiorization of the dominant moral code. Rather, Nietzsche made use of the re-elaboration of Schiller's philosophy that is to be found in the work of Emerson.

In *The Conduct of Life* Emerson makes a clear, if implicit, reference to Schiller by calling the great men whom he discusses in this book "fine souls"

(CL, 131; FL, 171). Nevertheless, what Emerson means by this term is something completely different from what Schiller had meant by it. For Emerson the "fine [or beautiful] soul" is the person who instinctively chooses whatever accords with his or her own individual nature and promotes its development. One might indeed say that for Emerson just as for Schiller the "beautiful soul" is a soul that acts morally by instinct. But to act "morally" means, for Emerson, not to act in conformity with any moral code but rather to act in accordance with Nature—more precisely, in accordance with one's own inner nature. In the essay *Self-Reliance* Emerson declares, "No law can be sacred to me but that of my nature. Good and bad are but names very readily transferable to that or this; the only right is what is after my constitution; the only wrong what is against it" (E I, 42; V, 37; Nietzsche underlined "the only wrong what is against it" and marked the passage with a vertical line drawn in the margin and the numeral "27"; it was included in his notebook of extracts from the year 1882).[61] We can identify Nietzsche's source of inspiration for the parable *On the Sublimes Ones* in a passage from the essay *Spiritual Laws* which he had, in fact, vigorously underlined in his copy of the *Essays*. In this passage Emerson argues that truly virtuous persons are not those who strive and struggle effortfully to act morally, dominating their own instincts in order to do so, but rather those persons who no longer need to engage in any such struggle, since their instinct itself will unfailingly guide them toward what is truly good for them:

> People represent virtue as a struggle, and take to themselves great airs upon their attainments, and the question is every where vexed, when a noble nature is commended, Whether the man is not better who strives with temptation? But there is no merit in the matter. . . . The less a man thinks or knows about his virtues, the better we like him. . . . When we see a soul whose acts are all regal, graceful and pleasant as roses, we must thank God that such things can be and are, and not turn sourly on the angel, and say, "Crump is a better man with his grunting resistance to all his native devils." (E I, 109; V, 99; Nietzsche underlined "represent virtue as a struggle" and "noble nature," as well as the phrases "The less a man . . . like him," "such things can be," "represent virtue as a struggle").

In the last analysis, then, Nietzsche follows Emerson in rejecting the traditional definition of virtuous action as "acting in obedience to a moral code" (be this a moral code imposed on the individual from outside or a moral code imposed by the individual on himself or herself) and offering a new definition of it as "acting spontaneously in accordance with one's own nature."[62]

Clearly, the two thinkers differ regarding the way such an "accordance" is to be achieved. For Emerson, the individual enters into contact with his or her own true self by means of intuition and inspiration and remains faithful to this self by means of a constant effort of will. For Nietzsche, however, "to act in accordance with one's own nature" must necessarily have a quite different meaning, since for the younger philosopher this "nature" is not anything that is already given and present in advance. For Nietzsche, it means that the individual's conscious thought approves those things which the instincts are already pursuing and aspiring to. Clearly, this accordance can be properly established only in cases where the individual's instincts are healthy ones— that is to say, where the individual has achieved dominance over his or her drives and has selected, individually, which ones are to be allowed free rein (see Richardson 2004, 96).[63]

Only, then, when the instincts have been modeled and organized harmoniously—and not before—can conscious thought approve whatever instinct suggests to it. In a note from 1885–1886 Nietzsche explains this very clearly: "Overcoming of the affects?—No, not if it means weakening and annihilating them. Rather, take them into one's service, which may include exercising a long tyranny over them. . . . In the end we can, ever more trustingly, give them back their freedom: they love us now like good servants and voluntarily go there where the best of us wishes to go" (NL 1885–1886 1[122], WLN, 63).

We may conclude, then, that the notion of spontaneity—a spontaneity which Nietzsche conceives of as the highest stage of morality or, better put, as an overcoming of "morality" altogether as this latter has traditionally been understood—is in large part borrowed from Emerson. Let us reemphasize at this point that this highest stage can emerge only as a development from and crowning of the two prior stages. "Spontaneity" cannot just mean being the prey and plaything of one's own drives and instincts. In order to be truly spontaneous it is necessary first to bring to maturity in oneself an ability to dominate these drives and instincts (stage 1: the camel); then to take up a stance in opposition to predominant values and to impose upon oneself a long training and discipline in order to teach oneself to feel differently from the way in which one may have been taught to feel by these values hitherto predominant in one's world (stage 2: the lion); and finally, to let go even of this self-imposed "you must be" so as to simply "be" (stage 3: the child). In this last and highest stage the individual no longer dominates and commands his or her own instincts but lives spontaneously in accord with them.

3.5. Conclusion

In conclusion, then, we can define both Emerson's ethics and Nietzsche's as forms of "virtue ethics." There is, however, a key difference between the two. Whereas Emerson's ethics presupposes (even if only as a regulative ideal) a telos which corresponds to the full expression of a particular individual's true self, Nietzsche's ethics takes the form of an "ethics of becoming" (Swanton 2015, 195). "Becoming what you are presupposes that you have not the slightest inkling what you are" (EH, Clever 9), declares Nietzsche in *Ecce Homo*. Nevertheless, even though Nietzsche's ethics involves no final state of perfection toward which moral development might be claimed to tend, this ethics is still and all an ethics of self-development which proceeds through successive acts of self-overcoming (Swanton 2015, 197).

Moreover, both Emerson's virtue ethics and Nietzsche's virtue ethics are pluralist virtue ethics: if each individual is different from all other individuals, he or she will have different qualities to develop to their highest state of perfection. The universal content both of Emerson's and of Nietzsche's ethical ideal concerns, therefore, solely that process which leads one to mature as an individual, that is to say, to detach oneself from that which Emerson calls "social conformism" and Nietzsche "the morality of customs." In other words, we may say that self-reliance is the sole universal value, since it inheres in the very process of becoming an individual, whereas the results that will be produced by acting as an individual will be different from person to person. This self-reliance comprises a reverence vis-à-vis one's own distinctive individuality and a desire to develop this individuality; a receptivity to the points of view of others and an ability to use these points of view of others as stimuli to broaden and deepen one's own way of looking at things; a "naive inconsiderateness" such that, in every one of one's actions, it is one's whole self that is fully and authentically expressed. Self-reliance is the parameter by which to judge "the value of values" or, in other words, by which to carry out that "transvaluation of all values" that Nietzsche hoped to see come about. In actions and attitudes where self-reliance is lacking (as in the cases of envy, vanity, and dogmatism, but also in the case of nihilism) we have to do with vices, but in actions and attitudes where self-reliance is present (as in the cases of nonconformism, skepticism, abnegation, and magnanimity) we have to do with virtues.

To mature as an individual, or to become an individual in the true and full sense, means to achieve moral autonomy. Emerson and Nietzsche, however, in sharp contrast to Kant, understand "moral autonomy" to consist not in a giving of commands to oneself—not, that is to say, as an act of obedience, be it even of the self to the self—but rather as an act of spontaneity or, in other words, an act of creativity. Emerson and Nietzsche differ, indeed, as to the manner in which this moral autonomy is to be achieved. For Emerson, spontaneity is achieved by removing the various forms of social conditioning that crowd in and weigh on the individual so that he or she can get into contact with his or her own true self: through an act of intuition and free volition. For Nietzsche, by contrast, spontaneity arises from a coordination between drives and conscious thought which establishes itself as the result of that operation of self-creation we examined in chapter 2.

4

Society or Solitude?

Self-reliance is not just the parameter by which there can be judged which attitudes contribute to the ideal of self-perfecting or, in other words, to the process of the maturation of one's own individuality and of the actualizing of all this individuality's potential. It is also the parameter by reference to which one can judge whether the ways in which we relate to other people are virtuous or vicious. In this chapter I want to examine two values that Nietzsche "transvalues"—that is, reinterprets in a radically different way—using as criterion for this "transvaluation" the Emersonian notion of self-reliance.[1] These are compassion, or pity (*Mitleid*), and egoism.

Following Swanton (2015, 111), I argue that Nietzsche distinguishes between, on the one hand, a nonvirtuous and immature egoism, understood as "instant gratification and a lack of social feeling" (127), and, on the other, a virtuous egoism in which the goal personally useful to oneself that one pursues contributes at the same time to the well-being of society. I will demonstrate that Nietzsche's reading of Emerson played an essential role in allowing him to bring these thoughts to maturation. For Emerson, but also generally speaking for the entire American culture of Emerson's age, what Nietzsche calls "healthy egoism" is nothing other than individualism, one of the cornerstone values of a healthy democratic society.

The other value that Nietzsche "transvalues" is altruism. Nietzsche is critical of compassion and of pity inasmuch as these moral attitudes denote a will to flee from one's own self or, in other words, denote a lack of self-reliance. Nietzsche does not, however, exclude from his ethical vision a concern for the other; he merely insists that this concern should be expressed in different ways and forms from those in which it has traditionally been expressed. According to Nietzsche, those who sacrifice themselves for the sake of the "needy" have no respect for their own distinctive individuality, nor are they animated by any desire to develop this individuality; in short, they lack self-reliance. Similarly, those who, in offering help, wish to flaunt their own superiority lack self-reliance, since they are affirming themselves by degrading someone else. This indicates that they lack faith in their capacity to develop their own distinct individuality, or that they lack the disposition necessary to bear the effort and frustration that such a self-development would involve. None of this means, however, that the self-reliant individual has no concern for others. There is, for Nietzsche, a genuinely virtuous form of altruism, and this consists in offering help and support to people whose needs and goals one understands, while having at heart these people's true interest and benefit, which is not avoiding pain and displeasure but rather developing, also on their side, their own individuality to its full potential. These people are called friends. Whereas compassion is a form of love for the other which is born only once individuality has been removed (this compassionate love being in fact directed toward a merely generic "other" going under the name of "thy neighbor"), friendship, by contrast, is a form of love which is directed toward the distinctive individuality of the other person. The love that is offered to the friend is, as Nietzsche puts it, not a "sharing of suffering" (*Mit-leid*) but rather a "sharing of joy" (*Mit-freude*).

In a first stage of development of his philosophy Nietzsche tended to conceive of the profitable and constructive relations that the true individual is able to form with others as indeed confined to the sphere of this individual's friends in the strict, traditional sense of this term. I want to demonstrate, however, that Nietzsche's reading of Emerson directed him toward the notion of the extension of the relation of friendship to society as a whole or, in other words, toward the elaboration of an "ethics of friendship" in which this latter relationship becomes the model for all social relations. Such an "ethics of friendship," in which "friendship" is taken to mean a love for the distinctive individuality of the other person, takes the form of an encounter-cum-confrontation, hard but loyal, wherein the persons involved have as their aim and goal a perfecting both of their own selves and of the selves of others.

4.1. More Egoism, Less Compassion

Nietzsche criticizes traditional morality for having led to a dramatic weakening of individuality. This result, he argues, is due, on the one hand, to the fact that this type of morality has obscured the human origin of moral values and presented them as absolute and transcendent, thus preventing the individual from becoming aware that he or she can aspire to personal moral autonomy. But on the other hand, he goes on, it is due also to the very content of the values proposed to the individual. The values of Socratico-Christian morality are founded on an opposition established between altruistic attitudes, which the individual adopts vis-à-vis others, and egoistic attitudes, which involve the individual pursuing his or her own profit or benefit alone. The former are praised as virtues, the latter deprecated as vices. Hitherto, Nietzsche observes, selfless actions have been "universally commended and accorded distinction" (HH 95) on the grounds that they are the most useful to society. Conversely, acting out of personal interest has been called "egoism" and judged to be "bad." "One never tires of enumerating and indicting all that is evil and inimical, prodigal, costly, extravagant in the form individual existence has assumed hitherto" (D 132). The goal of Socratico-Christian morality—promoting, as it does, altruism and discouraging egoism—has been to increase social cohesion and participation in the life of the collective. Individuals, in short, have been drawn forcibly away from themselves and induced to offer themselves "as a sacrifice to the state, to science, to those in need" (HH 95). But this sacrifice of the individual, observes Nietzsche, has not led to the desired result—namely, an improvement of society—but rather to society's ruin. Nietzsche, therefore, raises questions regarding the quality of the criterion which lies at the foundation of Socratico-Christian morality's evaluation of egoism as evil and altruism as good. This criterion is compassion, which had hitherto been generally viewed as the true source of moral action.

The principal theorist in the modern era of an ethics based on compassion, and thus the principal target of Nietzsche's critique, is Schopenhauer. In Schopenhauer's ([1840] 1995, 132) view, egoism is the main motor of human action. "Colossal" and "natural," it "towers above the world." Just like animals, human beings are egoistic by nature. A blind, insatiable will to live drives them to desire and to seek, under all circumstances, the greatest possible amount of well-being and pleasure. Nevertheless, in pursuing these desires human beings very often come into collision with the desires of others, and through this collision into conflict. From the conflict, in turn, there ensue suffering and frustration. But suffering and frustration, says Schopenhauer, are already inherent in desire itself, which can never be definitively sated and satisfied. Hardly will one have attained the thing one desires than one's desire will turn toward other objects. Human beings will not cease suffering, says Schopenhauer, until that very will to live that prompts them to desire has been eliminated. To this end, he urges that we pursue an ascetic program of gradual detachment from the world which will free the intellect from its usual state of servitude to the will. If the individual succeeds in coming to awareness of the fact that individuality is just an illusion (*Schein*), and that ultimately every individual is a victim of the same "will to live" that leads all human beings to desire and to suffer, then the individual will feel he or she forms a single entity with other human beings. From this premise there is born compassion, which consists—as the term itself (*Mit-leid*) implies—in a "suffering with" others, that is to say, in a feeling of other people's pain as if it were one's own, because one identifies with them.[2] To feel the pain of others as if it were one's own will tend to prompt the individual to acts of altruism and philanthropy; one will seek not only to ensure that one's actions cause no harm or suffering to others but also to alleviate, as far as possible, others' sufferings. Ultimately, then, Schopenhauer ([1840] 1995, 138–139) considered compassion to be the sole authentic source of moral action, and this moral action indeed to consist entirely and exclusively in acts of altruism.[3]

After a short period of infatuation with Schopenhauer's philosophy, Nietzsche resolutely distanced himself from Schopenhauer's morality of compassion.[4] Nietzsche contested the claim that compassion is "good" in both senses of this term, namely that (1) compassion was born of a mental disposition that was benevolent with regard to the other and (2) that it produced positive effects and results. Contrary to this claim, he showed, (1) following La Rochefoucauld, that the motor driving compassion is nothing other than the desire for self-enjoyment and self-aggrandizement and, (2) following Emerson, that pity tends to be something pernicious both for the person to whom it is accorded and for the person of whom it is demanded.

Parallel to this, Nietzsche proceeds to reevaluate that "egoism" which is viewed, in Schopenhauer's philosophy and in Socratico-Christian morality generally, as the polar opposite of compassion. The contribution made by Emerson to this reevaluation is a fundamental one. Following Emerson, Nietzsche sheds light on the facts that (1) there exists, beside the nonvirtuous form of egoism, also a virtuous form, and (2) altruism as it is normally understood is a nonvirtuous, or perverted, form of altruism. Finally, still making use of ideas which he had derived from his reading of Emerson, Nietzsche also sheds light on the fact that (3) there does, after all, exist a virtuous, or nonperverted, form of altruism.

4.1.1. Nietzsche's Critique of Compassion

Nietzsche contests the assumption that compassion is a "good" thing, both in the sense of its having been born out of a disposition of mind which was essentially benevolent toward the other person and in the sense of its being useful. He concludes instead that (1) compassion is not born out of a concern for the other person but out of a desire for self-enjoyment and self-aggrandizement; (2) the effects and results of compassion tend to be pernicious both (2a) for him or her who receives it and (2b) for him or her on whom it is imposed as a value, that is to say, for him or her from whom it is demanded.

Let us first consider (1). In *Daybreak* 133 Nietzsche contests the false notion that compassion and altruism are born out of an attitude of benevolence toward one's fellow man. He observes that one throws oneself into the water to save a drowning man not because this man's safety and well-being are really matters of concern for one; if one makes the effort to save or succor others, this is most likely because one has the sense of reaffirming thereby one's own sense of superiority vis-à-vis those in a state of need; such "altruistic" actions, in short, serve to allow one to present oneself to one's own mind's eye "as the more powerful and as a helper." We might say that the stance of "offering help," in such a case, represents a reactive form of self-affirmation: an enhancement of one's own self that actually diminishes the other person. In the absence of self-reliance—that is to say, of an active affirmation of one's own self—that "altruistic" comportment which consists in helping and succoring others is, it seems to Nietzsche, not a virtue but rather a vice.

The fact that compassion is not "good" in the sense of being "born of a benevolent attitude of mind" does not, of course, exclude the possibility that it might be "good" in the sense of being "useful to other people" (see Foot 2003, 109). The second prong of Nietzsche's critique of this moral attitude consists, therefore, in contesting just this: whether compassion is efficacious even in this Utilitarian sense. In other words, it consists in demonstrating (2a) how compassion and the actions that originate from it are, in fact, of no help to those to whom this compassion is shown but rather actually tend to do them harm.

This harm is inflicted essentially in two ways: (1) in the form of personal humiliation. Compassionate individuals violate the privacy of the person to whom they show compassion and reveal this person's pitiful condition to the world (GS 338). The suffering of the intended beneficiary is thus not alleviated but, on the contrary, increased, inasmuch as his or her pride is wounded. The humiliation and the suffering that are hereby caused do not diminish but increase still further when the compassion is accompanied by concrete actions. In the parable *On the Pitying*, Zarathustra states, "Great indebtedness does not make people thankful, but vengeful instead; and if the small kindness is not forgotten then it will become a gnawing worm" (Z II, On the Pitying). To have to accept an offer of help means admitting one's own condition of indigence and neediness or, in other words, one's own position of inferiority vis-à-vis the person offering you this help. In order to formulate this point Nietzsche makes use of certain insights of Emerson's developed in his essay *Compensation*. Emerson observes that, each time someone gives and someone else takes, "there arises on the deed the instant acknowledgment of benefit on the one part, and of debt on the other; that is, of superiority and inferiority" (E I 93; V, 85; Nietzsche underlined "superiority and inferiority"). In consideration of the relation of implicit subordination that tends to be created by a gift, Emerson further observes, it would be naive to expect gratitude from any truly noble person for any gift that one might give him or her; rather one must already count oneself fortunate "to get off without injury and heart-burning from one who has had the ill-luck to be served by you" (E II, 95; V, 388–389; marked by Nietzsche in the margin with many vertical signs). To be trapped in a condition of subordination tends to offend a person's sense of his or her own dignity and thus to give rise to pain and anger. Emerson states, "We wish to be self-sustained. We do not quite forgive a giver. The hand that feeds us is in some danger of being bitten" (E II, 94; V, 387; Nietzsche heavily underlined the phrase "We do not quite forgive a giver" and the word "bitten"; he glossed the whole passage in the margin with the letters "N.B."; see Appendix Figure 28).[5] This anger over being trapped in a condition of subordination, where it is sustained over a lengthy period of time without being able to express and discharge itself through action, tends, in its turn, to develop into a sort of subdued but persistent malevolence toward the benefactor. For this reason, Emerson advises whoever receives a benefit to "pay it away" immediately: "Beware of too much good staying in your hand. It will fast corrupt and worm worms. Pay it away quickly in some sort" (E I, 94; V, 86; Nietzsche heavily underlined this whole passage).

In the United States in Emerson's era, of course, the question of equal opportunities had not yet arisen. People's lives were characterized by an exceptional well-being. The many natural resources the country offered made people think that it could easily satisfy the expectations of all its citizens. The choice of occupation was unrestricted. Crises were momentary, corruption only occasional, and most Americans were confident in the justice of their institutions (Aaron 1962, 85).[6] Entirely comprehensible in this context is Emerson's exhortation to be self-sufficient, inasmuch as self-sufficiency represents the precondition for independence both moral and intellectual.[7] The poor, the destitute, and the less well-off classes were generally looked on as morally responsible for their own poverty, which was taken to be the result of a lack of determination and ambition.

It can also be argued that pity harms the person to whom it is accorded because (2) succoring those in a state of need or distress and removing them from this state deprives them of the benefits that persisting in such circumstances might potentially have brought them. Here, clearly, Nietzsche is not referring to the mere psychological-emotional relation of compassion but to the concrete acts by which one intervenes in the life of another person in order to alleviate a situation of suffering or distress. In GS 338 he states that those who rush to the aid of the needy and distressed "have no thought that there is a personal necessity of misfortune; that terrors, deprivations, impoverishments, midnights, adventures, risks, and blunders are as necessary for me and you as their opposites." As we saw in chapter 2, Nietzsche, making use of ideas suggested to him by Emerson, accords a positive value to the presence of pain and suffering in a human life, provided only that this pain and suffering find their place within a broader context of ongoing self-improvement and self-perfection.[8]

When Nietzsche calls into question the supposed benefits of compassion he does not restrict himself to observing that (2a) compassion and the actions it gives rise to are pernicious for those who form their intended objects. Making use of the many reflections on this question that are to be found in Emerson,

Nietzsche (2b) critiques compassion also, and indeed above all, on account of the pernicious effects that it tends to have on the person from whom compassion is demanded, that is, on the person on whom compassion is imposed as a value.

In *On the Genealogy of Morality* Nietzsche traces compassion back to the extremely hostile and destructive attitude that he calls *ressentiment*. This attitude is characteristic of the weak and the degenerate, who, being unable to assert themselves in any positive way, seek to weaken others. So as to drag the strong individual down to their level the weak try to convince this individual that, in a world where pain is so widely prevalent, the only morally acceptable behavior is compassion: "It's a disgrace to be happy! There is too much misery!" they say (GM III 14). Thus, the strong and happy people, constrained to feel ashamed of their own strength and happiness and to take upon themselves the pain of those who suffer, soon ruin and destroy also themselves and end up in the very same state as the needy people they were called upon to help.[9]

Emerson had formulated many very interesting thoughts on this topic, and on these Nietzsche extensively and enthusiastically drew. Emerson too considered devoting oneself to others to be a vice rather than a virtue. Those who devote themselves to others, he believed, not only fail thereby to help these others but also rob themselves of time and energy that they might have devoted to the perfecting of their own self and the pursuit of their own goals. For this reason, Emerson tends to view indulging in feelings of compassion and acts of altruism as a lack of self-control. Of his encounters with the many beggars who filled the streets of New England at the time, he writes, "I confess with shame I sometimes succumb and give the dollar, [but] it is a wicked dollar, which by and by I shall have the manhood to withhold" (E I, 43; V, 38). Zarathustra echoes Emerson's words when he exclaims that beggars "should be abolished completely! Indeed, one is angered in giving and angered in not giving to them" (Z II, On the Pitying).

Emerson acknowledges, indeed, that to ask for help shamelessly and uninhibitedly is a constitutive characteristic of the suffering human being: "The sufferers parade their miseries, tear the lint from their bruises, reveal their indictable crimes, that you may pity them" (CL, 70; FL, 92). In other words, Emerson appears to suggest that the suffering individual simply cannot refrain from asking help of others: "For sickness is a cannibal which eats up all the life and youth it can lay hold of . . . afflicting other souls with meanness and mopings, and with ministration to its voracity of trifles" (CL, 139–140; FL, 182–183). It is up to the person who is not sick, then, to refuse to allow himself or herself to be "eaten up" in this way.

Those who are pursuing the ideal of self-cultivation must drive back and defend themselves against anyone who attempts to steal from them their time and energy. Nietzsche summarized in his 1882 notebook of excerpts from the *Essays* this passage of Emerson's: "At times the whole world seems to be in conspiracy to importune you with emphatic trifles. Friend, client, child, sickness, fear, want, charity, all knock at once at thy closet door and say, 'Come out unto us.'—Do not spill thy soul; do not all descend.... The power men possess to annoy me, I give them by a weak curiosity. No man can come near me but through my act" (E I, 59; V, 36–37; see NL 1882 17[37], KSA 9: 672).

Emerson compares the "sympathetic" person to a "swimmer among drowning men, who all catch at him, and if he give so much as a leg or a finger they will drown him" (E II, 47; V, 331–332; Nietzsche marked the passage with three heavy vertical lines in the margin). Nietzsche once again uses this very metaphor to communicate this concept in a preparatory draft version of the fourth book of Zarathustra:

> My serpent speaks to me secretly of drowning people: the sea drags them down—so that they willingly grasp at a strong swimmer.
>
> And in truth, those who are drowning extend arms and legs towards a saviour and a man of good will so blindly and so violently that they drag down with them, into their depths, even the strongest man. Are you—those who drown?
>
> I already hold out my little finger to you. O pity on me! What else will you take from me and seize for yourselves! (NL 1884–1885 31[62], KSA 11: 391)[10]

In short, it is through his reading of Emerson that Nietzsche gradually brings to maturity in himself the conviction that not compassion but the overcoming of compassion is a virtue; such an overcoming is achieved through an intensification of self-mastery brought about by focusing on the thought of the perniciousness of the effects of compassion both on the person who receives it and the person who accords it. In his 1882 notebook of excerpts Nietzsche writes, summing up Emerson's remarks on the topic, "It demands a godlike nature of him who has gotten rid of the common motives of humanity. High-heartedness [*Hochherzigkeit*], abiding will [*Willenstreue*] and a clear understanding [*und ein klarer Verstand*]: these must be his qualities, if he wants to be doctrine, society and law unto himself: so that a simple purpose is to him as strong as iron necessity is to others. p. 57" (NL 1882 17[38], KSA 9: 672; see E I, 61; V, 57; Nietzsche marked this passage in the margin with a vertical line and enclosed it in brackets).

4.1.2. The Transvaluation of Egoism

Parallel to his critique of compassion Nietzsche also proceeds to a radical reevaluation of egoism, viewed by Socratico-Christian morality as the exact opposite of compassion and thus as the origin of every action contrary to morality itself.

Put more precisely, Nietzsche distinguishes two types of egoism, the one fundamentally different from the other. "Egoism" in the sense of a greed for material goods Nietzsche defines as "a hungering" selfishness "that always wants to steal" (Z I, Bestowing Virtue 1). This first type of egoism is detrimental both to the individual—because it distracts him or her from his or her true good, namely self-perfection—and also to the social collective, because it brings each individual into conflict with all others. Nietzsche, however, also identifies a second type of egoism: that absolute concentration upon one's own self that is needed if one is to perfect one's own individuality and effectively pursue one's own vocation. This egoism—if one can still really speak of "egoism" in such a case—deserves, he says, the appellation "holy" (Z I, Bestowing Virtue 1) or "divine" (KSB 6: 452, n. 471).[11] The individual seeks here too his or her own interest, but since this interest coincides with his or her maturation as an individual, it brings benefit also to others. It is in the following terms that Zarathustra addresses the individual who is an "egoist" in this latter sense:

> Insatiably your soul strives for treasures and gems, because your virtue is insatiable in wanting to bestow.
>
> You compel all things to and into yourselves, so that they may gush back from your well as the gifts of your love.
>
> Indeed, such a bestowing love must become a robber of all values, but hale and holy I call this selfishness. (Z I, Bestowing Virtue 1)

What is the criterion by which we might distinguish between the first and the second type of egoism? It is the virtue that Emerson calls self-reliance. In the first type of egoism the individual is not pursuing the affirmation and the development of his or her own distinctive individuality. Rather, he or she is acting with a view to the immediate satisfaction of his or her impulses, that is, simply seeking pleasure. The fact that this first type of egoist acts, as it were, in ignorance of his or her own self—that is to say, in ignorance of the value of his or her own distinctive individuality—tends to lead him or her to remain morally blind also in respect of others. For this reason, as Swanton (2015, 112) writes, this first type of egoism can be defined as an "unsocialized egoism."

The second type of egoism, by contrast, proceeds from the recognition of one's own value and from the desire to devote oneself to perfecting oneself as an individual. The path to this goal is not pleasurable or easy, and to travel it requires a great abnegation, that is to say, a capacity to control one's own drives and impulses. What the individual who sets out on it is seeking can indeed be rightly described as his or her own satisfaction, but this personal satisfaction is at the same time a benefit bestowed upon humanity as a whole. The personal action of such an "egoistic" individual, therefore, is an action that, rightly understood, takes place on a plane that is more than just personal; that is, it takes place (even if only indirectly) in relation to the entire collectivity which surrounds the individual in question.[12]

Nietzsche's reevaluation of egoism—or, put more precisely, his identification of a virtuous form of egoism existing side by side with its nonvirtuous form— would not have been possible if his reading of Emerson had not drawn his attention to a meaning of the term "individualism" with which he would doubtless not have been familiar, had his reading been restricted to the literary and philosophical legacy of the "Old World" alone.

In the middle of the 19th century the term "individualism" was used in Europe exclusively in a pejorative sense: as meaning either egoism in the first of the two senses we have just reviewed (i.e., the greedy pursuit of material advantages regardless of the interests of others) or a deliberate standing apart from society and a confining of oneself to the secure sphere of private life (Aaron 1962, 88). This being the case, individualism was looked upon as one of the major causes not only of moral corruption and depravity but also of atomism, anarchy, and, ultimately, social disintegration (Urbinati 1997, 33). The situation was quite different in the United States. As is shown by Alexis de Tocqueville's memorable analyses, individualism arose spontaneously as a lifestyle within the colonies of the New World long before there was any word to define it.[13] The wide-open spaces and the absence of any strong state presence particularly in the territories farther to the west not only allowed the individual to be self-sufficient and self-governing but positively demanded that he or she be so. "Every man for himself and the devil take the hindmost" was the pioneers' motto. Moreover, the absence in America of any noble or aristocratic class ensured that each individual saw his or her own life as subject to no interference by any other person—though at the same time also standing under nobody else's protection. Given this spontaneously individualist approach to life, maintains Tocqueville in his survey *Democracy in America*, life in political and civil association was understood as a matter of free cooperation between individuals who each continued to pursue therein their own individual aims. It was this particular model of a common life that the system of democratic government was born to protect and promote. Along with Whitman, Emerson was the first herald of this new culture of individuality. In the essay *Historic Notes of Life and Letters in Massachusetts* (which Nietzsche took the trouble to have specially translated for him in 1883) Emerson describes the new political awareness of his times as follows: "The former generations acted under the belief that a shining social prosperity was the beatitude of man and sacrificed uniformly the citizen to the State. . . . The modern mind believed that the nation existed for the individual, for the guardianship and education of every man" (HNLLM, 529). In other words, Emerson recognized as the distinctive sign of the age he lived in the individual's recognition that he himself or she herself was the source of all power and political authority. On this basis, the individual demands the right to govern himself or herself and grants legitimacy to the state only to the extent that it defends and promotes this aspiration (see Whitman [1871] 1945, 411). To pursue the development of his or her own distinct individuality is, Emerson maintains, a veritable moral duty for every human being, and a duty owed, moreover, by each individual not just to themselves but to society. For indeed, it is only by following one's own vocation that one can obtain the best from one's own self, something from which not just the individual alone but the whole society benefits. "Society can never prosper, but must always be bankrupt, until every man does that which he was created to do," declares Emerson (CL, 60; FL, 79).[14] To become an individual also means to develop an independent and critical style of thinking, and it is only on condition that he or she succeeds in doing this that the individual will be able to exercise an active citizenship and thus contribute to the good functioning of democratic life. "The root and the seed of democracy is the doctrine: 'Judge for yourself. Reverence thyself.' It is the inevitable effect of that doctrine . . . to make each man a state" (JMN 4: 342, quoted in Miller [1953] 1962, 78), observes Emerson in his *Journals*.[15]

In short, then, taking advantage of the suggestions derived from his reading of Emerson, Nietzsche develops an evaluation of individualism completely opposed to the evaluation of this attitude predominant in his time and place. In *Human, All Too Human* Nietzsche argues that "the pillars of a strong civilization" can only be "self-reliant, independent, unprejudiced" individuals (D 163). Where individuality proves to be lacking, society itself begins to collapse. This is why Nietzsche concludes that the best contribution one can make to one's society is "to make of oneself a complete person, and in all that one does to have in view the highest good of this person" (HH 95). In other words, Nietzsche contests traditional morality's assumption that the interest of the individual and the interest of society are essentially opposed to one another. Rather, he insists, where the two are correctly understood, personal utility coincides with social utility. This is the value that Nietzsche establishes as the basis of his own conception of ethics, as an alternative to the value of compassion and in direct contrast to it: not "love of one's neighbour [*Nächstenliebe*]" but rather "love of the *farthest* [Fernsten-*Liebe*]," that is to say, the pursuit of one's own highest self:

> Do I recommend love of the neighbour [*Nächstenliebe*] to you? I prefer instead to recommend flight from the neighbour [*Nächsten-Flucht*] and love of the farthest [*Fernsten-Liebe*]!

Higher than love of the neighbour is love of the farthest and the future; higher still than love of human beings is love of things and ghosts. (Z I, On the Neighbour)

4.1.3. Virtuous Forms of Altruism

As Swanton (2015) observes, the virtuous egoism on which Nietzsche founds his ethics is in opposition both to (1) the nonvirtuous form of egoism and (2) the nonvirtuous forms of altruism, that is, to all those forms of altruism which express the desire to flee from one's own self; it is not, however, in opposition to (3) the virtuous forms of altruism. The individual who concerns himself or herself with the process of self-perfection is not, in fact, at all indifferent to the sufferings of other people. Such an individual is, however, able to control his or her impulses to run to the aid of these suffering others by remaining mindful that (a) running to their aid in this way will not, ultimately, be helpful to them, and (b) such action would also distract him or her from the pursuit of his or her own personal goals. That the self-reliant individual is not indifferent to the sufferings of others is demonstrated by the fact that Nietzsche describes the overcoming of compassion as a "test of strength" (i.e., as a test and proof of self-mastery): "To stay in control, to keep the height of your task free from the many lower and short-sighted impulses that are at work in supposedly selfless actions, this is the test, the final test, perhaps, that a Zarathustra has to pass—his real proof of strength" (EH, Why I Am So Wise 4). Giving in to compassion, on the other hand, is considered a sign of "an inherent weakness" or "a case of being unable to defend oneself against stimuli" (EH, Why I Am So Wise 4). Which, then, are the forms of interest taken in the fates of distressed and needy people that do not collide either with (a) or with (b), that is to say, that do harm neither to the person to whom compassion is displayed nor to the person displaying it?

There are essentially two such forms: (1) offering to such people one's own joy in life and giving them the chance to share in it; (2) spurring them on to overcome, by their own efforts, their distress and their difficulties.

Let us consider the former of these first. Nietzsche maintains that those who wish to help others does so more usefully by cultivating their own joy in themselves than by attempting to share others' pain and misery. In the parable *On the Pitying* Zarathustra declares, "I probably did this and that for sufferers, but I always seemed to do myself better when I learned to enjoy myself better." In the first place, a happy, fulfilled, fully self-realized person will tend not to engage in forms of behavior inspired by envy or resentment and thus aimed at harming others. But above and beyond this, such a person will provide a kind of solace and spiritual reinforcement to the suffering individual simply by his or her presence alone. To take upon oneself the sufferings of others makes one sick and sad; conversely, the mere exposure to a being full of joy tends to produce the opposite result: it has a stimulating effect. "Pity [*Mitleid*]," writes Nietzsche in a note of 1880, ". . . increases the suffering of the world. . . . Shared joy [*Mitfreude*], on the other hand, increases the world's strength" (NL 1880 7[285], KSA 9: 377).[16] Should one wish to do good to others, then, one is well advised to "create something out of oneself that the other can behold with pleasure: a beautiful, restful, self-enclosed garden perhaps, with high walls against storms and the dust of the roadway but also a hospitable gate" (D 174).[17] In other words, one should make of oneself a perfected and joyful individual and make a gift to others of this restoring and reinvigorating sight.

This is precisely the strategy adopted by Nietzsche's Zarathustra in the fourth part of the book that bears his name, when he receives into his cavern a company composed of suffering and despairing "higher men." For indeed, rather than attempting to take their suffering upon himself and thereby lower himself to their level, the attitude Zarathustra adopts is that of trying to infect them with his own spirit of joy and thereby raise them to his level. As if he were a fisherman, Zarathustra casts his joy out like bait on a hook.

> My very happiness I cast far and wide, between sunrise, noon and sunset, to see if many human fishes learn to jiggle and wiggle on my happiness.
>
>   Until, biting on my sharp hidden hooks, they have to emerge into my height, the motliest gorge gudgeons to the most spiteful of all fishers of human fish. (Z IV, The Honey Sacrifice)

This whole episode, however, of Zarathustra's receiving of the "higher men" in his cavern, as indeed the lesson that Nietzsche tries to convey through it, is in fact inspired by the story of Osman,[18] which Emerson recounts in the *Essays*:

> The Shah at Schiraz could not afford to be so bountiful as the poor Osman who dwelt at his gate. Osman had a humanity so broad and deep, that although his speech was so bold and free with the Koran as to disgust all the dervishes, yet was there never a poor outcast, eccentric, or insane man, some fool who had cut off his beard, or who had been mutilated under a vow, or had a pet madness in his brain, but fled at once to him, —that great heart lay there so sunny and hospitable in the centre of the country, —that it seemed as if the instinct of all sufferers drew them to his side. And the madness which he harbored, he did not share. Is not this to be rich? this only to be rightly rich? (E II, 90; V, 383–384; Nietzsche marked this passage with many vertical lines in the margin)

The moral that Emerson wanted to convey with this story was this: "Without the rich heart, wealth is an ugly beggar" (E II, 90; V, 383). In other words, Emerson counterposes the "giving of something" to the "giving of oneself." The former of these two gestures merely humiliates; the latter is a true comfort to the "other." Moreover, "giving of oneself" here clearly does not mean "sacrifice oneself for the other person" but rather "give the gift of oneself to the world as a mature individual." Osman does not devote himself to solving the problems of the suffering and the needy; he simply offers himself to their view and allows them the possibility of sharing his joy.

Let us look now at the second way in which the self-reliant individual succeeds in actually aiding the suffering and needy. This aid consists in spurring them on so that they overcome difficulties by their own strength and efforts. This "spurring on" can take the form either of (a) indirect encouragement, by example, or (b) direct encouragement, by advice and exhortation. As regards (a), this type of aid is offered, together with the possibility of sharing the self-reliant individual's joy, when this mature, fully developed individual offers himself or herself to the view of the suffering and needy ones. As regards (b), let us consider the fact that Nietzsche chooses to personify this superior stage of morality represented by the fully mature individual in the figure of a teacher, namely Zarathustra. What Zarathustra teaches is simply that course and journey toward true individuality that he himself has traveled. He teaches the Overman. Or, in other words, he teaches the series of "self-overcomings" that is necessary if one is really to develop one's own distinctive individuality. In this respect, we find another very interesting reference to Emerson in a note of Nietzsche's from 1883: "Make the poor rich, Emerson p. 383" (NL 1883 17[39], KSA 10: 551). What we find on page 383 of Nietzsche's German copy of the *Essays* is precisely the parable of Osman I cited earlier. The correspondence, of course, is striking between these words committed to Nietzsche's notebook and the words spoken by Zarathustra in the Prologue to the eponymous text, namely, that the poor "must learn once again to enjoy their wealth" (Z, Prologue 1). The poor discover themselves to be rich as soon as they come to understand that true wealth is not material wealth but rather the interior wealth that is true individuality and begin to devote themselves to perfecting their own individual selves. This is the message that Osman imparts to the poor and wretched people who arrive in his dwelling place and that Zarathustra imparts in his discourses.

There is, however, a significant dissymmetry between the parable of Osman and the episode of Zarathustra in his cavern. It is a dissymmetry which appears to reveal an important difference between Emerson's vision and Nietzsche's. Osman receives and welcomes every kind of "outcast and eccentric"; Zarathustra, however, receives only "higher men." In other words, for Emerson the self-reliant thinker has the duty to form some sort of relationship with absolutely everyone regardless of who they are, so as to spread and promote as far as possible the culture of individuality. In Nietzsche's work, by contrast, this question of whom the mature individual should and should not enter into relation with is a much more difficult and complex question. At GS 338, for example, Nietzsche speaks of offering aid only to a specific category of people, namely "friends": "You will also want to help—but only those whose distress you properly under-stand . . .—your friends—and only in the way you help yourself: I want to make them braver, more persevering, simpler, more full of gaiety. I want to teach them what is today understood by so few, least of all by these preachers of compassion [*Mitleiden*]: to share not pain, but joy [*Mitfreude*]!" In this aphorism Nietzsche clearly reiterates his conviction that the other person can really only be "helped" in two ways: (1) spurring him or her on in such a way as to increase his or her perseverance and courage in confronting difficulties, and (2) offering him or her the chance to share in one's own joy. Nietzsche, however, makes it equally clear that the "help" in question here is a help accorded solely to our friends, whose needs and goals we understand because they are also our own. As we will see in the next section, these "friends" of the self-reliant individual can only be a group composed of persons who possess a certain level of maturity and who, like the self-reliant individual himself or herself, are pursuing the goal of perfecting their own individuality. These people, in Zarathustra, are representatives of the "higher men," that is to say, of people who are pursuing the development of their own distinct individualities but are going through moments of difficulty and bewilderment.

4.2. Ethics of Friendship

As has been eloquently demonstrated by Ruth Abbey (1999, 2000), friendship is a central concern of Nietzsche's in the works of his middle period. Not only does he personally confer a great importance on this type of relation; he also makes it the object of his philosophical reflection. Although Nietzsche considers solitude—that is, a voluntary distancing of oneself from the masses—to be a necessary condition for the bringing to maturity of one's own individuality, friendship does not seem to him to disturb the pursuit of this objective but, on the contrary, assists it. It appears, then, to be a condition compatible with soli-tude. The solitude which Nietzsche recommends as conducive to the pursuit of individuality is not, in fact, isolation or unrelatedness but a sort of spiritual pri-vacy that allows one to keep one's own individuality distinct from that of others. Friendship does not intrude into this privacy but rather respects it, while at the same time bringing forms of stimulation that contribute to remedying the po-tential inconveniences of this state.

Abbey (1999, 51) holds that the importance Nietzsche accords to friendship, especially in the works of the middle period, "requires a revision of the common interpretation that he is unremittingly sceptical about pity and other forms of fellow feeling." She is partly wrong and partly right here. She is right to say that in the works of the middle period Nietzsche's condemnation of compassion has not yet acquired clear shape. He condemns certain manifestations of this sentiment while allowing validity to others (see HH 46, 49). Abbey is wrong, however, in holding that friendship is somehow founded in compassion. Following the traces of Nietzsche's reading of Emerson, I shall show that, on the contrary, Nietzsche describes and defines friendship as the exact opposite of compassion both as regards its conditions of possibility and as regards its goals. I shall furthermore show that, contrary to Abbey's view, Nietzsche does not suddenly, after 1883, become skeptical with regard to the possibility of friendship. On Abbey's (1999, 65) account, in the works following Zarathustra, "it is enemies, not friends, who spur higher individuals on." "In the later works, then," she goes on, "friendship seems to be the prerogative of the herd" (66). Pointing up the importance of the contribution made by his readings in Emerson to the evolution of Nietzsche's position on this question of friendship, I shall show that, after 1883, far from reducing the role accorded to friendship in his philosophy, Nietzsche in fact increases it. He gives full realization to a proposition already formulated during his middle period: that of making friendship the basis of a new type of ethics, opposed and alternative to the Socratico-Christian ethics of compassion and altruism. Following Emerson, Nietzsche denies and rejects the traditional distinction between friend and enemy and assumes that the way true friends relate to one another can become the model for relations between every type of person, provided only that the people concerned are mature individuals or are pursuing the goal of becoming such.

4.2.1. Friendship (*Mitfreude*) versus Compassion (*Mitleid*)

What is friendship for Nietzsche? We can find some indications regarding the trait that Nietzsche considers to be the defining characteristic of this sentiment at HH 499, in an aphorism entitled, precisely, "Friend": "Fellow rejoicing [*Mitfreude*], not fellow suffering [*Mitleiden*], makes the friend." This aphorism clearly stems from a note made two years previously, in which he had expressed this same vision in rather less succinct form: "Those who can rejoice with us stand not only higher but also closer to us than those who suffer with us. Fellow-rejoicing [*Mitfreude*] makes the 'friend' (the companion in joy [*den Mitfreuenden*]), compassion [*Mitleid*] the companion in suffering [*den Leidensgefährten*]. —An ethics of compassion [*Eine Ethik des Mitleidens*] must be complemented by an even higher ethics of friendship [*Ethik der Freundschaft*]" (NL 1876 19[9], KSA 8: 333). Leaving aside this last suggestive remark regarding friendship as a foundation for ethics (which I shall develop below), we can clearly see from this note of 1876 and from the *Human, All Too Human* aphorism that is drawn from it that Nietzsche conceived of friendship as the exact opposite of compassion and placed the former on a higher level than the latter. As we have noted, the German term for "compassion" (*Mitleid*) conveys particularly clearly and immediately the underlying sense of "suffering with"; particularly perspicuous in the language of his works' composition, then, is Nietzsche's conceiving of friendship as the opposite of *Mit-Leid*, namely, as *Mit-Freude*, a "rejoicing with." Whereas the compassionate person feels the other's suffering as if it were his or her own, the friend feels the same regarding the other's joy.

Initially, Nietzsche conceives of friendship as just a necessary complement to compassion. Very soon, however, he realizes that these two attitudes are in fact incompatible with one another—indeed, that they represent attitudes characteristic of two directly mutually opposed human types. It is the weak and suffering type of human being that is typically inclined to compassion, and this type is basically incapable with friendship in Nietzsche's sense.

In HH 321 Nietzsche describes the compassionate precisely as "natures who are full of sympathy and always ready to assist in misfortune," but "when others are fortunate they . . . feel they have lost their position of superiority and thus can easily exhibit displeasure."[19] The suffering types need another being to be suffering along with them in order to feel good about themselves—so that if one allows them to see that one is not suffering, but rather happy, they suddenly become "malicious and envious" (AOM 334; see Abbey 2000, 56). This suffering type of human being is not capable of friendship, then, because they are not capable of feeling others' joy as if it were their own. Underlining this fact, Zarathustra says in the speech entitled *On the Pitying*, "May my destiny always lead those like you, who do not suffer, across my path, and those with whom I may share hope and meal and honey" (Z II, On the Pitying). In order to feel someone else's joy as if it were one's own—or, in other words, in order to be capable of friendship—one must oneself be a happy person. The happiness to which Nietzsche implicitly alludes here is the profound happiness which derives from one's bringing oneself to expression as an individual. It is that feeling of a growth in personal power to which we alluded at in section 3.2.1: a feeling which is experienced during one's own "overcomings of oneself." Since very few people in the modern world are, in fact, fully mature individuals or are pursuing the goal of becoming such, the ability to feel joy for and with the other person—and thus the ability to be a "friend" to him or her in Nietzsche's sense at all—is extremely rare. In AOM 62 Nietzsche writes, "To imagine the joy of others and to rejoice at it is the highest privilege of the highest animals, and among them it is accessible only to the choicest exemplars—thus a rare humanum."

4.2.2. Higher Friendship (*Mitfreude*) versus Lower Forms of Friendship

It is not just to compassion that Nietzsche counterposes friendship as *Mitfreude*. He counterposes it also to certain inferior forms of friendship, that is, interpersonal ties that do not involve fully mature individuals. Abbey (1999, 50–51) argues that Nietzsche, in his distinguishing between higher and lower forms of friendship, is basically following Aristotle. It seems to me much more probable, however, that Nietzsche is following the Emerson who, in his essay *Friendship*, takes up and develops that treatment of the theme of friendship that had been proposed by Aristotle in the *Nicomachean Ethics*.

Aristotle had distinguished in this famous text among three different types of friendship. The first kind of friendship is that based on utility. People involved in this type of friendship are not interested in each other per se, but rather, as if they were trading partners, in the profit they can potentially derive from each other. The second kind of friendship is friendship based on pleasure, where two people love to spend time together because of the pleasure that they derive from one another's wit, good looks, or other qualities. The third kind of friendship is friendship based on virtue, in which friends are bound together by mutual esteem, originating from their common striving for perfection. According to Aristotle, this is the only authentic form of friendship and also the only really enduring one, because it originates from an authentic interest in the substantial being of the friend and not from any merely accidental quality or factor (see Aristotle 1999, 121–124).[20]

Following Aristotle, Emerson observes that many of the ties that are given the name of "friendship" do not, in fact, deserve this appellation. One of these, he says, is indeed, as Aristotle had argued, the interhuman tie that has been entered into for the sake of some mere utility: one person seeks out another not for this other's own sake but in order to make up for some lack in himself or herself. Emerson argues that, to be truly friends with someone else, one must have no need of this other person either from a material viewpoint (as a means to fulfilling one's needs) or from a psychological one (as a prop for one's own convictions). "The condition which high friendship demands," he writes, "is, ability to do without it. To be capable of that high office, requires great and sublime parts. There must be very two, before there can be very one. . . . Yet the least defect of self-possession vitiates, in my judgment, the entire relation. There can never be deep peace between two spirits, never mutual respect until, in their dialogue, each stands for the whole world" (E I, 173, 176; V, 155, 157; Nietzsche underlined "ability to do without it" and marked this whole passage, which appears on page 155 of the German translation of the *Essays*, with a vertical line, as he does the passage on p. 157 of this volume; see Appendix Figure 18). In the essay *Character* Emerson reiterates this idea in verse form: "When each the other shall avoid, / Shall each by each be most enjoyed" (E II, 65; V, 353; the passage was left in English by the translator).

We may assume that Nietzsche had displayed an almost obsessional interest in this dictum of Emerson's since Marie Baumgarten, writing to him in December 1879 to express her admiration for his just-published *Human, All Too Human* and hoping thereby to please him, poses the question of whether a certain aphorism in this new book did not perhaps contradict that passage in Emerson in which the American "describes it as the acme of the most noble friendship when one can—'simply do without the friend! [*wo er es als Hohepunkt der edelsten Freundschaft bezeichnet wenn man den Freund— 'entbehren koenne'!*]" (KGB II/6.2: 1245, n. 1266). At HH 360 Nietzsche had in fact written, "When good friends praise a talented nature he will often exhibit pleasure at it, though he does so out of politeness and benevolence: in truth he is indifferent to it." The "indifference" here may at first sight appear deeply puzzling. Nietzsche is not speaking of any praise that might be heaped upon a "talented nature" by the masses but rather of praise accorded to this individual by his or her "good friends." As we explained in sections 3.2.3 and 3.2.4, the masses are bearers of values that are utterly different from those cherished by the true individual. The praises received from the masses, then, go only to nourish and sustain that social image of oneself which is precisely what one should refrain from cultivating and concerning oneself with if one wishes to develop one's own distinctive individuality. Given this presupposition, it makes complete sense that whoever is pursuing this latter objective should feel only indifference with regard to praise emanating from the masses. One's "good friends," however, as we have seen, will necessarily be, on Nietzsche's account of them, mature individuals who share with one the objective of self-perfection. For this reason, their opinion of one would seem to have to be held in high esteem. What can it mean, then, when Nietzsche speaks of an individual's being "indifferent" to the praise of "good friends"? It means that the individual in question is sufficiently self-possessed to not have need of the approval even of friends as an imprimatur for his or her own choices and decisions (see also Abbey 1999, 57). This interpretation is confirmed also by a passage from Zarathustra, in which Nietzsche refers to the passage in Emerson's *Essays* which reiterates that, if the relationship between two people is to be an authentic one, each must be a whole and perfect individual and "in their dialogue . . . stand for the whole world" (E I, 176; V, 157). Zarathustra says, "I teach you the friend in whom the world stands complete, a bowl of goodness—the creating friend who always has a complete world to bestow" (Z I, On Love of the Neighbor). In the last analysis, then, Nietzsche, following Emerson, assumes that the primary characteristic of true friendship is that the people involved in it are self-sufficient or aspire to self-sufficiency. This characteristic is always a consequence of self-reliance: whoever has reverence for his or her own distinctive individuality and wishes to develop it will naturally aspire to render himself or herself self-sufficient.[21]

The second type of interhuman tie or bond that Emerson is careful to distinguish from true friendship is the tie or bond that is established, to use Aristotle's terms, with a view to pleasure alone: the pleasure of spending time with someone who shares our tastes and opinions. A "friendship" defined in these terms involves two affirmations that Emerson rejects: (1) that the friend is someone with whom we typically spend our time, and (2) that the friend is someone with whom we share tastes and opinions. Above all, Emerson is skeptical about "sharing a life in common" with one's friends. He is convinced that to live with others is inevitably to limit our autonomy. "Almost all people descend to meet. All association must be a compromise, and, what is worst, the very flower and aroma of the flower of each of the beautiful natures disappears as they approach each other" (E I, 166; V, 147; Nietzsche underlined the words "disappear" and "as they approach each other"; see Appendix Figure 14). A sharing of daily life is, for Emerson, not a part of true friendship because this latter is a bond of a kind which does not require a constant keeping of company, in contrast, for example, to the bonds of family. This, indeed, is what makes it possible to keep a real friendship free from all those trivialities into which familial ties and relations tend inevitably to descend: "Why should we desecrate noble and beautiful souls by intruding on them?" Emerson writes. "Why insist on rash personal relations with your friend? Why go to his house, or know his mother and brother and sisters? Why be visited by him at your own? Are these things material to our covenant? Leave this touching and clawing. Let him be to me a spirit." Indeed, from a friend, I want "a message, a thought, a sincerity, a glance," not "pottage" (E I, 174–175; V, 156). True friendship for Emerson, then, is an almost ideal bond in which friends tend each to follow their own path, which is always unique to them alone.

> I do then with my friends as I do with my books. I would have them where I can find them, but I seldom use them. We must have society on our own terms and admit or exclude it on the slightest cause. . . . In the great days, presentiments hover before me in the firmament. I ought then to dedicate myself to them. . . . Then, though I prize my friends, I cannot afford to talk with them. . . . It would indeed give me a certain household joy to quit this loftily seeking, this spiritual astronomy, or

search of stars, and come down to warm sympathies with you; but then I know well I shall mourn always the vanishing of my mighty gods. (E I, 178–179; V, 160; Nietzsche marked this passage with a vertical line in the margin from the words "In the great days" right up to the end)

Nietzsche—who, in the margin of the passage in which Emerson speaks of the compromises demanded by a life in common, wrote, "γέγραφά που (gevgrafav pou)," "I once wrote the same somewhere" (E I, 117; V, 147; see Appendix Figure 14)[22]—likewise considered solitude to be an essential condition for the development of one's own individuality. Solitude is a virtue of the "free spirit." In other words, the "free spirit" does not suffer from the state of solitude but rather pursues it in order to distance himself or herself from the pressures of society, free himself or herself from social obligations and expectations, and facilitate thereby the emergence of his or her own requirements and aspirations. The connection between solitude and "freedom of the spirit" emerges in exemplary manner in BGE 44:

> At home, or at least having been guests, in many countries of the spirit; having escaped again and again from the musty agreeable nooks into which preference and prejudice, youth, origin, the accidents of people and books or even exhaustion from wandering seemed to have banished us; full of malice gains the lures of dependence that lie hidden in honors, or money, or offices, or enthusiasms of the senses. . . . We are born, sworn, jealous friends of solitude, of our own most profound, most midnightly, most middaily solitude: that is the type of man we are, we free spirits!

Nevertheless, for Nietzsche solitude does not exclude friendship, if by "friendship" we mean that highest form which we reviewed above. As Abbey (1999, 62) observes, "As this sort of intimacy keeps a respectful distance and does not totally subsume individuality, it is unlikely to be the sort of intrusion from which solitude is usually sought." A solitude without "friends" or "books," writes Nietzsche in WS 200, gives rise to "much ennui, ill-humor and boredom." For this reason, friendship can be considered a state intermediate between life in the interior of mass society, in which the person who aspires to live as a true individual is necessarily subject to innumerable distracting attachments and temptations, and a life of complete isolation, which, where it is protracted over time, can turn out to be equally alienating. Nevertheless, the person who is pursuing the development of his or her own distinctive individuality will tend to shun any ties that are based on the assiduous keeping of company with others. "If we live together with another person too closely," opines Nietzsche, "what happens is similar to when we repeatedly handle a good engraving with our bare hands: one day all we have left is a piece of dirty paper. The soul of a human being too can finally become tattered by being handled continually. . . . One always loses by too familiar association with friends and woman" (HH 428). In short, as Abbey (1999, 63) aptly notes, with regard to the friend Nietzsche "adduces an ideal of intimacy that is simultaneously lovingly close and respectfully distant." Following Emerson, Nietzsche also numbers privacy among the characteristics of true friendship. Like self-sufficiency, a sense of privacy also tends to show it-self among those self-reliant persons who aspire to affirm their own individuality.

Let us now move on to examine the second "prong" of that critique that Emerson directs toward that interhuman tie that is described as "friendship" but is based, in fact, on the search for personal pleasure: his critique of the notion that we can call someone a "friend" simply because he or she shares our tastes and opinions. For Emerson, true friendship is born out of reverence for the dis-tinct individuality of the other person. The true friend, therefore, never seeks to draw others toward him or her but rather lets them be themselves. As had already been observed by Aristotle, true friendship "is a mutually mediated, mutually shared freedom," that is to say, "a bi-lateral relation of recognition of reciprocal alterity, wherein nobody wants to control or dominate anyone else" (Williams 2012, 65). Different tastes, views, and values, Emerson says, are nothing but "tents of a night" that cannot distract us from contemplating the "overarching vault, bright with galaxies of immutable lights'" (E I, 155; V, 139), namely, the beauty of our friend's complete and mature individuality. In a true friendship, indeed, the more the respective, distinct individualities of the two friends man-ifest and assert themselves, and the more their opinions diverge, the stronger the bond of friendship becomes. Looked at superficially and from the outside, the two friends in question may well seem, since they are now professing dif-ferent opinions from one another, to have parted ways. But in reality, observes Emerson, they part "only to meet again on a higher platform, and only be more each other's because [they] are more [their] own" (E I, 178; V, 160). This love-within-difference also ensures that the bond of friendship can endure through the years and survive the necessary and inevitable evolution in the two friends' tastes, opinions, and habits. The friends we lose by evolving spiritually were not really friends at all: we should, therefore, not fear this loss but rather rejoice in it: "A man's growth is seen in the successive choirs of his friends. For every friend whom he loses for truth, he gains a better" (E I, 254; V, 225; Nietzsche underlined the second phrase; see Appendix Figure 22).[23]

Nietzsche accords a positive reception to these observations of Emerson's. For Nietzsche, friendship is distinguished from romantic love precisely by reason of the fact that the former does not express itself as a desire to possess the other party or to "be one" with him or her—that is to say, as a desire to assimilate the other to oneself. In friendship the "greedy desire of two people for each other gives way to a new desire and greed, a shared higher thirst for an ideal above them" (GS 14, 41). This ideal is that of individuality.[24] Nietzsche likewise distinguishes true friendship from the relation called "comradeship," specifying that the former, unlike the latter, is not based on agreement and does not fail or lessen when agreement ceases to be. Where the relation of friendship is a false one, disagreement often results in hostility and even in an end to the relationship altogether. This is why such false or merely superficial friends usually try to soften their true opinions in their dealings with one another, or even to hide them entirely (see HH 376, 148). True friendship, by contrast, is only made stronger the more the two parties develop their own personalities and thereby their own fully formed views and opinions. Echoing Emerson's words, Nietzsche declares, "It is not in how one soul approaches another but in how it distances itself from it that I recognize their affinity and relatedness" (AOM 251). Indeed, he goes so far as to make the degree to which an individual can take joy "in the fact that another lives, feels, and acts in a way different from and opposite to" his or her own way of living, feeling, and acting the very measure of that individual's maturity (AOM 75). In other words, true friends can be recognized by the fact that they are not afraid, when they take their distance from one another, that they will thereby lose one another altogether. For the greater the apparent distance between them, the stronger does the tie of friendship become. Nietzsche compares true friends to stars, who are attracted to one another though separated in fact by distances almost unimaginably vast.

> We were friends and have become estranged. But that was right. . . . We are two ships, each of which has its own goal and course. . . . The almighty force of our projects drove us apart . . . into different seas. . . . That we had to become estranged is the law above us; through it we should come to have more respect for each other. . . . There is probably a tremendous invisible curve and stellar orbit in which our different ways and goals may be included as small stretches—let us rise to this thought! . . . Let us then believe in our star friendship even if we must be earth enemies. (GS 279)

Nietzsche reveals himself, therefore, to embrace, above and beyond self-sufficiency and privacy, also a third characteristic of friendship as Emerson had understood it: reverence for the "other" as an individual different from myself. This too is a manifestation of self-reliance. "Self-reliance applied to another person is reverence" (JMN 7: 371), says Emerson, that is, reverence for another's distinctive individuality. I revere another as different from myself just as I revere myself as an original and unique human being.

4.2.3. The Goal of True Friendship

By following the traces of his readings in Emerson we can identify what conditions form, for Nietzsche, the conditions required for friendship in the true sense; we can also identify what Nietzsche held to be the purpose or results of this true friendship. For Emerson true friendship makes a contribution to the development of one's own distinctive individuality. In the first instance, this contribution is made in terms of an augmentation of the individual's awareness or knowledge of his or her own self. As Emerson writes, "The soul environs itself with friends, that it may enter into a grander self-acquaintance" (E I, 164–165; V, 145; Nietzsche underlined this whole passage heavily and marked it in the margin with four vertical lines). In the second instance, the contribution that the friend makes to the development of our own distinctive individuality consists in the fact that it becomes possible for us to confront our own views and opinions with the friend's. An open and honest confrontation with a true friend can serve to broaden our perspective and help us to identify the weak points in the positions we ourselves hold. If this end is really to be achieved, of course, it is necessary that the friend adopt with us a form of communication that is open and sincere.

A friend who refrains from being sincere and open with us for fear of losing our affection cannot claim to be truly a friend. "Let me be alone to the end of the world, rather than that my friend should overstep by a word or a look his real sympathy," writes Emerson (E I, 173; V, 155; Nietzsche underlined this whole passage as well, marking it in the margin with a vertical line and writing "bravo!"; the word "overstep" is underlined twice; see Appendix Figure 18). "Let him not cease an instant to be himself. The only joy I have in his being mine, is that the not mine is mine. It turns the stomach . . . where I looked for a manly furtherance, or at least a manly resistance, to find a mush of concession. Better be a nettle in the side of your friend than his echo" (E I, 173; V, 155; Nietzsche marked the passage "It turns . . . concession," in the margin, with a vertical line and wrote "Bravo," while the passage "Better . . . echo" is marked in the margin with two vertical lines and a kind of spiral; see Appendix Figure 18). In the last analysis, concludes Emerson, those pursuing the goal of perfecting their own self will appreciate in the true friend his or her role as a kind of enemy; in other words, they will appreciate the friend as someone who is prompted by love for them to attack them and to call them into question: "Let him be to thee forever a sort of beautiful enemy, untamable, devoutly revered and not a trivial conveniency to be soon outgrown and cast aside" (E I, 175; V, 157; Nietzsche marked this passage in the margin with a vertical line and a kind of spiral).[25]

As is shown by the many underlinings and marginal notes, Nietzsche was in enthusiastic agreement with Emerson's position regarding the purpose and the ends of friendship. Zarathustra declares that the true friend is a bridge to the Overman; that is, he provides an infinitely precious contribution to our own endless process of self-overcoming. The friend also helps us to avoid the dangers of introspection. "For the hermit the friend is always a third," declares Zarathustra in the section of the eponymous book entitled *On the Friend*; "the third is the cork that prevents the conversation of the two from sinking into the depths" (Z I, On the Friend). The friend, furthermore, serves to safeguard the solitary person who is pursuing the project of expressing his or her own individuality from the perils of self-deceit (see HH 491), of "presumptuousness" (HH 316), and of "underestimation" (HH 625), and wards off "boredom" (AOM 337) and dogmatism (see Abbey 2000, 55). Clearly, if such a frank and open confrontation is really going to occur, the friend must have no fear of expressing criticism; indeed, as Emerson had already remarked, he must not draw back even from behaving like an "enemy":

> If one wants a friend, then one must also want to wage war for him: and in order to wage war, one must be able to be an enemy.
>
> One should honor the enemy even in one's friend. Can you step up to your friend without stepping over to him?
>
> In one's friend one should have one's best enemy. You should be closest to him when you resist him. (Z I, On the Friend)

In short, by tracing Nietzsche's reading of Emerson we can form a fairly exhaustive picture of just what Nietzsche meant by "friendship," just what conditions he posed for its existence in a true and authentic form, and just what ends and purposes he thought could be pursued and achieved through it. The conditions that must obtain in order for two people to form a bond of friendship are the following: they must each be self-reliant, that is to say, self-sufficient; they must each be respectful both of their own and of the other's privacy; they must each esteem the other as distinct and different from themselves and rejoice, therefore, each time this other gives expression to his or her personality in a way original to him or her. The effects of this bond of friendship, once established, are that it enables each participant to know himself or herself ever better, and it reinforces each participant's own sense of his or her distinctive individuality. The apparent paradox involved in positing individuality as at the same time condition and result of true friendship is only apparent; if the "true friendship" described here is looked on as a regulative ideal, the paradox is immediately dissolved. In other words, we may state that to be a true friend and to find a true friend are no more than goals that are to be pursued—but goals that one necessarily draws closer to achieving the more fully one becomes, for one's own part, a true individual.[26]

4.2.4. Friendship and Society

At this point the question arises of how many different people can be contained within this bond of friendship. Is friendship always a matter of an intimate and exclusive relationship between two individuals? Or can this type of relation be established between a larger number of people? As Paul Van Tongeren (2000) has pointed out, there are fundamentally two different ways of thinking about this question within the philosophical tradition. The first originates with Aristotle, who considers friendship to form the basis of the ties of political association. In book VIII of *Nicomachean Ethics* he states that every kind of community is based on two requirements, justice and friendship, and that friendship is even more essential to community than is justice: "Moreover, friendship would seem to hold cities together, and legislators would seem to be more concerned about it than about justice. For concord would seem to be similar to friendship, and they aim at concord among all, while they try above all to expel civil conflict, which is enmity" (Aristotle 1999, 119–120). The opposite view of the question is represented by Montaigne, who considers friendship to be a private relation that can even come into conflict with the bond of social and political association. Thus, he defends Gaius Blosius, who says he would have obeyed his friend Tiberius Gracchus even if he had asked him to set the temples on fire, and comments, "They were more friends than they were citizens" (Van Tongeren 2000, 215). In this case, friendship is seen as an alternative to society, which is inevitably corrupt.[27]

Nietzsche cannot be easily situated within either one or the other of these two currents. On the one hand, he shares Montaigne's disappointment with society and his idea of friendship as a refuge from it.[28] Nietzsche thinks of the friend as a correction to the solipsism of the nonconformist individual who has distanced himself or herself from society in order to "become who they are." On the other hand, the Nietzschean "free spirit" appears to yearn for a community of friends who would share with him his ideal of self-perfection and indirectly support and sustain him in the pursuit of this goal. There are various aphorisms which suggest that the "free spirit" is in search not just of a friend but indeed of an entire community of friends.[29] In HH 638 Nietzsche presents the "free spirit" as a solitary wanderer forced endlessly to traverse "the desert," as he is not welcome in the town. But in fact, it is the "free spirit" himself who is unable to find any rest or ease in the town, that is, in contemporary society. This "free spirit," however, is not content to be alone but rather, says Nietzsche, looks out for "wanderers and philosophers" who, just like him, feel at home "in mountain, wood and solitude" (HH 638). In other words, the "free spirit" appears to refuse society as an alienating dimension of human experience while at the same time positively demanding for himself a society or community of some different type. Nietzsche seems to confirm this hypothesis—namely, that the "free spirit" is in search not just of a friend but of an entire community of friends—also in the following note from 1881: "Make oneself indifferent toward praise or blame: formulae [*Recepte*] in order to achieve this. To establish for oneself, on the other hand, a circle of people that will be aware of the goals and the standards [*Maaßstäbe*] that we have set for ourselves and that will, thenceforth, alone signify praise and blame for us" (NL 1881 11[1], KSA 9: 441). It emerges clearly from this note that the "free spirit" does not pursue the recognition or acknowledgment that might be accorded him by society; he is indifferent to the praise or censure of the masses because he does not, for his part, acknowledge the worth of those who compose them. On the other hand, however, the "free spirit" yearns to be recognized and acknowledged by certain "selected" people, people at his own level, that is to say, by his friends. In short the "free spirit" appears to yearn, as Derrida (2005, 37) has keenly observed, for "a community of solitary friends, friends 'jealous of solitude' . . . the 'community of those without community.' "[30] The aim of this community is to support and assist the pursuit of virtue. Indeed, writes Nietzsche, "how could the individual keep himself aloft and, against every current, swim along his own course through life if he did not see here and there others of his own kind living under the same conditions and take them by the hand?" (HH 261).

In the last analysis, then, during his middle period Nietzsche is of the view that the best way to pursue virtue is to do so within a community of friends, that is, the company of a "select few" who are each likewise pursuing the goal of perfecting their own respective individualities. Whereas living in society forces one to standardize one's opinions and lowers the exceptional individual down to the level of the norm, confrontation with selected persons, respectful of the inviolable limits that safeguard individual freedom, tends, on the contrary, to stimulate one to strengthen one's own individuality and thus enhances one's virtues. In this "close-knit society," the "free spirits" that compose it "have need of one another, they have joy in one another, they understand the signs of one another—but each of them is nonetheless free, he fights and conquers in his own place, and would rather perish than submit" (HH 261).

Within this community of "free spirits" the foundation of ethics is not compassion, as it has been in hitherto existing society, but rather friendship, understood in terms of the model Nietzsche derived from Emerson. In other words, all interhuman relations come to fit the model of a "hard but loyal encounter and confrontation with the other," which Emerson recognizes as the distinguishing quality of true friendship, wherein love for one's friend is demonstrated through the contribution that this love makes to the development of his or her distinctive individuality (see NL 1876 19[9], KSA 8: 333).

This "encounter and confrontation" between true friends is inspired by the Classical Greek model of the *agon*, a dimension of human experience to which Nietzsche assigned great importance. From the time of his early essay *Homer's Contest* (1872) onward, Nietzsche drew a distinction between two distinct types of "confrontation," motivated by two types of feeling apparently similar to one another but in fact very different in nature. In order to arrive at this distinction he drew on the account given by the Greek historian Pausanius of Hesiod's *Works and Days*. Pausanius tells of how Hesiod splits the goddess Eris, who personifies envy and the discord inspired by envy, into two sisters of the same name; he does this, suggests Pausanius, in order to point up how envy and discord can in fact take on different forms and how these forms need not in every case bear negative connotations. Hesiod portrays the "first Eris" as a malevolent deity, tradition- ally identified with jealous rage and associated with war. This malevolent deity's "good sister," however, represents envy's other, more positive aspect: that desire to excel and to outdo one's loved and respected peers, which gives rise to a fair and productive confrontation between individuals (Acampora 2013, 18). On this basis Nietzsche distinguishes the "fight to the death [*the Vernichtungskampf*]" (KSA 1.787), wherein the motivating desire is truly to destroy one's adversary, from the fight that takes the form of a competition (the *Wettkampf*, or, to use the ancient Greek term, the *agon*), wherein the motivating desire is to overcome one's adversary by an acknowledged superior performance. It is this latter type of confrontation—the *agon*—much more than a quiet life free of all conflicts that is, in Nietzsche's view, the ideal context and environment for the cultiva- tion of virtue. To compete in order to excel just for excellence's sake will tend, in fact, to stimulate productive and creative forms of behavior.[31] A community of friends, each pursuing virtue on their own and for their own sake, will none- theless tend indirectly to help each other to achieve their goals, inasmuch as all will be spurred on to give the best of themselves. This dream of a community of "free spirits" seemed, in 1876, to be on the point of becoming a concrete reality for Nietzsche.[32]

4.2.5. The Dream of a Community of "Free Spirits"

In the summer of 1876 Nietzsche returned home from the first Bayreuth Festival disappointed and disgusted. The festival had brought home to him that to con- tinue to support Wagner's great project would mean too great a sacrifice of his own intellectual honesty. Added to this personal crisis was the crisis in his phys- ical well-being. His health had deteriorated so gravely that he was obliged to ask Basel University for an extended period of leave. On the invitation of his friend Malwida von Meysenbug he went to stay for several months in Sorrento in the company of Malwida, Paul Rée, and a Basel student by the name of Albert Brenner. This stay in Italy marks the beginning of a new phase in Nietzsche's thinking. The Sorrento Notebooks, written in October of this year, form the initial nucleus of *Human, All Too Human* (D'Iorio 2012, 17) and represent Nietzsche's first step toward total intellectual independence. Nietzsche and his friends stayed at the Villa Rubinacci, a boardinghouse run by a German lady, on the first floor of which Malwida had reserved various bedrooms and a common living room to house their "little colony" (Meysenbug 1898, 44–45). From the balcony of his room, which looked out on the Gulf of Sorrento, Nietzsche could see the island of Ischia, which became a model for the "Blessed Isles" described in Zarathustra (D'Iorio 2012, 17).[33] This sun-kissed volcanic island became the symbol of the new culture that Nietzsche believed he saw emerging: a southern, Mediterranean culture opposed to the decadent Germanic culture of the North, already sinking into its twilight.[34] The communal life at the Villa Rubinacci was structured in the following way: during the morning hours the friends were free to devote themselves to their own occupations; they came together for their midday meal and, after this meal, often went walking together in the orange groves that surrounded the town or ranged out further onto the promontories overlooking the sea. In the evening they once again ate together and then gathered in their common salon to read together and engage in animated discussions (Meysenbug 1898, 47–48).[35] Nietzsche and his friends took enormous pleasure in this style of life and formed plans to extend their little community to others. Nietzsche's letters from this period are full of references to this intention to establish a small community of friends, a ' "school of educators (also called a modern cloister, an ideal colony, a *université libre*)" (KSB 5: 216, n. 589), where "they would educate themselves" (KSB 5: 189, n. 554; see also NL 1875 5[25], KSA 8: 46–47). As Nietzsche explains in his private notes, this project was born out of the recognition that, in the modern world, the people assigned the task of educating others are usually not truly educated themselves: this "educator" will tend to be a specialist in his or her own field but completely lacking in broad and general culture (see NL 1876 23[136], KSA 8: 452). A life led in common was intended to make up for this general cultural failing.[36] Clearly, however, this was conditional upon each participant's freedom of thought being respected, indeed encouraged, by the community. Writing to his friend Seydlitz to inform him of his project and to invite him to join the community of educators, Nietzsche explains his purpose: "I am always hunting for men like any pirate, but not to sell them as slaves, rather to ransom myself with them in liberty" (KSB 5: 188 n. 554; see also Gilman 1987, 339; Treiber 1992, 331–349).

In a letter to Rée, Nietzsche refers to his plan for a community of "free spirits" as "my Epicurean garden" (KSB 5: 460, n. 899). The garden of Epicurus was a small community in which a few individuals gathered around their philosophical master and teacher with the aim of "self-improvement and the improvement of others by mutual admonition and correction" (Campbell 2010, 222). Since the most important virtue that a person needed to cultivate was, according to Epicurus, ataraxy—a kind of imperturbability—and since day-to-day life in society was especially apt to provoke emotional turbulence and perturbation, Epicurus believed that it was imperative for the individual aspiring to virtue to remove himself or herself from the day-to-day social world.[37] Epicurus's idea of a retreat from the world, and the formation of a community based on friendship, so as to be better able to cultivate virtue, was an idea that exerted enormous fascination on Nietzsche. In one of the aphorisms composing *The Gay Science* he recommends to "free spirits":

> Live in seclusion so that you are able to live for yourself. Live in igno-
> rance of what seems most important to your age! . . . And let the clamor
> of today, the noise of wars and revolutions, be but a murmur to you.
> You will also want to help—but only those whose distress you prop-
> erly understand because they share with you one suffering and one
> hope—your friends—and only in the way you help yourself: I want
> to make them braver, more persevering, simpler, more full of gaiety.
> I want to teach them what is today understood by so few, least of all by
> these preachers of compassion [*Mitleiden*]: to share not pain, but joy
> [*Mitfreude*]! (GS 338)

To live separated from the world in this way appears to be the most effective possible defensive measure to shield oneself against the wounds which are inflicted on the superior individual—be it in the form of a choking contempt or in the subtler form of the temptation to compassion—by the mere sight and presence of the modern "man of the masses."[38] After the first experiment in Sorrento, Nietzsche planned to form various "cloisters for free spirits" all over Europe that would gather people who "no longer want to have anything to do with the world" (NL 1876 17[50], KSA 8: 305).

That this "community of educators" had necessarily to represent not a permanent way of life but rather only a formative stage leading to something else was clear to all the participants in this "Sorrento experiment." Malwida herself wrote in her memoirs that the idea was that of "establishing a sort of 'mission station' intended to lead adults of both sexes toward the free development of the very noblest of intellectual lives in order that they could then go back out into the world to spread the seeds of a new and more spiritual culture" (Meysenbug 1898, 57–58). In the works of his middle period Nietzsche himself also indicates that these communities of "free spirits" are to be thought of as a merely transitory measure, suitable for a "moral interregnum" (D 453), which must last until humanity is able to "construct anew the laws of life and action" (D 453). He defines the envisaged "cloisters for free spirits" as "little experimental states" (D 453) in which ways of living could be worked out which would perhaps later be adopted on a broader scale. Nietzsche explains this very clearly:

> We withdraw into concealment: but not out of any kind of personal ill-humour, as though the political and social situation of the present day were not good enough for us, but because through our withdrawal we want to economize and assemble forces of which culture will later have great need, and more so if this present remains this present and as such fulfils its task. We are accumulating capital and seeking to make it secure: but, as in times of great peril, to do that we have to bury it. (WS 229; see Ansell-Pearson 2015, 222; Hutter 2006, 5)

Ultimately, then, we can say that, after his break with Wagner and his loss of faith in collective action for the reform of society, Nietzsche came to understand that, in an age of such extensive moral corruption, great individuals can emerge only in opposition to the general institutional design. It was for this reason that he formed the plan of small communities of the virtuous, in the hope that the achievement of excellence by some "happy few" would, in the long term, also provoke a transformation of society as a whole. This means that the "free spirit," though living above and outside of society, becomes, nonetheless, the force which propels the reform of society. As Conway (1997, 10) writes, "Far from the mere ornaments to which they have been reduced in late modernity, superlative human beings are in fact responsible for the catalysis of culture itself."[39]

4.2.6. The Utopian Communities of New England

The "communities of 'free spirits'" that Nietzsche merely imagined had in fact become, in Emerson's New England, a reality—at least for a period of time. In the 1840s, disgusted by the depravity of a society which was avidly materialistic and dominated by the inhumane laws of the marketplace, some friends belonging to the Transcendentalists group decided to withdraw from this society and set themselves up as independent farmers. In May 1840, the pastor George Ripley resigned from the ministry. He wanted to find "a more concrete means of reforming American society" than the sermons he had been delivering—in vain, he now felt—from the pulpit of his chapel (Richardson 1995, 337). In April 1841 he purchased a dairy farm near West Roxbury and established there the community called Brook Farm. His aims in doing so were the following:

Our objects . . . are to ensure a more natural union between intellectual and manual labor than now exists; to combine the thinker and the
worker, as far as possible, in the same individual; to guarantee the highest
mental freedom, by providing all with labor, adapted to their tastes and
talents, and securing to them the fruit of their industry; to do away with
the necessity of menial services, by opening the benefit of education and
the profit of labors to all; and thus to prepare a society of liberal, intel-
ligent, and cultivated persons, whose relations with each other would
permit a more simple and wholesome life than can be led amidst the
pressures of our competitive institutions. (Richardson 1995, 340)

In June 1843 another member of the Transcendental Club and a dear friend of
Emerson's, Bronson Alcott, established the farming community Fruitlands (in
Nashua Valley, Massachusetts). Alcott wished to carry out the experiment of a
way of life that would be completely innocent, founded on conversation about
elevated topics and intended to promote individual liberty.[40] These initiatives
pioneered by Ripley and Alcott were further developed thanks to the spread,
in this period, of the ideas of Fourier, a development due, in the States, to the
efforts of his disciple Albert Brisbane.[41] On account of Brisbane's efforts, over
forty Fourierist communes were formed in the United States during the 1840s
(see Richardson 1995, 365).[42] It was a decade of great euphoria, characterized by
the widely shared, powerful conviction that the structure of society really might
be radically transformed within just a short space of time. "We are a little wild
here," Emerson wrote to Carlyle, "with numberless projects of social reform.
Not a reading man but has a draft of a new Community in his waistcoat pocket.
I am gently mad myself and am resolved to live cleanly" (Richardson 1995, 341).
However, Emerson's attitude toward these utopian communities was an ambiv-
alent one. He was "not indifferent to the dream of community" (369). Together
with his friends Alcott and Ripley, he spent the summer of 1840 thinking of
forming "a community of like-minded souls," a sort of free university, "without
charter, diploma, corporation, or steward" (337). "What society shall we not
have! . . . We shall sleep no more and we shall concert better houses, economies,
and social modes than any we have seen" (337), wrote Emerson to Margaret
Fuller, seeking to involve her in their project. However, when Ripley launched
the Brook Farm community, Emerson unexpectedly held back from taking part.
Ripley had hoped that Emerson would assume a leading role within the community, given that he had been one of its main inspirations. But to everyone's
surprise he refused, in the end, to become a full participant in the project. His
friends at Brook Farm said of him, "He liked to stay with us sometimes, but not
to be one of us" (Van der Zee Sears 1912, 34).

As he clearly explained in his article *Historic Notes of Life and Letters in Massachusetts*, Emerson shared with his reforming friends the demand that a revolution should occur in contemporary society, but he did not share their methods for achieving this. In the first place, Emerson criticized the utopian communities of New England for the strict regimentation that communal life necessarily involved. Ultimately, Emerson believed, such regimentation ended up negating that very freedom to determine one's own individual life and destiny that these communities had been founded to defend. While appreciating Fourier's intelligence and his carefully planned-out system, Emerson concluded that when people are treated as vegetables to be cultivated or as gears within a mechanism, their dignity as human beings is violated. [43] As Kateb (1992, 87) has written, "good people are insulted when commanded" because their capacity to be autonomous moral subjects is thereby implicitly denied. Every time one insists on imposing a role or a certain conduct on others—even with the best of intentions—one inevitably makes them into slaves. It was for this reason that Emerson resolutely affirmed that no law that has not been given to the individual by himself or herself can be anything but a lie and an unforgivable limitation upon this individual's freedom:

> Whilst I do what is fit for me, and abstain from what is unfit, my neighbour and I shall often agree in our means and work together for a time to one end. But whenever I find my dominion over myself not sufficient for me, and undertake the direction of him also, I overstep the truth, and come into false relations to him. I may have so much more skill or strength than he, that he cannot express adequately his sense of wrong, but it is a lie, and hurts like a lie both him and me. . . . I can see well enough a great difference between my setting myself down to a self-control, and my going to make somebody else act after my views: but when a quarter of the human race assume to tell me what I must do, I may be too much disturbed by the circumstances to see so clearly the absurdity of their command. Therefore, all public ends look vague and quixotic beside private ones. For any laws but those which men make for themselves, are laughable. (E II, 125; V, 424–425; Nietzsche underlined this passage at several points, marked it in the margin with a vertical line, and also wrote in this margin, "Above morality [*über der Moral*]"; see Appendix Figure 29)[44]

Emerson's mistrust of the utopian undertakings of 1840s New England extends, in fact, to the ideal itself of "community." Unlike in merely temporary associations, formed to achieve a particular end or aim (such as the abolition of slavery), in associations proper, that is, in communities, individuals actually define themselves in terms of their membership in the group. This means that they do not autonomously develop their identity as unique and original human beings, but rather passively receive their worldview and values as an unquestionable dogma or ideology from the group that they are a member of. Inevitably, then, "communities will never have men in them, but only halves and quarters," since "they require a sacrifice of what cannot be sacrificed without detriment," that is, individuality (LL, 159).[45]

In fact, in Emerson's view, the sole form of "common life" in which individuals are both able to express themselves as individuals and at the same time perform an educational role vis-à-vis those who have not yet learned to share this aspiration is democratic society.[46] In contrast to a "community" in the sense we have just examined, in which tasks and duties are assigned rigidly "from above" and every detail even of the private lives of the members is meticulously organized, in a democratic society each person lives "in obedience to his most private being," though "acting in strict concert with all others who follow their private light" (HNLLM, 538). This does not mean that Emerson saw American democracy "through rose-tinted spectacles." In more than one passage of his writings he expresses his disgust at the fact that in American society decisions were made by a "sometimes ruthless and mindless majority" (Aaron 1962, 86; see also Urbinati 1997, 123) and that, by a sort of Darwinism in reverse, the few men of worth were crushed by "the fools." In other words, Emerson was fully aware that, in the hands of people who are not capable of thinking independently or of exercising true self-determination, democracy can be a dangerous weapon. But despite his despair over the present state of things, Emerson trusted in the possibility of transformation and improvement.[47] The sober awareness that most of his fellow citizens were presently absolutely unprepared for self-rule was accompanied by the hope that they could one day become "free and responsible actors on the public stage" (Zakaras 2009, 7). It was precisely in order that they might exercise the office of educating others in autonomy, Emerson believed, that the self-reliant individual ought not to retreat from society in order to live alone, or with some few personal friends, but should rather stay and endure within it. In a passage from *Self-Reliance* that Nietzsche summed up, along with some other excerpts from Emerson, in his notebook for 1882, the American philosopher writes, "It is easy in the world to live after the world's opinion; it is easy in solitude to live after your own; but the great man is he who in the midst of the crowd keeps with perfect sweetness the independence of solitude" (E I, 44; V, 39).[48] With these words Emerson challenges those who have brought their own character to maturity in solitude to remain faithful to themselves even in society and thereby indirectly— through the example they provide in and by their own person—to spur others on to become true individuals themselves.

4.2.7. Overcoming Friendship

Nietzsche became aware of Emerson's essay *Historic Notes of Life and Letters in Massachusetts*, in which, as we have seen, the American philosopher critiqued the utopian communities of New England, only in December 1884. Nietzsche did not read English but, given the great interest he had in Emerson, he decided to have the piece specially translated for him, suspecting that this essay would help him to a "better understanding of [Emerson's] development" (KSB 6: 573, n. 566).[49] What Emerson had written in the *Essays*, however, surely already more than sufficed to prompt Nietzsche to reflect on the fact that shutting oneself up in a community of friends could not be a permanent solution to the problems that concerned him. The development of Nietzsche's position on this question emerges clearly enough from book 3 of Zarathustra. Let us recall that, in the Prologue to this work, Zarathustra had taken the decision to go down from his mountain into the great city to preach his doctrine to all who dwelled there. At this point in the narrative, he had adopted a simplified form of expression in order to make what he said comprehensible to all who heard him. Nevertheless, he had found himself misunderstood and derided. He had decided, therefore, to direct thenceforth his efforts toward those alone who might be able truly to understand him. These were his friends: those who, like him, were pursuing the ideal of moral perfection and personal autonomy. To these friends—or "brothers"—to whom he addresses the speeches delivered from book 1 onward Zarathustra advises a withdrawal from society and a retreat to the "Blessed Isles," the imaginary scene of all the events narrated in book 2. Nevertheless, at the end of book 2 Zarathustra decides to abandon both the "Blessed Isles" and his group of friends.

Why does Zarathustra make this decision? We can understand the considerations that played a role here by examining a note from 1883 in which Nietzsche alludes to the necessity of "overcoming friendship" and includes a reference, once again, to Emerson's *Essays*: "Zarathustra recognises that he does not exist even for his friends: 'Who are my friends!' Neither for the people, nor for individuals! *Neither for the many, nor for the few! To overcome friendship! Signs* of his self-overcoming at the beginning of III. Emerson p. 426: description of the _wise man_." (NL 1883 16[37], KSA 10: 512). On the particular page of his German copy of the *Essays* to which Nietzsche refers in this note of 1883 Emerson enunciates the principle that it is not the individual who must serve the state but rather the state that must be at the service of the individual. The state, in other words, must promote a culture of true individuality and the pursuit, by each individual, of moral autonomy. Once each citizen of a state has achieved this goal, the state itself will cease to exist because it will have fulfilled, and thereby exhausted, its function.

Hence, the less government we have, the better, —the fewer laws, and the less confided power. The antidote to this abuse of formal Government is the influence of private character, the growth of the Individual; the appearance of the principle to supersede the proxy; the appearance of the wise man, of whom the existing government, is, it must be owned, but a shabby imitation. . . . To educate the wise man, the State exists; and with the appearance of the wise man, the State expires. The appearance of character makes the State unnecessary. (E II, 126; V, 426; Nietzsche heavily underlined the passage "To educate the wise man . . . unnecessary" and marked it in the margin with four vertical lines)[50]

Emerson goes on to describe in more detail this "wise man," i.e. the mature individual that the state only exists in order to educate:

The wise man is the State. He needs no army, fort, or navy, —he loves men too well; no bribe, or feast, or palace, to draw friends to him; no vantage ground, no favourable circumstance. He needs no library, for he has not done thinking; no church, for he is a prophet; no statute-book, for he has the lawgiver; no money, for he is value; no road, for he is at home where he is; no experience, for the life of the creator shoots through him, and looks from his eyes. *He has no personal friends, for he who has the spell to draw the prayer and piety of all men unto him, needs not husband and educate a few, to share with him a select and poetic life.* (E II, 126; V, 426, italics added; Nietzsche underlined certain passages here, among which was "He has no personal friends . . . poetic life"; he also marked this passage with heavy vertical lines in the margin)

The "wise man" is the man who knows how to govern himself and who, therefore, no longer has any need of the State. He no longer needs an army because he has good relations with the whole world. Finally, he has no need of friends of his own because he knows how to derive benefit from every encounter and from every type of experience. Wisdom, for Emerson, consists precisely in the ability to derive enjoyment from every circumstance and to find in every encounter a precious opportunity for one's spiritual development (see section 2.3.5).

In the light of Nietzsche's readings in Emerson, then, we can better understand just why Zarathustra leaves the "Blessed Isles." He does not leave them because he is discontented there; on the contrary, he feels all too contented there in the midst of people who stimulate and support him; he realizes, however, that precisely this privileged state of stimulation and support is one which draws him away from his true task. Zarathustra's task is to announce the "eternal return of the same," and to affirm this "eternal return of the same" with joy means to accept reality just as it is: it means to say "Yes and Amen" (Z III, Before Sunrise) also to the "smallest and pettiest man," that is, the "man of the masses." In the third book of this work that bears his name, Zarathustra, like Emerson's "wise man," finally succeeds in recognizing every encounter as an opportunity for growth and self-enrichment. He then no longer has any need to surround himself with just a "selected few," that is to say, with personal friends alone. This is what Nietzsche is alluding to when he speaks of "the overcoming of friendship."

When we place things in this context we can also better understand why, as Abbey (1999, 66) has well noted, the references to friendship become less frequent in Nietzsche's work. If already in *Zarathustra* and *Beyond Good and Evil* "the friend" tends to be praised only to the extent that he or she behaves like an adversary, in the works that follow in the final years of Nietzsche's conscious life "it is rare to find friendship lauded in any way" (66). In my view, this does not occur because Nietzsche's thought, as Abbey claims, involves an "autarchic" and "rabid" individualism (67). Rather, what emerges if we follow the traces of Nietzsche's reading of Emerson is that, after 1883, Nietzsche overcomes the conception of friendship as purely personal and exclusive and arrives at the conclusion that, if "the friend" is the person who spurs us on to self-overcoming, then every human being is, to a certain degree at least, a friend.

4.2.8. The Living Fool versus the Dying Sage

The position that Nietzsche arrived at in 1883 had already been announced and prepared in the works of the middle period. Besides the note from 1876 (mentioned above) in which he alludes to friendship as a possible foundation for ethics (NL 1876 19[9], KSA 8: 333)—that is to say, as a model by reference to which there might be structured one's relations with all people generally—we might also mention an aphorism in *Human, All Too Human* in which he alludes to a future "higher stage of human culture" in which all members of society will behave toward one another as friends behave. At that time, writes Nietzsche, modern humankind—typically "consumed with envy whenever competitors or neighbours achieve a success," with each individual violently opposing "all opinions not his own"—will be replaced by a type "who readily rejoices with his fellow men, wins friends everywhere, welcomes everything new and developing, takes pleasure in the honours and successes of others and makes no claim to be in the sole possession of the truth" (HH 614). In other words, Nietzsche, in this aphorism, hopes for a future stage of humanity in which the distinction between friend and enemy will be erased, since all human beings will then behave toward one another in that mode of "higher friendship" described by Emerson.[51]

Aphorism 376 of *Human, All Too Human* likewise clearly drives in this direction of an overcoming and transcendence of "friendship" in the purely personal sense of this term. In this aphorism Nietzsche speaks of how uncertain must be the ground on which we attempt to build any friendship, since none among us seems to be that truly mature individual that true friendship requires. He concludes, however, with an exhortation to "endure other people," that is to say, tolerate their weaknesses, just as we endure or tolerate ourselves. In this way "perhaps to each of us there will come the more joyful hour when we exclaim: 'Friends, there are no friends!'[52] thus said the dying sage; 'Foes, there are no foes!' say I, the living fool" (HH 376).

This aphorism has been interpreted in various ways. According to Van Tongeren (2000, 217–220) it shows that, for Nietzsche, friendship demands that we do not reveal ourselves completely to our own friend. If we succeed in seeing our friends as what they truly are, we will necessarily be disappointed by them and conclude that friendship does not exist. Derrida (2005, 28), on the other hand, places the accent on the second part of the phrase and claims that, with the exclamation "foes, there are no foes!" Nietzsche is expressing a complaint regarding the fact that modernity lacks grand personalities to confront: the individual pursuing virtue cannot find worthy adversaries.

However, when we consider the contribution Emerson made to Nietzsche's reflections on friendship, we are able to interpret this aphorism in quite another way. Above all, from the analysis of the text it clearly emerges that Nietzsche cites the position of "the dying sage" only in order to set himself against it. He clearly states that, if one takes into account the fact that no one can be held responsible for his or her own actions, one can "get free of that bitterness of feeling with which the sage cried: 'Friends, there are no friends!' " (HH 376, 148). Nietzsche, in other words, is criticizing something that is commonly accepted as wisdom. This supposed "wisdom" appears to him to be a kind of cynicism which serves to protect one from disappointments but, in the last analysis, only limits and restricts one's experience of life. To this traditional pseudo-wisdom he opposes wisdom as Emerson had understood it, as the capacity to draw advantage and benefit from every set of circumstances. He personifies this true wisdom in the figure of the "living fool," who, even in the face of all disappointments, goes out without prejudice to encounter and confront the world and all those in it. We find a confirmation of this interpretation in aphorism 195 of *The Gay Science* in which Nietzsche declares himself an "indestructible fool and sage" on the basis of the fact that, despite having had to swallow so many disappointments, he has not yet become a cynic. The idea of the "sage who is also a fool"—of the sage who is not, and will never become, a cynic—was probably sparked in Nietzsche by his reading in 1876 of Emerson's *Letters and Social Aims*. In the essay that opens this collection, *Poetry and Imagination*, Emerson recounts a story from

Morte d'Arthur by Sir Thomas Malory ([1485] 1976). Malory re-elaborated, in
the 15th century, some of the most important of the Breton Cycle of legends
dealing with the fortunes and misfortunes of Arthur, Guinevere, Merlin, and
the Knights of the Round Table. The story cited by Emerson tells of one of
these knights, Sir Gawain, who went in search of Merlin after the wizard had
disappeared from the court of King Arthur. While riding in the forest, Gawain
heard a voice calling him. Initially disoriented, he quickly realized that Merlin
was talking to him, although he could not see him. Merlin then revealed to him
that he had been bewitched and was now condemned to remain invisible to everyone except for the woman who had bewitched him. Gawain then questioned
him as follows: "'How, Merlin, my good friend . . . how can this have happened,
seeing that you are the wisest man in the world?' 'Rather,' said Merlin, 'the
greatest fool; for I well knew that all this would befall me, and I have been fool
enough to love another more than myself, for I taught my mistress that whereby
she hath imprisoned me in such a manner that none can set me free'" (LSA 35).
Merlin, despite having so much experience of life (that is to say, despite being so
wise), has not yet become cynical and goes out to encounter others always with
the most sanguine of expectations.

We may conclude, then, that the figure of the "wise fool" (or "living fool"),
precisely inasmuch as this figure personifies wisdom as Emerson understood it,
preludes and prepares the attitude that Nietzsche was to adopt in 1883: that of
knowing how to treat every person one meets as a friend, since every kind of encounter represents a useful opportunity for (self-)enrichment.[53]

4.3. Conclusion

As regards the question of the value of egoism, then, the positions of Emerson
and Nietzsche basically coincide with one another: both draw a distinction between egoism in the popular and narrow sense and a certain virtuous egoism,
the latter being distinct from the former by reason of the fact that, in the case
of virtuous egoism, the profit or benefit that the individual pursues works out
also to the advantage of the collectivity. Nevertheless, it must be observed that,
whereas in Emerson the individual who is pursuing the project of his or her
self-perfection finds an additional spur to persist in this project in the fact itself
that he or she is contributing to the good of society, in Nietzsche the reform
of society—and this is the case already in the works of the middle period, although it becomes ever more marked in the works of Nietzsche's maturity and
in his late works—appears rather to be a mere collateral effect of the individuals'
achieving of personal virtue, these individuals being portrayed as living "for
themselves alone and for the sake of their own joy" (WS 350). Also regarding

the question of altruism, Emerson and Nietzsche have substantially the same position: on the one hand, they consider compassion to be a form of humiliation and the offering of help to be a kind of depriving of the other person of the chance to grow stronger by confronting adversity; on the other hand, however, they also envisage a form of concern for the "other" that is more personal—in the sense that it is not directed to some impersonal "neighbour" but rather to some person whom we know well—and which is called "friendship." In friendship, one relieves the pain of the "other" not by sharing his or her suffering but rather by showing him or her one's own joy, which the friend can then share, raising thereby his or her spirits. Moreover, pain is relieved by spurring someone on to "overcome" his or her own self.

Both Nietzsche and Emerson hold that the bond of friendship can be established only between a "selected few"—between people who possess a sufficient level of maturity and who are pursuing the same goal: self-perfection. Since these conditions are only rarely fulfilled, both Emerson and Nietzsche consider true friendship to be something very rare. The recognition of this fact, however, does not lead them to adopt a closed-off attitude vis-à-vis other people but rather one of great openness. Rather than lament the absence of friends truly deserving of the name, both arrive at the conclusion that whoever is pursuing the goal of self-perfection can draw benefit for himself or herself from every person whom he or she may encounter, even from the very worst.

As regards, however, the question of the relationship between the fully mature individual and the masses, the respective positions of the two philosophers differ quite considerably. Emerson despises the masses and sees in the political power they possess a great danger for society. But he remains, nonetheless, confident that each and every person, if properly educated, is capable of maturing into true individuality: "Masses are rude, lame, unmade, pernicious in their demands and influence, and need not to be flattered but to be schooled. I wish not to concede anything to them, but to tame, drill, divide, and break them up, and draw individuals out of them" (CL, 132; FL, 173).

In Emerson the wise man—that is to say, the mature individual—continues to live in society, in the midst of people in whose values he does not recognize himself nor his own values, with a view to educating, through his own example, other people to become mature individuals themselves. In the position adopted by Emerson here we can recognize the Confucian ideal of the wise man who refuses to withdraw from society. In an entry in his *Journal* for 1843, Emerson wrote, "Reform. Chang Tsoo and Kee Neih retired from the state to the fields on account of misrule and showed their displeasure at Confucius who remained in the world. Confucius sighed and said, 'I cannot associate with birds and beasts. If I follow not man, whom shall I follow? If the world were in possession of right principles, I should not seek to change it!'" (JMN 6: 403, quoted in Christy

1960, 126–127). This was the reason Emerson was so severely critical of the way of life of his friend Thoreau, who lived in total solitude and self-reliance at Walden Pond, and of that of his friends Ripley and Alcott, who had quit the normal social structures of the day to establish self-sufficient communities.[54] In other words, Emerson's self-reliant individual, although he or she refrains from dedicating his or her life to helping the needy, nevertheless feels a moral responsibility to contribute to the good of society as a whole.

Nietzsche's position here is much more nuanced. In the works of his middle period he conceives of the community of educators as "engines," as it were, propelling a general reform of culture; that is to say, he sees the project of self-perfection as serving a function conducive to a general improvement of society. The "free spirits" do not concern themselves about others, but in concerning themselves about their own selves they are aware that this, as is prescribed by the morality of the mature individual (HH 95, see section 4.1.2), is the highest good that can be contributed to society. In his very last period, however, Nietzsche loses all hope of a general reform of culture and entirely gives up the idea of educating the masses. After leaving the "Blessed Isles" Zarathustra does not go back to live in the city but rather returns to the solitude of his cave. It is to this cave that, in part 4 of the book, the "higher men" will have to ascend to hear his announcement of the doctrine of the Eternal Return. This indicates that Zarathustra believes that it is, in fact, only a small, select number of people who "have ears to hear" what he has to say, that is, who are able to receive certain of his teachings. Nietzsche's wise man—quite different in this respect from the wise man of Emerson—rather than lowering himself to the level of the petty masses, expects that he who is ready to receive his wisdom should rise to his level.

5

Making History and Writing History

5.1. Nietzsche's Position(s) on History and Historiography

Let us now turn to look at the development of Nietzsche's philosophical attitude to the topic of history by examining, in depth, three phases of his treatment of this theme: the period of the second of the *Untimely Meditations*, the middle period (i.e., the period running from *Human, All Too Human* up to *The Gay Science*), and the late period (comprising published works and unpublished notes composed between 1883 and the end of 1888).

The first thesis I want to demonstrate is that reading Emerson played an indispensable role in Nietzsche's moving from the position on the question of history which he had expounded in the second of the *Untimely Meditations* to that which characterizes the works of the middle period. Proceeding from a general comparison between the thought of the two authors, Stack (1992, 120–133) overestimates the importance of the theory of "active forgetting" that Nietzsche expounds in the former text and assumes it to be representative of his general position on history. But by following the real traces of Nietzsche's reading of Emerson I will show that this active forgetting is a virtue (Swanton 2015, 163) only for the Nietzsche of the early writings, when he was still partly under the influence of Schopenhauerian metaphysics and of Wagner.[1] From *Human, All Too Human* onward Nietzsche, through reading Emerson, begins to be open to the idea that history is not a burden weighing on Man but rather an inestimable source of intellectual and moral wealth, and that the more extended our historical horizon is, the greater is the power to which we can attain. More specifically, through reading Emerson Nietzsche succeeds in identifying the criterion by which it is possible to distinguish a healthy, and thereby virtuous, relationship with history from an unhealthy, and thereby vicious, relationship with it. He discovers self-reliance to be this criterion. Whoever lacks self-reliance will focus on history in order to lose themselves, but whoever possesses self-reliance will turn to history in order to find themselves. Taking his lead from ideas he had found expressed in Emerson, Nietzsche elaborated, in the works of his middle period, an alternative to the historiographical canon of the 19th century: an active, empathetic reading of historical events in which these events are relived "in the first person." Nietzsche personifies this model of historical knowledge first in the ideal historian whom he calls a "hundred-eyed Argos," evoked at AOM 223, then in the portrait of an idealized Goethe, which he sketches in *Twilight of the Idols*. Far more than does the historical Goethe the figure sketched here resembles the voracious nomadic character whom Emerson had presented in his essay on the great German poet and author, who yearns to draw from history as much experience, and thereby as much power, as is humanly possible.

5.1.1. The Malady of History: Diagnoses and Remedies

In the second of the *Untimely Meditations*, which Jensen (2018) proposes should be translated as *Of Uses and Disadvantage of History for Life*,[2] Nietzsche deplores the fact that the most prominent personalities in his era's cultural panorama consist of scholars and "men of letters" alone, and that there is no sign, far and wide, of original thinkers. Nietzsche believes the fault lies with the excessive importance that his era tends to confer upon the past and upon tradition; in other words, the fault lies with an excessive preoccupation with the study of history. The precepts of "historical man" dictate that a phenomenon is "understood" only when every single event which contributed to its formation has been painstakingly reconstructed. In the 19th century this approach came gradually to be applied to every sphere of culture, to such an extent that this century came to be remembered as "the historical century [*das historische Jahrhundert*]," as opposed to the "philosophical" 18th century that had preceded it (Sandberger 1997,11). Nietzsche criticized not just the excessive attention that the intellectuals of his era were paying to the past but also, and indeed above all, the methodology with which the historical research of the day was being conducted. The quality of a historiographic description was measured based on these two parameters: exhaustiveness and objectivity. The more details such a description contained, and the fewer traces it bore of any personal interpretation on the part of the historian, the more valuable it was considered to be.[3] First, as regards this requirement that a description be exhaustive, Nietzsche makes the observation that to store up a mass of information greater than the quantity that one is able personally to assimilate—that is to say, able to make actual use of in one's own life—is extremely harmful. Just as a spring that remains constantly compressed under an excessive load will, over time, lose its elasticity, so too will the scholarly "historical man," crushed under an excessive quantity of notions and ideas, eventually become incapable of thinking for himself and in his own right.[4] As to the second requirement—objectivity—Nietzsche makes the observation that imposing upon scholars the rule that they maintain a completely passive attitude vis-à-vis all that they study—that is to say, that they should have no emotional reaction or response to any of the historical events with which they concern themselves— will, over time, tend to render such scholars incapable of expressing personal judgments at all and thereby incapable also of using the things that they study to develop their own future plans and projects. All in all, then, Nietzsche concludes that the study of history, carried out according to the precepts dear to the "historical man" of the 19th century, does not help or support the development of human personality but rather hinders it. The portrait he draws of the historians of his era is that of "idlers" who loiter "in the garden of knowledge [*verwöhnte Müssiggänger im Garten des Wissens*]" (HL Foreword), making use of the noble excuse of science as a mask for their own incapacity to act.[5]

Needless to say, Nietzsche never hated historians or historiography. In the second *Untimely Meditation* he is simply deploring the way that history is studied and lamenting the fact that the historian has lost sight of the connection linking his or her field of study to the formation of human personality (*Bildung*) and to life itself. Nietzsche's contention is not that we should dispense with history but simply that the study of history should be subordinated to the education of the individual. This is why he concludes his essay *Of Uses and Disadvantage of History for Life* with the declaration "We want to serve history only to the extent that history serves life" (HL Foreword).

The "balsam" that Nietzsche prescribes "against the malady of history" (HL 10) is "the unhistorical and the suprahistorical" (HL 10).[6] Put briefly, Nietzsche recommends to the educated modern individual that he or she draw a limit to his or her own historical horizon and remain focused solely on events that might prove to bear some relation to his or her own life, that is, events from which he or she might potentially derive some practical and immediate lesson or instruction with regard to questions that interest and concern him or her on a personal level. All the rest can and must be forgotten.

During the period of the *Untimely Meditations* Nietzsche considered this "active forgetting" to be necessary to the health of the mind, just as sleep is necessary if one is going to lead an active life by day. In 1883, however, looking back, he was to take a stance opposed to this theory of "active forgetting" and to define it as a deliberate attempt on his part to "base culture on illusion" (NL 1883 16[23], KSA 10: 507) ascribable to the pernicious influence that Wagner was still exerting upon him at the period of the *Untimely Meditations*. On closer examination, it can be seen that already at this period Nietzsche had looked upon "active forgetting" as an extreme remedy for an extreme malady, or, in other words, as an "emergency measure." It was for this reason that he had, as he put it, here and there left himself "exit strategies [*Ausfallspforten*]" (NL

1876 17[36], KSA 8: 303) in the *Untimely Meditations*. By this he meant that he had introduced into the texts certain "clauses," as it were, which specified the conditions of applicability of the solutions that he proposed. One of these "exit strategies" is to be found at that point in the second *Untimely Meditation* when, after having declared that, if one is not to succumb under the enormous quantity of information that it is possible to draw from books, then one must define and limit one's historical horizon to whatever can be useful for one's own life, Nietzsche goes on to specify that the usefulness that one can succeed in deriving from events depends upon one's own capacity to assimilate and to transform. And this capacity, in its turn, depends upon the strength of one's own personality: the stronger a person's personality is, the less risk he or she runs of losing his or her own independence through coming into contact with the views of others or with the models that others take for their lives. And all the more numerous, thereby, will be this person's opportunities to learn from such views and models. For the weak personality of the modern scholar, "active forgetting" is a necessity. Nietzsche concedes, however, at least in principle, that there might exist a personality so strong that it would not need to draw any limit at all to its personal historical horizon. Such an enormously powerful nature "would draw to itself and incorporate into itself all the past, its own and that most foreign to it, and as it were transform it into blood" (HL 1). In other words, an individual constituted in such a way would be able to make use of all the notions that he or she had learned and acquired from books as nutriment for his or her own original thought and action.

Just what characteristics this "enormously powerful nature" would need to possess, and just how it would "draw to itself all the past" and gain nourishment from it—these are things that Nietzsche does not explain in the second *Untimely Meditation*. As we shall see, this ideal was to be further developed in the period of *Human, All Too Human*, once again taking certain cues and clues from Emerson. In fact, in sharp contradistinction from his contemporaries, Emerson had elaborated an approach to history characterized by a great reverence for the past, surpassed only by the reverence that he believed was owed to that present task that each individual is called upon to carry to completion.

5.1.2. Making a Clean Break with the Past

The historical-cultural climate in which Emerson was immersed was a million miles from that stagnant cultural atmosphere that characterized Nietzsche's Germany of the second half of the 18th century. The New England Transcendentalists, in Herbert Wallace Schneider's (1946, 281) words, "were confident that they were still in the centre of creative activity, too busy for reminiscence and too hopeful for regrets." Emerson and his friends were united in the wish to make a clean break with the past and to initiate something radically new in world history. Particularly representative of the spirit of their time is a short story by Hawthorne entitled "Old Esther Dudley." The protagonist, Governor Hancock, declares to the old woman Esther, a symbol of the past, "I, and these around me—we represent a new race of men—living no longer in the past, scarcely in the present—but projecting our lives forward into the future. Ceasing to model ourselves on ancestral superstitions, it is our faith and principle to press onward, onward!" (quoted in Kerkering 2003, 78). American intellectuals identified Europe with a past with regard to which they repeatedly affirmed their difference and exteriority. By crossing the Atlantic their forefathers had forever taken their distance from this tradition. They saw the New World as a completely blank page upon which they could freely invent the social and cultural forms that corresponded best to their requirements. As Thoreau wrote in his essay *Walking*, "We go eastward to realize history and study the works of art and literature, retracing the steps of the race; we go westward as into the future, with a spirit of enterprise and adventure. The Atlantic is a Lethean stream, in our passage over which we have had an opportunity to forget the Old World and its institutions" (quoted in Bercovitch and Patell 1995, 134). Emerson shared with the Transcendentalists the wish to free oneself from cultural servitude to the past and to initiate something radically new. At the very beginning of the essay *Nature* (1836), considered to be the manifesto of American Transcendentalism, he provocatively raises the following demands:

> Our age is retrospective. It builds the sepulchres of the fathers. It writes biographies, histories, and criticism. The foregoing generations beheld God and nature face to face; we, through their eyes. Why should not we also enjoy an original relation to the universe? . . . Why should we grope among the dry bones of the past, or put the living generation into masquerade out of its faded wardrobe? The sun shines to-day also. There is more wool and flax in the fields. There are new lands, new men, new thoughts. Let us demand our own works and laws and worship. (NAL, 7)

With this statement Emerson invites his contemporaries to establish a firsthand relation to Nature, a relation that is not weighed down by the burden of the past. But Emerson also asks himself just how all this will be brought to pass. Is it really possible to get rid of the past? And even if it were, would it really be the best choice to do so? On the one hand, Emerson observes that in "idiots," children, and "savages" the true self speaks out much more clearly and audibly than it does in the "dissector or the antiquary," the modern man of letters or man of science, whose mind tends to be crowded and jammed with an infinity of voices foreign to his own inward being. To immerse oneself in Nature and to live in the present, oblivious to both past and future, might seem, then, to be the best way to be happy and to express oneself in a free and original way. The individual would then be freed from the anxiety of having to conform to already existing models and would develop his or her own particular nature in spontaneity. As a kind of exhortation to rediscover this sense of freedom, Emerson writes in one passage, "These roses under my window make no reference to former roses or better ones; they are what they are; they exist with God to-day. There is no time to them. There is simply the rose; it is perfect in every moment of its existence" (E I, 55; V, 50). On the other hand, however, Emerson is absolutely aware of the fact that it is simply not possible to live completely nonhistorically: we are no longer "savages" and cannot return to our prehistoric state of "savagery." Like it or not, we find ourselves immersed in tradition. Therefore, rather than trying to ignore this fact of our condition, it is better to accept it and to try to draw some benefit from it. In other words, consistently with his basic philosophical approach, Emerson urges that we do not attempt to deny inevitably existing circumstances but rather use them to our own advantage. With regard to this specific case, Emerson explains that, where we transform our way of relating to tradition and to history, these in turn can be changed from burdens or obstacles into treasures of inestimable value. What, then, according to Emerson, is the proper way of relating to tradition?

Emerson provides a practical example of the right attitude to adopt with regard to tradition in the very passage we cited earlier, which opens the essay *Nature*. Surprisingly, his famous declaration of the need always to think and act in an original way consists of a collage of quotations from some of his best-loved authors. Whereas the first sentence, "Our age is retrospective," echoes William Hazlitt's chapter on Coleridge in *The Spirit of the Age*, the second, "It builds the sepulchres of the fathers," echoes not only Luke 11:47 but also Daniel Webster's 1825 speech on the occasion of the laying of the cornerstone of the Bunker Hill Monument (JMN 3, 38; see Keane 2005, 162).[7] This is certainly no demonstration of the fact that Emerson was incapable of expressing himself using his own words. Rather, through his use of quotations he wanted to demonstrate that there is no incompatibility between quotation and originality: tradition can and must be used as material for every new creation. In other words, the voice of tradition must neither replace that of the individual nor be ignored. In the essay on Shakespeare included in *Representative Men* Emerson defines "originality" as the ability to take already existing elements and assemble them in some new way. He argues that if what we mean by "originality" is merely individuals' "weaving like a spider their web from their own bowels," then we must declare that "no great men are original" (RM, 109; UGS, 49). The true genius "did owe debts in all directions" (RM, 112; UGS, 57) because he used all that he happened to find as material for his own creation. At the same time, however, as Emerson adds in his essay on Goethe, the genius does not resemble another, that is, has never copied nor imitated anyone (RM, 15).[8] What Emerson argues here with specific limited reference to the field of literary creation can easily be extended to our relations with the past in all its forms and aspects: whoever decides to initiate an original action never does so ex nihilo but rather in drawing inspiration from what has been done by others.

Ultimately, then, Emerson turns completely on its head the Transcendentalist dream of making a clean break with the past and freeing oneself from tradition. For Emerson, the individual liberates himself or herself from the authority of tradition not by seeking to forget tradition but rather by making use of it in order to create something new. This is the dimension through which humankind can tap into the maximum degree of power that we are capable of: "The new position of the advancing man has all the powers of the old yet has them all new. It carries in its bosom all the energies of the past yet is itself an exhalation of the morning" (E I, 264; V, 236; Nietzsche marks this passage in the margin with two vertical lines).

Obviously, if one is not to remain crushed by the weight of the past and if one is to succeed in using the past for one's own life mission, one must approach it under a certain precondition: that of a persisting reverence for oneself and for one's own vocation. "The Past is for us," Emerson states, "but the sole terms on which it can become ours are its subordination to the Present" (LSA, 107; NE, 189). In other words, only the self-reliant individual is able to profit from the study of history.

In what way does this self-reliant scholar relate to history? Since the focus of his or her interest in history is the lessons that can be drawn from it, this scholar will relate back every event and personality of the past to himself or herself and to his or her own life. In short, he or she will develop an active, empathetic reading: a reading in which one seeks to actually identify with the events narrated and to live them as things that might have befallen one's own self:

> The student is to read history actively and not passively; to esteem his own life the text, and books the commentary. Thus compelled, the muse of history will utter oracles, as never to those who do not respect themselves. I have no expectation that any man will read history aright, who thinks that what was done in a remote age, by men whose names have resounded far, has any deeper sense than what he is doing to-day.... He [the scholar] should see that he can live all history in his own person. He must ... transfer the point of view from which history is commonly read, from Rome and Athens and London to himself.... We are always coming up with the facts that have moved us in history in our private

experience, and verifying them here. All history becomes subjective; in other words, there is properly no History; only Biography. Every soul must know the whole lesson for itself [the German translation of this passage is *Jeder Mensch muss seine ganze Aufgabe erkennen*]. . . . What it does not see, what it does not live, it will not know. . . . All inquiry into antiquity . . . is the desire to do away this wild, savage and preposterous There or Then, and introduce in its place the Here and the Now. (E I, 7–9; V 5–8; Nietzsche underlined "what he is doing to-day" and marked the passage "I have no expectation . . . to-day" with two vertical lines in the margin and the numeral "5"; he underlined "there is properly no history, only biography" and "for itself" and marked the passage "All inquiry . . . the Now" with a vertical line in the margin and the number "7")

With this active reading of history Emerson wants to present an alternative to the scientism which dominated historiography in the 19th century and which he had already critiqued in an early lecture series titled *The Philosophy of History* (EL II, 3; see Van Cromphout 1990, 104). His point of reference here is Goethe, of whom he was a great admirer. In fact, Emerson began to meditate on this theme of "reliving history at first hand" after his first tour of Europe, during which he read Goethe's *Italian Journey*. There Goethe (1948–1971, IX, 160, 167) tells of how, during his stay in Rome, he began to see history not from the outside but from the inside, or, in other words, to relive it in his own mind and soul. Just at the time that he was reading Goethe's book, Emerson notes, in his journal for the year 1834, his resolution in future to consider every fact always and only with reference to his own life (see JMN 4: 272).

In *Representative Men* Emerson sketches a portrait of Goethe as the "ideal scholar," that is to say, as the scholar who had best known how to place himself in a proper relation to tradition. On the one hand, Goethe wished to draw from tradition as much information as he possibly could; on the other hand, the knowledge he drew from the past interested him only insofar as it could be utilized for all the things that he wanted to create in the present. Regarding every doctrine he studied he always posed the question "What can you teach me?" (RM, 163; UGS 37). In *Representative Men* Emerson portrays Goethe as "hundred-handed, Argus-eyed [*mit nimmermüde Augen begabt* in the German text], able and happy to cope with this rolling miscellany of facts" the cultural tradition made available to him "and, by his own versatility, to dispose of them with ease" (RM, 156; UGS 18). The genius of Goethe would have been "impossible at any earlier time" (RM, 156; UGS 18). In other words, his view would not have been so powerful and effective if it had not been nurtured by centuries of tradition. At the same time, his vision is completely original.

It might be argued that, in the last analysis, Emerson does no more than re-state Goethe's position on the question of history and historiography. And certainly, Emerson and Goethe shared the fundamental notion that only an individual endowed with an original creative strength and committed to developing it could possibly derive any benefit from the study of history, since it would only be such an individual who would possess the energy required to assimilate the stimuli emerging from such a study and fertilize with them his or her own creative thought. Nietzsche, in fact, in the second *Untimely Meditation*, cites not Emerson but Goethe himself in this connection: "In any case, I hate everything that merely instructs me without augmenting or directly invigorating my activity" (HL Foreword).

The substantial difference between Emerson's position and Goethe's here, and the reason Nietzsche found himself drawn to the former rather than to the latter, is the voracity which, in Emerson's writing, is characteristic of that individual who turns his or her attention to history. Goethe (1948–1971, XXI: 892; IXX: 670), for his part, is an advocate of the notion of active forgetting; that is to say, he recommends that we restrict the consideration we accord to historical events to those that might possibly have some relation to our own lives. Emerson, by contrast, maintains that there are no historical events that do not somehow concern us; even those historical figures who exemplify characteristics as distant from our own as can be imagined embody and represent possibilities that we have not yet, but still might, actualize, or circumstances that we have not yet, but still might one day, encounter. In other words, for Emerson, provided only that one possess a great degree of self-reliance and thus runs no risk of "losing oneself" thereby, it is to be hoped and wished that one should relive, as if it were one's own experience, the entire history of humanity.

5.1.3. Universal History as Biography

Nietzsche takes advantage of cues and clues arising from his readings in Emerson above all during his middle period, when he begins reevaluating the importance of historical knowledge for the fundamental philosophical task of "knowing thyself." During the period of the *Untimely Meditations* he tends still to define the philosopher by counterposing this figure to that of the "historical man" (in the sense of the man "born for history"). The true philosopher is the genius who attains to knowledge by the path of intuition. "He who lets concepts, opinions, past events, books, step between himself and things—he, that is to say, who is in the broadest sense born for history—will never have an immediate perception of things and will never be an immediately perceived thing himself" (SE 7), declares Nietzsche in the third of the *Untimely Meditations*.[9] The figure of "Schopenhauer as educator" is described exactly in these terms: "Most of the instruction he receives he has to acquire out of himself and . . . he serves himself as a reflection and brief abstract of the whole world" (SE 7). In the period of *Human, All Too Human* Nietzsche distanced himself from the Schopenhauerian theory of the genius as someone whose superior intuitive capacity was supposed to allow him a direct and immediate access to truth without any need for study. He arrived now rather at the conclusion that history and science were the sole sources of reliable knowledge. He even went so far as to doubt the effectiveness, as regards the basic philosophical task of "knowing thyself," of the revered method of introspection: "Direct self-observation is not nearly sufficient for us to know ourselves: we require history, for the past continues to flow within us in a hundred waves" (AOM 223). What does this mean, that "the past continues to flow within us"? It means that, as much from the cultural as from the biological[10] point of view, we are the heirs of the generations that have preceded us. Looked at in this way, the study of history no longer appears as an idle pastime or a distraction from our true mission in life but rather—to the extent that it helps us to better understand our own selves—as a precondition for fulfilling this very mission. The greater our knowledge of the past, the greater will be our knowledge of our own selves and thereby also our ability to act effectively.

By examining the notebook of excerpts from Emerson that Nietzsche compiled in 1882 we can clearly recognize that Nietzsche used the American philosopher's *Essays* to bring into focus in his own mind both the presuppositions from which one should proceed in the study of history and the method that needs to be applied in pursuing this study.

In one of these excerpts Nietzsche loosely summarizes the argument of Emerson's which we cited earlier regarding the methodology required in order effectively to perform a personal reading of history. Nietzsche's paraphrase of this Emersonian argument, translated back into English from the German, runs: "The creative instinct of the mind betrays itself in the use we make of history: there is only biography. Everybody must know his or her whole task [*seine ganze Aufgabe*]. —This unplanned, wild, meaningless [*planlose rohe widersinnige*] There and Then must disappear and be replaced with the Here and the Now" (NL 1882 17[5], KSA 9: 666).[11] In another of these excerpts Nietzsche adopts as his own the Emersonian thesis whereby, in order to stand in a healthy relationship to history, one's own current-day life goal must be clearly present to one's mind. And for this, in turn, there is needful a great degree of self-reliance; in other words, it is necessary that individuals should have the greatest respect for themselves and for their mission. Once again drawing, somewhat freely, his inspiration from what Emerson says in the essay *History*, Nietzsche writes in his notebook of 1882, "That which I do today has as deep a meaning as anything from the past [*Das, was ich heute thue, hat eine so tiefe Bedeutung als irgend etwas Vergangenes*]" (NL 1882 17[3], KSA 9: 666).

These excerpts really do no more than recapitulate certain propositions that Nietzsche had already assimilated from his readings in Emerson's work some years earlier. In *Assorted Opinions and Maxims*, Nietzsche expounds his new notion of an ideal historical knowledge by recurring to the portrait of Goethe that Emerson had advanced in *Representative Men* and combining this with the reflections on an active reading of history contained in the essay of Emerson's bearing just this title (*History*):

> He who, after long practice in this art of travel, has become a hundred-eyed Argos, will in the end be attended everywhere by his Io—I mean his ego—and will rediscover the adventurous travels of this ego in process of becoming and transformation in Egypt and Greece, Byzantium and Rome, France and Germany, in the age of the nomadic or of the settled nations, in the Renaissance and the Reformation, at home and abroad, indeed in the sea, the forests, in the plants and in the mountains.—Thus self-knowledge will become universal knowledge with regard to all that is past. (AOM 223)

The "ideal historian" is now, for Nietzsche, an individual who contains within himself or herself a great multitude of different individuals—namely, all those men and women of the past with whom he or she has succeeded in empathizing—and who has developed the same sort of feeling toward universal history as he or she would have toward his or her own individual biography. In short, during his middle period Nietzsche, drawing on Emerson, worked out a model for the study of history alternative to the "scientific" model which had predominated throughout his own century. This consisted in an empathetic reading of historical events, a reading as it were "in the first person," in which the preoccupation was no longer "establishing what really happened" but rather "what I can learn" from whatever happened (Jensen 2013, 94–95). Above all, however, in this period Nietzsche draws from Emerson the conviction that the limitation of one's historical horizon is not at all something to be wished for or pursued, since it means limiting also the power that one can draw from history; provided only that one possess a sufficiently strong personality, the vaster the span and body of tradition that one cognitively attains to and embraces, the better for oneself. There is thus concretely developed, in the portrait of the ideal historian as a hundred-eyed Argos who is able to relive empathetically the entire history of humanity and to assimilate all humanity's experiences, the very image of that supremely "powerful and tremendous nature" (HL 1) that Nietzsche had longed to see realized several years before, in the period of the second of the *Untimely Meditations*.

5.1.4. Thirst for Power

Already in the second of the *Untimely Meditations*, but above all starting from the middle period works, what impels, in Nietzsche's vision, the scholar to turn to the past is precisely a hunger to increase his or her own power. The men and women of the past do not, in themselves, interest the individual, but only with regard to the treasure trove of experience they have accrued and which this individual can now make his or her own. From *Zarathustra* on, Nietzsche was to define the will to truth as a form of the will to power. The will to historical knowledge can therefore also be considered a form of the will to power. As we pointed out in section 3.1.2, the will to power is not to be understood as some mental or spiritual force that governs all Nature, after the manner of Schopenhauer's "Will." Rather, "will to power" is an expression that Nietzsche uses to indicate the quality—or, better put, the structure—of all that exists. At the level of the self, increase of power is obtained by the acquisition of new points of view and perspectives, a process in which the "foreign" or "alien" element (i.e., the points of view of others) is subjugated, incorporated, and, in the moment in which it is incorporated, also re-elaborated and appropriated by the incorporating subject, that is, united with this subject's own total vision of the world. The extent of the plurality of world interpretations that a self can contain and manage determines this self's degree of power. Within such a framework, the broader the historical knowledge possessed by an individual, the greater will be his or her power.

It seems a plausible supposition that Nietzsche may have drawn inspiration both for the expression "will to power" and for the concept this expression conveys from Emerson's essay *Power* included in the collection *The Conduct of Life*. In this essay Emerson identifies as a distinctive characteristic of a living being that it displays a tendency to expand and grow through the subjection and acquisition of that which is foreign and "other" to it: "Life is a search after power; and this is an element with which the world is so saturated . . . that no honest seeking goes unrewarded" (CL, 28; FL 36).[12] It is precisely this search after power, argues Emerson in the essay *Compensation* (included in the *Essays*), that also motivates our interest in history. If history is a precious treasure house of different experiences that we might make use of, it is only natural that there should be ignited in the mind an avid thirst to study as much of it as possible. "It is the eternal nature of the soul to appropriate and make all things its own. Jesus and Shakespeare are fragments of the soul, and by love I conquer and incorporate them in my own conscious domain" (E I, 102; V, 94).[13] That this thirst for power is also, for Emerson, the motor driving the acquisition of historical knowledge clearly emerges also from the poem that he places at the head of his essay *History*, in which he yearns to possess "Plato's brain," "Lord Christ's heart," "Caesar's hand," etc. Nietzsche writes the following comment on this poem in the margin: "Oh our greed! I sense nothing of selflessness, but rather an all-desiring self, which through many individuals—sees as with its eyes and grasps with its hands, is also a self which wishes to regain the whole past, one which does not want to lose anything which could belong to it" (NL 1881 13[7], KSA 9: 619, V, 1; see Appendix Figure 2).[14] On the reverse side of the title page of Nietzsche's copy of the *Essays*, we also find the following note: "Do you want to become a universal, impartial eye? Then you shall have to do it as an individual that has gone through many individuals and whose latest individuality [*Individuum*] requires all previous ones as functions" (NL 1881 13[5], KSA 9: 619).[15] Nietzsche worked up the annotations he made to Emerson's *Essays* into a series of notes dating from the summer of 1881, probably composed in conjunction with the annotations made to his copy of Emerson's *Essays*, in which Nietzsche reiterates that, in order to train one's own interpretative capacities, it is necessary to "look into the world with as many eyes as possible" (NL 1881 11[141], KSA 9: 494) or "go through many individuals" (NL 1881 11[197], KSA 9: 520; see also NL 1881 11[65, 119], KSA 9: 466, 483). In the end, these notes resulted in GS 249:

> The sigh of the one who comes to know. —"Oh, my greed! In this soul there dwells no selflessness but rather an all-desiring self that would like, as it were, to see with the eyes and seize with the hands of many individuals—a self that would like to bring back the entire past, that wants to lose nothing it could possibly possess! Oh, this flame of my greed! Oh, that I might be reborn into a hundred beings!"—Whoever does not know this sigh from experience does not know the passion of coming to know.

This aphorism takes up and further explores that notion of an ideal historian already presented in the image of the "hundred-eyed Argos" in AOM 223. Nietzsche's polemical target here is not just the historicist ideal of an objective knowledge but that whole philosophical tradition which, from Locke to Kant, conceives of true knowledge as pure and disinterested. For Nietzsche, when we perform the act of knowing—that is to say, when we form for ourselves a vision of the things around us—it is not some supposed "mind" or "intellectual faculty" distinct from the body which interprets the world. Rather, it is the organism qua "Lebens-System" (NL 1881 11[7], KSA 9: 443) that places itself in an active relation to its external environment. In other words, we do not first form an image of the world and then, only afterward, express value judgments; rather, we form our image of the world on the basis of the value judgments which we have already all along unconsciously been expressing (Siemens 2006, 149).[16] For this reason, if we want to increase our knowledge it is not enough to "know" just what the facts were and how they came to be; rather, it is necessary to relive these facts, to transform ourselves, even if it is only momentarily, into the men and women of the past and to thus acquire their experience.

According to Jensen (2013), Nietzsche's critique of the ideal of a "pure historical knowledge"—a knowledge free of all emotional input from the knowing subject—was already present in the second of the *Untimely Meditations*. In this latter text, claims Jensen, Nietzsche outlines three different types of historian, each with his particular characteristic configuration of drives, and goes on to show how to each particular psychological configuration there corresponds a particular approach to history. For example, whoever is dominated by a drive toward truth will develop a critical approach to history; the "revering soul" (Jensen 2013, 85) will develop what Nietzsche calls an "antiquarian" approach; and the individual of the active type will develop a "monumental" approach. Jensen claims that Nietzsche did not intend, with this typology, to criticize the subjectivism of these various visions but rather only to emphasize the fact that "the subjectivity of the observer is absolutely essential in the process of constructing a historical account" (87). In any case, in the works of the middle period Nietzsche makes fuller and more explicit his critique of the ideal of "pure objective knowledge" in general and of the scientistic ideal of "historical knowledge as impersonal knowledge" in particular. He uses Emerson's observations to redefine the historian's ideal of "objectivity": this is no longer conceived of in terms of the achievement of some suprapersonal—and thereby supposedly "pure"—point of view, imagined to be free of all emotions and affections; on the contrary, it is now conceived of in terms of the multiplication of personal perspectives and thereby of the emotions and affections that necessarily characterize them. By immersing ourselves, in a highly personal way, in the men and women of the past, we can feel what they felt and thereby see things as they saw them. The historian is thus enabled to elaborate a point of view of his or her own, which will be comprehensive of all the points of view and visions that had preceded it, and thereby indeed be "supremely powerful" but not assimilable to any of these latter and thus entirely original.

5.1.5. Historical Sense versus the "Humanity" of the Future

Those who wish to immerse themselves in the lives of as many men and women of the past as possible, with a view to expanding as far as possible the range of their own experience, will have necessarily also to confront an enormous amount of suffering and frustration. History does not, in fact, consist just in moments of glory but also in a great mass of errors with tragic consequences. In part 4 of *Thus Spoke Zarathustra* Nietzsche shows us the danger that history contains of crushing the individual who studies it under the weight of human suffering. He does so with the figure of the Ugliest Human Being, who represents the historical sense or, more precisely, the historical sense in its negative and pernicious aspect.[17] This Ugliest Human Being, who sees history as a series of senseless massacres and disappointed hopes, suffers from this vision so intensely that the notion of the Eternal Return appears unacceptable to him. Through this figure Nietzsche wants to suggest that, if one simply takes upon oneself the emotions of people who have lived before one without knowing how to transform these emotions, one will surely be destroyed by them. To assimilate something means to accept and embrace it, but, at the same time, it means inserting this old thing into some new order or structure and thereby altering its meaning. If he or she is not to collapse under the weight of pain and sorrow, the historian must bear in mind that every negative experience contains a lesson to be learned, one which can increase the historian's own power and ability to act. It is in the name of his or her own future action that whoever undertakes to study history succeeds in resituating each historical event within some new perspective, and thereby in giving it some new value. Once again it is Emerson who enables Nietzsche to achieve these insights. In a passage from the essay *Spiritual Laws* Emerson argues that our cognitive assimilation of the deeds of the men and women of past ages can be said to be completed only when we perform an original action of our own:

> If the poet write a true drama, then he is Caesar, and not the player of Caesar; then the selfsame strain of thought, emotion as pure, wit as subtle, motions as swift, mounting, extravagant, and a heart as great, self-sufficing, dauntless, which on the waves of its love and hope can uplift all that is reckoned solid and precious in the world, palaces, gardens, money, navies, kingdoms, —marking its own incomparable worth by the slight it casts on these gauds of men, —these all are his, and by the power of these he rouses the nations. (E I, 135; V, 123; Nietzsche marked this passage with many vertical lines; see Appendix Figure 13)

Nietzsche wrote in the margin, "Sum felix [I am happy]" (see V 123; Appendix Figure 13). This passage from Emerson can be considered the point of departure for the reflections that Nietzsche presents in GS 337, an aphorism in which he describes what is indeed an experience of great happiness. GS 337 bears the title "The 'Humanity' of the Future." The German term Nietzsche used is *Menschlichkeit*, which designates not the human species in the bare biological sense (which in German would be *Menschheit*) but rather the special sensibility that is supposed to follow from being a "human being" in the full meaning of this term. Nietzsche considered that a higher form of this sensibility might evolve— and ought, indeed, to be hoped and wished to evolve—from the "historical sense" that characterized his own epoch. This "historical sense" as it has manifested itself up until now, observes Nietzsche, has produced a form of knowledge which has had no vitalizing effect upon human action. On the contrary, it has had the effect of making people "poorer and colder" in their actions and feelings. In this remark we can see a reference back to that critique of the "scientific" practice of historiography which Nietzsche had already himself developed in the second of the *Untimely Meditations*. He even adds, in this aphorism, that this "scientific" historiography can be perceived as a sign of the approaching senility of our culture or as a sign of its having become a sickly invalid, writing up its past in order to forget its wretched present. To this "historical sense" in the "scientific" form predominant in his own age Nietzsche counterposes the sensibility characteristic of the person who reads history "in the first person" or, in other words, the self-reliant individual described by Emerson in his *Essays*:

> He who is able to feel the history of man altogether as his own history feels in a monstrous generalization all the grief of the invalid thinking of health, of the old man thinking of the dreams of his youth, of the lover robbed of his beloved, of the martyr whose ideal is perishing, of the hero on the eve after a battle that decided nothing but brought him wounds and the loss of a friend. But to bear and to be able to bear this monstrous sum of all kinds . . . to take this upon one's soul—the oldest, the newest, losses, hopes, conquests, victories of humanity . . . and compress it into one feeling—this would surely have to produce a happiness unknown to humanity so far: a divine happiness full of power and love. (GS 337)[18]

The self-reliant individual, sympathizing and empathizing as he or she does with the men and women of the past, surely must initially take upon himself or herself an enormous accumulation of sufferings and frustrations. But in the moment in which he or she actually succeeds in assimilating the experience of history, he or she experiences a sense of increase in power which gives rise to a feeling of great happiness.[19] In short, Nietzsche, taking and making his own the above-cited passage from Emerson—and this he does, indeed, both on the stylistic level and in terms of its actual philosophical substance—uses it to answer a question which Emerson himself, in his own essays, had not only not resolved but never even posed: the question of how to transform the great mass of pain and sorrow that history necessarily contains in such a way as not to be destroyed by it.

In *Twilight of the Idols* Nietzsche presents this ideal sensibility that he calls "the humanity [*Menschlichkeit*] of the future" as finding exemplary personification in the figure of Goethe. In this choice we must surely recognize a will on Nietzsche's part to make reference to the ideal that Emerson before him had already chosen to personify through a portrait of the great German author. Nietzsche's Goethe here does not, in fact, resemble in the least the actual historical Goethe, the representative of Weimar Classicism;[20] rather, he recalls the portrait of Goethe as a "nomadic subject" sketched out by Emerson in *Representative Men*: a subject constantly desirous of experiencing in his own person all the conditions under which the men of the past had lived, thus increasing, to the very limit of the possible, his own present power. In order to achieve this aim, Nietzsche's Goethe is willing to put up with even the greatest sufferings. This is why he no longer says no to anything, excludes no event from his personal horizon; each event, however dramatic it may be, is an opportunity for him to gain new knowledge. Goethe, writes Nietzsche, "did not remove himself from life, he put himself squarely in the middle of it; he did not despair, and he took as much as he could on himself, to himself, in himself. . . . Goethe conceived of . . . a person who is tolerant out of strength and not weakness because he knows how to take advantage of things that would destroy an average nature" (TI, Skirmishes 49). It can be said that Nietzsche's Goethe succeeded in the very attempt in which his character Faust had failed, namely, that of gathering in himself all Mankind's experience without getting crushed under the huge amount of suffering and failures involved therein. Says Faust in the dramatic poem that bears his name:

> My heart, now free of the longing for learning,
> shall close itself to no future pain.
> I mean to enjoy in my innermost being all that is offered to mankind,
> to seize the highest and the lowest, to mix all kinds of good and evil,
> and thus expand my Self till it includes the spirit of all men—
> and, with them, I shall be ruined and perish in the end. (Goethe [1808]
> 1949, 55; see Campioni 1987, 218)

The Goethe whose portrait is sketched by Nietzsche in *Twilight of the Idols*, on the pattern of the Goethe previously sketched by Emerson, surpasses the actual historical Goethe, who held it to be impossible to relive within oneself the entire history of humanity without being destroyed by it. The arrival at this "benedictory" perspective—which is characterized by a rejection of nothing at all in Mankind's past and a turning of absolutely everything in this past into useful material for one's own original action, and which was brought to maturation in Nietzsche through his engagement with the work of Emerson— marks Nietzsche's definitive reconciliation with history and historiography and carries to its conclusion an itinerary begun in the period of the *Untimely Meditations*.[21]

5.2. The Example of "Great Men"

If it is true that there is contained in every historical event and personality a precious lesson for the life of the present-day human being, it is equally true that, for Nietzsche, it is above all the deeds of "great men" that have an edifying effect upon the generations now living. In the second *Untimely Meditation* Nietzsche states that those who feel filled with the desire to perform great deeds can be fortified and supported in their will to do so by examining the biographies of great men and women of the past. This will tend to allow to grow and ripen in them the conviction "that the greatness that once existed was in any event once possible, and may thus be possible again; [the person who wishes to do great things] thus goes his way with more cheerful step, for the doubt which assailed him in weaker moments, whether he was not perhaps desiring the impossible, has now been banished" (HL 2). Nietzsche does not explicitly inform his readers, however, of the presupposition upon which this claim rests: whoever has a great goal to achieve in the present can draw encouragement from the things achieved by the "great men" of the past because the present-day individual assumes there to exist a substantial identity between himself or herself and these historical figures. Certainly, both belong to the psychological type of the "man of action." But this is not sufficient. We may advance the hypothesis that Nietzsche, at a period when he was still the prisoner of a metaphysical perspective, adopted as his own certain notions put into circulation by his colleague and friend Jacob Burckhardt and viewed these "great men" as instantiations of universal human "types" that had appeared and reappeared at various moments in history. Could the encouragement and inspiration that Nietzsche imagines someone deriving from observing these "great men" of the past have been conceived of by him as an inspiration based on the person's believing himself or herself to be the latest instantiation of the universal type represented by this or that great figure from history?[22]

Such a hypothesis, as Jensen (2018) argues, is far from being fully convincing. Already in the second of the *Untimely Meditations* Nietzsche, although a great admirer of Burckhardt, does not embrace the thesis of an *überhistorische* historiography, the thesis that "the past and the present are one, that is to say, with all their diversity identical in all that is typical and, as the omnipresence of imperishable types a motionless structure of a value that cannot alter and a significance that is always the same" (HL 1). Nietzsche instead takes up a critical stance toward this approach, based on the consideration that the subject will tend to rapidly develop feelings of being surfeited and even nauseated by a history so understood. As Jensen (2018, 59) states, the "active" individual whom Nietzsche describes in the second of the *Untimely Meditations* does not seek types whom he might aspire to resemble but rather "types to overcome." In other words, he desires to bring to realization something that will be completely original and to surpass thereby the "great men" of the past.

The thesis that I want to demonstrate now is that it is only by taking into account Nietzsche's readings in Emerson that we can properly understand the dynamic that Nietzsche identifies as lying at the base of the fortifying effect produced on those looking back at the example of "great men." Borrowing from Emerson the notion of the "great man" specifically as "representative man," Nietzsche sees the fundamental identity that the present-day individual discovers himself or herself to share with the "great men" of the past to consist in the simple fact of both one and the other's belonging to the same category of being, namely, human being. Following the traces of Nietzsche's reading of Emerson is also fundamentally important if we are effectively to rebut those misinterpretations of Nietzsche that see in his doctrine of moral perfectionism a form of aestheticizing elitism and that confuse and confound his position with that of Carlyle.

5.2.1. Genius in the Third of the *Untimely Meditations*

Before examining the dynamic whereby the sight of a "great man" gives rise, within the so-called common man, to a "fortifying effect," let us look first at the presupposition upon which such a dynamic necessarily rests: the nature and being of this "great man" as Nietzsche conceived of him. In a first phase of his thought Nietzsche embraces the conception of genius that is to be found in Schopenhauer: the genius—whether a saint, a philosopher, or an artist—is an individual who is by nature more gifted than others and who, by reason of this innate superior endowment, possesses a privileged status as compared to other human beings. He or she is capable of intuiting the very essence of the world and has a vocation to extend the activity of this world-essence, that is, to construct "dream-images" which serve to make life bearable for his or her fellow humans. For several years Nietzsche saw Wagner as the incarnation of this "genius" as described by Schopenhauer. The whole Wagnerian project—which Nietzsche, despite his private doubts, continued to publicly embrace up until 1876—is effectively founded on just such a presupposition that the artistic genius enjoys a superior status vis-à-vis other human beings and thus has the task of elaborating a cultural and political project which it will then be incumbent on these other, lesser human beings to support. It was Wagner himself who convinced Nietzsche to write the *Untimely Meditations*, at a period in which the young philosopher's true interests were in fact tending in quite other directions, as a contribution to what was, in Wagner's eyes, the urgent task of reforming German culture and politics in terms of a model birthed by Wagner's own genius.[23] After 1876 Nietzsche abandoned all the hopes that he had placed in the Wagnerian project, discontinued his collaboration in it, and developed a critique of that metaphysical notion of genius from which this project had drawn its legitimacy.[24] His readings in Emerson were of fundamental importance for Nietzsche in bringing to birth, nurturing, and carrying through this important intellectual transition.

The thesis that I want to demonstrate is that already in the third *Untimely Meditation* this reading of Emerson is working its as it were "subterranean" effects as a counterweight to the influence exercised by the metaphysics of Schopenhauer and Wagner, whose positions Nietzsche at the time still publicly espoused. As we pointed out in section 3.2.2, Emerson was very much in the forefront of Nietzsche's mind during the composition of the third *Untimely Meditation*. In September 1874 Nietzsche recounts to his friend Gersdorff the theft of his traveling bag on his way back from his summer vacation, during which he had been working on the final revisions of this piece of writing. The bag, wrote Nietzsche, had contained "a fine copy of the *Ring of the Nibelung* (with a dedication by Wagner himself)," along with "the excellent Emerson," that is to say, Nietzsche's copy of the German translation of the *Essays: First and Second Series* (KSB 4: 258, n. 390). These two "bedside books" of Nietzsche in this period may well explain the "double soul" that inhabits the third *Untimely Meditation*.

The problem that interests and engages Nietzsche in the third *Untimely Meditation* is the regeneration of German culture by the production of great men. These great men, Nietzsche observes, tend to emerge randomly, as exceptions, in the various historical epochs. What Nietzsche hopes and wishes for is that the institutions should work in favor of the affirmation of these great men within the sociopolitical context. Nietzsche expounds his vision of things in this regard in the following passage:

> "Mankind must work continually at the production of individual great men—that and nothing else is its task." . . . The goal of its evolution lies, not in the mass of its exemplars and their wellbeing . . . but rather in those apparently scattered and chance existences which favourable conditions have here and there produced; and it ought to be just as easy to understand the demand that, because it can arrive at a conscious awareness of its goal, mankind ought to seek out and create the favourable conditions under which those great redemptive men can come into existence. But everything resists this conclusion: here the ultimate goal is seen to lie in the happiness of all or of the greatest number, there in the development of great communities; and though one may be ready to sacrifice one's

life to a state, for instance, it is another matter if one is asked to sacrifice it on behalf of another individual. . . . For the question is this: how can your life, the individual life, receive the highest value, the deepest significance? How can it be least squandered? Certainly only by your living for the good of the rarest and most valuable exemplars, and not for the good of the majority, that is to say those who, taken individually, are the least valuable exemplars. (SE 6)

This passage was taken up by John Rawls (1971) in his seminal *Theory of Justice* as a position representative of the moral theory of Perfectionism. Rawls considers Perfectionism to be a form of Utilitarianism in which the goodness of an action is to be assessed in accordance with the degree to which it maximizes cultural excellence, without taking into account the moral or political consequences of this action. To greatly compress Rawls's argument: Nietzsche, he claims, divides people into individuals of category A, the so-called geniuses, and individuals of category B, "common" men and women, and invites the latter to sacrifice themselves for the former, by reason of the fact that those belonging to category A have a greater probability of achieving exalted results in the field of "art, science, and culture" (Rawls 1971, 325). In this aestheticizing elitism "the capacity for a higher life is a ground for treating men unequally" (326). This assumption would obviously lay the basis for social inequality just as, in the city-states of ancient Greece, for example, slavery was morally and legally accepted in order to allow a greater degree of freedom to a minority.[25] Rawls concludes by rejecting the theory of Perfectionism, and Nietzsche as its representative, as antiliberal.

A very strong and passionate case has been made against this Rawlsian interpretation of Nietzsche, and against Rawls's condemnation of Perfectionism as an essentially anti-egalitarian theory, by Stanley Cavell (1990). In rehabilitating Nietzsche here, Cavell makes great play of the influence that Emerson exerted on Nietzsche's thought. First of all, Cavell observes that in the passage from the third *Untimely Meditation* which is cited by Rawls, the German word "Exemplar" is translated (by R. J. Hollingdale) as "specimen." This term has biological connotations and suggests that "great men" are of a different species from "common men," that is, that there exists a qualitative difference between them. It would have been more appropriate, claims Cavell, to translate the German "Exemplar" as (precisely) "exemplar," which would suggest rather that the great men in question are the best of their species (and therefore unequivocally of their species).[26] Second, Cavell argues that in this essay Nietzsche is defending a concept of genius that is specifically Emersonian, or, in other words, that what Nietzsche means by "genius" here is not some miraculous gift endowed by Nature on the few but rather that mixture of talents unique and peculiar to each individual. Expanding on Cavell's hypothesis, let us note that, according to Emerson, those personalities who have achieved excellence in some particular field—be it artistic or military or religious—are distinguished from those who have led merely ordinary lives not by their having been endowed with greater potential than other people but simply by their having believed in themselves and having dedicated all their energy to developing their potential. Ultimately, then, there do not exist, for Emerson, individuals belonging to "category A" and "category B"; so-called common men are simply people who have not yet even begun to bring to expression their own "genius," that is to say, their own distinct personality:

> As to what we call the masses, and common men; —there are no common men. All men are at last of a size; and true art is only possible on the conviction that every talent has its apotheosis somewhere. Fair play and an open field! and freshest laurels to all who have won them! But heaven reserves an equal scope for every creature. Each is uneasy until he has produced his private ray unto the concave sphere, and beheld his talent also in its last nobility and exaltation. (RM, 18)[27]

There can be no doubt but that Nietzsche is following Emerson's lead when, in the third Untimely Meditation, he defines "genius" as that "core of productive uniqueness" which every human being possesses but few, in fact, bring to expression. Out of fear—or, still more often, out of laziness—many prefer to ignore the fact that they have in them the capacity to achieve excellent results. They prefer to think that they are condemned to remain "little people," just as it is the "destiny" of great men to be great (see SE 4). If we consider, then, that Nietzsche embraced this specifically Emersonian conception of genius, the passage from Schopenhauer as Educator that Rawls takes as evidence of a fundamental antiliberalism can be interpreted in a radically different way. "Living for the sake of genius," claims Cavell (1990, 52), does not mean that "there is a genius such that every self is to live for it" but rather that "for each self there is a genius"; in other words, each one of us has a particular talent to bring to expression and must dedicate himself or herself entirely to this task. As Cavell observes, where it is interpreted in this sense Nietzsche's controversial declaration that one must "live for genius" not only becomes "tolerable to the life of justice in a constitutional democracy" but even proves "essential to that life" (56). The sacrifice in the cause of culture which Nietzsche recommends does not consist in the sacrifice of a majority of mere "common people" in favor of a few individuals extraordinarily gifted in the artistic field; rather, it consists in the effort that should be made by all to bring to perfection their own particular selves.

Making his own intervention in this dispute between Rawls and Cavell, Conway (1997, 50) observes that "Cavell conflates the moral perfectionism he champions with the political perfectionism Rawls rejects." Conway defines "political perfectionism" as a series of institutional measures intended to favor and promote the emergence and affirmation of great individuals. These institutional measures might, for example, include the rigid stratification and hierarchical organization of society and its resources which we observe in aristocratic regimes. "Moral perfectionism," on the other hand, can be broadly characterized in terms of the conviction that "one's primary, overriding—and perhaps sole—ethical 'obligation' is to attend to the perfection of one's ownmost self. Any 'obligations' that one might choose to observe to others are strictly derivative of, and secondary to, the imperative to perfect oneself" (51). These two forms of perfectionism "do not logically entail one another" (52). There are thinkers, such as Emerson and Mill, who defend moral perfectionism but decidedly reject political perfectionism; on the other hand, there are political thinkers, such as Machiavelli, who embrace political perfectionism without thereby having any great faith in the notion of citizens' being able to perfect themselves as individuals or achieve moral autonomy. Nietzsche, claims Conway, defends both these views. Put more precisely, he defends political perfectionism to the extent that he believes that it tends to further and promote moral perfectionism, although he does not consider the former to be an absolutely necessary condition for the attainment of the latter.[28] Conway considers the passage that Rawls cites to represent a defense of political perfectionism and concedes that Rawls is right to view it as essentially antiliberal. The fact that he also professes moral perfectionism, says Conway, and that this, as Cavell claims, perfectly expresses the spirit that lies at the basis of life in a democratic society,[29] does not in the least invalidate Rawls's critique (50–51).

In my own view, however, from the time Nietzsche, in the third *Untimely Meditation*, comes to embrace a specifically Emersonian concept of "genius" it is no longer possible to conceive of him as still holding to the position of political perfectionism (a position, nonetheless, which he certainly had endorsed in the past, specifically in the form of his support for the Wagnerian project). This interpretation is confirmed, moreover, by the fact that in the third of the *Untimely Meditations* Nietzsche does not mean by the term "culture" what Rawls takes him to mean by it—namely, literature and the fine arts. Rather, Nietzsche understands by "culture" the same thing as Emerson understood by it: the cultivation of the self. Culture is, for Emerson, primarily and fundamentally, the culture of individuality—that is to say, the cultivation of one's own distinct personality. To fight in the cause of culture means to defend, with heroic rigor and discipline, one's own authentic self against all social pressures. Institutions, argues

Emerson, exist precisely in order to defend and promote in every individual this aspiration to individuality in the truest and fullest sense. That Nietzsche intended the term "culture" to be understood in that sense of a "cultivation of true individuality" which it bears in Emerson is proven by the following declaration of Nietzsche's: "The goal of culture is to promote the production of true human beings and nothing else" (SE 6). Who are these "true human beings"? They are human beings who live as such, and not as mere animals. That is to say, they are those who live as individuals and not after the manner of the herd. To "live for culture" does not mean, then, to dedicate oneself to artistic activities. As we saw in section 3.2.2, in the third *Untimely Meditation* Nietzsche assigns a privileged status to artists by reason solely of the fact that, by expressing themselves in an original way, they provide an example of how every human being could, and should, live. What "living for culture" actually means, for Nietzsche, is pursuing with determination the project of perfecting one's own distinct individuality and helping those other people who are pursuing the same aim. This is indubitably the meaning conveyed by the following passage: "Anyone who believes in culture is thereby saying: 'I see above me something higher and more human than I am; let everyone help me to attain it, as I will help everyone who knows and suffers as I do'" (SE 6).

When Nietzsche, in the passage cited by Rawls, claims that institutions must favor the achievements of individual great men to the detriment of the well-being of the masses, he is not claiming that the "common man and woman" must sacrifice themselves to support the projects of certain individuals of especially great talent, the so-called geniuses. He is claiming that institutions should not take as their ultimate aim the well-being of "the masses": a well-being which would consist merely in continuing to live as "the masses," pursuing pleasure and avoiding all discomfort, particularly the discomfort that would be involved in the strenuous and thankless project of developing one's own distinctive individuality. Rather, social institutions ought to favor the emergence of great individuals and therefore, as Emerson had already argued, defend and promote in each human being the pursuit of the expression of his or her own personal "genius." In fact, in order to express his true philosophical views—views which he had formed, in large part, through his readings in Emerson—Nietzsche often uses at this time certain ambiguous formulations which might have led his readers to think that he still held to the metaphysical notion of genius and to the stance of political perfectionism. It seems to me that he most likely did this with a view specifically to avoiding alienating or antagonizing Wagner, whom he wished still to accommodate and please. As soon as this desire to please Wagner ceases to be a factor—that is to say, after the first Bayreuth Festival of 1876—the philosophical vision which had been slowly ripening in him, thanks to his readings in Emerson, can finally emerge fully into the light.[30]

5.2.2. The Genius in *Human, All Too Human*

In his philosophy of the middle period Nietzsche explores in greater depth and develops the position that he had already basically formulated in the third *Untimely Meditation*. He goes on to use his own reading of Emerson to critique the metaphysical notion of "genius" as a special gift ("genius 1a") granted solely to a few individuals, a notion on which there rests, in turn, the notion of "the genius" ("genius 2") as an individual qualitatively different from and superior to all "common people." Following Emerson, Nietzsche emphasizes that each person has his or her own specific "genius," a unique combination of talents ("genius 1b") which, if developed to the level of excellence, can rightfully secure for the person the designation "genius" ("genius 2") or "great individual."

In HH 162 Nietzsche states that the genius is not a "miraculum," or, in other words, not "a wholly uncommon accident, or, if we are still religiously inclined, a mercy from on high" (HH 162). With the expression "genius" here Nietzsche is clearly referring to a certain skill or prowess which reveals itself in the form of excellence in some particular field or other. An extraordinary personal skill or prowess of this sort should not make us think of divine intervention or some uncanny, miraculous exception to the laws of Nature. It is rather simply the result of an exclusive dedication to developing one's own individual predispositions. This interpretation is confirmed by the immediately following aphorism in which Nietzsche writes, "Do not talk of being gifted or of possessing innate talent! One can name great men of all kinds who were not very gifted. They acquired greatness, became 'geniuses' (as we put it), through making the most of qualities which no one would care to admit he did not have: they all possessed the seriousness of the efficient workman" (HH 163, translation amended; see Conant 2001, 212).

How exactly, then, is one to develop to perfection one's own natural predispositions? How is one to attain to that extraordinary ability that is called genius? In HH 162 Nietzsche draws up a precise list of the things that are required here: (1) one's thought must be "active in one direction"; that is, one must concentrate on a single goal; (2) one must "employ everything as a material," that is, be able to gather out of every experience useful impulses to propel oneself closer to the goals that one has set oneself; (3) one must "zealously observe [one's] own inner life and that of others," that is, take good care of oneself by means of close attention to the little details of daily life, as well as (4) "perceive everywhere models and incentives" (HH 162), that is, learn as much as possible from others. The thesis that I want to defend is that the influence of Emerson can clearly be seen in each of these points listed by Nietzsche.

Lysaker (2008, 55) observes that, for Emerson, the process by which one attains to that specific excellence which belongs to one's own particular nature involves two factors, both of equal importance: inspiration and conscious and sustained commitment. Emerson believed that each of us has moments in which we realize that there are certain activities which come easier to us than they do to others and in which we outperform other people. This is called "talent": "Each man has his own vocation. The talent is the call. . . . He inclines to do something which is easy to him, and good when it is done, but which no other man can do" (E I, 115; V, 104; Nietzsche underlined this passage from the word "easy" to the end; see Appendix Figure 7). Talent, once it has revealed itself, "calls out" to be developed, that is, carried to perfection. And this "calling out" is justly named a "vocation." To follow one's own vocation implies, as Nietzsche observes at point 2, using all the stimuli that reach one from one's external human and natural environment as "fertilizers" for one's own ideas. As we saw in section 5.1.2, for Emerson originality is born not out of a total absence of relations with one's external human environment but rather out of the assimilation and re-elaboration of as many stimuli reaching one from this environment as possible. As to point 4, as we saw in section 3.2.4, Emerson argues that the person who wishes to develop his or her own self to perfection must not pay heed to the judgments passed on to him or her by "the masses" but rather take as his or her models and examples those who have traveled this same road already, the "great individuals" of history.

As regards point 1 in the essay *Greatness*, published as part of the collection *Letters and Social Aims*, Emerson specifies that the things necessary in order to perfect a talent are concentration and absolute dedication: "If the first rule is to obey your native bias, to accept that work for which you were inwardly formed, the second rule is concentration, which doubles its force" (LSA, 172; NE 284; Nietzsche underlined the word "concentration").[31] Particularly interesting, however, is point 3, in respect of which Emerson surely made a truly unique contribution to Nietzsche's nascent ideas. In the essay *Prudence* (*Klugheit*)—almost every line of which Nietzsche's underlined and provided with marginal notes in his personal copy of the German translation—Emerson "transvalues," so to speak, the virtue from which the essay takes its name. He deliberately reassesses and transforms this virtue from a "silly, purely negative virtue, hovering somewhere between caution and timidity and hinting at failure" (Von Frank 1999, 112) to the first and most important virtue of the "great individual." "Prudence" is defined by Emerson as "the art of securing a present well being" (E I, 199; V, 178; Nietzsche underlined the word "prudence" and marked the passage with three vertical lines in the margin) through a meticulous attention to the smallest details of day-to-day life, such as diet, sleep, and climate: "We live by the air which blows around us, and we are poisoned by the air that is too cold or too hot, too dry or too wet," stated Emerson in a passage that Nietzsche marked with a vertical line in the margin and the note "bravo!" (E I, 186;

V, 166; see Appendix Figure 19). Any flagging of attentiveness in this regard will inevitably be punished by Nature with a diminution of one's personal energies. "On him who scorned the world," Emerson warns, "the scorned world wreaks its revenge. He that despiseth small things, will perish by little and little . . . like a giant slaughtered by pins" (E I, 192–193; V, 171–172; Nietzsche underlined the passage "He that despiseth . . . little" and marked it with a horizontal line in the margin; the passage "like a giant slaughtered by pins" he marked with two vertical lines in the left margin and one vertical line in the right margin). Emerson gives here the example of the court politician Antonio and the inspired poet Tasso in Goethe's drama *Torquato Tasso*. Whereas Antonio knows and pays attention to the natural rhythms of all the "organisms" both within and around him, Tasso, "fired with all the divine sentiments," believes himself to be exempt from any such precautions and disregards all natural and social structures. His destiny, then, proves to be that of every "man of genius, of an ardent temperament, reckless of physical laws, self-indulgent": he becomes "unfortunate, querulous, a 'discomfortable cousin,' a thorn to himself and to others" (E I, 192; V, 172; Nietzsche marked the passage from "man of genius" to the end with three vertical lines in the margin).[32]

Nietzsche takes up again and expands upon some of these observations that Emerson had formulated in the essay *Prudence* in the chapter of *Ecce Homo* entitled *Why I Am So Clever* (*Warum Ich So Klug Bin*). The chapter heading itself, indeed, might be interpreted as a sort of homage to Emerson, whose essay *Prudence* had been rendered into German, in Fabricius's 1856 translation of the *Essays: First and Second Series*, under the title *Klugheit*. Nietzsche sees the secret of his own success as lying precisely in the keen attention that—at least from 1876 onward—he paid to the small facts and matters of everyday life: "Nutrition, location, climate, mode of recuperation," often considered mere negligible details for the philosopher, are, for Nietzsche, "fundamental concerns of life itself" and are actually "far more important than all the concepts people have considered important so far" (EH, Why I Am So Clever 10). The intellectual dynamism that is commonly called "genius" is, for Nietzsche, nothing other than a great power and agility of mind which arises in individuals thanks to their having taken great care of the conditions of their own life (EH, Why I Am So Clever 2).[33]

In short, making use of ideas and sources of inspiration that he had found in Emerson, Nietzsche substantially overturned that traditional and stereotypical image of the "great man" as a supernatural being endowed with extraordinary energies which absolve him of the need to take the precautions that "ordinary mortals" are obliged to take. The "great man" is rather the individual who has dedicated himself strenuously to the development of his own individual talent, devoting the most meticulous attention to the small facts and details of everyday life.

5.2.3. How Does the Fortifying Effect of
Past Examples Come About?

The "great man," then, as Emerson and Nietzsche understand this notion, is in the last analysis nothing more nor less than the virtuous individual described in chapter 3, that is, the individual who expresses his or her whole self completely through his or her actions.

Such an individual, indeed, will not pose or parade as a master or mistress of virtue; nonetheless there will emanate from his or her person a certain moral teaching. This moral teaching will concern the process by which true individuality is achieved or, in other words, the process by which one "becomes what one is." Whoever observes an individual who has achieved, in this way, a complete expression of his or her true self will instinctively feel a desire to emulate this individual. Not, *nota bene*, a desire to imitate the person but rather a desire to emulate him or her by setting out on one's own road to bringing one's own individuality to full realization. It is this conviction that lies at the basis of Nietzsche's characteristic technique of creating symbolic "types," that is to say, his method of embodying specific moral teachings in real or imaginary figures or personalities which, as we pointed out in section 3.1.3, recalls in its turn the method employed by Emerson in *Representative Men*. Emerson had laid the foundations for this method as he himself employed it in his essay *Character*, in which he argues that "great men"—those who have achieved mastery over themselves and are able to act as true individuals—exert a great fascination upon all those who observe them: a fascination which Emerson compares to the force of natural magnetism. Such individuals, says Emerson, teach others not through words but through what they are.

In a passage that Nietzsche entered in summary form into a notebook from 1878 Emerson writes, "That which we are, we shall teach, not voluntarily but involuntarily. . . . If he have found his centre, the Deity will shine through him. . . . The tone of seeking, is one, and the tone of having is another" (E I, 236–237; V, 210–211; Nietzsche underlined this last sentence and marked it in the margin with a vertical line).[34] Summing up another passage from the essay *Character*, Nietzsche notes down in his notebook of excerpted passages from the year 1882, "There was always a joyful adherence to the man who moved according to self-created laws, who made his own value-table of people and things and overthrew the one already existing, and who represented the law in his own person" (NL 1882 17[33], KSA 9: 671).[35] To give an example of this, Emerson speaks as follows in his *Essays* of the original historical Zarathustra, the Persian prophet:[36]

> We require that a man should be so large and columnar in the landscape
> that it should deserve to be recorded that he arose and girded up his loins

and departed to such a place. The most credible pictures are those of ma-
jestic men [*grossen Menschen* in the German translation] who prevailed
at their entrance and convinced the senses; as happened to the eastern
magian [*Weise* in the German translation] who was sent to test the
merits of Zertusht [*Zarathustra* in the German translation] or Zoroaster.
When the Yunani sage arrived at Balkh, the Persians tell us, Gushtasp appointed a day on which the Mobeds of every country should assemble,
and a golden chair was placed for the Yunani sage. Then the beloved of
Yezdam, the prophet Zertusht [*Zarathustra* in the German translation],
advanced into the midst of the assembly. The Yunani sage, on seeing that
chief, said: "This form and this gait [*diese Gestalt und dieser Gang und
Haltung* in the German translation] cannot lie, and nothing but truth
can proceed from them." (E II, 63; V, 351; Nietzsche underlined the first
sentence of this passage; see Appendix Figure 27)

"It is this exactly! [*Das ist es!*]," noted Nietzsche approvingly in the margin of his
copy (see Appendix Figure 27).[37] Zarathustra is just this: a master and a teacher,
but one who teaches, as had the figure of "Schopenhauer as educator" before
him, above all through his personal example. In one of the preparatory notes
that fed into the published text of that third *Untimely Meditation* that focused on
Schopenhauer Nietzsche explains, "The nature of a man can stand as a warrant
for a hundred systems. In what he [Schopenhauer] teaches he may be a hundred
times wrong. But in what he is, he is right [*sein Wesen selber ist im Recht*]—and
this should be enough for us [*daran wollen wir uns halten*]. In a philosopher there
is something that could never be in a philosophy, namely the source [*Ursache*] of
many philosophies: the great man" (NL 1875 12[7], KSA 8: 247–248).[38]

What precisely is the dynamic that is established between the "great man"
and the "common man"? In the third *Untimely Meditation* Nietzsche claims that
observing a great man "bestows on the soul . . . not only a clear, discriminating
and self-contemptuous view of itself, but also the desire to look beyond itself
and to seek with all its might for a higher self as yet still concealed from it"
(SE 6). We have to do here, as Conant (2001, 220) correctly points out, with a
kind of "moral shame" concerning the potentialities, which we inwardly know
we possess but which we have not yet developed. Out of this shame there
results a desire to bring such potentialities to expression, which, in turn, we see
take more substantial form in a sort of envisaged perfected version of ourselves
(higher self). In other words, the "great man" should, according to Nietzsche,
spark a general reform of culture to the extent that these latter personalities
awaken in the so-called common man or common woman a desire to emulate
them, to perfect their own individual selves until they have raised themselves to
the level of the "great man."

To help us understand what Nietzsche means here it is useful to recall a passage of Emerson's essay *History* from which these reflections of Nietzsche's originate. In this essay Emerson claims that in great men and in the great moments of history we can see our own selves, improved and enlarged. We see in these great men, in other words, ourselves as we could be if we truly trusted in ourselves and acted with courage and determination. Likewise, in the great moments of history, in revolutions and in works of art, we see results that we have not yet achieved but that we have it in ourselves to achieve. Emerson declares:

> We sympathize in the great moments of history, in the great discoveries, the great resistances, the great prosperities of men; —because there law was enacted, the sea was searched, the land was found, or the blow was struck for us, as we ourselves in that place would have done or applauded. So it is in respect to condition and character. We honour the rich because they have externally the freedom, power and grace which we feel to be proper to man, proper to us. So all that is said of the wise man by Stoic or oriental or modern essayist, describes to each man his own idea, describes his unattained but attainable self [*unerreichtes, aber doch erreichbares Ich* in the German text]. All literature writes the character of the wise man. All books, monuments, pictures, conversation, are portraits in which the wise man finds the lineaments he is forming. (E I, 6; V, 4)[39]

By admiring the distant figures of the great men and women of the past, says Emerson, we can recognize qualities that are also our own but that we have not yet developed in ourselves. In other words, we can gain an intuition of that which we not yet are but which we might one day become. In essence, the "higher self" hypothesized by Nietzsche as the motor driving the project of self-perfection is nothing more nor less than a reformulation of the "unattained yet attainable self" Emerson wrote of.[40]

In order, however, for the "great individual" really to play the revitalizing role in our cultures that Nietzsche assigns to him or her, one thing is absolutely essential: that he or she not be perceived by the rest of us as essentially qualitatively different from us—that is, as a superhuman being endowed with powers which we neither possess nor can acquire. In *Human, All Too Human* 162 Nietzsche explains that if we think of the "great man" as "being very remote from us, as a miraculum," then he does not "wound" us. That is to say, he does not awaken in us that "moral shame" to which Nietzsche had alluded in the third *Untimely Meditation*. Aphorism 162 of *Human, All Too Human* continues, "To call someone 'divine' means: 'here there is no need for us to compete.'" The expression "to compete" allows us to understand that Nietzsche conceives of the psychological dynamic which is established in the mind and sensibilities of the "common man" when he is confronted with the sight of a "great man" as similar to the dynamic that arises between adversaries in that type of competition that the Greeks called the *agon*.

As I pointed out in section 4.2.4, as early as the piece *Homer's Contest*, written in his late 20s, Nietzsche drew an important distinction between two types of adversarial relation: the *Vernichtungskampf*, a "struggle to the death" in which one adversary aspires to gain victory by actually destroying the other; and the Greek *agon*, in which the aspiration is to gain victory simply by performing visibly better than one's opponent. Two different emotional experiences lie at the foundation of these two different types of behavior. In the first case the emotional driving force is "envy" in the sense in which this emotion is commonly understood. In the second case it is jealousy, a good, nondestructive envy.[41] The condition that must apply if a genuinely "agonal" contest or competition animated by this latter, nondestructive emotion is really to occur between two or more individuals is that something approximating to an equality or equilibrium must exist between the adversaries involved. In *Homer's Contest* Nietzsche recounts how the practice of ostracism, which came later to be used by tyrants to rid themselves of their political adversaries, had originally come into existence as a way of maintaining that equilibrium between the parties that allowed the agonal contest to take place. Diogenes Laertius, for example, tells of how Heraclitus complained that his friend Hermadorus was exiled from Ephesus by his fellow citizens when his personal achievements became so great that no one could any longer hope to surpass him (see KSA 1.788). The Ephesians—such was the implication—did not behave in this way because they hated or despised greatness but rather out of a concern that conditions be maintained such that this greatness would be striven for right across their society. If one individual surpassed others by such an enormous margin that the will to compete was blotted out in all his fellow citizens, the authorities took steps to remove him from the social "contest." For Nietzsche, this institution of ostracism showed (at least as long as it was applied as it had allegedly been applied by the Ephesian citizenry, that is, had not degenerated into a tool of tyranny) how much the ancient Greeks had relied on the *agon* for the preservation and the continued vitality of their culture (see Acampora 2013, 25).

The psychological dynamic, then, that gives rise to the *agon* is established only where the competing parties perceive themselves to be something close to equally matched. In other words, if one is to feel the desire to compete, one must have some faith in at least the possibility of emerging victorious. The same applies to the case of "great individuals." If they are really to have upon the "common man" the effect of drawing him out of his apathy and spurring him on to seek the excellences that might be developed out of his own qualities, these "great individuals" must, indeed, appear great, but not so great as to extinguish in others the desire to vie with them and to compete. What Nietzsche emphasizes in HH 162 is that to put "great individuals" on pedestals and venerate them as superhumans—to conceive of them as essentially different from ourselves—in fact deprives them of their function, which is that of stimulating an interior transformation. This is the reason he considers a cultish worship of "great men" of the kind promoted by Carlyle to be a very great danger to true culture.

Here too it was largely through meditating further on ideas which he had originally encountered in Emerson that Nietzsche was able to focus on the question of what was most essentially required in order that the "great man" should prove productive for culture and was able also, specifically, to develop his critique of Carlyle's influential "cult of the Hero."

The collection of essays in which Emerson specifically addresses the topic of "great individuals" is *Representative Men*. The majority of contemporary commentators and interpreters of this publication considered it to be essentially just an American echo of Carlyle's *On Heroes, Hero Worship, and the Heroic in History*. In reality, however, Emerson conceived of *Representative Men* as a polemical riposte to this highly influential work by his slightly older contemporary. The adjective itself which Emerson uses to designate the great men whom he discusses in this work expresses very clearly the function he assigns to them: great men *represent* human greatness; that is to say, they show what human beings can achieve when they live to the very maximum of their possibilities. In other words, for Emerson "great men" are not great because they partake of the superhuman, as had been the case for Carlyle's "heroes"; on the contrary, they are great because they are fully and truly human. In the introduction to this work Emerson declares the use that we must make of "great men": "Great men exist that there might be greater men" (RM, 20). In other words, great men, as Emerson presents them, are not idols to be venerated but examples to be followed and to be outdone through performances and achievements still greater than theirs.

Since Nietzsche did not read English, the only essays belonging to the collection *Representative Men* that he had linguistic access to prior to 1883 were those on Goethe and Shakespeare, which had been published in German translation in 1858 by Herman Grimm. In the autumn of 1883, however, Ida Overbeck, the wife of Nietzsche's close friend Franz Overbeck, decided to translate this entire collection into German, very possibly on the suggestion of Nietzsche himself. We do not know whether Ida Overbeck ever completed this translation nor, consequently, whether Nietzsche ever got to read Emerson's book in its entirety. He was, however, certainly able to read at least the translated introduction because around the middle of November of that year we find Franz Overbeck writing to Nietzsche, "My wife has begun translating and has already completed the introductory essay on *The Uses of Great Men*. We read through this incipit together yesterday. The matter is difficult to render into German, as indeed is the book's very title. What do you think of *Darstellende Menschen*?" (KGB III/ 2: 409, n. 215).[42] It was probably after reading Ida Overbeck's version of this introduction that Nietzsche wrote to her husband, on December 24, 1883, saying, "Tell your dear wife that I feel Emerson to be a '*brother* **soul**' to me" (KSB 6: 463, n. 477).[43]

Reading the introduction to *Representative Men* Nietzsche would surely simply have found confirmed there certain key notions that he would already have gathered from his readings in Emerson's *Essays*. In the *Essays*—even if he does not make this intention explicit—Emerson is concerned to reduce the distance between "great men" and "common men" by the use of a double strategy: on the one hand, he takes a sober and somewhat minimizing view of the widely vaunted achievements of the former; on the other hand, he seeks to reinforce the faith of the latter in their own potential. As an example of the first "wing" of this double strategy we can cite a passage from the essay *Character*. "History has been mean; our nations have been mobs," exclaims Emerson indignantly, "we have never seen a man: that divine form we do not yet know, but only the dream and prophecy of such. . . . What greatness has yet appeared, is the beginning and encouragements to us in this direction" (E II, 66; V, 354– 355).[44] As an example of the strategy's other "wing" let us take a passage from *Self-Reliance*: "Why all this deference to Alfred, and Scanderbeg, and Gustavus? Suppose they were virtuous: did they wear out virtue? As great a stake depends on your private act to-day as followed their public and renowned steps" (E II, 36; V, 47).[45]

It is only in the light of Nietzsche's readings in Emerson that we can correctly interpret the significance of the reply that Zarathustra gives to the figure called "the Magician" in the eponymous parable in Nietzsche's great work of the mid-1880s. Zarathustra comes upon this figure, midway through the book's fourth and final part, in a condition of extreme sadness, abandoned by all, shivering with cold, and appealing to be loved. This Magician can be considered an incarnation of Wagner or, more generally, of the ideology of the artistic genius as the legitimate head of a community of adepts, all submissive to him in their venerating adoration. As this figure of the Magician clearly reveals, there had been a period in which Nietzsche himself had believed in this lie. "And just admit it," says the Magician to Zarathustra, Nietzsche's alter ego, "it took you a long time . . . before you saw through my art and lie!" (Z IV, The Magician). Now, however, Zarathustra merely beats the Magician with his stick and, "with grim laughter," begins to call him an actor and a counterfeiter. Zarathustra, in other words, refuses to consider the Magician as a great man and refuses to "heat him up"—cover him with praise and veneration—as the old "counter-feiter" desires. Similarly, Zarathustra succeeds in evading the temptation to consider himself a great man—a temptation to which the Magician, as a last deceitful expedient, hopes to make him yield. After having raised himself from the ground, the Magician says to Zarathustra, with a charming glint in his eye, "Oh Zarathustra, I seek someone who is genuine, proper, simple, unequivocal, a human being of all honesty, a vessel of wisdom, a saint of knowledge, a great human being!" But Zarathustra replies, "For my part—I've never seen a great human being" (Z IV, The Magician 2). If we trace Zarathustra's words back to the source from which they originate—namely, Emerson's *Essays*—we can grasp the fact that, with such an utterance, Nietzsche is not expressing a lack of respect for the great individuals of history but is simply warning against the danger of idolizing them.

Emerson's critical stance toward "great men," which Nietzsche calls his "scepticism," is made the object of a psychological analysis in *Twilight of the Idols*. Emerson's "sceptical" stance here is sharply contrasted with the fanaticism of Carlyle. In *Twilight* Carlyle is portrayed as "a man of strong words and attitudes, a rhetorician out of necessity who is constantly harassed by a yearning for a strong faith and the feeling that he is not up to the task (—which makes him a typical Romantic!)" (TI, Skirmishes 12). In other words, Carlyle's need to exalt and adulate great men, portraying them as supernatural beings, and his urging of the "common people" to place their trust uncritically in "heroes," denotes, according to Nietzsche, a profound lack of faith in the value of human beings. "Carlyle anaesthetizes something in himself," continues Nietzsche, "with both the for-tissimo of his worship for people who have strong faith and his fury at people who are less naive" (TI, Skirmishes 12). The truth is really the contrary: "If you have a strong faith you can allow yourself the beautiful luxury of scepticism: you are certain enough, stable enough, committed enough for it" (TI, Skirmishes 12). "Faith" is surely intended to be understood here in a double sense: faith in oneself and also faith in human potential. The person who possesses confidence in these two things is not afraid of pointing up the limitations of "great men" be-cause he or she has a "strong faith" in his or her, and humanity's, capacity to over-come and surpass these limitations. In Nietzsche's view, Emerson is the ideal representative of this stance (TI, Skirmishes 13).

5.2.4. From Metaphysics to Biology

How, though, can the scholar "enter into contact" with the great men and women of the past so as to assimilate their experience? On this point we must recognize that there exists a very significant difference between Emerson's position and Nietzsche's.

According to Emerson, the "great men" of history were great because they rose above the search for petty satisfactions onto the plane of a desire to fulfill their own individual vocation for the advantage of all humanity. Every enlightened person—that is to say, every person who succeeds in getting their own petty ego out of the way so that they can listen instead to the voice of their true self—enters into contact with a sort of Universal Spirit which Emerson calls the Over-Soul. It is to the extent that individuals participate in this Over-Soul that they are also in contact with one another.[46] Whoever wants, then, to make their own the experiences of history's great men need do nothing other than raise themselves to this universal viewpoint:

> There is one mind common to all individual men [the German translation runs *Es ist ein Geist, der alle Menschen beseelt*]. Every man is an inlet to the same and to all of the same. He that is once admitted to the right of reason[47] is made a freeman of the whole estate. What Plato has thought, he may think; what a saint has felt, he may feel; what at any time has befallen any man, he can understand. Who hath access to this universal mind, is a party to all that is or can be done, for this is the only and sovereign agent. (E I, 3; V, 1; Nietzsche underlined "universal mind" [*allumfassende Geiste* in the German translation])

Nietzsche writes in the margin of the passage from the essay *History*: "No! But it is an ideal [*Nein, aber es ist ein Ideal*]" (see Appendix Figure 2). That is to say, Nietzsche reacts negatively to Emerson's expressed belief that one can tap into the experience of great men of the past by virtue of a sort of "mystical" participation in some supernatural entity. Emerson's "Over-Soul" is clearly a metaphysical idea, and so Nietzsche, of course, could not possibly embrace it. In a note from the year 1878 Nietzsche explains better what he thought of Emerson's key idea: "Emerson p. 201 the 'Over-Soul' is really the highest result of culture, a ghost which all the best and greatest men created together" (NL 1878 32[13], KSA 8: 562).[48] In short, for Nietzsche, Emerson's Over-Soul is a phantasm, an imaginary entity, created by adding together the greatest results achieved by all human beings at all times. Nevertheless, Nietzsche's gloss on the passage from Emerson—"No! But it is an ideal"—suggests that Nietzsche was willing to allow and accept the Over-Soul as a regulative ideal. In other words, if the individual transcends his or her petty ego and posits his or her own activity as something that exists in continuity with the activity of the great men of the past, it may be that this individual will not, thereby, enter magically into contact with the spirit of these great men, but such an individual will certainly derive therefrom a certain impulse or inspiration to "overcome his or her own self." In short, then, Nietzsche believes that the notion that we are able to establish an ideal continuity between the lives of the great men of the past and our own can produce positive effects—even if this co-belonging to a great encompassing Over-Soul is a merely "regulative ideal" (i.e., nothing more than a "ghost"). This was already the intuition that prompted Nietzsche, in the second of the *Untimely Meditations*, to recommend a monumental approach to history: to allow oneself to be inspired by grand designs so as to raise oneself above the meanness and pettiness of a materialistic mass society.

This idea, presented by Nietzsche already in the second *Untimely Meditation*, of a connection between a present-day individual aspiring to realize some great project and the great men of the past, is complemented, from the period of *Human, All Too Human* onward, by a belief in a real biological continuity between past generations and the men and women of the present day.[49] In the second half of the 1880s, in light of some reading in contemporary scientific authors such as Haeckel and Roux, Nietzsche pushed on still further with this line of research. Following Haeckel, Nietzsche now assumes that memory pertains not just to human beings but to the entire organic realm. Clearly, the memory of a plant will not be the product of the voluntary act of a mind which, "outside time, reproduces, recognizes, etc." (NL 1885 40[29], KSA 11: 644). Rather, the "memory" concerned here will be a matter of unconscious information contained within the organism's biological makeup. According to Haeckel, every living being conserves a memory of every one of the evolutionary stages which have carried it to its present form and state. In other words, for Haeckel ontogeny recapitulates phylogeny. Embracing this theory, Nietzsche writes in 1883, "Everything organic differs from the inorganic due to the fact that it collects experiences. . . . Every smallest cell is in this precise moment the heir of the entire organic past" (NL 1883 12[31], KSA 10: 406). As regards human beings in particular, Nietzsche supposes that the presently living individual conserves within himself or herself a memory of all the individuals that have gone before. This memory, however, will not be part of the conscious contents of the mind. Rather, the "memory" concerned here will be a matter of unconscious information deposited within the present-day individual's biological makeup. "In every judgment of the senses [*Sinnes-Urtheil*], the whole pre-history of the organism is at work. . . . Memory in instinct" (NL 1885 34[167], KSA 11: 476), writes Nietzsche in 1885. In other words, he assumes that the organic memory of the species manifests itself in the present-day individual in the form of instincts.[50] When, in his 1882 notebook of excerpts from Emerson's *Essays,* Nietzsche writes, "In every action is the abbreviated history of all becoming. Ego" (NL 1882 17[1], KSA 9: 666),[51] he means something rather different from what Emerson had meant by these words. With this statement Emerson wanted to suggest that, since human nature is universal, the present-day individual is able to enter into a relation of empathy with all the different forms of feeling and thinking that have manifested throughout history. For Nietzsche, however, this statement is true in a literal sense; he genuinely believes that every action performed or judgment passed by the present-day individual is guided by instincts that matured during the whole evolution of the human species.[52]

Where this perspective of an organic memory passed down from generation to generation is adopted, the greatness of the men of past ages truly no longer overawes or intimidates the individual of the present, who now recognizes himself or herself to be the former's legitimate heir. On the endpapers of his copy of the *Essays* Nietzsche wrote:

> Not to see the new greatness above oneself, not to see it outside of oneself, rather to make of it a new function of one's self.
> We are the ocean into which all rivers of greatness must flow.
> How dangerous it is when our faith in the universality of our Self is lacking! A plurality of faiths is required. (NL 1881 13[19], KSA 9: 621; see also NL 1881–1882 16[9], KSA 9: 660)

Nietzsche gives Emerson's theory of self-reliance a biological foundation. In Nietzsche's view, the individual of the present day can achieve results still greater than those which were achieved in the past because this individual contains within himself or herself, in the form of instincts, the experience of all who have lived before. "We contain within ourselves a multiplicity of instincts since we are the heir of generations who lived in the most various conditions of existence" (NL 1884 25[462], KSA 11: 136). The awareness of this organic heritage gives to the individual an inebriating sense of power. In some fragments from autumn 1881 Nietzsche declares himself "proud of humanity [*stolz auf die Menschlichkeit*]" (NL 1881 12[52], KSA 9: 585), and in some notes from the same year he declares himself proud of having in his veins the blood of "Plato, Pascal, Spinoza, and Goethe" (NL 1881 12[52], KSA 9: 585). "My pride . . . is: 'I have an origin [*Herkunft*]'—therefore I do not need fame. I already live in that which moved Zarathustra, Moses, Muhammad, Jesus, Plato, Brutus, Spinoza, Mirabeau, and many things are coming to fruition in me that slumbered embryonically for a few millennia. We are the first aristocrats in the history of spirit—the historical sense begins right now" (NL 1881 15[17], KSA 9: 642). This inebriating sensation was to become insanity in the letter written to Burckhardt in January 1889: "What is unpleasant and a strain on my modesty is that, in fact, I am every name in history" (KSB 8: 578, n. 1256).

5.3. Conclusion

Ultimately, then, Nietzsche's description of the relation established by the self-reliant individual to history and, in particular, to the "great men" of the past finds its point of departure in a philosophical stance developed by Emerson but is supplemented and rounded off by ideas drawn from Nietzsche's own readings in the latest scientific literature of his day. For Emerson the self-reliant individual—that is to say, the individual who feels reverence for himself or herself and for the task which he or she wishes to carry to its completion—is someone who knows how to establish a healthy relationship with history: a relationship that is neither one of refusal nor one of subjection. Putting himself or herself, by an act of empathic imagination, "in the shoes" of these great men and women of the past, the self-reliant individual seeks to assimilate their experience and thus to increase his or her own power. According to Emerson, if the self-reliant individual perseveres, on the one hand, in developing his or her own individuality and perfecting his or her own specific talents while, on the other hand, confronting and learning from that which is "other" than himself or herself, he or she will also one day be able to be called a "great individual" or a "genius."

For Nietzsche too the genius, or the "great man," is the individual who has absorbed to the greatest degree possible the lessons to be learned from those who came before. The assimilation of the knowledge of past generations has, however, on Nietzsche's view, occurred unconsciously, on the organic level; these bodies of knowledge now manifest themselves in the form of instincts. Clearly necessary, however, in order to make good use of this multiplicity of instincts that we carry inside ourselves, is the most meticulous attention to our own selves and to the way these selves function. Borrowing an expression from the scientist Buffon, Nietzsche declares, "Le génie n'est qu'une longue patience [Genius is just enduring patience]" (NL 1887 9[69], KSA12: 372).[53] In other words, genius, is conceived of by Nietzsche as the result of a long accumulation of energies and bodies of information from generation to generation, which can, however, be made use of only through an equally patient and meticulous work performed by present-day individuals upon themselves.[54]

Given the existence of a close linguistic affinity between the two terms, we are obliged, finally, at least to touch on the question of the relation between Emerson's Over-Soul (*Überseele* in its German translation) and Nietzsche's *Übermensch*, and to ask whether the former notion might have had any influence on the genesis of the latter. We have seen that Nietzsche radically rejected any and every idea of a suprapersonal dimension in which there might be realized a mystical union between all individuals, or rather between all "great men and women." For Nietzsche, then, Emerson's Over-Soul is simply a fantasy, a "ghost," created by abstracting and hypostatizing all the best results achieved by human beings throughout history. But the Over-Soul is more than this, inasmuch as it potentially also comprises results that have not yet been achieved but may be achieved in the future. In other words, the Over-Soul is a symbol of human potential: a potential that actual human beings have by no means yet exhausted with what they have so far historically performed. As Robinson (1993, 89) recounts, the idea for the essay collection *Representative Men*, and for the series of lectures on the theme of genius from which it arose, was born in Emerson's mind out of a "long engagement with the idea of the universal or central man." This "central man" is nothing more nor less than a symbol of human potential (90). In an entry in his *Journals* from the year 1846—contemporary, that is to say, with the above-mentioned lecture series—Emerson tells of how he had dreamed of a man who had taken on alternately the appearances of Socrates, Shakespeare, Raphael, Michelangelo, Dante, and Jesus Christ. "These great secular personalities," recounts Emerson, "were only expressions of his face chasing each other like the rack of clouds" (JMN 9, 395). In short, this dream image of a "central man" can be considered an indication of the evolution of the Emersonian notion of the Over-Soul. In the second phase of his philosophical production, in which he rejects the metaphysics that had characterized this production's first phase, Emerson recognizes that the Over-Soul that he had written of is indeed more appropriately considered a "dream," a mere product of the human imagination.

Nietzsche's notion of an *Übermensch* is certainly inspired by this nonmetaphysical version of the Emersonian Over-Soul. This is the case inasmuch as the *Übermensch* is not at all to be understood as a precise human type, a sort of demigod who stands above "common men." As Oskar Ellwald noted already in 1903, the Overman "is not at all an object that can be conceived of with concrete evidentiality and that possesses a corresponding perceptible appearance" (Fornari 2004, 45).[55] Nor is the Overman to be conceived of as the final result of the process of natural evolution (because, were this the case, the Overman would be all too similar to the one Zarathustra calls "the last human being"). Rather, the Overman is to be understood as a regulative ideal that invites the individual to a constant self-overcoming. The Overman represents the spur that drives us or draws us on to rise above the form in which we presently exist.

Conclusion

Individuality and Beyond

"Emerson, with his essays, was always a good friend to me and one who brightened even my darkest times. . . . Truly a unique case. . . . Even as a boy I listened gladly to what he had to say" (KSA 14. 476–477). Nietzsche wrote these words in that section of the draft manuscript of *Ecce Homo* (dating from October 1888) in which he recalls his intellectual "masters."[1] In the passage just quoted he calls his philosophical amity for Emerson "a unique case," and this it surely was both in its intensity and in its duration. No other author was so important for Nietzsche over so extended a span of time. His reading of Emerson, begun when Nietzsche was indeed a "boy," continued almost without interruption to the end of his conscious life, becoming most intense during Nietzsche's greatest difficulties, such as the break with Wagner in 1876 and the bitter disappointment that resulted from his discovery, in 1882, of the affair between the woman he loved, Lou von Salomé, and his best friend, Paul Rée. As Stack (1992, 311) has rightly observed, Nietzsche found in Emerson not just a thinker with whom he could engage and compare his own ideas but also a kind of personal friend who, from the pages of his essays, proffered to him useful pieces of advice on how to comport himself in the face of the challenges of his own life. Ultimately, when one traces Nietzsche's reading of Emerson the line of a dialogue takes shape which, like one of those rivers that pass underground only to emerge again under another name, becomes from time to time invisible only because it has descended to a greater depth.

Many exegetes have judged the two philosophers' respective visions of the world to be "drastically distant" from one another (see Hubbard 1958, 2) and limited Emerson's influence on Nietzsche to a few stylistic motifs. But if Nietzsche really had appreciated nothing in Emerson but a few particularly well-turned phrases and images, then he would not have read and reread, acquired and reacquired his works over the years, nor striven to gain information about him by commissioning translations. There exists in fact a profound affinity between the two thinkers which persists even despite their individual diversity. As is implied by Nietzsche's image (inspired by Emerson) of an "amity of star for star," this affinity proves all the stronger the more one acknowledges the irreducibility of one of these two distinct individualities to the other and abstains from all superficial assimilations.

The many ideas and sources of inspiration that Nietzsche, in the course of the years, drew from his intense and passionate reading in the work of the American essayist can, to sum up very briefly their quantity and complexity, be organized in terms of two main lines of thought. The first line leads in the direction of the development of the individual personality; the second leads in the direction of a surpassing—or, to use Nietzsche's preferred term, an "overcoming"—of this very individual personality once it has been developed.

The development of true individuality represents the response to many of the questions raised in the virtual dialogue between Nietzsche and Emerson.

In the first place, the construction of individuality is the response to the question of how to emerge victorious from the struggle against fate. As we have seen, Emerson—despite his having found no terms except metaphysical ones in which to conceive of the freedom of the will and of the intellect—nonetheless helped Nietzsche to focus on the fact that freedom is not a matter of our acting without limitations of any sort but rather a matter of our becoming "agents of our own actions" and of our acquiring the feeling that the force of our own will is prevailing over the resistances opposed to it by our external environment, both natural and human (i.e., a matter of a sense of personal efficaciousness). Both of these—that is, both freedom as agency and the feeling of freedom as the absence of all feeling of constriction—we acquire through becoming individuals. One becomes "the agent of one's own actions" when one succeeds in mastering one's own natural instincts and the ingrained tendencies that have been inculcated in one by society—above all the tendency to conform to social norms—and in living according to a standard and a law that are one's own, that is to say, in an autonomous and original manner. And the feeling of efficaciousness—the feeling that one is able to achieve the goals that one has set oneself—is acquired only when one sets these goals not arbitrarily but rather in accordance with one's own specific nature. In other words, the feeling of being free is acquired only by recognizing and making the most of one's own unique individuality.

This same achievement of a condition of true individuality likewise represents an effective answer to the question of how to overcome traditional morality (i.e., Socratico-Christian morality or the morality of customs). Emerson's thoughts were of fundamental importance for Nietzsche in his establishing both the ultimate goal of this overcoming and the steps by which it would be achieved. One's overcoming of traditional morality, as we have seen, can be said to be consummated once one is regularly acting in conformity with one's own nature, that is to say, in accordance with values which have their origin in one's own conditions of existence. In order to bring these values to maturation it is necessary, in the first place, to become aware of having conditions of existence peculiar and specific to oneself and to take up a stance, in the name of these specific and individual values, against the "morality of the herd." Second, it is necessary to overcome also the negative, reactive feelings that will necessarily have arisen precisely as a result of this taking of a stance against the "herd"; should one fail to do this, the new values that one establishes for oneself will be nothing more than a simple reversal of traditional values. The coercion that one imposes on oneself can only be abandoned, finally, once one has attained to a perfect mastery of one's own drives and to an absolute accord between these drives and one's conscious thought. In this condition, which corresponds to the condition of freedom in the sense of agency or to life as a true individual, one can finally rightly claim to have surpassed and transcended the morality of customs.

The achievement of true individuality is also a fundamental premise and precondition for maintaining fair and just relations with other people. Reading Emerson played a fundamental role in bringing Nietzsche to focus on the idea that it is only the person who defends his or her own value as an individual, as well as the value of the goals that he or she is pursuing, that can bring any real benefit to the society in which that person lives. Conversely, whoever forfeits their own individuality through feeling the pain of others as if it were their own and throwing away their energy and substance in attempts to alleviate this pain, really ends up doing harm and damage to these others. Likewise, it is that person alone who has attained to true individuality who can be a good friend to someone else, since it is only such a person who will treat others not as a means to an end but rather as an end in themselves. That is to say he or she will not seek out the company of other persons as a way of making up for what he or she lacks, be it materially or psychologically; nor will he or she demand that others support the causes that he or she supports; the true individual will seek in the friend nothing other than the joy that is brought to him or her by the opportunity to admire another consummate individual in all the latter's inevitable difference from himself or herself.

Finally, the achieving of true individuality also constitutes the answer to the question of how one becomes a "great man." It was reading Emerson that prompted Nietzsche to develop his critique of the metaphysical notion of "the genius" as a more-than-natural being who, by virtue of his innate superiority, can claim a privileged status within society. And it was likewise ideas that he discovered in reading Emerson that helped Nietzsche to redefine, in parallel with this critique, "genius" as that talent or mixture of talents that every individual, already qua individual—that is, qua unique being who will only ever exist once upon this earth—possesses. Those, then, that each age has referred to as "great men" were simply human beings who dared to live as individuals and who, without imitating anyone, focused on perfecting their own peculiar talents so as to develop them to the level of excellence.

The construction of individuality, however, is not possible without establishing a relation to that which is "other" than, and to, oneself. The second line of thought, then, in terms of which we can organize the ideas and inspirations that Nietzsche drew, in the course of the years, from Emerson is the overcoming of individuality, that is to say, the need to transcend one's own individual—and thus by definition limited—view of the world. If the American philosopher insisted, on the one hand, on the need to form one's own independent vision of things, he also stressed, on the other hand, the equally urgent need to continually confront and engage with visions different from one's own, to put into question and debate one's own values and certainties, and thus to acquire, over time, an ever broader and ampler perspective on the world. This confrontation can either be a real one, an engagement with actual living individuals of one's own era, such as one's own friends and enemies, or a "virtual" one, an engagement, through books, with the views of the men and women of the past. The image of the strong individuality which Nietzsche forms thanks to his reading of Emerson takes on—ultimately—the appearance of a nomadic subject who, constantly confronting himself or herself with that which is "other" to him or to her, equally constantly acquires the knowledge of different emotional attitudes to and visions of the world and is able to confront and compare these attitudes and visions to his or her own. In this way "individuality" becomes something that is ever more difficult to attain, since the elements that must be managed and governed in order to do so tend to become ever more numerous, but it thereby also becomes something that is ever richer and more potent. Clearly, since the configuration of drives that characterizes it will undergo continual modification through contact with external stimuli, such an individuality will never be statically identical with itself but will rather be subject to a constant process of evolution. "*Yo me sucedo a mi mismo* [I am my own successor]" (TI, Skirmishes 13): these words, taken from Lope de Vega, that Nietzsche uses to describe both Emerson and himself sum up also the main lesson that Nietzsche drew from the American philosopher's work: that becoming an individual means to undergo constant transformation through contact with that which is other than and to oneself.[2]

A note jotted down by Nietzsche on the endpapers of his German copy of Emerson's *Essays* sums up the "recipe" for the construction of true individuality that he had gleaned from his reading of this book:

> Proceed from the smallest/nearest
>
> (1) Become aware of the whole mass of dependencies into which one was born and in which one was raised.
>
> (2) The accustomed rhythm of our thinking, our feeling, our intellectual needs and ways of nourishing ourselves.
>
> (3) Attempts [*Versuche*] at change; first, attempts to break with old habits (e.g. diet).
>
> For a time, to "lean intellectually upon the shoulder" of one's adversaries, to try to live in their air;
>
> To journey, in every sense
>
> "A fugitive and a vagabond in the earth"[3]—for a time.
>
> From time to time to rest upon one's experiences, to digest them.
>
> (4) Attempts at the composition of an ideal and later at the living out of this ideal [*Versuche der Idealdichtung und später des Ideal-Lebens*].
>
> (NL 1881 13[20], KSA 9: 621–622)[4]

With the first line of this note, Nietzsche alludes to that close attentiveness to the "little things" of life that Emerson had recommended in his essay *Prudence* (*Klugheit*), an attentiveness especially necessary for anyone who aspires to achieve high goals. In point 1 Nietzsche refers to the need to identify the circumstances in which one was born and educated, so as to understand what sort of influences have been exerted upon one. Identifying these, as Emerson explains in *Self-Reliance* and other essays, is the first step toward freeing oneself from them. In point 2 he references the need to become aware of one's own personal and peculiar conditions of existence so that one may learn to act always in a manner that accords with these. This too is a recommendation that Emerson makes over and over again in the essay *Self-Reliance*. Point 3 refers first to that "experimental" attitude that distinguishes the "honest thinker" to whom Emerson alludes in the essay *Circles*; it then goes on to reference the need to confront and engage with visions of the world different from one's own (i.e., draw benefit and advantage from one's adversaries) to which Emerson alludes in the essay *Friendship*; and finally, it refers to the practice of "intellectual nomadism" that Emerson also described, namely, in his essay *History*. In point 4 Nietzsche's implicit reference is to Emerson's essay *Art*, in which the American thinker reminds us that our creative powers ought really to be employed not in the creation of works of art but in transforming ourselves and our lives.

The ideal result of the process of the construction of individuality which Nietzsche sketches out here, using ideas and reference points taken from Emerson, is that "human being who has turned out well [*der Wohlgeratene*]," who, in *Ecce Homo*, is presented as the antithesis of the "décadent." The "person who has turned out well," writes Nietzsche,

> does our senses good: by the fact that he is cut from wood that is simultaneously hard, gentle, and fragrant. He only has a taste for what agrees with him; his enjoyment, his desires stop at the boundary of what is agreeable to him. He works out how to repair damages, he uses mishaps to his advantage; what does not kill him makes him stronger. He instinctively gathers his totality from everything he sees, hears, experiences: he is a principle of selection, he lets many things fall by the wayside. He is always in his own company, whether dealing with books, peoples, or landscapes: he honours by choosing, by permitting, by trusting. He reacts slowly to all types of stimuli, with that slowness that has been bred in him by a long caution and a willful pride, —he scrutinizes whatever stimulus comes near him, he would not go to meet it. He does not believe in "bad luck" or "guilt": he comes to terms with himself and with others, he knows how to forget, —he is strong enough that everything has to turn out best for him. (EH, Why I Am So Wise 2)

It goes to confirm how important a role Emerson played for Nietzsche in the working out of this image of a truly strong individuality which he counterposes to the image of the "décadent" that so very many of the characteristics of this "person who has turned out well" evoked in *Ecce Homo* coincide with the characteristics of Emerson's "self-reliant individual." As Emerson explains in the essay *Character*, this individual is beautiful to behold because his posture and gait reflect his inner harmony. As he explains in *Self-Reliance*, this individual instinctively chooses what is right for him and what concords with his own nature, and with magnanimity—that is, without wearing himself out in strife and struggle against it—simply refrains, and turns away, from whatever is not good for him. Moreover, as Emerson explains in the essay *Fate*, he knows how to use circumstances, even the most apparently negative, to his own benefit and advantage. He does not believe in personal misfortune because all that which would kill a weaker nature goes only to strengthen his own. He is able, as Emerson explains in the essays on Goethe and on Shakespeare, to draw from everything that he experiences elements that are useful for the great work of his own that he had originally undertaken. He does not live in the midst of society but, as Emerson recommends in the essay *Friendship*, in a solitude made bearable by good books and good friends, both of which he selects with the utmost meticulousness. Finally, he has learned, as Emerson urges his readers to do in the essay *Experience*, how to master his own impulses and to refrain from allowing his energies to be drained away by the needy and the suffering in those cases where he recognizes that according help to them will harm both him and them.

The great spiritual proximity between Emerson and Nietzsche, which emerges as soon as one reconstructs the virtual dialogue that the latter conducted with the former, should not, however, lead us to forget how different were their respective historical-cultural contexts and how different also, consequently, were the solutions they offered in response to the same needs and demands. As is only consistent with the strongly religious upbringing and education that he received, Emerson believes in the intrinsic goodness of human nature and has confidence in mankind's perfectibility. He also believes that the process of self-culture, aimed at drawing the authentic core of a person's individual nature back into the light and freeing it from its concealment under social conditioning, can be set in motion and brought to fruition just by an appeal to the will and to the faculty of reason, which he holds to be unconditionally free. In addition to these we have the clearly "democratic" tenor that Emerson gives to his conception of the great man: for Emerson every individual has the capacity—indeed the duty—to perfect his or her own self up to the point where he or she achieves excellence.

Nietzsche, on the other hand, is led by his awareness of how urgent it is that individuality be strengthened to dig down deep into the nature of subjectivity so as to measure the real impact on the human being of the constraints that have been laid upon this person's thought and action. And the results of this digging-down into subjectivity undermine at its very foundations the belief in the will as the faculty of free decision, just as they do the Cartesian notion of the transparency of consciousness to itself. There ensues from this, in Nietzsche's work, a ruthlessly deterministic perspective on the question of the human individual's capacity to change himself or herself and possibly thereby to achieve greatness. For Nietzsche, it is that organism alone which happens to be endowed with a fortunate configuration of drives, and which happens to encounter on its life path certain circumstances rather than others, that is likely to succeed in becoming a true individual—that is to say, likely to become an individual who is truly the agent of his or her own actions and to develop to the maximum his or her intrinsic talents.

Ultimately, then, it would be inexact to speak of the effect of Nietzsche's reading of Emerson in terms of the latter's having exerted an "influence" on the former. Because these readings in Emerson did not, in fact, lead to Nietzsche's adopting Emerson's point of view. Rather, they led him to elaborate a philosophy authentically his own—that is to say, to free himself from every kind of influence. In essence Emerson, like every genuine educator, pushed Nietzsche on down a road that was Nietzsche's alone to travel. He urged him, as a true friend does, to seek and to become his own self. The younger thinker's reading of his American elder, then, did not result in Nietzsche's becoming a second Emerson; rather, it saw to it that Nietzsche became Nietzsche.

NOTES

Introduction

1. Nietzsche purchased a copy of *Versuche* during his school years at Schulpforta, probably in 1864. This copy was stolen from him in 1874. Some time between 1874 and 1878 (the date at which we find him quoting once again from this collection) he bought a second copy, which is the one presently preserved in Weimar and the one whose underlinings and marginal glosses we will analyze here.

2. When the Italian team of Giuliano Campioni, Paolo D'Iorio, Maria Cristina Fornari, Andrea Orsucci, etc. undertook their study of Nietzsche's personal library, they discovered several pages of this book still uncut. This fact is documented in Campioni et al. 2003, 212. Some years later, these uncut pages were opened on the orders of the director of the Duchess Anna Amalia Library, with a view to making a microfilm record of all the books.

3. The notebook containing the translation was discovered by Baumgarten in 1938 (see Baumgarten 1956, 58) but its contents were identified and published only in 1980, by Sander Gilman (see Gilman 1980).

4. According to the catalogue made by Rudolf Steiner, one copy was bound together with *Über Goethe und Shakespeare*, the other together with Rée's *Psychologische Beobachtungen*. The latter copy of *Die Führung des Lebens*, Steiner's catalogue records, showed signs of having been heavily read and several marginal notes appear (see Campioni et al. 2003, 211–212).

5. The notebook in question is a quarto (16 x 20) notebook with a black cover, consisting of 32 lined pages. As was generally his practice, Nietzsche wrote in this notebook beginning in its backmost pages and moving toward the front and using one side of the page only (in this case the even-numbered pages). The excerpts from Emerson are to be found on pp. 32–26. Baumgarten, who was the first to examine Nietzsche's copy of the *Essays*, noted that, before selecting the excerpts in question, Nietzsche had marked certain passages of the book with numbers in the margin. Only some of these were actually copied into the notebook; others were copied into it without being numbered beforehand (Baumgarten 1957, 25). The excerpts numbered 1 to 19 are drawn from the essay *History*; those numbered 20 to 39 from the essay *Self-Reliance*. Baumgarten counted 40 excerpts rather than 39 because he wrongly interpreted the final line of the 27th excerpt as forming a separate excerpt in itself. As is noted already by Golden (2013, 405) many commentators, basing themselves on Baumgarten's faulty work, perpetuate his error and speak of "40 entries." In addition to the 39 excerpts, Golden (2013, 405) mentions an "additional entry not collated with the others but noted by them [= Colli e Montinari], (Commentary to Volume 4, 6[451], KSA 14.638)." In reality, however, the "entry" referred to here is not an excerpt but rather a marginal note which should rather have been inserted into that part of the Critical Edition that is devoted to the "Emerson Exemplar" (NL 1881 13[11–22]; KSA 9: 618–622).

6. When Montinari, who was in Weimar at the time working on producing the Critical Edition, realized what a mass of underlinings, exclamation marks, question marks, and annotations Nietzsche had added to his copy of this book, he wrote to Colli in Pisa, "Emerson is a goldmine *for all our volumes!*" (Montinari to Colli, December 14, 1964, in Campioni 1992, 116–117). In other words, Montinari immediately understood that Emerson's influence on Nietzsche was not restricted to any particular period nor to any specific idea but was relevant to all the volumes of the edition he was preparing. In short, he recognized that the influence of Emerson pervaded Nietzsche's thought in its entirety. Montinari was able to decipher the greater part of the annotations that Nietzsche had made to the Emerson volumes in his library. It was only when he had finished his work that Montinari became aware of Baumgarten's researches and of the fact that these marginal glosses had already been deciphered. See Montinari's letter to Giorgio Colli, August 2, 1965, in Campioni 1992, 374.

7. In 2013 there appeared an English translation of this material by Mason Golden, who provided it with a brief introductory commentary. As Golden (2013, 399) himself declares, his intention in this short introduction is not "to chart potential lines of Emerson's influence on Nietzsche" but simply that of "contextualizing and clarifying, briefly, when possible, Nietzsche's often cryptic marginalia." Golden painstakingly compares the excerpts that Nietzsche made from his personal copy of *Versuche* (the 1858 German translation of Emerson's essays) both with the text of the first, 1841 edition of the *Essays: First Series* (on which the German translator Fabricius had based his work) and with the second, revised edition of the *Essays: First Series* from 1847, to which Emerson scholars usually refer and which is included in the standard Critical Edition of this latter's works. The revisions made by Emerson in new editions of his own work were highly significant, involving changes not only to the style but also to the substance of the argument. Remarkably, indeed, as Golden observes, the modifications that Nietzsche makes when he copies passages from Emerson into his own notebooks often coincide to an uncanny degree with the revisions that Emerson himself made when he reworked the texts of his essays for republication. Still more astonishingly, at places where the German translator Fabricius interprets Emerson's text poorly and produces a misleading rendering, the modifications that Nietzsche makes to the German text in copying it often draw it back closer to the spirit of Emerson's original. In short, "Nietzsche instinctively brings us closer to Emerson as we know him" (Golden 2013, 404).

8. It is important to distinguish between the essay *Nature* that Emerson wrote in 1836 and the essay of the same title which he included in the first series of the *Essays* (1841). A German translation of the essay *Nature* (1836) was published in 1868, but any trace of Nietzsche's having read it is lacking. Stack (1992) perceives a strong analogy between the argument of the 1836 *Nature* and that of Nietzsche's early (but only posthumously published) essay *On Truth and Lies in a Non-Moral Sense*. Stack's grounds here, however, consist only in the fact that, in this essay, Emerson alludes to the theory that the origin of abstract terms is to be sought in more concrete ones, above all in the observations that human beings make about their own selves, so that we tend naturally to form an "anthropomorphic" image of the world around us (147). There must be opposed to Stack's view, then, the considerations that, first, this theory was already widely diffused among the authors of German Romanticism, with whom Nietzsche would certainly have been familiar, and, second, the same notion is in fact expressed much more eloquently by Emerson himself in the piece *The Poet*, also included in the *Essays*. Stack furthermore maintains that Emerson's *The American Scholar* likewise exerted an important influence on Nietzsche (155). But, given that no German translation of this work was available at the time, we suggest this possibility can be excluded.

Chapter 1

1. See Biedenkapp 1902; Michaud (1910) 1924; Worthington Smith 1911; How 1911; Royce 1917.

2. Grimm's specific approach to the history of art consisted in summing up the basic characteristics of each era in accounts of their most representative personalities. This was probably the reason Grimm took an interest in Emerson and particularly in the book *Representative Men* (1850), which, soon after its publication, received laudatory reviews in all the major

European cultural periodicals. In 1856 this collection of essays was published in the original English in the *Standard American Authors* series brought out by the Leipzig publishing house Dürr. Grimm was so impressed by it that he translated a large extract into German himself. *Über Goethe und Shakespeare*, his German version of the essays Emerson had devoted to these two personalities, appeared in 1857, provided with a lengthy introductory essay by Grimm himself. The first full translation of *Representative Men* was to appear only 30 years later, in 1895. Already in 1856, however, Grimm began a substantial correspondence with Emerson that continued right up until the latter's death (see Holls 1903).

3. In fact the German public had a first opportunity to become acquainted with Emerson's life and works in 1854–1855, thanks to the travel diary of a Swedish writer, Frederike Bremer, who traveled for two years across North America and Cuba. During her journey she had the opportunity to meet the most significant personalities of New England, including Emerson, with whom she had inspiring conversations about his country. She portrayed Emerson as a "cordial, quiet, honest man, whose thinking had the same refreshing and invigorating effect as the water of a mountain spring" (Bremer 1854–1855, 72). Bremer's diary, which was published at a time when many Germans were thinking about emigrating to the United States, was a great literary success.

4. The preface to Emerson's *Versuche* (1858) was not signed. However, Gisela von Arnim's letters to Moritz Carrière in spring 1858 reveal her authorship: "How much I love Emerson is proven by the Preface, that I wrote" (see Simon 1937, 113).

5. In Germany Positivism took the specific form of a materialist monism in which all mental and spiritual processes were reduced to physiological ones. Representative of this new "spirit of the age" were the works of Karl Vogt, who denied all autonomy to the mental processes. Instead he held thoughts to be secretions of the brain in just the same way as bile is a secretion of the liver and urine a secretion of the kidneys.

6. The first work of Emerson's to be translated into German, in 1856, was his *English Traits*—a translation commissioned by the publisher Carl Mayer of Hannover, who numbered among the very few admirers of Emerson in Germany. There then followed, in 1857, a translation of the *Essays: First and Second Series*, along with Hermann Grimm's own translation of extracts from *Representative Men* (*Über Goethe und Shakespeare*). In 1865 a translation of Emerson's famous *Divinity School Address* (1838) appeared in Karl Scholl's collection *Freie Stimmen aus dem heutigen Frankreich, England und America über Lebensfragen der Religion* under the title *Die zwei Hauptfehler des geschichtlichen Christentums*, and a translation of the essay *Nature* (1836), the manifesto of American Transcendentalism, was published in 1868. All of these translations enjoyed only very limited readership and success. Neither, however, did Emerson find much favor in the German-speaking world as a poet. In 1859 a few of his poems were included in the collection *Amerikanische Gedichte*, edited and translated by the German writer Friedrich Spielhagen. This book, however, enjoyed no resonance at all. This was not the case, however, as regards the works Emerson wrote in the second half of the 19th century, namely *The Conduct of Life* (1860) and *Society and Solitude* (1870). These received a much broader and more positive reception in Germany. The German translation of *The Conduct of Life*, for example, was embraced by the German public, running into two editions in 1862 and then a third in 1885. Even more successful was the collection *Society and Solitude*, first translated into German in 1871 and reprinted in 1876 and 1885. The better reception accorded to the so-called second Emerson, that is, to the works written in the second half of his life, is probably due to the different approach that characterizes these works. In these later writings Emerson rejected his earlier naturalistic mysticism and limitless faith in human potentialities in favor of a more realistic and pragmatic approach, one conscious of the difficulties and frustrations inevitably involved in the journey toward self-realization. These two collections, though published 10 years apart, display a similar spirit, since both were based on lectures that Emerson gave in the 1850s (Robinson 1993, 5–6). On the other hand, *Letters and Social Aims* (1875), which was translated as *Neue Essays* a few months after the publication of the original in English, was not positively received by the German public. This collection gathers together some of Emerson's early essays that were not originally intended for publication.

7. Between 1894 and 1907, 18 translations of Emerson's works appeared, among which four were reprinted within a short time. In 1903, the centenary of his birth, more than 30 essays

were published in magazines and journals, and a complete critical edition and a paperback edition of his works were published by Eugen Diederich (Simon 1937, 146).

8. Emerson was widely read and appreciated by Rudolf Steiner, who was a close friend of Herman Grimm. Steiner became a passionate reader of Emerson after he found Nietzsche's annotated German copy of the *Essays* in the Nietzsche-Archiv. He counted Emerson among the most important minds of the 19th century and often quoted from his works (in German translation) (see Steiner 1925, 177). Musil and Rilke were also great admirers of the American writer. Emerson was very much appreciated also within the circle around Stefan George. One of the members of the so-called George-Kreis, Friedrich Gundolf, published an essay on Emerson in 1918, praising the American writer's celebration of spontaneity, intuition, and mystical communion between individuals (see Gundolf 1918).

9. Due to the feeling of power and growth it gave rise to, this type of ethics was highly attractive to the merchant middle classes of Massachusetts, who now began to convert en masse to Unitarianism. "Calvinism, or orthodoxy, was (now) the despised and persecuted form of faith. It was the dethroned royal family wandering like a permitted mendicant in the city where once it had held court, and Unitarianism reigned in its stead. All the literary men of Massachusetts were Unitarians. All the elite of wealth and fashion crowded Unitarian churches. The judges on the bench were Unitarian, giving decisions by which the peculiar features of Church organization, so carefully ordained by the Pilgrim Fathers, had been nullified" (Wilbur 1952, 436–437).

10. According to David Robinson, what rendered Emerson anathematic to the Unitarians was not so much his refusal to grant the authority of the Bible but rather his faith in intuition as a means of attaining to that Divine which already dwells within each individual. Unitarianism was, in fact, a kind of natural religion of strongly rationalist bent. In later stages of his intellectual development, when the mystical component of his thought came to play a less predominant role, Emerson, argues Robinson (1993, 5), reincorporated many basic elements of Unitarian doctrine into his philosophy, such as, for example, the "ethos of character-building and self-culture through ethical action." Robinson, in other words, sees Emerson's thought, considered in all its unfolding stages, as ultimately more a development of the Unitarian doctrine than a rupture with it.

11. Hedge's essay was published in *The Christian Examiner,* which was at the time the organ of what Perry Miller (1950, 12) calls "literate Unitarianism." In this essay Hedge explained and praised the "transcendental" method that had been introduced in the philosophy of Kant and his "followers" (by which Hedge meant Fichte and Schelling) and disseminated among cultured English-speaking circles by Coleridge. This method, as Coleridge had presented it and Hedge received it, consisted in acknowledging the superiority of Reason (intuition) over Understanding (ratiocination). Whereas Understanding is bound to empirical data alone, Reason can transcend these and gain access directly to those principles or ideas which all human beings intuitively recognize to be true. This "transcendental" vision completely undermined the empiricist philosophy underlying Unitarianism and for this reason caused no small amount of scandal.

12. Some conversancy with German literature and culture was in fact to be found already in the generation of American scholars preceding Hedge's and Emerson's. Edward Everett (1794–1865), professor of Greek at Harvard University and one of the first great American orators, had actually gained a doctorate from the University of Göttingen after several years' study there, in 1817, the year that Emerson entered Harvard.

13. Among the active members of the group were Orestes Brownson, Theodore Parker, Bronson Alcott, Margaret Fuller, and James Freeman Clarke. Jones Very, Thoreau, Hawthorne, Longfellow, and Whitman also occasionally took part in the meetings. The meetings were devoted to topics of an educational, ethicomoral, or religious nature. For example, at the meeting held on October 3, 1836, at Alcott's house in Boston the topic was "American Genius—the causes which hinder its growth, and give us no first-rate productions." On October 18, 1836, at Brownson's house in the same city it was "the education of Humanity." And on May 29, 1837, once again in Boston at the house of George Ripley, the question discussed was "What is the essence of religion as distinct from morality?" In the summer of 1837 at Emerson's house it was "Does the species advance beyond the individual?" On May 20, 1838, at Caleb

Stetson's house in Medford, it was "Is mysticism an element of Christianity?" In June 1838, at Cyrus Bartol's house in Boston, it was "On the character and genius of Goethe." In December 1838, at the same place, the topic was "Pantheism." And on May 13, 1840, again at Emerson's house, it was "the inspiration of the prophet and the bard, the nature of poetry, and the causes of the sterility of poetic inspiration in our age and country" (Richardson 1995, 246).

14. Hedge was indeed an exception, at first, among the Transcendentalists in possessing a deep scholarly knowledge of the new German philosophy. In 1842 he published in *The Dial* a translation of the epoch-making inaugural lecture that Schelling had given at Berlin University late in the previous year. He also published a philosophical anthology, *Prose Writers of Germany* (1847), containing translations from Kant's *Critique of Judgment*, Hegel's *Philosophy of History*, and Fichte's *The Destiny of Man*. Late in life he became a professor of German literature at Harvard University and published scholarly contributions on Leibniz and Schopenhauer (see Wellek 1965, 158–160). Emerson too, however, had engaged in a deep study of German literature, using the reference works most widely available at the time. He was, in particular, a great admirer of Goethe—with whom he first became acquainted through Carlyle's translations but whose works he later read, almost in their entirety, in the original German (Van Cromphout 1990, 1–3)—and of Schelling. When this latter philosopher was appointed to Hegel's former chair in philosophy at the University of Berlin late in 1841, Emerson received from an American friend in Germany the text of his inaugural address along with some other material. What is more, when, some years later, in 1845, Emerson's biographer J. E. Cabot lent him the manuscript of his translation of Schelling's *Philosophical Inquiries into the Nature of Human Freedom*, Emerson appreciated the work so enormously that he held onto it for almost an entire year (Wellek 1965, 198–199).

15. Nietzsche had this 1883 essay of Emerson's translated for his own use already at the end of the following year, in December 1884. When Nietzsche saw how poor and fragmentary Emerson's education had been and how little cultural stimulation his environment had provided, he realized also how large a part of the American's talent had been wasted. "I do not know how much I would give," writes Nietzsche to the Overbecks, "if only I could bring it about, ex post facto, that such a great and magnificent nature, rich in soul and spirit [*eine solche herrliche große Natur, reich an Seele und Geist*], might have had the benefit of some strict discipline, a really scientific education. As it is, in Emerson we have <u>lost</u> a philosopher [*So wie es steht, ist uns in Emerson ein Philosoph <u>verloren</u> gegangen!*]" (KSA 6.573, n. 566). In a letter from 1883 where he expressed to Franz Overbeck his admiration for the American, Nietzsche added the remark, "But his mind [*Geist*] has been badly formed" (KSB 6: 463, n. 477). With this observation, Nietzsche was very probably referring to Emerson's lack of what he, Nietzsche, considered to be a really adequate academic training and of really competent partners with whom the American thinker might have conducted a dialogue.

16. Other journals related to New England Transcendentalism were *The Western Messenger* (1836–1839), edited by James Freeman Clarke and Bronson Alcott; the *Boston Quarterly Review* (1838–1842), edited by Orestes Brownson, which later merged with the *Democratic Review*; *The Harbinger* (1845–1849), the official bulletin of Brook Farm, edited by George Ripley; and the *Massachusetts Quarterly Review* (1847–1850), edited by Theodore Parker.

17. Despite their profound acquaintance with German philosophy, neither Emerson nor Hedge appears to have been capable of grasping the distinction between "transcendent" and "transcendental." They used this latter term to refer loosely and generally to any and every philosophical approach of an intuitionistic kind. In his essay *The Transcendentalist* (1842) Emerson wrote, "The extraordinary profoundness and precision of that man's [Kant]'s thinking have given vogue to his nomenclature, in Europe and America, to that extent, that whatever belongs to the class of intuitive thought is popularly called at the present day *Transcendental*" (Wellek 1965, 193).

18. Emerson's disciple and biographer Cabot made translations into English of Hegel's *Philosophy of Right* and *Logic*. Emerson himself, however, found these post-Kantian works of speculation absolutely unintelligible. As Frothingham (1959, 43) notes, "To comprehend or even to apprehend Hegel requires more philosophical culture than was found in New England half a century ago." Moreover the basically conservative spirit that pervades Hegel's philosophy was as far removed as it was possible to be from the revolutionary aim cherished by

the Transcendentalists. In a journal entry from 1870 Emerson explicitly criticizes Hegel's compromises with the autocratic Prussian government of his day and favorably contrasts with this attitude the American values of freedom and liberty (see Wellek 1965, 208).

19. Versluis argues that the sacred texts of the East were received and absorbed by the American Transcendentalists in a way that was philologically inaccurate, that is, that failed to pay sufficient attention to these texts' original cultural contexts. The Transcendentalists took from these texts only those notions that they felt could be integrated with the key notions of Christianity so as to form a sort of "literary religion" which they imagined to be a universal religion reflecting fundamental truths supposed to be innate within every human being (see Versluis 1993, 51, 70).

20. During the last two years of *The Dial*'s publication, when its direction was taken in hand by Emerson himself, he entrusted to Thoreau a regularly appearing section of the journal entitled "Ethnical Scriptures" devoted to identifying the principal religious and moral teachings lying at the base of the different religions of the world. Emerson also published in *The Dial* selections from such classics of Oriental literature as the *Hitopadesha*, a condensation of material from the *Panchatantra* of the Sanskrit poet Vishnu Sharma (July 1842), the so-called *Institutes of Hindu Law*, nowadays usually called *The Laws of Manu* but referred to in Sir William Jones's late 18th-century English translation as *The Ordinances of Menu* (January 1843), the sayings of Confucius (April 1843), the Zoroastrian *Desatir* (July 1843), the broader Confucian canon called the *Four Books* (October 1843), and the sayings of Buddha (January 1844). The "Ethnical Scriptures" section in the final, April 1844 issue of *The Dial* was devoted by Emerson to the sayings of Zoroaster himself, as mediated to the modern world by Thomas Taylor (Richardson 1995, 379).

21. A happy exception to the general hostility to the notion that it might be possible to discover certain filiations between Emerson's ideas and Nietzsche's is to be found in Salter (1917), who recognizes that there do indeed exist several parallelisms between the key conceptions of the two philosophers. Paradoxically, Salter was completely in the dark regarding the fact that Nietzsche had ever read Emerson and that, therefore, the affinities with Emerson's work which he discovered in Nietzsche's were actually the result of a direct influence.

22. This is certainly true, for example, of the eminent midcentury Harvard scholar Matthiessen (1941), who, in his influential standard work *American Renaissance*, cites Emerson's mild and gentle temperament and his innocent, childlike way of looking at the world as reasons enough to exclude any *rapprochement* between his thought and that of Nietzsche, seen by Matthiessen as the fanatical theorist of the Superman.

23. The first author to inquire in depth into these events was Victor Farias (1987). Farias's study, however, was heavily criticized by several philosophers and intellectual historians, and its 2nd edition the following year contained many revisions. Much more information, brought into line with the present state of research, is to be found in O'Brien 2015, 117–120.

24. Needless to say, in Heidegger's (1961) monumental interpretation of Nietzsche, Emerson is not even mentioned. Less self-evident, perhaps, is the neglect of Nietzsche's relation to Emerson in the work of the poststructuralist current of French Nietzscheans (Derrida, Deleuze, Foucault, Bataille, etc.). This might be due to the fact that these writers relied on Heidegger's interpretation of Nietzsche, though critically attacking it.

25. Regarding the whole history of the book *The Will to Power*, assembled by Elisabeth and Peter Gast (Heinrich Köselitz), see D'Iorio 1996 and Montinari 1996b. For a history of the Critical Edition see Montinari 1996a and Campioni 1992.

Chapter 2

1. Katsafanas (2016, 138) cites D 124, in which Nietzsche denies the existence of any connection between willing and action, and D 130, in which Nietzsche questions the very existence of such a thing as "the will."

2. Nietzsche had intended these essays as contributions to the literary club Germania. Schulpforta had a rigorous academic schedule and the pupils' lives were regulated with almost military discipline. They had little free time to spend on extracurricular reading or on literary or musical compositions of their own. To remedy this lack, Nietzsche, together with

two fellow pupils he had known since childhood, Krug and Pinder, founded a club in 1860 devoted to discussing just such original compositions in prose, poetry, or musical form. Thus, although immature and fragmentary, *Fate and History* and *Freedom of the Will and Fate* anticipate many of the important themes of Nietzsche's mature philosophy, from the critique of morality and religion, through the notion of time as circular and the repudiation of teleology and the idea of inherent "ends," to the criticism of the thesis of natural evolution. As Stack (1992, 12) has observed, they "presented a brief overture that sounded many of the themes of his later philosophical symphony."

3. Further evidence of Emerson's having been present to Nietzsche's mind during the writing of these two essays is a self-penned report on his literary activity in 1862 (NL 1862–1863, 14[1], KGW I/3: 3) in which he mentions that, at the same time as he was composing them, he was also reading the American essayist Emerson (misspelled "Emmerson").

4. Volkmann, who came from a prestigious family of Bremen merchants, had also mastered several modern languages. In Nietzsche's time at Schulpforta he was also the school's teacher of French, English, and German (Beheim-Schwarzbach 1943, 24). In a letter to his sister from November 1861, Nietzsche mentions Volkmann's English classes and writes that he hopes to attend them starting in the spring (see KSB 1: 188, n. 288). There can be little doubt but that Volkmann would have introduced his pupils not only to the classics of English literature, such as Shakespeare and Byron, but also to an author who was, at this time, the object of huge public acclaim both in England and the United States: Ralph Waldo Emerson. In these years around 1870 Emerson was so famous in his own country that he was already considered a national icon and venerated as enjoying an authority on a par with the Buddha's (Porte 1999, 1). He was hardly less well-known and appreciated in England where, in 1847–1848, he had given, with great success, a series of public lectures and entered into contact with the major literary personalities of the age (Richardson 1995, 523). Moreover, Volkmann must surely have heard much about Emerson from his own brother, Johann Hermann Volkmann (1840–1896), who was the US consul in Odessa. The supposition that Volkmann would likely have introduced his pupils to Emerson either in his classes or in private chats is further supported by the fact that other pupils besides Nietzsche and Gersdorff expressed interest in this author, who was little known in Germany at the time, and were in the habit of referring to him as a philosopher, whereas most Germans (if they spoke of Emerson at all) tended, by reason of his markedly literary style, to speak of him rather as a writer. This is the case, for example, of Heinrich Wendt, who, in July 1879, reminds Nietzsche in a letter of their conversations about "the American philosopher Emerson" under the linden and chestnut trees in the grounds of Schulpforta (KGB II/6.2: 1141, n. 1215). It is also the case of Carl von Gersdorff, who was to become one of Nietzsche's dearest friends and one of his principal interlocutors in his discussions of the American author's ideas. In a letter to Nietzsche dating from 1874, Gersdorff told of how he had begun once again to read *The Conduct of Life*, a book he had acquired while a pupil at Pforta merely out of curiosity, only for it to become one of his favorite and most constantly consulted books (KGB II/4: 544, n. 569). Gersdorff and Nietzsche shared a passion for the American essayist over a period of twenty years and were in the habit of regularly exchanging opinions on all they read by or about him (Hummel 1946, 71). Unfortunately we can trace this exchange of views on Emerson only through Gersdorff's letters to Nietzsche, as Nietzsche's replies have been lost. *Nota bene*: The correspondence between the two friends was interrupted from 1877 to 1881 for personal reasons.

5. As he clearly states in another contribution, from the same period, to the literary club Germania, he had come by this time to be of the view that the principles of Christian doctrine were nothing other than symbols serving to express certain "fundamental truths of the human heart" (KSB 1: 202, n. 301).

6. Stack (1992, 12) commits the error of reducing "fate" to just these restrictions imposed by the personality alone, whereas, in Emerson's actual view, these restrictions were only added to, without entirely replacing, "fate" in the more traditional sense of the totality of events befalling the individual from outside, such as natural catastrophes.

7. Emerson anticipated in this regard certain important modern discoveries about the stability of personality and is "perhaps the first to decry personal stability as the enemy of freedom, creativity, and growth" (McCrae and Costa 1994, 173).

8. Spurzheim's ideas had gained some popularity in America already as early as the 1820s (see Walsh 1972, 188), although their scientificity was questioned by many (see 204). In August 1832 Spurzheim disembarked in Boston, having come to America to carry out research on the indigenous peoples of the continent and on the slaves still held in the southern states, and also in order to promulgate his doctrines more widely (see 187). Many people followed his public lecture tour, although we do not know if Emerson was among them. Stack (1992, 87) inclines toward this hypothesis but does not provide any proof. Stern (1984, 214), on the other hand, considers it unlikely that Emerson attended Spurzheim's public lectures in Boston because in this period he was in very poor health and was also in the course of severing his ties with the Second Church. In any case, the great interest Emerson took in the science of phrenology is evident in numerous journal entries, as well as in the many books in Emerson's personal library that were devoted to this topic (see 214). Quetelet's most important book, *Sur l'homme et le développement de ses facultés, ou Essai de physique sociale*, was published in 1835 and translated into English in 1842. Emerson read this work while he was working on his own *Representative Men* and was deeply impressed by it (see Richardson 1995, 467–469). Quetelet was accused of being a determinist, a fatalist, but in reality his predictions applied only to "the average man," that is to say, to an abstraction intended to be representative of the "social body" in general; with actual individuals he declared himself not to be concerned (see 468). He stated that, whereas the actions of a single individual are impossible to predict, those of a supposed "average man," gleaned from statistical data relative to each social body, are calculable to a high degree of accuracy (see 469; Quetelet 1842, 96).

9. It was Spurzheim (1832, 12) who coined the term "phrenology" for this new discipline, which he defined as follows: "the doctrine of the special phenomena of the mind, and of the relations between the mental dispositions and the body, particularly the brain."

10. Embracing Lamarck's theory of the inheritability of acquired traits, Emerson maintains that we inherit from our ancestors not only a certain genetic patrimony but also habits, vices, and virtues: "We sometimes see a change of expression in our companion, and say, his father, or his mother, comes to the windows of his eyes, and sometimes a remote relative. In different hours, a man represents each of several of his ancestors, as if there were seven or eight of us rolled up in each man's skin, —seven or eight ancestors at least, —and they constitute the variety of notes for that new piece of music which his life is" (CL, 5; FL, 7). It was surely through Emerson, then, that Nietzsche became acquainted with this theory long before he encountered it in Lamarck. Moreover, Lamarck is an author whom Nietzsche cites only very rarely (see Hubbard 1958, 32, 80; Stack 1992, 169).

11. Precisely because of this misunderstanding, the essay *Fate* was, for a long time, misinterpreted as a confession of impotence by a defeated idealist, or even as a modern version of the Calvinist theory of predestination (e.g., Whicher 1953, 123–140).

12. As Robinson (1993, 136) ironically observes, speaking of Fate in American culture always amounts to a form of political dissent.

13. In the essay on Napoleon included in *Representative Men* Emerson tells of how the French soldier-cum-emperor was called "the Child of Destiny" (RM, 133) since everything seemed somehow always to turn in his favor. He seemed, for long periods, invulnerable to any harm: even the royal armies sent against him cast down, amazingly, the colors they were marching under and, instead of enemies, became friends to him. Napoleon said of himself that he was born under a lucky star. According to Emerson, however, his success was due rather to the fact that Napoleon well understood how to interpret the dominant trends and tendencies of his epoch and to use these to his advantage. He always "marched ... with events" (RM, 133), wrote Emerson.

14. In the German text the expression "evil is good in the making" is rendered as "das Böse Gutes befördert" (FL, 25). Emerson employs this same expression once again in the following passage: "If Fate is ore and quarry, if evil is good in the making, if limitation is power that shall be, if calamities, oppositions, and weights are wings and means, —we are reconciled" (CL, 19; FL, 25).

15. As Goethe interprets the myth of Prometheus, this figure is the progenitor of a "new race of men" who must learn to cope with a hostile universe devoid of all divine benefactors. Nietzsche held Goethe's interpretation of the Greek myth in very high esteem and devoted

an essay to it in 1859 (NL 1859 6[2], KGW I/2: 36; on Goethe's *Prometheus* as an anticipation of Nietzsche's *Übermensch* see Lecznar 2013, 39). The character developed in Goethe's poem—which, composed in the 1770s and first published in the 1780s, was a key work of the proto-Romantic *Sturm und Drang*—was a profound inspiration to many writers of the Romantic movement proper, such as Coleridge, Byron, Shelley, Schlegel, and Schelling (Dougherty 2006, 91–115). All those who wanted to rebel against the authority of religious belief or political oppression saw it both as an encouragement of and a warning against human aspirations to total self-sufficiency. Nietzsche also wrote, in this same year of 1861, an essay on Byron's *Manfred* (NL 1861–1862 12[4], KGW I/2: 344).

16. On Schiller's *Robbers*, see NL 1859 6[77], KGW I/2: 119; on Byron's *Manfred* see NL 1861–1862 12[4], KGW I/2: 345, 348, 349.

17. This early work has been translated into English as *On Moods*. But in view of the remarks that we will have to make about this piece, the reader should be aware that the notion evoked by the German term *Stimmungen* is more complex: that of the "disposing" of the mind into a specific "mental disposition" or even that of a "tuning" or an "attunement" of the mental and spiritual faculties.

18. Stack argues that Nietzsche must have known Emerson's *Essays* as early as 1862. He bases this argument on the fact that the description of the relation between the individual and universal history that we find in Nietzsche's *Fate and History* of April of that year appears to be inspired by Emerson's *Circles*, included in the *Essays: First Series*. In this essay Nietzsche writes that the universe can be imagined as a series of concentric circles: the innermost represents the life of the individual, the others that of the species, universal history, etc. In *Circles*, however, Emerson had used the image of the circle to convey quite a different idea: that of the horizon that limits our point of view. Emerson wrote that around every circle there can always be drawn a still greater circle, that every way of looking at things can always be disconfirmed by a way of looking at things acquired by adopting a broader perspective. The present study, then, inclines toward the hypothesis that Nietzsche's and Emerson's both using the image of concentric circles was merely a coincidence, and that Nietzsche's first reading of the *Essays* is, consequently, to be dated back only to 1864 (not 1862). This hypothesis seems confirmed by the fact that we find Gersdorff and Nietzsche exchanging views on the *Essays* only in the first months of 1864 and by the fact that Nietzsche, during the whole of 1863, was concerned exclusively with *The Conduct of Life*, never once mentioning the *Essays*. It must have been Nietzsche who advised Gersdorff to buy this book because, in December 1864, Gersdorff writes to Nietzsche, "I promptly followed your friendly advice to buy Emerson's *Essays*" (KGB I/3: 23, n. 91).

19. Nietzsche wrote in the margin of this passage, "This is true also of Mankind as a whole! Out of all the variety of things Mankind takes *that which is its own*—all the rest *remains within the things! [Die Menschheit auch! Sie nimmt ihr* Eigenes *aus dem Mannigfaltigen—alles andere* Besitztum bleibt in den Dingen zurück]" (V, 108; see Appendix Figure 10). This gloss on Emerson can be seen as a provisional draft of Aphorism 242 of *The Gay Science*: "However great my greed for knowledge may be, I cannot take anything else out of things than what already belongs to me—what belongs to others remains behind. How is it possible for a human being to be a thief or a robber?" See also Baumgarten 1956, 32–33.

20. In October 1865 Nietzsche transferred from Bonn University to Leipzig so as to remain with his philological mentor Ritschl, who had been appointed to a chair there. It was during this period that Nietzsche happened, in a secondhand bookstore, on a book that had hitherto been unknown to him: Schopenhauer's ([1819] 1969) *World as Will and Representation*. Enraptured by the philosophy of this "morose and vigorous genius," Nietzsche immediately acquired and devoured all his other writings. In 1874 he himself confessed, "I am one of those readers of Schopenhauer who, once they had read a single page of him, knew for certain that they would go on to read and pay heed to every word he wrote" (SE 2). The discovery of Schopenhauer brought about a real spiritual revolution in Nietzsche and reinforced that sense of a philosophical vocation which he had first felt on discovering Emerson. He lost all interest in his Greek and Latin studies and in the other courses taught at the university. More important to him than the day, devoted to curricular activities, became the night, which he spent "in the narrow chambers of his own brain [*in den engen Hirnkammern*]" meditating on

Schopenhauer (KSB 2: 94, n. 486). His Emersonian readings did not even now take second place, but Emerson's influence melded and combined with that of Schopenhauer. In a letter to Gersdorff of April 7, 1866, Nietzsche makes use of a fine image from Emerson's essay *Nature* to convey an idea that he had in fact found in Schopenhauer: the condition of the mind when, freed of its usual servitude to the will, it is finally able to adopt toward the world an attitude of disinterested equanimity. "Dear friend, from time to time come hours of quiet contemplation in which, with mixed feelings of joy and sorrow, one stands, as it were, above one's own life— like those beautiful summer days so wonderfully described by Emerson as 'sleeping over the broad hills.' In such hours, as Emerson says, 'the world reaches its perfection.' And us? We find ourselves freed, in such hours, from the spell of the ever-watchful Will and become but a pure, disinterested, contemplating eye" (KSB 2: 119–120, n. 500).

21. According to Schopenhauer, our actions are often not motivated by abstract grounds clearly formulated as such by our faculty of reason but rather by impressions received in the present moment, by emotions awoken by these impressions, or by prejudices derived from our cultural surroundings. In such cases, we do not act as individuals—that is to say, on the basis of reasons for action that we have formulated by a personal process of decision—but rather as members of a "herd." It is only when one's reasons for acting are "distinctly known" to oneself that one can be said to be an agent in the authentic sense, inasmuch as one's individual character will then be manifest in one's actions (Schopenhauer [1841] 2009, 303–304). I thank João Constâncio for help on this point.

22. In the *Critique of Pure Reason* Kant ([1787] 1999, A539/B567, 185) explains the difference between empirical and intelligible character as follows: "In a subject of the world of sense we would have, first, an *empirical character*. Through this character the subject's actions, as appearances, would, according to constant natural laws, stand throughout in connection with other appearances and could be derived from these appearances as the actions' conditions; and thus these actions would, in combination with those other appearances, amount to members of a single series of the natural order. Second, one would have to grant to the subject also an *intelligible character*. Through this character the subject is indeed the cause of those actions as appearances, but the character itself is not subject to any conditions of sensibility and is not itself appearance."

23. Nietzsche likewise refuted the inference whereby an individual character was judged to be "good" or "bad": "First of all one calls individual actions good or bad . . . on account of their useful or harmful consequences. Soon, however, one forgets the origin of these designations and believes that the quality 'good' and 'evil' is inherent in the actions themselves, irrespective of their consequences. . . . Then one consigns the being good or being evil to the motives. . . . One goes further and accords the predicate good or evil no longer to the individual motive but to the whole nature of a man out of whom the motive grows as the plant does from the soil. Thus, one successively makes men accountable for the effects they produce, then for their actions, then for their motives, and finally for their nature" (HH 39).

24. Nietzsche seems to want to draw a distinction between "instinct" and "drive" (*Trieb*). The "drive" can be thought of as the axis of transmission of an informational content from one part of the body to another—for example, from the brain of the pianist to his fingers (see NL 1883 7[211], KSA 10: 308: "Separate parts of the body telegraphically linked—i.e. 'drive'"). The "drive," qua process of information-transmission, contains within itself a value judgment, an "interpretation of the stimulus [*Auslegung des Reizes*]" (NL 1881 10[F100], KSA 9: 437). One has to do with an "instinct," however, in cases where such an interpretation acquires autonomy and no longer has any need of a stimulus in order to be spontaneously passed. "I speak of *instinct* in cases where a judgment of some kind (*taste* at its lowest level) is embodied in such a way that it goes into motion spontaneously and no longer needs to wait for the stimulus to trigger it" (NL 1881, 11[164], KSA 9: 505; see also NL 1884 26[94], KSA 11: 175).

25. Emerson too believed that the individual qualities and dispositions which compose the nature of each individual are things inherited from one's ancestors and progenitors. Nevertheless, he added, the combination of these qualities and dispositions is in each case unique and unrepeatable. It is for this reason that each individual is different from every other. See CL, 5; FL, 6.

26. If a person's character is in constant evolution, it follows that one can never know what type of behavior is to be expected from this person. This is a philosophical position which Nietzsche, even if he held to a conception of "character" very different from that which was to be found in Emerson, nevertheless shared with him. It is a position that opposes both thinkers to Schopenhauer. According to Schopenhauer, since character is immutable, one must always expect of a person who has, on one occasion, committed a crime that he or she will, if placed in the same circumstances, commit this same crime once again. Schopenhauer is not denying thereby the possibility of a criminal's being "reformed" and ceasing to engage in criminal behavior; he is simply arguing that, if such a change in behavior occurs, it might possibly be attributed to a growth in knowledge and awareness on the part of the individual in question, but never to a change in this individual's fundamental character. In a notebook from the autumn of 1878, Nietzsche writes, "Emerson says: 'the value of life (lies) in its *inscrutable* possibilities; in the fact that I never know, in addressing myself to a new individual, what may befall me.' This is the mental disposition [*die Stimmung*] of the 'wanderer.' Page 311 in Emerson is important: *the fear of 'the so-called sciences'*—the creator finds a door through which to pass into each individual" (NL 1878 32[15], KSA 8: 562). In the passage to which Nietzsche alludes here Emerson is putting his readers on their guard against such pseudo-sciences as phrenology, which claimed to be able to infer an individual's capacity for thought from the dimensions of his or her cranium. He tells of a "gracious gentleman" who "adapts his conversation to the form of the head of the man he talks with," imagining this to be an indication of his interlocutor's mental capacity. But Emerson, for his part, insists on the human individual's infinite capacity to transfigure and transform his or her own circumstances. "Into every intelligence," concludes Emerson, "there is a door which is never closed, through which the creator passes" (E II, 32; V, 311; Nietzsche marked this passage in the margin with vertical lines and exclamation marks). Emerson rejected phrenology because he refused to look upon thought simply as a product of matter. According to Emerson, thought belongs to a different order of reality altogether from that of the material world and is unconditionally free. Nietzsche does not share Emerson's theoretical presuppositions here. But inasmuch as he sees, like Emerson, the human character as something constantly in transformation, he does share with the American author the conclusion that people are to be judged solely on the basis of our present experience of them. This attitude, which has freed itself of all prejudice, is considered by Nietzsche to be the characteristic attitude of the figure he calls "the wanderer" (see section 3.3.1).

27. Golden (2013, 427) suggests that in NL 1881 13[3] Nietzsche is responding to a passage in Emerson's *Experience*, to which Nietzsche had added, in his personal copy, along with various other markings, some vertical underlinings in the margins. In this passage Emerson maintains that our most formative experiences tend to be the "casual" ones: "We thrive by casualties. Our chief experiences have been casual" (E II, 39; V, 322).

28. Except, perhaps, in the early work *Schopenhauer as Educator*, as we shall see in section 3.2.2.

29. This is why Christine Swanton (2015, 196) defines Nietzsche's ethics as a "virtue ethics of becoming" as opposed to a "virtue ethics of perfection" of the sort propounded by Aristotle and Aristotelians. We shall go further into this question in chapter 3.

30. In the course of his or her life an individual can form very many such "aspirational selves," and they can often be very different one from the other.

31. Nietzsche proposes that we think of the conscious purpose thus arising as like a match which, set to a powder keg, triggers an explosion (the "explosion" here being the individual's action). The idea of "catalytic force" had been suggested to Nietzsche by Julius Robert Meyer (1845, 80; see Abel 1998, 43–49). In other words, a purpose is "something quite insignificant, mostly a small accident," as compared to its effect. Alternatively, one might think of the "conscious purpose" as the helmsman of a boat: although the helmsman determines the direction of the boat's voyage, the force that powers this voyage and makes it possible—the steam (*Dampf*)—is provided by the circumstances and events of the individual's life (GS 360, 225, translation emended: in the English text the term *Dampf* has been erroneously translated as "stream" instead of "steam"). In other words, the conscious purpose, according to Nietzsche, intervenes within an already existing stream of forces rather than generating them. The conscious purpose "does not initiate action; rather, it intervenes in a continuous stream of behaviour that is

prompted by the agent's motives. It reshapes and redirects them, but does not generate them ex nihilo" (Katsafanas 2016, 160).

32. Emerson recommended that the individual should not deny his own constitution but rather make of it "an outlet for his character, so that he may justify his work to their eyes for doing what he does" (i.e., to the eyes of his fellow men; E I, 116; V, 105; Nietzsche underlined "an outlet for his character" and marked the whole passage in its margin with three vertical lines). At the bottom of this page, Nietzsche wrote, "My way of being sick and healthy represents my character to a great degree [*ist ein gutes Stück meines Charakters*]—it justifies itself, and me" (NL 1881 13[10], KSA 9: 620). Nietzsche recognized in this singular condition of a "basically healthy" (EH, Why I Am So Wise 2) nature wracked by chronic illness the very trait that distinguished him from other thinkers and writers. It was from this very unusual set of life conditions, he suggested, that he was able to draw the special plus of his philosophy: the ability to look at life from the viewpoint of sickness and, conversely, sickness from the viewpoint of life. Still in *Ecce Homo*, he writes, "This double birth . . . simultaneously decadent and beginning—this, if anything . . . is, perhaps, my distinction. . . . To be able to look out from the optic of sickness towards *healthier* concepts and values, and again the other way around, to look down from the fullness and self-assurance of the *rich* life into the secret work of the instinct of decadence—that was my longest training, my genuine experience, and if I became the master of anything, it was this. I have a hand for switching *perspectives*: the first reason why a 'revaluation of values' is even possible, perhaps for me alone" (EH, Why I Am So Wise 1).

33. A note of Nietzsche's from 1888 confirms that he was of the view that a strong will leads one to pursue one's objectives with resilience, while a weak will causes one to be a slave of one's own impulses, unable to "keep faith" with the intentions that one has oneself formed: "Weakness of the will: this is a metaphor which can be misleading. For there is no will, and hence neither a strong will nor a weak one. Multiplicity and disaggregation of the impulses, lack of system among them, results as 'weak will'; their coordination under the dominance of a single one results as 'strong will'—in the first case it is oscillation and the lack of a centre of gravity; in the second precision and clarity of direction" (NL 1888 14[219], WLN, 266). This interpretation is confirmed also by what Nietzsche writes in *Twilight of the Idols*: weakness is the "inability not to respond to a stimulus" (TI, Morality as Anti-Nature 2), while strength, on the contrary, is the capacity "not to react at once to a stimulus, but to gain control of all the inhibiting, excluding instincts" (TI, What Germans Lack 6).

34. This training consists in two elements: fear (fear of such public punishments as torture) and guilt (in which the individual inflicts a private, internal punishment on himself or herself). See Richardson 1997, 140.

35. In the first of the three essays forming *On the Genealogy of Morality* Nietzsche observes that if the human being who has been rendered "good," that is to say no longer "dangerous," no longer inspires fear, he thereby no longer inspires respect either: "in losing our fear of man we have also lost our love for him, our respect for him, our hope in him and even our will to be man. The sight of man makes us tired" (GM I 12).

36. Already in a note of 1881 Nietzsche had picked out the capacity to sublimate one's animal drives as that which makes all the difference between "self-tyranny" and "self-mastery": "We *resist* all savage energies for just so long as we do not understand how to make use of them (as force); and for just so long, likewise, do we speak of them as 'evil.' But once we have understood this (i.e. how to use them), we do so no longer!" (NL 1881 11[169], KSA 9: 506). Nietzsche also made use of Emerson's reflections on the potential usefulness of forces which, if they are properly and punctually channeled, can become dangerous in commenting on a phenomenon that had become still more marked in his heyday than it had been in Emerson's, namely, socialism. Nietzsche writes, "To men who with regard to every cause keep in view its higher utility, socialism . . . represents not a problem of *justice* . . . but only a problem of *power*; the situation is the same as in the case of a force of nature, for example steam, which is either pressed into service by man as god of the machine or, if the machine is faulty, if that is to say human calculation in its construction is faulty, blows the machine and man with it to pieces" (HH 446). The comparison between steam and other natural forces on the one hand and certain social and political forces on the other is very likely inspired by Emerson, who had drawn a very similar comparison in his essay *Fate*. As Stack (1992, 140) writes, "He pictures

the 'Fultons and Watts of politics' as controlling the dangerous social and political forces that threaten to topple governments or turn societies upside down."

37. Zarathustra can also be considered the "heir" of the idealized Wagner of the fourth *Untimely Meditation* inasmuch as Zarathustra has proven able to give form to his own character and to acquire "the grand style."

38. It is in this direction that there goes, for example, an excerpt that Nietzsche made from Emerson's *Essays*: "Fashion from the remnants of our animal nature [*Thierheit*] one's own most precious ornament: as with Isis, who had nothing of her metamorphosis left but the lunar horns" (NL 1882 17[6], KSA 9: 666). Emerson's text reads, "In man we still trace the rudiments or hints of all that we esteem badges of servitude in the lower races, yet in him they enhance his nobleness and grace; as Io, in Aeschylus, transformed to a cow, offends the imagination, but how changed, when as Isis in Egypt she meets Jove, a beautiful woman, with nothing of the metamorphosis left but the lunar horns" (E I, 12; V 10).

39. This analysis will offer arguments in support of the thesis advanced by Katsafanas (2016, 152), according to which, for Nietzsche, conscious thought is causally efficacious in modifying our emotions and thereby in forming the motive forces which trigger action. Katsafanas's view here is directly contrary to that of Leiter ([1998] 2001, 294), to the effect that all conscious mental states are, in Nietzsche's estimation, ephiphenomenal. It is a view that is also at odds with the revised view of Leiter (2007, 10–11), according to which the conscious states related to willing are ephiphenomenal. And indeed, several of Nietzsche's aphorisms do appear to support the "epiphenomenalist" thesis of Leiter, for example, D 124, BGE 21, and TI, The Four Great Errors, 3. In fact, I tend to concur with Katsafanas in holding that Nietzsche was neither arguing that conscious thought is totally causally in-effective nor that experiences related to willing, such as intentions and choices, are purely epiphenomenal (Leiter 2007). It was simply that Nietzsche criticized our "ridiculous over-estimation" of the *role* played by consciousness in the production of human action (GS 11). As Katsafanas (2016) rightly observes, our recognition of the fact that conscious thoughts have a causal impact on our motives, and thus on our actions, should not make us forget that (1) "conscious thoughts are not special . . . they are continuous with the rest of the agent's mental economy" (154); (2) they make up only a small part of this mental economy and, as regards the production of action, are only one causal factor among many others (154, 156); and (3) they do not operate in an instantaneous fashion; rather, their effects are actually "gradual and incremental" (156).

40. These observations of Emerson's made a strong impression on Nietzsche right from the day of his first encountering them as a very young man. In his school essay *Freedom of the Will and Fate* (1862) he contrasted the attitude of these peoples distinguished by "energy and force of will" with the attitude of the Christian, in which, he believed, there could be recognized the typology of "the weak and the lazy" as described by Emerson. What Christians, Nietzsche observes, hide behind their mask of humility and acquiescence in God's will is, in the end, nothing other than weakness and cowardice (FWF, 157, translation slightly emended).

41. Obviously, these two notions of the "strong" and the "weak" organism exist on a vast spectrum of different degrees and admixtures of strength and weakness. What is more, these two types, "strong" and "weak," should not be conceived of as stable in themselves: every individual is in constant evolution and undergoes phases throughout life of greater or lesser strength (that is to say, of greater or lesser coordination of their internal drives).

42. I am inclined to agree with the thesis advanced by Acampora (2008, 41) to the effect that the "sovereign individual" is "the goal or the ultimate fruit sought by the process of moralization and refinement of conscience," so long as this "sovereign individual" is not read "as Nietzsche's Ideal." Nietzsche's moral ideal (if one can speak of such a thing at all) is personified rather by Zarathustra or by the characters that prefigure him (the "Free Spirit," etc.). See chapter 3.

43. The notes Nietzsche made in the margins of his personal copy of the German translation of Emerson's *Essays* display a strict thematic unity with the notes contained in the notebook M III 1 of his *Nachlass*, in which there are to be found the first outlines of his notion of the "eternal return" and of the book *Thus Spoke Zarathustra*, which he still planned, at this point, to entitle *Midday and Eternity*. This shows that reading Emerson likely also played a decisive role in the process by which Nietzsche conceived of his newest and most revolutionary book.

44. Fabricius's translation diverges at several points from the English original, which runs, "The world . . . will certainly accept your own measure of your doing and being, whether you sneak about and deny your own name, or whether you see your work produced to the concave sphere of the heavens, one with the revolution of the stars" (E I, 124). The German, for example, clearly omits what is arguably Emerson's central point in this passage: that "the world always accepts" the measure that the individual applies to his or her own work. Fabricius's German conveys only the idea that this measure can easily be gauged from the individual's own attitude. It is this latter idea—really Fabricius's rather than Emerson's—that Nietzsche appears to take up.

45. Given the similarity between the above-cited passage from Emerson and Nietzsche's GS 341, we cannot assume that Nietzsche's writing "Ecce Homo" in the margin of his copy of Emerson indicated merely an intention to cite or refer to the Emersonian passage in question in his own later book of that name (which in any case lay, in the early 1880s, several years in the future and which Nietzsche could hardly have known that he would eventually write). We may rather suppose that Nietzsche believed that, in the passage in question, he had glimpsed the man Emerson, that is to say the essence of the American's philosophy. This essence, as we shall see more clearly in the following chapter, consists in exhorting the individual to be himself or herself, that is to say, to act on the basis of values that he or she has consciously and autonomously chosen.

46. The ascetic priest too offers an interpretation of suffering designed to render it acceptable (Katsafanas 2016, 153). It is for just this reason that Reginster adds that Nietzsche's specific "transvaluation" is distinguished by the fact of its being guided by an "ethics of power" (Reginster 2006, 185).

47. This gloss unmistakably represents a preliminary draft of aphorism 318 of *The Gay Science*, entitled *Wisdom in Pain*. And the fact that we have a published (and therefore presumably proofread and perfected) version of the same set of thoughts goes at least a long way to clearing up some interpretative doubts about the gloss itself. Nietzsche's jotting on the title page of his German copy of the *Essays* reads, "Die Fähigkeit zum Schmerz ist ein ausgezeichneter Erhalter, eine Art Versicherung des Lebens: *dies ist es, was der Schmerz erhalten hat.*" Since the substantive "der Schmerz" is in the nominative case, we are, prima facie, obliged to read this as meaning "This is the thing that pain has sustained" ("the thing," in turn, having presumably to be understood to mean the last-mentioned "Leben" ("life"). The opening of aphorism 318 of *The Gay Science*, however, reads, "Im Schmerz ist so viel Weisheit wie in der Lust: er gehört gleich dieser zu den arterhaltenden Kräften ersten Ranges. *Wäre er dies nicht, so würde er längst zugrunde gegangen sein.*" These last eleven words would amount to an exact paraphrase of the "dies ist es, was der Schmerz erhalten hat" of the Emerson jotting *if* it had been written with just a single letter's difference, as "dies ist es, was *den Schmerz erhalten hat*" (i.e., with the substantive "Schmerz" in the accusative case). Both enunciations would then mean "This (the requirement that life be preserved) is the thing that has sustained pain." With the benefit of the hindsight of this published aphorism, then, it appears at least probable that the first lines of this note, jotted down in his personal copy of Emerson, contain a slip of the pen on Nietzsche's part (which he did not revise since the jotting was intended only for his own use) and that Nietzsche did indeed intend to write "dies ist es, was *den* Schmerz erhalten hat" (i.e., the demands of life have sustained the human capacity for pain). This seems all the more likely given that the jotting on the title page of Nietzsche's copy of the *Essays* is also at other points rather "relaxed" in its adherence to grammatical rules and structures. Toward the end of the note, for example, Nietzsche writes, "Denn die Gerechtigkeit würde wissen, dass der Schmerz und das Übel," an enunciation which breaks off at this point, in disregard of all grammar, without Nietzsche's specifying exactly what it is that justice would know pain and evil to do.

48. In that 318th aphorism of *The Gay Science* already discussed at length in the preceding note Nietzsche points out how pain and suffering are also useful for the conservation of the species. Pain is a kind of alarm bell that alerts us when we are drawing near to our physical limits, and for this reason it is very useful from an adaptational perspective. Certain individuals, however, continues Nietzsche, do not draw back in the face of pain but rather push on forward. These individuals, in other words, have a different emotional reaction to the prospect of suffering. They do not fear it but, on the contrary, interpret it as an indication that they are attempting

enterprises that lie beyond the limits they have hitherto recognized for themselves. These, says Nietzsche, are the "heroic human beings. . . . They are eminently . . . species-enhancing forces" (GS 318). In the 12th aphorism of *The Gay Science*, by contrast, Nietzsche chooses to employ the argument that to make oneself insensible to the experience of pain, as the Stoics teach we ought to do, would also make it impossible for a person to perceive and experience pleasure (see GS 12, but also NL 1881 15[55], KSA 9: 653). Nietzsche is referring here to the Stoics specifically as they were interpreted by Schopenhauer. Schopenhauer ([1819] 1969, 113) praised Stoic ethics highly, taking the Stoic ethical ideal of *ataraxia* as the basis for "a life as free as possible from pain and therefore as happy as possible." In the 324th aphorism of *The Gay Science*, Nietzsche identifies what he calls "the great liberator" in the adoption of a perspective on life as a means to the end of knowledge (GS 324): if the goal and purpose of life is to know and understand as much as possible, then all experiences, even those involving suffering, are to be considered precious. "No, life has not disappointed me. Rather, I find it . . . more desirable . . . every year—ever since the great liberator overcame me: the thought that life could be an experiment for the knowledge-seeker—not a duty, not a disaster, not a deception! *'Life as a means to knowlege'*—with this principle in one's heart one can not only live bravely but also *live gaily and laugh gaily!*" (GS 324, 181).

49. The idealized version of Wagner that Nietzsche presents as a moral example in the fourth of the *Untimely Meditations* is just such a personality: one so strong in its fundamental nature that it is able to draw nourishment even from "poison and misfortune" and grow "strong and healthy in the process" (WB 6).

50. Emerson criticizes modern society, which, by accustoming those who dwell in it to an easy life, tends to weaken their character. Nietzsche, in his 1882 notebook of excerpts from Emerson, summarizes the passage from *Self-Reliance* in which the American philosopher presents this argument in the following way: "Our housekeeping is mendicant, our arts, our occupations, our marriages, our religion we have not chosen, but society has chosen for us. . . . The rugged battle of fate, where strength is born, we shun" (E I, 61–62; V 57). Nietzsche omitted, in the version of this passage that he entered in his notebook, "religion," underlined "rugged battle of fate," and expanded Emerson's "strength" to read "our inner strength [*unsere innere Kraft*]"; see NL 1882 17[39], KSA 9: 672.

51. Also based on this "law of cause and effect" is the key Oriental notion of karma, or rather of karmic retribution, which Emerson mentions in the essay *Fate*. Karma is the effect of our own acts, be they committed in this life or in past ones. When someone dies, the effect of his or her acts does not simply dissolve but passes on as a kind of "inheritance" to the beings in whom his or her soul is reincarnated. Apparently the child inherits the traits of his or her physical parents. But in reality the child inherits the karma of his or her own past lives, and it was indeed as a function of this karma that the soul came to settle upon the new body in which it is reincarnated (Sharma 2005, 227).

52. The word "drei" is not clearly legible. Nietzsche did not write down the two other "errors." As is shown by this note from autumn 1881, he read Emerson at this time also as an antidote to a German culture that he had come to look upon as toxic, characterized as it was by abstract speculation, vain erudition, and sonorous but hollow ideals. The note reads in full: "Of all our present century's authors, the richest in ideas [*der gedankenreichste Autor dieses Jahrhunderts*] has been an American (though his thought too was dimmed and obscured [*verdunkelt*] by German philosophy—Milk glass [*Milchglas*])" (NL 1881 12[151], KSA 9: 602). The "milk glass" referred to here was a kind of glass made in Venice, very fashionable at the time, characterized by an opaque, milky-white tint obtained by the addition of an opacifying powder tin. Inversely, then, to the general reception of Emerson in Germany, which esteemed him only as a follower and imitator of Goethe, Nietzsche praised rather the distinctively American traits in Emerson's thought and deplored German philosophy's influence on him as harmful. It is interesting to note that Gersdorff follows Nietzsche's interpretation here. Early on in Nietzsche's authorial career (on December 3, 1874, to be precise) we find Gersdorff writing to him, "Every day, I read a few pages, or at least a few sentences, of yours, of Emerson's and of Goethe's," as a way of resisting his surrounding German culture or, as Gersdorff calls it in this letter, "the empire of German grandeur [*Reich der deutschen Herrlichkeit*]" (KGB II/4: 616, n. 609).

53. Also in a later note, from 1888, Nietzsche writes, as if as a further commentary on Emerson's claim that there exists a Providence-like "law of compensation," "An external observer would not be able to see in my life any move which didn't hit the mark—like the masters of music, I am able to instantly reinterpret and insert every mistake and randomness within the main thematic structure. In this way, I succeeded even in recognizing a providential fate for myself, that 'everything is for the best'—and thus in deceiving my own self" (Commentary to Volume 4, preliminary version of GS 303; KSA 14. 267; on "unsuccessful attempts [*verunglückten Würfe*]" see also GS 109).

54. Baumgarten (1956, 97) was the first to identify and draw attention to this passage in the *Journals* in which Emerson declares himself to be "a professor of the Joyous Science." This might prompt scholars to ask themselves whether Nietzsche had access to Emerson's *Journals* and drew from these his inspiration for the title of his work of 1882—were this not clearly impossible, since the *Journals* were published only many years after Emerson's death (and even then only in English). Emerson advocates once again the professing of a "Joyous Science"— in opposition to the "tone of sorrow and anxiety" that Alexis de Tocqueville had adopted when speaking of the future of the United States—in the lecture *Prospects*, from January 1842 (EL III, 367–368; see also Tocqueville 1840, 144). Emerson repeats this claim also in the *Discourse at Middlebury College* (July 22, 1845) and in the essay *The Scholar* (see JMN VIII: 9). Nietzsche, however, could not possibly have had access to any of these texts. Baumgarten was forced to conclude, then, that the use of the term *gaya scienza* by both Emerson and Nietzsche was simply a coincidence. Gay Wilson Allen (1981, 468–489), in his monumental intellectual biography of Emerson, comes to the same conclusion. In reality, however, Nietzsche would at least have been aware that the *gaya scienza* of the Provençal poets was also an essential reference in Emerson's philosophy, since he certainly had read the essay *Poetry and Imagination*, contained in the collection *Letters and Social Aims,* which Nietzsche can be proven to have read as early as 1876 (see Zavatta 2006a, 94). Recently, Grimstad (2013, 156) identified the expression "poetry is the *gai science*" in Emerson's lecture *Poetry and English Poetry* (1854). He failed to realize, however, that this lecture was later reprinted in the collection *Letters and Social Aims* under the title *Poetry and Imagination.* Thus, Grimstad finally ends up endorsing the "coincidence" hypothesis. Robert Pippin (2010, 34) excludes, with good reason, the possibility that Nietzsche could have read Emerson's *Journals.* But he assumes, without sufficient evidence, that Nietzsche "could have" been familiar with the lecture *Prospects* (1842). In fact, the editors of the volume of Emerson's *Early Lectures* which contained this lecture stated very clearly that their edition (1972) represented its first publication. A report on the lecture as Emerson delivered it, for the second time, in New York in March 1842 was printed in the *New York Tribune* for March 17, 1842 (EL III, 366), but it would be a stretch of the imagination to believe that Nietzsche could have had access to it. Emerson also uses the term "the Joyous Science" in a lecture entitled *The Scholar* that he gave in 1876, but it is, once again, extremely unlikely that Nietzsche had any access to this. Golden (2013, 406) correctly cites the essay *Poetry and Imagination* as a source of Nietzsche's but, like Grimstad, fails to correctly identify the significance that the term "gay science" bore for Emerson. Grimstad (2013, 32–33) claims, "For both Emerson and Nietzsche, to practice *gaia scienza* is to become attuned to the rhythm of poetry (in the broad sense Emerson uses the word, which would include prose) as it is being set down sentence by sentence." Golden (2013, 406) believes he can corroborate this (erroneous) interpretation and repeats that *gaia scienza* is, for both Emerson and Nietzsche a "method of versification."

55. Nietzsche read the *Neue Essays (Letters and Social Aims)* between April and May 1876. It was Gersdorff who informed him of the book's recent publication. "In a bookshop window," wrote Gersdorff to Nietzsche in the middle of April 1876, "I found R. W. Emerson, *Neue Essays,* translated by Julian Schmidt, 1876; that is to say, the latest news from our magnificent friend" (KGB II/6.1: 312, n. 763). Nietzsche promptly bought the book and devoured it in the space of a month. On May 26 he wrote to Gersdorff, "The *new* Emerson has become a bit old, do you not think? The earlier essays were much richer. He is just repeating himself now. And in the last analysis he is all too much in love with life" (KSB 5: 164, n. 529). Stack (1992, VIII) relates Nietzsche's remarks on the "new Emerson" rather to the Emerson of the second series of the *Essays.* But this hypothesis is easily disconfirmed by the fact that Emerson's first and

second series of essays had been published in Germany together, in the collection *Versuche* (*Essays: First and Second Series*), which Nietzsche had known since his youth. Moreover, the adjective "new" alludes quite explicitly to the title of the German translation of *Letters and Social Aims, Neue Essays*. Nietzsche was right to see in these "new" essays no evolution of Emerson's thought—though not for the reasons he believed. The collection in question in fact consisted of essays from Emerson's younger years not originally intended for publication. They had all been liberally revised by Emerson's young friend James Elliot Cabot, who had been entrusted with this task by Emerson's family after a fire had destroyed the older author's home and, stricken by depression, he felt himself no longer able to work. Emerson always refused to recognize *Letters and Social Aims* as his own work and, in his correspondence with Cabot, consistently refers to it as "your book" (see Emerson 1903, viii).

56. Nietzsche acquired this book in January 1880 and continued to read it at least up until the autumn of 1881 (see Campioni 2010, 15–37; D'Iorio 2013).

57. The values exalted by the Provençal *canzoni* were those composing the knightly virtues and excellences that Nietzsche, in *On the Genealogy of Morality*, considered to be typical of "master morality" (*Herrenmoral*): "war, adventure, hunting, dancing, jousting and everything else that contains strong, free, happy action" (GM I 7).

58. Emerson had long been interested in the fragments of ancient Welsh poetry that he found in Turner (1799–1805). Also in the poem that introduces *Considerations by the Way* he refers to the figure of ancient British myth, Merlin, associating him with a certain "joyful" or "delightful" wisdom:

> Hear what British Merlin sung,
> Of keenest eye and truest tongue.
> . . . Live in the sunshine, swim the sea,
> Drink the wild air's salubrity:
> Where the star Canope shines in May,
> Shepherds are thankful, and nations gay.
> The music that can deepest reach,
> And cure all ill, is cordial speech:
> Mask thy wisdom with delight." (CL, 129; FL, 169)

59. Emerson writes, "There is higher work for Art than the arts. They are abortive births of an imperfect or vitiated instinct. Art is the need to create. . . . Nothing less than the creation of man and nature is its end" (E I, 299; V 265; Nietzsche underlined the second part of this passage, from "Art is the need" up to "end").

60. Oddly, in the draft version of this aphorism Nietzsche had included Emerson among the "poetical men" who seek out spheres where scientific knowledge has not yet penetrated so as to fill these spheres with their own fantasies: "The poet as impostor: he pretends to be a man with knowledge. . . . He makes things more valuable; and people believe that whatever appears more valuable is thereby 'truer,' 'realer.' —Still today, poetical men (e.g. Emerson, Lipiner) like best to seek out those places where our knowledge finds its limits—preferably, indeed, those places where knowledge yields entirely to scepticism. They do this to get out from under the sway of logic. Uncertainty is what they want, since then wizards, premonitions and all that exerts a great effect upon the soul become possible once again" (Commentary to volume 2, KSA 14.165; this draft version of AOM 32 is contained in notebook P II 13c, which would mean that it was written in 1875–1876; see KGW IV/4. 260). According to Nietzsche, then, those who emphasize the limits to scientific knowledge—among whom he counts Emerson—aim, in doing so, to create a space in which ideas can be affirmed that have a fortifying effect upon the human soul. The aim, indeed, is a noble one, but the fact remains that the poet, by doing this, deceives both himself and his fellow human beings. In the published version of *Assorted Opinions and Maxims*, however, Emerson's name disappears from aphorism 32. This could be due to the fact that Nietzsche, prior to his actually publishing this work, reread Emerson's essay *Art*. In this essay Emerson insists that art must not be confined, in order to comfort human beings in their misery, to some sphere distinct and separate from daily life; on the contrary, it must be applied to this daily life in order to shed light on life's inherent value. That Nietzsche read this essay at some point between his composing the

draft version and his composing the definitive published version of AOM 32 is confirmed by a note from the autumn of 1878: "Poets and fanciful philosophers *dream* that Nature (animals and plants) can be understood by love and intuition alone, without any need of science or method. This is the very same position as the metaphysicians adopt with regard to Man" (NL 1878 32[25], KSA 8: 564). At first glance, we might see in this observation the case of a scientist, Nietzsche, criticizing a poet, Emerson. But it was in fact Emerson himself who wrote in the essay *Art*, "We do not know the properties of plants and animals and the laws of nature through our sympathy with the same; but this remains the dream of poets" (E I, 191; V, 170; as a sign of his approval Nietzsche had written in the margin next to this passage the word "good [*Gut!*]"; see Appendix Figure 20).

61. In aphorism 299 of *The Gay Science* Nietzsche explicitly states that what we need to learn from artists is their artistic technique but not in order to employ this ourselves in the creation of such things as statues or paintings; rather we must employ this technique in (re-) creating ourselves and the reality in which we live. "To distance oneself from things until there is much in them that one no longer sees and much that the eye must add *in order to see them at all*, or to see things around a corner and as if they were cut out and extracted from their context, or to place them so that each partially distorts the view one has of the others and allows only perspectival glimpses, or to look at them though coloured glass or in the light of the sunset, or to give them a surface and a skin that is not fully transparent: all this we should learn from artists, while otherwise being wiser than they. For usually in their case this delicate power stops where art ends and life begins; *we*, however, want to be poets of our lives, starting with the smallest and most commonplace details" (GS 299). The participants in Provençal culture are themselves an example here: by creating "courtly love" they also created a new way of looking at relations between the sexes, and thereby a new kind of interaction between men and women: "We owe to the spirit of Provençal culture—which remained pagan (I mean, '*not* Germanic')—the spiritualization of *amor*, or sexual love. All that classical antiquity had achieved was instead a spiritualization of pederasty" (NL 1885, 34[90], KSA 11: 449; see also BGE 260).

62. See also NL 1882 16[5], KSA 9: 673. As a motto for the second edition of the *Gay Science* Nietzsche replaced the quotation from Emerson with the following verse: "I dwell in my own house, / Minding my own ways and no one else's / And I laugh at any master who lacks / The grace to laugh at himself" (Stack 1998, 59, translation slightly emended). Stack proposes the idea that, with this affirmation of independence, Nietzsche was in fact still making reference to Emerson, given that in a note from 1881 Nietzsche had spoken of feeling as if he were "in his own home" in Emerson's *Essays*. And indeed, the *Gay Science* is so permeated by Emerson's influence that it would be vain to deny it (Stack 1998, 61). The great literary critic Harold Bloom has nonetheless interpreted the change of epigram as an instance of what he famously calls "the anxiety of influence" (Stack 1998, 59). Nietzsche, claims Bloom, wanted to declare hereby his independence from all literary models, Emerson included. Even Bloom concedes, however, that in making this declaration of independence Nietzsche became more Emersonian still (Stack 1998, 59).

63. As we have seen in section 2.2.3, for Emerson such a choice is always a free choice, inasmuch as he situates human thought and human will on the "spiritual" as opposed to the "material" plane. For Nietzsche, on the other hand, this choice is determined by a very large range of causes.

64. In 1883, when Nietzsche discovered the etymology of the name Zarathustra, "namely 'golden star' [*Gold-Stern*]," he called it a very happy coincidence and declared that "the whole idea" of his "little book" was already announced in the etymology of this name (KSB 6: 366, n. 406).

65. The same notion had already been expressed by Nietzsche in the example of "*the fruitful field*. —All rejection and negation points to a lack of fruitfulness: if only we were fruitful fields, we would at bottom let nothing perish unused and see in every event, thing and man welcome manure, rain or sunshine" (AOM 332).

66. These are images drawn from *The Conduct of Life* and from the *Essays*: "We live amid surfaces, and the true art of life is to skate well on them" (E II, 35; V, 335); "We must fetch the pump with dirty water, if clean cannot be had" (CL, 32; FL, 41). For the image of the lightning see section 2.2.5.

67. Most people however, complains Emerson, are possessed by illusions which prevent them from appreciating reality: "Men live in their fancy, like drunkards" (E II, 35; V, 315). As a comment on this claim, Nietzsche wrote on the cover of his copy of the *Essays*, "You go through life like drunkards, unconscious [*besinnunglos*]—occasionally you fall down the stairs and, thanks to your drunkenness and unconsciousness, do *not* break your limbs.—Here lies OUR danger! Our muscles are not lax and are terribly much more affected [*leiden furchtbar viel mehr*] than yours!" (NL 1881 13[2], KSA 9: 618; this marginal annotation is then blended into the text of GS 154). With this remark, Nietzsche probably wanted to convey the idea that these people who do nothing but constantly complain tend to provoke discomfort and suffering even in those whose desire is to enjoy and appreciate life. These people, who are continually lamenting about all that is negative in life, are weak personalities who lack the ability to interpret necessity to their own advantage. Nietzsche calls them the "preachers of death" (Z I, On the Hinterwordly), that is to say, those who make of suffering an argument against life and who imagine, as "compensation" for this life painted in the darkest colors, an "afterworld" (*Hinterwelt*) of eternal, immutable essences. Emerson goes on, in the same piece, to say this of such people: "The fine young people despise life, but in me, and in such as with me are free from dyspepsia, and to whom a day is a sound and solid good, it is a great excess of politeness to look scornful. . . . Leave me alone, and I should relish every hour and what it brought me" (E II, 306; V, 316). The "dyspeptic" here is the person who does not know how to draw "nourishment" from the circumstances which surround him or her. Nietzsche was to say, in *Zarathustra*, "Life is a well of joy; but for those out of whom the ruined stomach speaks, the father of gloom, all wells are poisoned" (Z III, Old and New Tablets, 16).

Chapter 3

1. As Simon May (1999, 108) has very correctly explained here, for someone to "become what he or she is" means "to actualize his or her highest possibilities—i.e. to find the most life-enhancing way(s) in which someone with his or her particular endowments of nature, nurture, and life-circumstances (and hence particular historical inheritance) could live."
2. Within Nietzsche's "trilogy of the Free Spirit" (a term with which Nietzsche scholars have come to distinguish and designate the subcorpus formed by the two volumes of HH, D, and GS 1–4), *Daybreak* marks the point at which Nietzsche ceases to use the term *Ehrlichkeit* and puts in its place the term *Redlichkeit* (probity, integrity) (see Lane 2007). In D 456 Nietzsche describes *Redlichkeit* as "*a virtue in process of becoming*" and as "the youngest virtue, still very immature." Whereas *Ehrlichkeit* seems still to belong to that system of customary morality which Nietzsche has undertaken to critique, the same cannot be said of *Redlichkeit* (see Bamford 2015, 89). We may suppose that *Ehrlichkeit* represents "honesty" specifically in the sense of a transparency of the human conscience in the face of God, while *Redlichkeit* represents that "will to truth" which motivates the scientific spirit. In GS 357 Nietzsche in fact explicitly points out that it is the "Christian conscience," sublimated and refined, that lies, in the last analysis, at the origin of the "scientific conscience," this latter consisting in a will to "intellectual cleanliness at any price."
3. By discovering the origin of our values we will judge these values differently and, in time, adopt new ones. This is a perfect example of how conscious thought—in time—is capable of modifying our emotions and our drives. See also Katsafanas 2016, 150.
4. Swanton (2015, 158) observes that Aristotle too assumes that there exist differentiated forms of universal virtues. For example, "magnificence is a differentiated form of the universal virtue of excellence in dispositions to spend resources. Only those possessing great resources should be magnificent; those of more modest means should be merely liberal."
5. Identified as prominent among such "formal excellences" in Nietzsche's moral teaching have been such qualities as creativity (BGE 212; see Reginster 2007), the capacity to give form to things, in particular to oneself (GS 290; see Ridley 1998, 136), health (GM I 7, GM III 15–16; see Harcourt 2011), self-love or self-affirmation (GS 341; see Janaway 2007, 253), freedom or self-rule (TI, Skirmishes 38; see Pippin 2010, 108), self-overcoming (BGE 257; see Pippin 2010, 120; Reginster 2007, 51), the capacity to seek out and overcome obstacles

(Swanton 2005, 189; Reginster 2007, 36), and ("undistorted") will to power (Reginster 2007, 42; Swanton 2005, 179).

6. According to Swanton (2015, 120), will to power is distorted when it is (a) "unsublimated," as in the case of episodes of physical aggression, or when it is (b) "neurotically expressed," as in the case of the resentment of the weak individual toward the strong. Swanton views as cases of distorted will to power also those cases in which this latter is (c) "enfeebled" or (d) completely absent. Swanton classifies (c) and (d) as "forms [of will to power] which are distorted but not quantitatively powerful," while (a) and (b) are "forms [of will to power] which are distorted but quantitatively powerful" (120). It seems to me that it is simpler to say that at the basis of virtue there must be an undistorted will to power, that is to say, this must be (1) present in some significant way (a condition that rules out (c) and (d)) and (2) not distorted (a condition that rules out (a) and (b)).

7. In a note of 1888 Nietzsche defines the universe as a formation constituted by "quantities of force [Kraft-Quanta] the essence of which consists in exercising power over all other quantities of force" (NL 1888 14[81], KSA 13: 261). In this way Nietzsche simply removes from the philosophical equation that "being" which metaphysicians had hitherto postulated to exist behind all "becoming." He is very clear about this. In a note from 1887 we read, "If I think away all the relationships, all the 'qualities,' all the 'activities' of a thing, then the thing does *not* remain behind: because thingness was only a *fiction added* by us, out of the needs of logic, thus for the purpose of designation, communication" (NL 1887 10[202], WLN, 206). Müller-Lauter (1998, 36) comments that will to power "is not something that forms the foundation of the world, that produces life, or expresses itself as art, or is realized in the form of humanity." Rather, to say that Nature, art, life, religion, morality, etc. (see NL 1888 14[72], KSA 13: 254) "are" just will to power means saying that all these things are structured in a certain way. Likewise, when Nietzsche writes that a nation or an individual "has" its own will to power this means that this nation or this individual *actually consists* in a specific will to power, that is to say, in a particular configuration of forces (39).

8. "Pleasure and unpleasure are mere consequences, mere accompanying phenomena—what man wants, what every smallest part of a living organism wants, is an increment of power" (NL 1888 14[174], WLN, 264).

9. With this expression ("One thing is needful [Eins ist Noth]") Nietzsche is alluding specifically to a passage from the Christian gospels (Luke 10: 42) in which Jesus uses these words to respond to Martha, who complains that her sister Mary, instead of helping her to serve and minister to Jesus, who has entered their house as a guest, is simply sitting at Jesus's feet and listening to all He has to say. Jesus says, "Martha, thou art careful and troubled about many things. . . . But one thing is needful."

10. That these three figures are closely linked to one another and represent, indeed, three stages on a single path is stated explicitly by Nietzsche in a letter to Peter Gast from April 1883. Giving his friend suggestions as to how to interpret his latest book, *Thus Spoke Zarathustra*, Nietzsche writes, "Everything was already present as a promise in *Schopenhauer as Educator*, but from *Human, All Too Human* to the Overman [Übermenschen] there was quite a long way still to go" (KSB 6: 364, n. 405). As always, Nietzsche builds into his philosophy autobiographical points of reference. "Schopenhauer as educator," the "free spirit," and "Zarathustra" in fact personify three stages in that journey toward full self-realization as an individual that Nietzsche himself had traversed. In a certain sense these three figures represent Nietzsche's alter egos. He writes to Overbeck in 1884, "I *lived as* I had prefigured (above all in *Schopenhauer as Educator*). In case you bring *Zarathustra* on holiday with you, bring along the aforementioned piece of writing as well to make a comparison between them (its *defect* is that it actually speaks almost only about me, not about Schopenhauer—but I did not yet know it when I wrote it)" (KSB 6: 518, n. 524).

11. During the summer holidays of 1863 Nietzsche had planned to compose for his "friends" a résumé of *The Conduct of Life* along with "extracts from all the essays" (NL 1863 15[17], KGW I/3: 144). As a reminder, he noted the titles of those two essays by Emerson which had perhaps left the deepest impression on him—namely, *Wealth* and *Beauty*—as well as the topic "on philosophy in life." In the end, Nietzsche compiled only two series of extracts: the first from the essay *Beauty* alone (NL 1863 15[36], KGW I/3: 180–182), and the second mixing

extracts from *Beauty* (not included in the first series or repeated here in slightly divergent formulations) with extracts from the essay *Power* (NL 1863 15A[5], KGW I/3: 227–228), which evidently must have supplanted *Wealth* by this time in Nietzsche's personal grading of the various essays' worth and importance. For the most part Nietzsche follows Emerson's text to the letter. If he makes changes, these never significantly alter the meaning. It was this second series of excerpts that Nietzsche used some months later as catalysts for his own reflections during the composition of the essay *Can the Envious Man Be Really Happy?*

12. As Lasch (1991, 270) observes, Emerson seems to issue a sort of "tax on desire" that forbids people to yearn for whatever they have not worked for. This principle is the perfect basis for the political morality of "producerism" (265), which condemns every attempt to get something for nothing. "Unearned increment" is the producer's version of hubris, or pride, which defies limits, overrides natural boundaries, challenges fate, and thus provokes the retaliation of the gods (270).

13. The original English passage runs, "Any real increase of fitness to its end is an increase of beauty" (CL, 154).

14. He then goes on to add a few more deviations from Emerson's text—for example by shortening Fabricius's (faithful) rendering of Emerson's "no kernel of nourishing corn [*kein Samenkörnchen des nährenden Getreides*]" to simply "kein Samenkörnchen."

15. Nietzsche had already written in *Schopenhauer as Educator*, "There exists no more repulsive and desolate a creature in the world than the man who has evaded his genius and who now looks furtively to left and right, behind him and all about him" (SE 1).

16. In a passage that Nietzsche summed up in his notebook of 1882 (NL 1882 17[20], KSA 9: 668) Emerson states that the trait which is common to all great men of all eras is precisely this fact, that they rely on themselves alone, calling into question all the truths received from others: "To believe your own thought, to believe that what is true for you in your private heart, is true for all men,—that is genius ... the highest merit we ascribe to Moses, Plato, and Milton, is that they set at naught books and traditions, and spoke not what men but what they thought" (E I, 37; V 32).

17. The first work of his in which Emerson confronts the necessity of defending one's own right to individuality, that is to say, one's right to independence of thought and moral autonomy, against external pressures, is the *Divinity School Address* of 1838. In this lecture Emerson accuses Christianity of maintaining humanity in a state of moral immaturity inasmuch as it does not allow people to seek the truth, autonomously, themselves but rather forces them to receive this truth "at second hand": "Men have come to speak of the revelation as somewhat long ago given and done" (NAL, 84). In reality, Emerson maintained, God reveals Himself directly to every human being in his or her best moments. To seek Him elsewhere than within oneself is to lose Him. For this reason, Emerson exhorts young men aspiring to become pastors to assign more importance to those things which they personally, inwardly believe to be true than to anything they find in Holy Scripture. "The sublime is excited in me by the great stoical doctrine, Obey thyself. That which shows God in me, fortifies me. That which shows God out of me, makes me a ward and a wen" (NAL, 82–83). In 1865 a translation of Emerson's *Divinity School Address* (1838) appeared in Karl Scholl's collection of *Freie Stimmen aus dem heutigen Frankreich, England und America über Lebensfragen der Religion* under the title *Die zwei Hauptfehler des geschichtlichen Christentums*. There is no direct evidence that Nietzsche bought this book or read it. Nevertheless, he had surely already acquired some news of Emerson's *Divinity School Address* through Philip Schaff's (1855) book *Amerika, die politischen socialen, kirklich-religiösen Zustände in den Vereinigten Staaten von Nordamerika*, which, during the early months of 1865, he used to prepare a lecture delivered to the Gustav-Adolf Verein in Bonn. This was an association established by Bonn's Protestant community, a minority in the predominantly Roman Catholic city and region (KSB 2: 26, n. 454). Its members contributed either financially or by offering courses on subjects in which they possessed some special competence. Nietzsche had begun to study philology and theology at Bonn University the previous year, and in March 1865 he gave a lecture there on "the religious-denominational situation of Germans in North America" (KSB 2: 47, n. 464), which was intended to provide a panoramic view of the various Protestant denominations spread across the United States. Preparing this lecture, Nietzsche had read Schaff's essay (see KSB 2: 46, n. 463). Schaff

praised the freedom of religion that reigned in the New World, attributing to this freedom the continuing vitality of religious feeling in the United States, which stood in such sad contrast to the decline of this feeling in Europe. Schaff's weighty study also included information on the "scandalous" case of Emerson. It told how Emerson, having been ordained a minister of the Unitarian Church in 1829, quit his ministry only three years later, speaking out against such key items of Christian faith as the authority of Scripture, the divinity of Christ, and the notions of guilt and penance. Schaff also told how, in the *Divinity School Address* he went on to give in 1838 in the capacity of a free and unaffiliated man of letters, Emerson propounded the notions of a divinity inherent in each individual and the equal capacity of all individuals to become recipients of divine ideas and insisted, on this basis, on every individual's right to moral autonomy. Schaff's (1855, 142) account concurred in the view that this course taken by Emerson was a "scandal," stating that the "dangerous scepticism and pantheism" that he had propounded in his writings and public lectures and sometimes even from the pulpit had spread from New England into the other states of the United States "to the great sorrow not only of the orthodox Puritans, but even of all earnest and sober-minded Unitarians." Although the Unitarian Church was extremely tolerant as regards dogmatic issues, added Schaff, it was left with no choice in the end but to excommunicate Emerson. Without ever explicitly mentioning the name "Emerson," Nietzsche recounted all this to his audience at the Gustav-Adolf Verein as proof of the fact that the United States, for all its vaunted religious freedom, was a country where, once one had chosen one's religious denomination, one was obliged to adhere strictly to that denomination's principles. "A minister who did not believe in the divinity of Christ, in the inspired nature of Scripture, or in the necessity that all be converted," said Nietzsche, "would perhaps not be imprisoned there nor burnt at the stake; but he would most certainly be removed from his position and, if necessary, excommunicated" (KGW I/4, 20–21).

18. It was this that Nietzsche tried to explain to his friend Deussen, who had urged him to write a refutation of Schopenhauer's philosophy: "We cannot criticize a vision of the world, we can just share it, or not. . . . He who cannot smell a rose has not the right to criticize it. And if he can smell it, *à la bonne heure,* he will not feel like criticizing it any longer" (KSB 2: 328, n. 595). Nietzsche had reached this conclusion already in 1866, following his reading of Friedrich Albert Lange's *History of Materialism* (KSB 2: 159–160, n. 517).

19. Emerson was familiar with the central themes of Schopenhauer's philosophy and shared with him the notion that Nature was entirely informed by a spiritual force definable as "Will." Nevertheless, as Stack (1992, 7) observes, "No doubt but that [Emerson] would have sighed when he discovered that Schopenhauer had concluded that this cosmic 'Will' in the form of the 'will to live' had to be stilled, denied. For what Schopenhauer condemned, he praised; what Schopenhauer thought should be denied, he affirmed."

20. Emerson's doctrine of self-reliance has, nonetheless, been misunderstood by many. For example, in his address to the Yale class of 1981, President A. Bartlett Giamatti defined this doctrine as a "ruthless worship of power and justification of brutality and force." In other words, Giamatti sees Emerson's "self-reliant individual" as the precursor of the modern unscrupulous businessman: the profoundly egotistical entrepreneur who, in pursuit of his own interest, will not hesitate to perpetrate any and every sort of abuse in "contemporary politics and economy" (Giamatti 1981, quoted in Kazin 1982, 3).

21. "For the most part we but half express ourselves and are ashamed of that divine idea which each of us represents. —One must give his whole heart over to his work: in the mere attempt our genius deserts us; no muse, no hope stands by us," summarizes Nietzsche in his 1882 notebook (NL 1882 17[23], KSA 9: 669).

22. As Mikics (2003, 117) has very correctly remarked, the freeing of oneself from inauthenticity that Nietzsche urges in the third *Untimely Meditation* "requires an anti-Schopenhauerian definition of how and why we might discover that we still lead a guilty or inadequate existence: not a realization of universally shared human weakness, but a confrontation with one's own answerable nature, its promises and avoidances. . . . This hope is deeply Emersonian, and not at all Schopenhauerian."

23. The theme of the conflict between the authentic thinker and society is addressed also in the next paragraph, which deals with the clash between free spirits and fettered spirits.

24. In 1882 Nietzsche copied into his notebook, "To be obliged to worship is oppressive for him; he would like to steal the fire from the Creator and live apart from him" (NL 1882 17[16], KSA 9: 668; see E I, 25; V 23). See GS 300: "Did Prometheus first have to *imagine* having *stolen* light and pay for it before he could finally discover that he had created light *by desiring light*, and that not only man but also *god* was the work of *his own* hands and clay in his hands?"

25. Here, Emerson is using the term "skepticism" in the following sense: refusal to make one's own the dominant opinion without first having subjected it to critique. Skepticism, in other words, is for Emerson the opposite of veneration of and submission to authority; it is a placing in doubt of that which had hitherto been considered incontrovertible. This, however, is not the only sense in which Emerson uses the term "skepticism." As we shall see in the next chapter, he also uses "skepticism" to mean the refusal to look upon any vision of the world, even one's own, as final and definitive.

26. Nietzsche in fact slightly miscites this German edition of Emerson. Fabricius's translation reads (p. 43) "gross sein ist missverstanden sein"; Nietzsche's note reads "Gross sein ist missverstanden *werden* (italics added)."

27. Nietzsche's excerpt comprises only the first part of this remark: "When a God comes among men, they do not recognize him" (NL 1882 17[17], KSA 9: 668).

28. In a passage heavily underlined by Nietzsche, and in the margin of which the younger man wrote "Ego" as a sign of his strong approval, Emerson states, "Those who live to the future must always appear selfish to those who live to the present" (E II, 60; V, 347; Nietzsche also wrote "1881" in the margin here; see Appendix Figure 26).

29. Nietzsche did not just use Emerson's observations to give form to the figure of the "self-reliant thinker" as a militant thinker engaged in a struggle with his own era. These observations were also useful to Nietzsche in interpreting his own personal experience and bringing his courage and resilience to maturity. In fact, the "philosophy for free spirits" that he elaborated from 1876 onward was neither understood nor appreciated by the readers he had acquired as a classicist and a Wagnerian. The publication of *Human, All Too Human* (1878) was described by the publisher himself as "a terrible failure": of the print run of 1,000 copies, only 120 were sold (KSB 5: 419, n. 857). "Were it not for the feeling I have of the great fruits that my new philosophy will surely bear," wrote Nietzsche to his friend Malwida in 1878, "I might well feel frightfully alone" (KSB 5: 331, n. 725). Having recourse once again to Emerson, Nietzsche reminded himself that, if society is characterized by mediocrity and conformism, the "untimeliness" evidenced by his isolation and by the lack of response to his books could be interpreted as a sign of high moral and intellectual stature. Later Nietzsche was to welcome the resounding failure of *Thus Spoke Zarathustra* to win over the reading public as an encouragement to continue down the road he had set out on: "Every word of my *Zarathustra* is victorious scorn, and more than scorn, for the ideals of this age," he wrote to his sister in 1883. "It is absolutely *necessary* that I be misunderstood; indeed, I must myself see to it that I am *badly* understood and *despised*" (KSB 6: 439, n. 459).

30. Nietzsche himself was to remind himself of this truth in the very darkest years of his *Freigesterei* when, through his insistence on following his vocation, he ended up uncomprehended and abandoned not just by the reading public but even by his dearest friends. In a private note to himself written in 1881 Nietzsche exhorted and encouraged himself in words that might have been Emerson's: "Go on becoming what you are [*Werde fort und fort, der, der du bist*]—the teacher and builder of yourself [*der Lehrer und Bildner deiner selbst*]. You are not a writer, you write just for yourself!" (NL 1881 11[297], KSA 9: 555). In a letter from July 1882 Nietzsche informs his friend Erwin Rohde of the publication of his latest book, *The Gay Science*, and adds that this book represents the completion of a journey on which he had set out in 1876. From this date on, writes Nietzsche, he had followed nothing but his own inward necessity, without any further thought of what might please any potential audience. He closes with the formulation "Mihi ipsi scripsi" (KSB 6: 226, n. 267; the same formulation recurs in KSB 6: 199, n. 235 and KSB 6: 202, n. 238).

31. "The way to speak and write what shall not go out of fashion, is, to speak and write sincerely. The argument which has not power to reach my own practice, I may well doubt, will fail to reach yours. But take Sidney's maxim: 'Look in thy heart and write.' He that writes to himself writes to an eternal public" (E I, 125).

32. Emerson read the *Confessions* of Saint Augustine in 1839 (see Richardson 1995, 316).

33. The passage from Emerson actually runs, "A wise and good soul [*frommer Mensch* in the German text] ... never needs look for allusions personal and laudatory in discourse. He hears the commendation, not of himself, but, more sweet, of that character he seeks, in every word that is said concerning character, yea, further, in every fact that befalls,—in the running river, and the rustling corn" (E I, 6–7; V 4–5; Nietzsche partially underlined this passage).

34. "A man" said Oliver Cromwell, "never raises so high as when he knows not whither he is going" (E I, 265; V 237; Nietzsche marked this passage in the margin with no fewer than seven vertical lines). In fact, as has been pointed out (see Cavell 2005, 216; Conant 2001, 236), Emerson was most likely not quoting Cromwell directly but rather his younger contemporary, the Cardinal de Retz, who quoted, or possibly invented, these alleged words of Cromwell in his *Memoirs*, composed some years after the latter's death.

35. In September 1875 Nietzsche was informed by Gersdorff of the appearance in German translation of yet another collection of Emerson's writing: *English Traits*, a collection of lectures that Emerson had given during his second tour of England in 1847–1848 and that had been published in English in 1856. It was a work that enjoyed little resonance in Germany. Gersdorff, however, wrote of it with great enthusiasm: "With Emerson's *Englische Charakterzüge* I have succeeded in giving great joy and entertainment to my family. My dear aunt, who is very well acquainted with England, its language and literature, always thanks me for introducing her to this book" (KGB II/6,1: 223, n. 712). We do not, however, know whether Nietzsche read this book, given the absence of documentary evidence either way. Gersdorff wrote to Nietzsche about Emerson again in April of the following year, saying, "Emerson's essays have been a daily source of strength to me even during this hard military service. One breathes a fresher air when one is acquainted with this pure and free soul. I have not lived, then, totally in vain" (KGB II/6.1: 316, n. 766). It is not clear which essays of Emerson's Gersdorff is referring to here: whether *English Traits*, as Hubbard (1958, 10) supposes; Gersdorff's already beloved *Essays: First and Second Series*; or the *Neue Essays*, the German translation of *Letters and Social Aims*, which Gersdorff had recently discovered by pure chance (KGB II/6.1: 312, n. 763).

36. We concur with Stack's (1992, 27–29) thesis to the effect that it was Emerson who suggested to Nietzsche a central theme of the latter's middle period, namely, that, while illusions are necessary to life, the true philosopher nonetheless has the duty to free both himself or herself and others of the self-deception involved in them. In the summer of 1878 Nietzsche made reference in his notebook to the little anthology *Über Goethe und Shakespeare*, which gathered together Emerson's essays on these two writers published in *Representative Men*. Nietzsche's note, clearly truncated or left incomplete, reads, "I know that independence of thought upon this earth has been increased and that whoever declares himself against me— see Emerson, Goethe, p. 9" (NL 1878 27[12], KSA 8: 488). We do not know exactly what meaning Nietzsche intended to convey with this phrase, also—indeed, above all—because it breaks off without being completed in a grammatically satisfactory way. On the particular page of the essay on Goethe to which Nietzsche refers Emerson wishes for the emergence of "one sane man with adequate powers of expression to hold up each object of monomania in its right relations" (RM, 153; see GS 9). By detaching any object from the web of relationships that link it to other objects, Emerson goes on, one makes of it a little idol. What is needed, then, is a person of sufficiently broad vision to unmask this idolatrous illusion and restore the judgment of the many to some form of sobriety. Nietzsche must have found in these pages of Emerson's a perfect description of the task he had set himself: to develop "a *chemistry* of the moral, religious and aesthetic conceptions and sensations" which would show the "human, all too human" origin of all "higher values" (HH 1). Such an enterprise, as we read in the passage from Emerson, adds to "the independence of thought on earth" but is inevitably bound to meet with incomprehension and even condemnation.

37. In Golden's (2013) view, Nietzsche is making a critical reference to Emerson at D 111, where he speaks of the "admirers of objectivity," that is to say, of those who aspire to achieve "*neutrality of feeling* [Neutralität der Empfindung] or 'objectivity.'" These people believe that such a condition is reserved for the genius alone, or for people gifted with a special intellectual integrity. In reality, however, concludes Nietzsche, objectivity is the fruit of training. In *On the Genealogy of Morality* Nietzsche expounds the theory that "objectivity" is not secured merely

by the absence of emotional reactions vis-à-vis the objects of our cognition but rather by the ability to dominate these objects and evaluate them critically. This being the case, the greater the range of different emotional reactions we are able to draw into consideration, the closer we will approach true "objectivity" (GM III 12). In short, for Nietzsche, neutrality of feeling and emotion is not just something impossible to attain; it is not even something that ought to be aspired to. Nevertheless, in the passage that Nietzsche recopied into his notebook, we do find Emerson defining just what he himself means by "objectivity": the ability of a certain kind of "eye" to find nourishment in everything. This "objectivity" of Emerson's is certainly not identical with the "neutrality of feeling" toward which Nietzsche adopts a critical stance; on the contrary, it closely approximates Nietzsche's own definition of objectivity as the ability to draw into consideration a wide range of different points of view without making any one of them a cognitive "absolute." On the other hand, Golden (2013, 400) himself acknowledges that Emerson is a "philosopher of moods," as Cavell (2003, 26) defines him, who praises "objectivity" at no other point anywhere in the *Essays* than the one we have just discussed and who, moreover, in the second edition of 1847 (see next note) decided to eliminate even this one reference to the notion in question. For this reason, Golden's thesis to the effect that Nietzsche is making, at D 111, a polemical reference to Emerson, or at least distancing himself from the position taken by Emerson, appears to me to be untenable.

38. This passage had been omitted from the second, revised English edition of the *Essays* (1847). In this revised text Emerson's intention seems rather to be to emphasize the potential dangers of "intellectual nomadism," so that he writes, "The pastoral nations were needy and hungry to desperation; and this intellectual nomadism, in its excess, bankrupts the mind through the dissipation of power on a miscellany of objects. The home-keeping wit, on the other hand, is that continence or content which finds all the elements of life in its own soil; and which has its own perils of monotony and deterioration, if not stimulated by foreign infusions" (E I 2nd edition, 13). Nietzsche's paraphrase of this Emerson passage in his 1882 notebook, when retranslated into English from the German, is as follows: "Intellectual nomadism is the gift of objectivity or the gift to find everywhere a feast for the eyes. Every human being, every individual thing, is my discovery, my possession: the love which is inspired in him for everything *smoothes* his forehead" (NL 1882 17[13], KSA 9: 667).

39. Emerson maintained that whoever sought truth had necessarily to cease to concern themselves with their "image in society." Society demands coherence and consistency, but those who are pursuing truth, in order to remain true to themselves, must be constantly changing their opinion. "A foolish consistency is the hobgoblin of little minds, adored by little statesmen and philosophers and divines," writes Emerson, "With consistency a great soul has simply nothing to do" (E I, 47; V 44). Nietzsche follows Emerson here, writing that the "knowledge-seeker" does not concern himself or herself about the censure of society he or she might receive for having changed his or her views and opinions (GS 324; see D 56). Rather, the "knowledge-seeker"—the free spirit—interprets this censure as a sign of merit, because it indicates that his or her knowledge is growing. "We are misidentified—for we ourselves keep growing, changing, shedding old hides; we still shed our skins every spring; we become increasingly younger, more future-oriented, taller, stronger. . . . Like trees we grow . . . like all life!" (GS 371).

40. In a notebook that he kept during the autumn of 1878 Nietzsche set down the following brief reference to the *Essays*: "Emerson, p. 331 of the *Essays*: 'The life of truth is cold and so far mournful; but it is not the slave, etc.'" (NL 1878 30[103], KSA 8: 540). The reference here is specifically to the essay *Experience*, which Nietzsche had already used during his Schulpforta years to work out some ideas regarding the impossibility of achieving any objective knowledge of reality (i.e., any knowledge of it not mediated by our own psychophysical state). To know oneself to be subject to such grave cognitive limitations tends to cast most human beings into despair and make them doubt whether such a thing as "knowledge" is possible at all. Only the strongest of personalities will continue, in awareness of such limitations, still to pursue truth undaunted. Emerson recommends, "We must hold hard to this poverty, however scandalous, and by more vigorous self-recoveries, after the sallies of action, possess our axis more firmly. The life of truth is cold and so far mournful; but it is not the slave of tears, contritions and perturbations" (E II, 46; V, 331).

41. I prefer to translate "geistige Nomadenthum" by "intellectual nomadism" (rather than by the "spiritual nomadism," chosen, for example, by Hollingdale in the text published as part of the Cambridge edition of Nietzsche's works) so as to bring out Nietzsche's intellectual debt to Emerson.

42. The ability to place one's own self and one's views in question corresponds to the second meaning that Emerson assigns to the term "skepticism," whereas the term in its first meaning is the "skepticism" that Emerson ascribes to Prometheus, that is, the ability to place in question the views of others (see section 3.2.5).

43. Golden (2013, 403) rightly observes that for Emerson, as for Nietzsche, "a persistent antagonism" is necessary if thought is really to develop. Emerson, in his *Journals*, often recurs to this theme, recognizing that what fascinates a thinker most is that which is different from him or her: "I see plainly the charm which belongs to Alienation or Otherism. 'What wine do you like the best, O Diogenes?' 'Another's,' replied the sage. What fact, thought, word, like we best? Another's" (JMN 5: 254).

44. For example, says Jensen (2013, 127–128), a person observing an object through the medium of water may be able to arrive at a consensus about this object with other persons observing it through the same medium, but he or she will not be able to arrive at such a consensus with people observing the same object through a different medium, such as air.

45. It is on the basis of this theory that Jensen (2013, 127) interprets the praise Nietzsche gives to the "objectivity" of Burckhardt. He sees Nietzsche's appreciation of this "objectivity" as having emerged from the fact that Burckhardt belonged to the same psychological type as Nietzsche himself; that is, Burckhardt had a "configuration of drives" similar to Nietzsche's one which resulted in the two men's sharing a similar distortion or diffraction of vision.

46. Even the "rich" self, however, will be constantly in danger of disintegrating under the pressure of opposed points of view. As Nietzsche writes at HH 230, "The free spirit is always weak, especially in actions: for he is aware of too many motives and points of view and therefore possesses an uncertain and unpracticed hand." See also BGE 42.

47. See also WS 249, in which Nietzsche says of the free spirit, "He needs no one to refute him: he does that for himself."

48. The title itself that Emerson chose for his collection, *Essays*, is intended to make clear the provisional status that he assigned to his own reflections. He also surely wanted to pay homage, with this title, to one of his own favorite authors, Montaigne, who had given this title to his principal work. In the essay devoted to Montaigne in *Representative Men*, which Nietzsche, however, could not have read before 1884, Emerson characterizes Montaigne as the skeptic par excellence, remarking that Montaigne knew how to "bear the disappearance of things he was wont to reverence, without losing his reverence" (RM, 105). In other words, the skeptic that Emerson has in mind does not lose faith in the notion of truth even when he is obliged to place in question things that he had formerly considered to be true; nor does he lose the ability to love and to venerate even when the objects toward which he directs his love or his veneration happen to change. This roughly corresponds to what Nietzsche defines as "the scepticism of strength."

49. Why, we may ask, is it necessary, in order to be an "experimenter," to overcome one's own emotions and values (to be "beyond love and hate, and good and evil"), to hide and dissemble (to be "a cheater with a clear conscience"), and, above all, what does it mean "to live on the blood of other souls"? In order better to understand what Nietzsche means here it is useful to place this gloss in relation to an unpublished note from around the same period in which he observes, "In order to know, I have need of all my instincts, the good ones as well as the bad ones, and I would very soon meet my end if I did not consent to be hostile toward the things around me, and mistrustful, cruel, malignant, vengeful, dissimulating of my true self etc." (NL 1881 11[73], KSA 9: 469–470). As Nietzsche eloquently explains at GM III 12, "knowing" is not a purely intellectual operation but also involves emotions and instincts. Whoever wants to achieve the broadest possible view of things or, as Nietzsche puts it at GM III 12, approximate to something that can be called "objectivity," must welcome within themselves a multiplicity of such emotions and instincts which will provide them with different viewpoints on the same thing. With the expression "live on the blood of other souls" Nietzsche means to convey the idea of momentarily transcending one's own restricted ego in order to immerse

oneself in the being of the "other soul" and, for a moment, to see the world as this "other soul" sees it, feel the world as this "other soul" feels it.

50. Nietzsche was to copy this marginal note made in his copy of the *Essays* into a notebook for the year 1882. (It is at this point that he added the word "ego," indicating that his opinion on this matter concorded with Emerson's; see NL 1882 17[18], KSA 9: 668.)

51. Nietzsche quotes Emerson's parable of the Sphinx once again in a note written on one of the blank pages at the end of his copy of Emerson's *Essays*: "Here you sit, relentless as the curiosity that compelled me to you: well then, Sphinx, I am, like you, a questioner: we have this abyss in common—is it possible we spoke with one and the same voice?" (NL 1881 13[22], KSA 9: 622). This time Nietzsche identifies not with the person to whom the riddle is posed but rather with the poser of it, the Sphinx herself. Perhaps he sympathizes with the Sphinx here because the doctrine of Eternal Return is also communicated to Zarathustra by way of a riddle: "To you, bold searchers, researchers [*Suchern, Versuchern*], and whoever put to terrible seas with cunning sails / . . . to you alone I tell the riddle that I *saw*" (Z III, On the Vision and the Riddle).

52. In the parable *On the Way of the Creator* Zarathustra says that, for those who wants to become creators, it is not enough that they free themselves from all constrictions and subjection. They must also be able to forget that they were ever constricted, so that their mind can become occupied exclusively by the positive thought of that which they want to express: "You call yourself free? Your dominating thought I want to hear, and not that you escaped from a yoke . . . / Free from what? What does Zarathustra care! But brightly your eyes should signal to me: free for what?" (Z I, On the Way of the Creator).

53. Nietzsche wrote "thierische Masse" where Fabricius's 1858 German translation of the *Essays* had had "thierische Macht." However, his change discloses the real meaning of the original English text, which the German translator had failed to catch: "For non-conformity the world whips you with its displeasure. . . . Yet is the discontent of the multitude more formidable than that of the senate and the college. It easy enough for a firm man who knows the world to brook the rage of the cultivated classes. Their rage is decorous and prudent, for they are timid as being very vulnerable themselves. But when to their feminine rage the indignation of the people is added, when the ignorant and the poor are aroused, when the unintelligent brute force that lies at the bottom of society is made to growl and mow, it needs the habit of magnanimity and religion to treat it godlike as a trifle of no concernment" (E I, 46). In this passage Emerson adds to the Greek virtue of "magnanimity" a reference to "religion," which Nietzsche, for obvious reasons, chooses to omit.

54. A further source of Nietzsche's here is book IV, chapter 3 (*Magnanimity*) of the *Nicomachean Ethics*, in which Aristotle gives embodiment to his own ideal of virtue in the figure of the *megalopsychos*, literally "the great minded" or "great souled" man. The "great minded man" of Aristotle is completely concentrated upon his own self. Such concentration is born out of an awareness of his own value and of the fact that he is destined to bring great things to consummation. "Magnanimity seems, even if we go simply by the name, to be concerned with great things," says Aristotle. "The magnanimous person, then, seems to be the one who thinks himself worthy of great things and is really worthy of them" (*Nicomachean Ethics*, IV, 3 1123b). Aristotle adds, "He is not prone . . . to remember evils, since it is proper to a magnanimous person not to nurse memories, especially not of evils, but to overlook them" (1125a). See Robert Solomon (1987, 115) on the similarities between Nietzsche's Overman and the "great-souled man" of Aristotle as moral and cultural ideals.

55. Endorsing Emerson's stance, Nietzsche exalts youth as pure energy which has not yet received a form and can thus burn convention as if it were dead wood. In a notebook from 1876 he quotes a dictum of Bacon's mentioned in Emerson's essay *Quotation and Originality* which had appeared in the collection translated into German as *Neue Essays* (*Letters and Social Aims*): "Consilia juventutis plus divinitatis habent" (NL 1876 16[19], KSA 8: 291; see NE, 171).

56. Emerson's original text reads, "Ah, that he could pass again into his neutral, godlike independence [*göttliche Unabhängigkeit* in the German text]! Who can thus lose all pledge, and having observed, observe again from the unaffected, unbiased, unbribable, unaffrighted innocence, must always be formidable" (E I, 40–41; V 36). According to Golden (2013, 401), Nietzsche,

in contrast to Emerson, saw childhood not as "a period . . . to experience nonconformity, but rather as a time of the most intense enculturation." Be that as it may, it is nonetheless in the image of a child that Nietzsche in *Zarathustra* chooses to embody that state of divine indifference that must be regained by whoever wishes to become the creator of his or her own values. Moreover, Golden contradicts himself regarding Emerson's position on children inasmuch as, on page 431 of his monograph, he interprets a passage from the *Essays* on the basis of the fact that, for Emerson, children are not objects of admiration but rather only a useful "case study."

57. In a passage to which Nietzsche appended, in the margin of his copy of the *Essays*, a mark of approbation, Emerson states, "To make habitually a new estimate,—that is elevation" (E I, 117; V, 106; Nietzsche underlined this passage and wrote in the margin: "Yes! [*Ja!*]"; see Appendix Figure 8). The German text runs, "A royal mind [*ein königlicher Geist*] will give a new value to accustomed things: this is elevation" (V, 106).

58. Emerson suggests the notion of a not merely negative but positive liberty not just through the image of a child but also through that of a fountain whose waters surge up not because they are pressed or pushed but because they are "self-moved": "The wise man not only leaves out of his thought the many but leaves out the few. Fountains, the self-moved [*die aus eignem Antriebe Handelnden* in the German text], the absorbed [*die in Gedanken versunkenen* in the German text] . . . announce the instant presence of supreme power" (E II, 59; V, 345). In his copy of the *Essays*, Nietzsche underlined the whole of this passage and wrote in the margin the word "Magnificent [*Herrlich*]!" (see Appendix Figure 25). However, perhaps because he recognized Emerson's image to be technically incorrect (because, strictly speaking, the water in a fountain does indeed surge up under pressure, not as something "self-moved"), Nietzsche replaced this image, in the parable of the *Three Metamorphoses* in Zarathustra, with that of "a wheel rolling out of itself." Zarathustra proclaims, "The child is innocence and forgetting, a new beginning, a game, a wheel rolling out of itself, a first movement, a sacred yes-saying" (Z I On the Three Metamorphoses).

59. Nietzsche read Schiller's *Letters on the Aesthetic Education of Man* in 1862, his 10-volume *Complete Works* in 1871, and his essay *On Naive and Sentimental Poetry* in the same year and again in 1873 (see Brobjer 2008, 254).

60. According to Katsafanas (2016, 185), "Nietzschean unity is not unity between particular drives, but unity between reflective judgment . . . on the one hand, and (the individual's) drives and affects . . . on the other hand." Katsafans defines disunity as "a kind of dissatisfaction with one's action. If an agent is disunified, he would cease to approve of his action, were he to know more about its etiology" (191). This is the case, for example, with the ascetic priest, who feels *ressentiment* vis-à-vis the warrior-aristocrat but at the same time finds his own *ressentiment* contemptible. In order to resolve this psychological conflict the priest-type carries out that "slave revolt in morality" whereby the values of strength and health become "evil" and the values of weakness and sickness become "good" (GM I 7). If the warrior-aristocrat is portrayed as "evil," then the *ressentiment* of the priest appears justified and his internal psychological conflict ceases (Katsafanas 2016, 187). On the basis of these theses, Katsafanas believes the conflict between the drives to be irrelevant to the attainment of the unity of the self (184). In my view the unity between conscious thought and the drives is a necessary but not a sufficient condition for a unitary self.

61. Nietzsche's summary runs, "No law can be sacred to me but that of my nature. The only right is what is according to my constitution, and the only wrong what is against it" (NL 1882 17[26], KSA 9: 669).

62. Clearly, Emerson recommends following one's instincts only in cases where this contact with one's true self has already been established. Otherwise, to "follow one's instincts" would simply be to exalt one's own animality. Emerson recounts a personal experience illustrating just this misunderstanding: "I remember an answer which, when quite young, I was prompted to make to a valued adviser who was wont to importune me with the dear old doctrines of the church. On my saying 'What have I to do with the sacredness of traditions, if I live wholly from within?' my friend suggested—'But these impulses may be from below, not from above.' I replied, 'They do not seem to me to be such; but if I am the Devil's child, I will live then from the Devil'" (E I, 41–42; V 37). Nietzsche was most likely thinking of Emerson when he drew his portrait of an "undaunted [*unverzagter*]" individual in the poem of this title printed as part

of the *Prelude in German Rhymes* (*Joke, Cunning and Revenge*) to *The Gay Science*. "Where you stand, there dig deep! / Below you lies the well! / Let obscurantists wail and weep: / 'Below is always—hell!'" (GS, Joke, Cunning and Revenge, n. 3 *Undaunted*; see also Baumgarten 1956, 43).

63. Clearly, to speak of an individual who dominates and disciplines the drives is misleading. There is, in reality, no faculty or agency "above" the drives which forms and orders them. As Acampora (2015, 201) very rightly points out, "there is no core subject, no one capable of the cultivation, no entity with sufficient independence to be the 'artist' of our lives, and certainly no one distinct from the organization one already is."

Chapter 4

1. Swanton (2015, 113) cites D 103, where Nietzsche explains that to "transvalue values" does not mean simply to turn topsy-turvy the "table of values" which has hitherto applied. In other words, we can say that "transvaluing values" does not mean calling, for example, altruism evil and egoism good. To "transvalue values" means rather to understand what lies at the origin of the values hitherto accepted and to alter the parameter on the basis of which certain attitudes or actions have hitherto been evaluated.

2. Compassion, argues Schopenhauer, is the highest form of love, because it is a form of love that is pure (*agapé*), that is, a form of love that is totally impersonal and disinterested. Compassion is impersonal in a double sense: first, because it is born in the mind only once one has freed oneself from one's individuality; and second, because it is directed toward "the other" as one instance of humanity in general, that is to say, toward a being who, also on his or her side, has been stripped of his or her distinct individuality.

3. For Schopenhauer, only actions born of compassion have any moral value. It is on this basis that he critiques Kant's "categorical imperative"; this latter, argues Schopenhauer, is still conditioned by the perspective of reward or punishment, or, in other words, still conceived of from an egoistic viewpoint.

4. He considered Schopenhauer's "*denial of the individual* ('all lions are at bottom only one lion'...)" (GS 99) as nothing but an aberration and "the instincts of compassion, self-denial, and self-sacrifice which Schopenhauer had for so long gilded, deified and transcendentalized" as the greatest "danger to mankind" (GM Preface 5).

5. Emerson believes he recognizes these two different attitudes, respectively, in the Christian and the Buddhist. Christians will shamelessly avow their state of neediness and their radical dependence upon God, praying constantly for God to fulfill their desires and praising Him whenever He appears to have done so. Emerson writes, referring to Christians, "A golden text for these gentlemen is that which I so admire in the Buddhist, who never thanks, and who says, 'Do not flatter your benefactors'" (E II, 95; V, 388–389; Nietzsche underlined "who never thanks" and "Do not flatter your benefactors"). In contrast to Christians, Buddhists look within themselves for their own resources and ask nothing of God. Nietzsche too identified the vulgar and the noble soul, respectively, with the Christian and the Buddhist and did so for the same reasons as Emerson. Nietzsche writes, "While Christians continuously praise God as their benefactor, Buddhists never flatter their benefactors" (GS 142).

6. Emerson wrote, "There is in America a general conviction in the minds of all mature men, that every young man of good faculty and good habits can by perseverance attain to an adequate estate; if he has a turn for business, and a quick eye for the opportunities which are always offering for investment, he can come to wealth" (LSA, 54; NE, 100).

7. "By diligence and self-command, let him put the bread he eats at his own disposal ... that he may not stand in bitter and false relations to other men; for the best good of wealth is freedom" (E I, 194–195; V, 174, where the same notion is expressed slightly differently). Emerson's profound approval of the ideal of self-sufficiency is also evident in the following passage: "The face which character wears to me is self-sufficingness. I revere the person who is riches; so that I cannot think of him as alone, or poor, or exiled, or unhappy, or a client, but as perpetual patron, benefactor, and beatified man" (E II, 58; V, 344). We must consider that Nietzsche viewed himself as having attained this admirable state on the day of his 37th birthday, given that he wrote in his copy of the *Essays* in the margin of this passage, "What

have I learned up to today (15 October 1881)? To derive *my own good* from every situation and to *have no need* of others." Nietzsche also underlined the passage from "so that" onward.

8. Nietzsche reiterates the notion of the potential benefits of distress and misfortune also on a collective level. In opposition to the modern Utilitarians, who wish for an easier and more comfortable life for everyone with a view to ultimately entirely eliminating the suffering and frustration of human existence, he emphasizes how overcoming difficulties can strengthen the character and advance the species much more effectively than such an "easy life for all" ever could. In *Beyond Good and Evil*, therefore, Nietzsche rails against that false type of "free thinker" who defends the modern ideas of "equal rights" and "sympathy for all that suffers." "We, who are quite the reverse, have kept an eye and a conscience open to the question of where and how the 'plant man' has grown the strongest, and we think that this has always happened under conditions that are quite the reverse. We think that the danger of the human condition has first had to grow to terrible heights, its power to invent and dissimulate (its 'spirit'—) has had to develop under prolonged pressure and compulsion into something re-fined and daring" (BGE 44).

9. In the morality of ancient Greece, compassion was considered not a virtue but a vice, a "morbid" indulging in sorrow (D 134). The Greeks, observes Nietzsche, well knew that to take upon oneself, on a regular basis, other people's suffering tends, in the long term, to make one "sick and melancholic" (D 134).

10. The drowning man appears in the parable *The Ugliest Human Being*, wherein Zarathustra warns himself against his own feelings of pity for the "many who are suffering, doubting, des-pairing, drowning, freezing" (Z IV, The Ugliest Human Being).

11. In a letter to his sister Elisabeth Nietzsche explains, "That which *turns my stomach* in *this* age is the untold amount of delicacy, unmanliness, impersonality, changeableness, good nature [*Gutmüthigkeit*]—in short, that whole enfeeblement of the individual's *intense attachment to his own self* [die Schwäche *der 'Selbst'-sucht*]—which parades itself around under the name of 'virtue.' . . . That which has hitherto *done me good* has been the sight of men with a *long will* . . . men who are honest enough to believe in nothing but their *Self* and their will. . . . That which drew me to Richard Wagner was *this*; Schopenhauer too had the same feeling all his life. . . . There are some *strong* 'selves,' whose selfishness one might call *divine (for instance Zarathustra)*" (KSB 6: 451, n. 471).

12. Clearly, this behavior of refusing all requests from "a world that seems to importune one" can be described as virtuous only on condition that such behavior does indeed proceed from self-reliance in the Emersonian sense: the will to devote oneself to the perfecting of one's own distinct individuality and to pursue one's own vocation. Should this not be the case, such be-havior would represent, simply a lapsing back into the first, "unsocialized" type of egoism (see Swanton 2015, 112).

13. The term "individualism" was imported into the United States from Europe in the mid-19th century. Henry Reeve, the first translator of Tocqueville's *Democracy in America* into English, explains in a footnote that he is coining the term "individualism" to render the French term *individualisme*, since there did not exist in English a term exactly equivalent (Tocqueville 1840, 104).

14. Emerson is so firmly set against the idea of individuals' devoting themselves to others be-cause those who live to help others will then no longer be in a position to fully develop their own talents, meaning that society too will be deprived of all the fruits and benefits that these undeveloped talents might potentially have yielded. Emerson observes, "In this our talking America, we are ruined by our good nature and listening on all sides. This compliance takes away the power of being greatly useful. A man should not be able to look other than directly and forthright" (E II, 47; V, 331–332; marked by Nietzsche with three heavy vertical lines in the margin).

15. As Zakaras (2009, 7) remarks, pursuing and expressing one's own distinctive individuality is precisely what a democratic society demands of us. Individuality, indeed, represents the very antithesis of docility, which, while it is praised as a virtue in nondemocratic forms of govern-ment ("the good citizen is the obedient one"), represents the greatest danger for a democratic society. Docility leads one to apathy, or withdrawal from active citizenship. Being docile, one abdicates responsibility for public decisions, which are left in the hands of others, and also

forgoes any attempt to control those who do exert political power, thus playing into the hands of organized economic interests (11). Docile people "unreluctantly accept being used" for political and economic ends that they fail to comprehend, writes Kateb (1992, 22). The self-reliant individual, by contrast, acting solely with a view to achieving his or her own particular goals and ends, refuses to be used as an instrument in this way.

16. The note in question is impossible to render adequately into English, since it is the German language that bears up Nietzsche's argument here and gives it its force. The English denominations of the attitude of mind in question here either (when it is termed "pity") reveal nothing about the inner structure of this attitude or (when it is termed "sym-pathia," recognizable to the scholar of Greek as meaning "suffering with") reveal its inner structure only to the ear trained in the classical languages. But the German term for "pity"/ "sympathy" (Mitleid) bears this latter signification ("suffering with" or "pain with") right on its surface, perspicuous even to a child. Nietzsche, then, is only following a train of thought, or linguistic association, that might occur to any native German speaker by coining the (somewhat odd and artificial-sounding) term Mitfreude ("rejoicing with") to designate an attitude of mind that produces the opposite effect to pity. Already in Daybreak Nietzsche had affirmed that compassion has the effect of increasing the "amount of suffering [Leiden]" in the world (D 134) and of weakening individuality: "Supposing it [compassion] was dominant even for a single day, mankind would immediately perish of it" (D 134).

17. See also AOM 187: "The men of the world of antiquity knew better how to rejoice: we how to suffer less; the former employed all their abundance of ingenuity and capacity to reflect for the continual creation of new occasions for happiness and celebration: whereas we employ our minds rather towards the amelioration of suffering and the removal of sources of pain."

18. Osman, or Othman, founded the Ottoman Empire in the 13th century. Emerson thought of him as his alter ego. See Richardson 1995, 350.

19. Hollingdale translates the title of this aphorism, Die Mitleidigen, as Sympathizers (HH 321). But so as to avoid introducing ambiguity into my argument, I prefer to translate it as The Compassionate.

20. In fact, this kind of friendship encompasses the other two, since from another's virtue one derives both benefit and pleasure, only one does so on a higher, less direct level. Moreover, this pleasure and this benefit are merely the consequences of the relation, not its grounds or motivating factor (see Aristotle 1999, 123).

21. Emerson argues that, however intense a desire one might have to share one's thoughts and feelings with a friend, it is always wrong to go seeking one. To pursue another person with a view to "having" them at any cost would be to divert from its object a precious energy that ought to be devoted to one's own individual life task, or to induce the pursued individual to betray his or her own nature to please the pursuer. Better, then, to devote oneself to one's own self-perfection, so that one day "we may congratulate ourselves that the period of nonage, of follies, of blunders, and of shame, is passed in solitude, and when we are finished men, we shall grasp heroic hands in heroic hands" (E I, 177; V 158–159; Nietzsche marked this passage in the margin with many vertical lines and underlined the words "in solitude," "finished men," and "we shall grasp heroic hands in heroic hands"). According to Emerson, friends must encounter one another without strain or effort, "with the simplicity and wholeness with which one chemical atom meets another" (E I, 168; V, 149). In other words, Emerson explained the bond of friendship by analogy with the sphere of chemistry, where atoms are drawn to one another by the "affinity" inherent in their respective natures. In Nietzsche's copy of the Essays we find this passage underlined with a heavy stroke of the pencil, and the marginal note: "This is not just an analogy but a literal description of how things really are. It is something from which I can profit that we now possess a language to express chemical facts [Dies ist die Sache und nicht nur das Gleichniß. Mein Verdienst, daß wir eine Sprache für chemische Thatsachen haben]" (see Appendix Figure 15). It may be that this gloss was written by Nietzsche during his stay in Sorrento with Rée and other friends. Malwida von Meysenbug relates that Rée was convinced to an almost ridiculous degree that absolutely every fact was explainable in terms of chemical affinities: "With Dr. Rée, a resolute positivist, we had endless discussions on philosophical questions, so that the phrase 'chemical combination' eventually became our private joke" (Meysenbug 1900, 86, quoted in D'Iorio 2012, 119). It almost seems that, with

his marginal note, Nietzsche wanted to make Emerson party to discoveries made by Rée and to convey to the American that the truth of his poetic intuition of years before was now confirmed by science.

22. My thanks for the deciphering of this marginal note go to Paolo D'Iorio and Francesco Fronterotta.

23. In the margin of this passage Nietzsche wrote "1883" (see Appendix Figure 22). In this date we can see a cryptic reference to Wagner, who died on February 13, 1883. Just a few days later Nietzsche, utterly distraught, wrote to Malwida von Meysenbug, "It was hard, very hard, having to be, for six whole years, the adversary of someone who was revered and loved as I loved Wagner" (February 21, 1883, n. 382). It was in order to bring to maturation his own distinctive individuality that Nietzsche was forced to abandon Wagner, who was unwilling to tolerate any divergence of opinion between himself and the younger man and put an end to their relations. Although he had seen it coming, Nietzsche was inconsolable over this loss. "I suffer terribly (from the loss of human sympathy) and nothing will ever be able to compensate me . . . for having lost, in these last few years, the sympathy of Wagner," he confessed to Peter Gast in 1880 (KSB 6: 36, n. 49). Once again, it is the reading of Emerson that sustains Nietzsche and gives him the courage to persevere on the path he has chosen. In autumn 1880 Nietzsche wrote, as a reminder to himself, in one of his notebooks, "Carry friendship to a higher level. N.B. Emerson p. 149" (NL 1880 6[451], KSA 9: 315). The reference is to a passage in Emerson which states that the friend is a person with whom one can be completely oneself, since this person's feelings for one do not depend on the fact of one's opinions coinciding with his or hers. This means that true friendship can bear discord. It is likewise in a notebook from the autumn of 1880 that Nietzsche writes, "Each time that a friend falls away from us we should aspire to gain something in barter, as it were, for this loss: namely, an ascent of our own soul to greater heights [*Für jeden Abfall eines Freundes eine höhere Seele eintauschen*]" (NL 1880 6[258], KSA 9: 265). If a friend abandons us because of a difference of opinion, then he or she was never a true friend. An estrangement under such circumstances, indeed, is not something to be lamented but must rather be seen as a positive development.

24. Developing and expressing one's own distinctive individuality—not, as Miner (2010, 57) assumes, the search for truth—is the shared goal that these friends pursue.

25. Emerson concludes that the friend, since he attacks us as if he or she were an enemy, is "a sort of paradox in nature" (E I, 169; V, 151; Nietzsche underlined "paradox in nature" here and wrote a large "Ja" of approval in the margin; see Appendix Figure 16).

26. In the essay *Friendship* Emerson considers the possession of a full and mature individuality to be a prerequisite for true friendship. But since this is only a regulative ideal, true friendship seems, in its turn, to be but a dream one pursues in full awareness of being unable to ever translate it into reality. "The higher the style we demand of friendship, of course the less easy to establish it with flesh and blood," writes Emerson. "We walk alone in the world. Friends such as we desire are dreams and fables" (E I, 177; V, 158). Emerson warns us against the illusions to which the great desire to have a friend can give rise and recommends that no attempt be made to form bonds of friendship with people who are incapable of friendship: "Only be admonished by what you already see, not to strike leagues of friendship with cheap persons, where no friendship can be" (E I, 177; V 159; Nietzsche marked this passage in the margin with two vertical lines and a kind of spiral). Already during their schooldays at Schulpforta the young friends Nietzsche and Gersdorff tried to model their behavior upon that suggested by Emerson. In 1863 Gersdorff wrote to Nietzsche that one cannot hurry the process of finding a friend if one does not wish to meet with ugly surprises in doing so. Gersdorff ends the letter by quoting Emerson himself: "Our impatience betrays us into rash and foolish alliances which no God attends" (KGB I/3: 26, n. 91).

27. These two different approaches to friendship suggest that, so far as there is a political community, friendship is to be considered as not foreign to the political sphere. But whenever society is seen as a jungle where nobody can trust anyone else, and people are disappointed by politics, then friendship is seen as securing that sense of community that can no longer be found in society (Van Tongeren 2000, 215).

28. Nietzsche, however, does not criticize society for having the character of a struggle but for exactly the opposite reason. He criticizes society insofar as it attempts to resolve the tension between different individualities and promotes uniformity and massification (Van Tongeren 2000, 216).

29. As Conway (1997) has observed, Nietzsche himself was always attracted by the idea of living a type of life that would have some social or communal dimension to it, perceiving this not as an alternative to solitude but as its necessary complement. There might be seen as evidence of this his "founding membership in Germania and the Leipzig Philological Society; his complicated Oedipal alliance with the Wagners in Tribschen; his fantasies (including Peter Gast, his friend and amanuensis) of a Knightly Brotherhood of the *gaya scienza*; his proposal to Lou Salomé and Paul Rée of an intellectual *ménage à trois*; and his imagination in 1887–1888 of a 'subterranean' Nietzsche cult growing among 'radical parties' in Europe (excepting Germany) and North America". The same desire is expressed in his habit of identifying "himself as party to a contrived or fictitious collective: 'we scholars,' 'we free spirits,' we Hyperboreans,' 'we Europeans of the day after tomorrow,' 'we philologists,' 'we psychologists,' 'we revaluers,' and so on" (Conway 1997, 31).

30. The notion of a "community of free spirits" may seem to be contradictory, but this is in fact not so, since what distinguishes these "free spirits" is not being entirely separate from their fellow men and women but just not being dependent on them. As Acampora (2015, 194) emphasizes, the *Unabhängigkeit* (independence) which Nietzsche praises so highly, and which he recognizes as the distinguishing characteristic of the "free spirit," does not mean that the "free spirit" is not in any relation to others, or does not love them, but only that he or she is not in a relation of dependency on them. "As Nietzsche appears to develop the idea, being unattached is not simply being *free from* others. It is not a matter of being radically unbound. Ideally, it includes being *enabled* in a certain way, that is, being *free to* form significant relations with others" (189).

31. In the *Wanderer and His Shadow* Nietzsche takes up once again this distinction between two types of confrontation or contest and between the feelings that motivate them: "The envious man is conscious of every respect in which the man he envies exceeds the common measure and desires to push him down to it—or to raise himself up to the height of the other: out of which there arise two different modes of action which Hesiod designated as the evil and the good Eris" (WS 29). In later years, Nietzsche was to conclude that the "evil Eris" (envy in the bad sense) is characteristic of weaker people: fundamentally herd-like animals who see in conformism their condition of existence. They feel another's strength to be a threat and desire to push the individual who "exceeds the common measure" down to their level. Conversely, the "good Eris" (envy in the good sense of respectful emulation and competition) is characteristic of strong individuals, who feel another's greatness to be a challenge to overcome their performance with a yet better one (see also NL 1882–1883 4[211], KSA 10: 170).

32. Nietzsche's claim that war is the essence of great politics should be interpreted precisely from this perspective of his affirmation of *agon*. "There will be wars such as the earth has never seen" (EH, Why I Am a Destiny 1). Whereas petty politics is built upon the division of the world into friends and enemies, and aimed at a pacific organization of human coexistence, great politics is based on individuals, and aimed at creating a stimulating tension and antagonism between them (see Van Tongeren 2008, 81).

33. In the summer of 1883, following advice from Malwida von Meysenbug, Nietzsche made plans to go and live on Ischia together with his sister Elisabeth. These plans had to be changed, however, when, on July 28 of that year, a terrible earthquake struck Ischia. In a letter dated August 16, he stated explicitly to his friend Peter Gast that the "Blessed Isles" evoked in *Zarathustra* were inspired by these islands (see KSB 6: 429, n. 452; D'Iorio 2012, 136).

34. Wagner and his family also stayed in Sorrento, for two weeks, during this period, specifically at the Hotel Vittoria (D'Iorio 2012, 47). Nietzsche met them there several times. It was in fact under these circumstances that Wagner confessed to Nietzsche his intention to embrace the Christian religion. For Nietzsche, already deeply disappointed by the Bayreuth festival, this was "the last straw." After Sorrento, Nietzsche and Wagner never met again (58).

35. For information on the books that the friends read during these sessions see D'Iorio 2012, 71, 73. On the resemblances between Nietzsche's project of a "congress of free spirits" and Weber's ideas on the "ideal type" of a Puritan sect, see Treiber 1992.

36. To realize this "school of educators," Nietzsche hoped ideally to involve people with very different personal competencies and skills: a doctor, a biologist, an economist, a historian of culture, a church historian, a Hellenist, a specialist in the study of politics and the state, etc. (see NL 1875 4[5], KSA 8: 40).

37. Whereas the Stoics had philosophized publicly in the *agora* of Athens, the followers of Epicurus were enjoined to "live unnoticed" and "not to get involved in political life" (Ansell-Pearson 2015, 206; see also Clay 2009, 16).

38. In *Zarathustra* Nietzsche observes that the small people, the people who make up the masses, are to the great individual like "poisonous flies" (Z I, *Market Place*, 39): their contempt causes little wounds, but the poison of these bites can dangerously accumulate in the strong individual until it makes him or her sick.

39. I go further into this question of the revitalizing function, for culture, of the "great man" in section 5.2.3.

40. For this reason, the members of the community neither ate meat nor made any use of wool or leather, nor did they engage in any form of agricultural production which involved the exploitation of animals, let alone of human beings (as cotton, for example, might have). One curious detail is that at Fruitlands it was permitted to eat only "aspiring vegetables and fruits, that is, those that grew upward" (Richardson 1995, 382). Potatoes, carrots, and other root crops were prohibited because of their "downward tendencies" (382).

41. The book that Brisbane wrote in order to popularize Fourier's ideas, entitled *The Social Destiny of Man*, quickly achieved wide readership, as did his column in *The Tribune*, entitled "Association," which began publication on March 1, 1842 (see Richardson 1995, 631).

42. Three years after its founding, Brook Farm was transformed into a Fourierist Phalanx. According to some historians, this was the beginning of the end of the undertaking, as the shift to industrial production entailed significant changes in membership: longtime members departed, and key supporters withdrew. In any case, in March 1846 a devastating fire burned the structure to the ground, and the community was never able to recover. The following year, Brook Farm was dissolved and its site sold (Delano 2004). Fruitlands, a smaller community than Brook Farm, was not able to grow sufficient food to get through the winter and failed in December 1843. After the collapse of this community, Bronson Alcott fell into a depression. A satirical portrait of the enterprise is to be found in Louisa May Alcott's *Transcendental Wild Oats* (1873). Ultimately, the failure of both Fruitlands and Brook Farm can be traced back to the Transcendental paradox of combining the exaltation of the individual with the search for perfect community (Francis 2007, ix–x).

43. Emerson met Brisbane in New York in 1842 during a lecture tour. The Fourierist had specifically requested a meeting with him in the hope of winning Emerson over to his ideas. Emerson commented on the meeting in his journal: "In a day of small, sour, and fierce schemes, one is admonished and cheered by a project of such friendly aims, and of such bold and generous proportion" (Richardson 1995, 369). Nevertheless, Emerson remained extremely skeptical about the method employed by Fourier and his disciples: "Fourier has skipped no fact but one, namely, life. He treats man as a plastic thing—something that may be put up or down, ripened or retarded, moulded, polished, made into solid, or fluid, or gas, at the will of the leader; or perhaps as a vegetable, from which . . . a very good peach can, by manure and exposure, be in time produced, but skips the faculty of life, which spawns and scorns system and system-makers, which eludes all conditions, which makes or supplants a thousand phalanxes and new harmonies with each pulsation" (HNLLM, 537–538).

44. Morality, as Nietzsche observes in his marginal gloss, is the primary form taken by that illegitimate domination whereby individuals seek to make universally binding that which is in fact a good only for themselves alone.

45. Emerson sometimes dreamed of a circle made up of a selected few who would lead together a purely poetic life, but he was aware that this was just a pipe-dream: "I please my imagination . . . with a circle of godlike men and women variously related to each other, and between whom subsists a lofty intelligence" (E I, 172; V, 153; Nietzsche underlined "circle of

godlike men and women" and "lofty intelligence" [*erhabenes Einverständniß* in the German translation]; at the bottom of the page Nietzsche wrote, "This is the essence of things" (see Appendix Figure 17), probably referring to what he experienced in Sorrento with his friends and planned to build up systematically elsewhere.

46. In a democratic society, the individual is not obliged to enter a group in order to receive an identity. Rather, in such a society, it is respect for themselves as unique human beings that prompts individuals to commit themselves to a cause and to enter into association with other men and women (Urbinati 1997, 5).

47. Deciding what Emerson's real position was regarding democracy remains quite a controversial issue (see Goodman 1998, 170). In any case, regardless of his political credo, Emerson is today recognized as the thinker who laid the foundations of democratic individualism (Kateb 2002, 197; Ezrahi 2012, 177; see also Brown 2009). Zakaras (2009, 22) makes an interesting observation regarding Emerson's vision of democracy: that Emerson thought of democracy as the possibility "[of] extend[ing] aristocracy to the whole society." He wanted "to expand rather than abolish aristocracy, to create an aristocracy of everyone. [Emerson] want[s] people to lead lives that are higher, more edified, more free and spontaneous." European intellectuals, by contrast—including Nietzsche—had formed an extremely negative idea of democracy, partly as a consequence of events associated with the Paris Commune. In Europe "the word 'democracy' was associated, at least until the mid-nineteenth century, with disrespectful abuse, aggressive anarchism, prevarication of property rights, and revenge against authority" (20).

48. "The fact that I consider only what appears to me to be my right [*was mir als mein Rechtes erscheint*], and disregard what people think about this—shows the difference between nobility and baseness [*zwischen Erhabenheit und Niedrigkeit*]. This is all the harder because you will find everywhere those who think they know your duty better than you. The great man is he who in the midst of the world's turmoil keeps with perfect clarity the freedom that solitude allows us" (NL 1882 17[27], KSA 9: 670).

49. During the winter of 1883–1884, spent in Nice, Nietzsche made the acquaintance of "an elderly American lady, wife of a clergyman," whom he had translate English books and articles for him "every day for about two hours" (KSB 6: 495, n. 504). It was most likely this same woman whom Nietzsche had translate for him, when he was back in Nice the following year, Emerson's essay from the *Atlantic Monthly*. On December 22, 1884, Nietzsche wrote to Overbeck telling him that the translation of the Emerson essay was under way and offering to send him a copy once it was completed (KSB 6: 573, n. 566). After the break with Lou von Salomé and Paul Rée, Nietzsche went through a very difficult period during which he was very reliant on Overbeck and his wife. They, in fact, became his principal interlocutors, also as regards his engagement with the ideas of Emerson.

50. Then "society" will be "maintained without artificial restraints, as well as the solar system" (E II, 128; V, 429; Nietzsche marked this passage with an "N.B."; see Appendix Figure 30). As Nadia Urbinati (1997, 111) has pointed out, it was in this spirit that had inspired and guided the thinking of the American revolutionaries. Already in Thomas Paine we find the idea that "the more perfect a civilization becomes, the fewer will be the occasions on which there is any actual need for government, because civilized society will then regulate its own affairs and be, as it were, its own government."

51. This ethical proposition would also have important consequences for political life. For centuries, political life has been regulated by the distinction between friend and enemy (i.e., the posing, one against the other, of contrary parties whose members share the same ideology), to such a point that Carl Schmitt came to recognize in this pair of opposed terms the very essence of "the political." One associates oneself with people who share one's ethnic origin and/or one's values and beliefs (and whom one calls "friends") in order to defend one's identity against foreigners (whom one calls "enemies"), particularly those who have a different ethnic origin and/or different beliefs and values from oneself. But if all individuals, instead of identifying with the principles of a party or a faction, concern themselves with bringing to full maturity their own distinct identity, the distinction between "friend" and "enemy" will gradually cease to have any significance. Everyone will consider themselves unique and different from every other person, while at the same time also equal to every other

person. This will have important repercussions on the political plane. There will no longer be any place for such phenomena as racial hatred or denigration of one's political adversaries. It will be possible to confront others politically without feeling offended when one is attacked and likewise without wishing to destroy those who think differently from oneself. Rather, the confrontation with people different from oneself will be welcomed as a precious opportunity for growth and self-enrichment. This, however, does not represent a threat to social cohesion but, on the contrary, an assurance that this cohesion will be maintained. As Urbinati (1997, 9) has written, in a properly functioning democratic society—that is to say, in a society of true individuals—social cohesion is ensured not by a uniformity of beliefs and values but by the good quality of dialogue within this society. A nation of true individuals will no longer be a homogeneous human mass sustained by the image of an "enemy" but "an accord between polyphonic people, respectful of their reciprocal foreignness" (Kristeva 2002, 64).

52. The doleful exclamation "My friends, there are no friends (*o philoi, oudeis philos*)" was originally attributed by Diogenes Laertius to Aristotle. Montaigne cites this (possibly apocryphal) dictum in chapter 28 of the first book of his *Essays*. According to Van Tongeren (2000, 216), Nietzsche himself, at times, took on this role of the cynical sage (see D 335).

53. To adopt the affirming attitude to life that Emerson recommends became especially difficult for Nietzsche when, toward the end of 1882, he discovered that the fascinating Russian woman whom he had fallen in love with, Lou von Salomé, was also involved in an amorous liaison with his closest friend, Paul Rée. His letter of Christmas Day 1882 to his old friend Franz Overbeck (also a passionate reader of Emerson) describes his innermost feelings of bitterness and despair in deeply poignant terms: "If I cannot somehow discover the alchemist's trick that will turn even this (to use no stronger word) filth into *gold*, then I am lost. —Well, I can ask, at least, for no better opportunity to prove that I really do count among those for whom 'every experience is useful, every day is sacred and every man divine'!!!!" (KSB 6: 312, n. 365). It is probably still in reference to these events that Nietzsche wrote "1882" in the margin of the following passage in Emerson's essay *Circles*: "I know and see too well, when not voluntarily blind, the speedy limits of persons called high and worthy. Rich, noble and great they are by the liberality of our speech, but truth is sad. O blessed Spirit, whom I forsake for these, they are not thee!" (E I, 254; V, 225; Nietzsche underlined the final phrase; see Appendix Figure 22). Unmistakable here is Nietzsche's deep disappointment in people whom he had held to be of high and noble character but who had behaved toward him in the basest possible way.

54. In one letter Emerson writes Thoreau, "Dear Henry, a frog was made to live in a swamp, but a man was not made to live in a swamp. Yours ever, R.W." (JMN 14, 203–204).

Chapter 5

1. In using the term "active forgetting" here we are referring to that willed and deliberate limiting of our historical horizon which Nietzsche invokes in the second of the *Untimely Meditations*, identifying it there with the term "unhistorisch." The "forgetting" invoked by Nietzsche as a quality of that "child" into whom the "lion" is transformed in the *Three Transformations of the Spirit* discourse in *Zarathustra* (see section 3.4.1) is, needless to say, quite another thing, as is the "forgetting" implicit in that process of the assimilation of experience that Nietzsche talks about in the second essay of *On the Genealogy of Morality* (see Acampora 2008, 41).

2. Jensen (2018, 11) believes that one of the most probable sources of inspiration for the title that Nietzsche gave to this essay was Henry St. John Bolingbroke's *Letters on the Study and Use of History*, written in English. The second of these "letters" of Bolingbroke's on history is called *Concerning the True Use and Advantages of It*. A German translation of this book existed during Nietzsche's lifetime, but Nietzsche cites it in English (NL 1873 29[177], KSA 7: 705). Moreover, the German translation of this second "letter," *Über den wahren Nutzen des Geschichtsstudiums*, does not seem to Jensen to suggest a connection with the title given by Nietzsche to the second *Untimely Meditation*. For this reason, Jensen (2018, 36) supposes that Nietzsche must be citing it secondhand from Emerson, who mentions Bolingbroke in the essay on Montaigne in *Representative Men*. During Nietzsche's lifetime, however, only the essays on Goethe and Shakespeare had been translated into German from this collection

(*Über Goethe und Shakespeare*, 1858). Nietzsche could have read the essay on Montaigne at the earliest only in 1883 (in the translation by Ida Overbeck, assuming that she did eventually complete it). Jensen's theses regarding Emerson as Nietzsche's source for the title of the second *Untimely Meditation* do not seem plausible.

3. Niebuhr, Mommsen, and Leopold von Ranke claimed that historiography emulated the natural sciences and thus held to be justified every claim that brought objective proofs (see Jensen 2013, 120). Ranke's famous dictum "Wie es eigentlich gewesen ist" evoked the notion of a historian who would be able, and obliged, to expunge from his work all elements of subjective characterization and thus present the past "as it really was" (120).

4. Already Schopenhauer ([1851] 2015, chap. 24, § 291) had reflected upon this set of problems, using the very same example.

5. Another of Nietzsche's complaints about 19th-century historians is that they interpret the events of history teleologically in such a way as to seek, in an unwarranted fashion, to justify the philistine culture of the present. "In sum, Nietzsche has two distinct critiques of the 'historical sense.' On the one hand, scientific historians are overly consumed by the culturally meaningless 'objective' details of their study while failing to recognize its true importance as a preliminary step in the education of authentic individuals. Nineteenth-century teleologists, on the other [hand], in interpreting the events of history as an aimed process whose goal turns out to be their own present age, either manifest a philistinism that justifies popular culture as rational and necessary or else fall into a nihilism which views individual willing as little more than a delusion. The 'historical sense' thus leads the modern man to pick his poison among stilted insignificance, philistinism, and nihilism" (Jensen 2013, 105).

6. "With the word '*unhistorisch*' I designate the art and power of forgetting and of enclosing oneself within a bounded horizon; I call '*überhistorisch*' the powers which lead the eye away from becoming towards that which bestows upon existence the character of the eternal and stable" (HL 10).

7. Hazlitt begins his essay by lamenting the intimidating burden of a monumental past: "The present is an age of talkers, and not of doers; and the reason is that the world is growing old. We are so far advanced in Arts and Sciences, that we live in retrospect, and dote on past achievements. The accumulation of knowledge has been so great, that we are lost in wonder at the height it has reached, instead of attempting to climb or add to it. . . . What is the use of doing anything, unless we could do better than all those who have gone before us? What hope is there of this? We are like those who have been to see some noble monument of art, who are content to admire without thinking of rivalling it" (Keane 2005, 165). Webster addressed his audience as a "race of children" who, "standing among the sepulchres of the fathers" and filled by the "pious feeling of dependence and gratitude" inspired by "this column, rising towards heaven among the pointed spires of so many temples dedicated to God," must feel themselves looked down upon by the watchful eyes of their dead forebears (165).

8. "Books are the best of things, well used; abused, among the worst. Which is the right use? . . . They are for nothing but to inspire" (NAL, 56), claims Emerson. In his famous 1838 lecture *The American Scholar* Emerson contrasts with the classic "bookworm" (NAL, 56) a new type of scholar, whom he calls "Man Thinking" (NAL, 53). This new type of scholar will be receptive to the tradition but at the same time original. He will be neither a slave to the authority of the past nor a savage who lives outside of history. He will know "how to use books," or, in other words, how to profitably relate to tradition.

9. In Nietzsche's essay *Philosophy in the Tragic Age of the Greeks* Heraclitus likewise embodies the Nietzschean prototype of the genius as antihistorical man: Nietzsche portrays him as a solitary figure whose "flaming eye" was constantly turned inward. To the "historical men" of his day, who were dedicating their lives to gathering and cataloguing facts, Heraclitus gave the proud reply, "I sought and consulted myself" (PTAG 8; see Campioni 1987, 211). This contraposition was to vanish, from the time of *Human, All Too Human* on, as a consequence of Nietzsche's reevaluation of the study of history.

10. Nietzsche came to realize that the categories (substance, causality, etc.) through which we form an image of the world are not, as Kant would have them be, eternal forms of the mind but rather structures that have evolved historically. Such categories are defined by Nietzsche as "habits of feeling [*Gewohnheiten der Empfindung*] acquired in primeval times" (HH 16),

that is to say, recurrent patterns of processing nerve impulses that had been worked out and built up in individuals living long before our time. In other words, Nietzsche hypothesized that just those responses to external stimuli which had shown themselves to be most effective were the ones picked out and memorized. These gradually consolidated themselves in the mind and became automatic response-routes, which, as such, facilitated savings in time and energy. Embracing Lamarck's theses on the heritability of acquired traits, Nietzsche then assumed that these proven effective ways of processing nerve impulses to form an image of reality were passed down to later generations in the form of a genetic heritage. These structures, since they govern, in ways that we are not conscious of, our mental representation of reality, provide the matrix for all our further reflections on the world around us (see Zavatta 2017).

11. See also NL 1878 32[21], KSA 8: 563: "History wants to overcome strangeness [*Befremden*], humans resist the past, everything ought to be 'ego,' 'biography' and 'long-since-known.'"

12. It is not a matter of a desire to exert one's own power over others; that the less powerful natures become subjugated here is rather merely a consequence. The effort that Emerson speaks of as characterizing all living beings from plants up to humans is an effort to develop, so far as possible, one's own nature.

13. Nietzsche underlined this passage extensively and wrote in the margin, "Naive and true [*Naiv und wahr*]" (see Appendix Figure 5). We may advance the hypothesis that with this comment "true" Nietzsche wanted to express his agreement with Emerson's thesis to the effect that what motivates us to study history is the self's natural tendency to grow, and to become vaster and more powerful, through the incorporation of the experiences of others. As regards the comment "naive," on the other hand, we may hypothesize that Nietzsche intended to express a certain dissent from Emerson's view regarding the exact manner in which this assimilation occurred. I shall go further into the question of this putative dissensus between Nietzsche and Emerson in section 5.2.4.

14. Nietzsche incorporated this marginal note into GS 249. This same thirst for possession and power can be felt in a note he made reformulating a passage from Emerson's *Essays* in 1882: "I want to live all history in the first person [*die ganze Geschichte in eigner Person durchleben*] and appropriate all power and glory, without bowing down in front of a king or any other greatness" (NL 1882 17[4], KSA 9: 666). Emerson's original passage runs, "The world exists for the education of each man. There is no age or state of society or mode of action in history, to which there is not somewhat corresponding in his life [i.e., the scholar's life]. Every thing tends in a most wonderful manner to abbreviate itself and yield its whole virtue to him" (E I, 7; V 5; Nietzsche underlined the words "education of each man" and "abbreviate"; he also marked the whole passage with a vertical line in the margin and added the number "6"). Nietzsche also summed up in his notebook another passage conveying a similar idea: "He shall be a Temple of Fame, he shall go along in a robe that is entirely covered and brimming with paintings, wonderful events and experiences" (NL 1882 17[19], KSA 9: 668; see E I, 32; V 29–30; the passage was underlined by Nietzsche and marked in the margin with a vertical line; he also added the number "23").

15. According to Golden, Nietzsche uses the term *Individuum* to refer to "Schopenhauer's understanding of *individuum* as 'only a particular example or specimen, so to speak, of the phenomenon of the will.' Nietzsche's 'individuum,' by contrast, has no universal metaphysical will behind it but past experience" (Schopenhauer [1819] 1969, I.4, 54; Golden 2013, 428). I share the view that we can read in the term *Individuum* a reference to Schopenhauer, but it seems to me to be rather a matter of a polemical reference to his theory of objectivity as the absence of the subject. According to Schopenhauer, it is only once the will to live has been extinguished that the intellect can finally contemplate the world in an objective way. Individuality, understood as the peculiar quality of one human being vis-à-vis another, falls away, and all that remains of what was once an individual is an agency of pure cognition. This hypothesis is supported, it seems to me, by the fact that in the same marginal note Nietzsche uses the expression (of Schopenhauerian inspiration) "universal, impartial eye" (see above). In his *World as Will and Representation* Schopenhauer ([1819] 1969, 185–186) defines genius as follows: "Genius is the capacity to remain in a state of pure perception, to lose oneself in perception, to remove from the service of the will the knowledge which originally existed only for this service. In other words, genius is the ability to leave entirely out of sight our own

interest, our willing, and our aims, and consequently to discard entirely our own personality for a time, in order to remain *pure knowing subject*, the clear eye of the world."

16. Nietzsche concurs with the empiricist assumption that all knowledge is based on sensation. Nevertheless, as Siemens (2006, 149) observes, in Nietzsche's vocabulary "Empfindung" (sensation) signifies "*both* a highly derivative, conscious state . . . *and* the 'far richer' unconscious processes or operations of perception anchored in the body, drives or instincts." Conscious sensation, then, is, for Nietzsche, a "sensation of sensation," a judgment formulated on the basis of unconscious sensations of pleasure/displeasure. Nietzsche arrived at this conclusion already in 1877 (see NL 1877 22[113], KSA 8: 400).

17. The fact that the Ugliest Human Being represents the historical sense and the assassin of God is confirmed in the drafts of book IV of Zarathustra (NL 1884–1885 31[10], KSA 11: 362; NL 1884 25[101], KSA 11: 36; NL 1884–1885 32[4], KSA 11: 400; see D'Iorio 2000).

18. Abbey (2000, 64–65) believes that, in his critique of compassion, Nietzsche contests also, and indeed above all, the possibility of one's taking upon oneself the pain and sorrow of another, an experience which presupposes the suspension of the *principium individuationis*. Since, then, in GS 337 Nietzsche supposes precisely this possibility, Abbey holds that he is contradicting himself. In reality, however, as we will see in section 5.2.4, for the mature Nietzsche the human being of the present day relives, inside of himself or herself, all the pains and sorrows of human beings of the past because this present-day human being contains these pains and sorrows within himself or herself in the form of drives. It is in this regard that the positions of Emerson and Nietzsche with regard to history lie farthest from one another: whereas Emerson is a mystic, Nietzsche is a physiologist.

19. Happiness is defined by Nietzsche as "the feeling that power is *growing*, that some resistance has been overcome. / *Not* contentedness, but more power" (AC 2). Nietzsche counterposes this, his own notion of happiness, to the traditional notion of happiness as the mere absence of pain. This latter Nietzsche sees as "the happiness of the herd [*Weide-Gluck der Heerde*]" (JBG 44; see Wienand 2008, 590–591).

20. In the period of the *Untimely Meditations* Goethe is for Nietzsche the ideal representative of the "monumental" approach to the past and therefore an ally in the Wagnerian mission in defense of the antihistorical and suprahistorical. In the period of *Human, All Too Human*, however, Nietzsche gives his predilection rather to the Classicist and formalist Goethe of the *Conversations with Eckermann*, who, in his significance as an antirhetorical and anti-Romantic figure, takes on the symbolic role of an "anti-Wagner" (see Vivarelli 1994, 276–278).

21. In book 5 of *The Gay Science* (1886) Nietzsche clarifies the fact that, in order to arrive at the approach to history outlined in TI and personified there in the figure of Goethe, a "great health" is required. "Anyone whose soul thirsts to experience the whole range of previous values and aspirations, to sail around all the coasts of this 'inland sea' [*Mittelmeer*] of ideals, anyone who wants to know from the adventures of his own experience how it feels to be the discoverer or conqueror of an ideal, or to be an artist, a saint, a lawmaker, a sage, a pious man, a soothsayer, an old-style divine loner—any such person needs one thing above all—the great health" (GS 382). As Marta Faustino (2009, 214) has explained, with this adjective "great" Nietzsche often indicated a notion that he meant to be understood in the opposite sense to that which is normally attributed to it (for example, the "great reason" of the body, as opposed to reason as normally understood). Thus, "great health is the health that, instead of being weakened or ruined by its apparent opposite (sickness), is even enhanced and reinforced by it." Faustino (2009, 213) asks herself why Nietzsche directly and expressly ascribes this "great health" only to the "free spirits" (HH I Preface 4), to the "redeeming man" (GM II 24), and to Zarathustra (EH, Why I Write Such Good Books, Zarathustra 2). It is a question that one can answer adequately only by considering "the great health" in relation to the practice that Emerson calls "spiritual nomadism." This "great health" is itself the result of intellectual nomadism. The person who has experienced in his or her own individual self the whole variety of possible human conditions of existence and the worldviews associated with them will have also passed through and overcome "sickness." That the "free spirit" and Zarathustra, as versions of such a personality, practice such "intellectual nomadism" has already been shown in chapter 3. As to the "redeeming man" in GM II 24, we read here precisely that there fall into this category "spirits who are strengthened by wars and victories, for whom conquest,

adventure, danger and even pain have actually become a necessity; they would also need to be acclimatized to thinner air higher up, to winter treks, ice and mountains in every sense" (GM II 24). In short, also in this case we have to do with "intellectual nomads."

22. Burckhardt's great contribution to the history of historical theory," observes Jensen (2018, 16), "is the notion of types." The "great individuals" who have "made history" represent, for Burckhardt, "timeless types," that is, "general concepts that are not exhausted by their historical context but who have formative value insofar as their meaning is timeless" (16). "In a curious sense," writes Jensen, "Burckhardt's great contribution to historiography was not historical at all. Burckhardt's historiography was *überhistorical*. . . . He sought the timeless and unchanging essences behind the passing façades of figures and events" (57).

23. See Zavatta 2015.

24. Conway (1997) holds that Nietzsche, even after 1876, while losing faith that such a regime could ever be brought to realization in the modern world, continued nevertheless to profess a doctrine of political perfectionism, that is to say, to sympathize with aristocratic regimes and even with the possibility of slavery. He cites in support of this thesis a passage from BGE 258 in which Nietzsche writes, "The essential feature of a good, healthy aristocracy is that it does *not* feel that it is a function (whether of the kingdom or of the community) but instead feels itself to be the *meaning* and the highest justification (of the kingdom or community),—and, consequently, that it accepts in good conscience the sacrifice of countless people who have to be pushed down and shrunk into incomplete human beings, into slaves, into tools, all *for the sake of the aristocracy.*" On the basis of this passage Conway claims that Nietzsche fully endorses the practice of political exclusion that the caste system developed by Manu was designed to convey and that, in particular, he endorses the practice of slavery. While recognizing that in certain passages in which Nietzsche appears to praise slavery (BGE 188) he is in fact speaking about "the sort of 'slavery' that one imposes on oneself in the cultivation of one's soul," Conway (1997, 35) remains nonetheless of the view that "if *real* slavery were possible in late modernity—that is, if the establishment of an aristocratic political regime were a viable option in the twilight of the idols—then [Nietzsche] would surely, and unabashedly, endorse it as a precondition of the perfectionism he advocates." In my view, however, Nietzsche did not, in reality, continue to hold to political perfectionism in his late work. Once he had abandoned the Wagnerian project, he became convinced that "great men" could emerge only in opposition to any and all institutional models, which tend to favor a "levelling down" rather than any excelling. In BGE 258 his intention is purely descriptive. He is merely explaining that a healthy aristocracy, as opposed to a "corrupt" one, lives out its privileges with a good conscience. Aristocracy lives upon the surplus produced by "the masses" and gives, in exchange for this, a meaning to their otherwise senseless existence. He is not hoping or wishing for the (re)establishment of an aristocratic political regime; he is merely explaining what the conditions are for maintaining such a regime. If Nietzsche had indeed remained a political perfectionist in his mature works, it would be impossible to explain his heated critique of Carlyle and of Carlyle's "cult of the Hero"—a critique developed in *Human, All Too Human* and taken up again in *Twilight of the Idols.* As we shall see in section 5.2.3, Nietzsche first takes up a stance against the "cult of the Hero" promulgated by Carlyle on the basis that this cult would represent a great danger for culture; he then goes on to analyze it from a psychophysiological point of view and describes it as something toward which a certain weak and decadent type of human being will show a predilection.

25. Some years later, Hurka (1993, 75–76) restates even more explicitly Rawls's interpretation of Nietzsche's Perfectionism as an anti-egalitarian, teleological theory: "There is a single goal for all agents to aim at, but not all agents figure in it. Global value is determined entirely by the good of the few best individuals." Contrary to Rawls, Hurka wants to defend Perfectionism, and to this end, he isolates Nietzsche as an unrepresentative perfectionist (Conant 2001, 189). Bertrand Russell's (1945) reading anticipates this "elitist" line of interpretation. Russell maintains that, for Nietzsche, the majority "should be only means to the excellence of the few, and should not be regarded as having any independent claim to happiness or well-being" (Conant 2001, 185). Still worse, Russell's Nietzsche legitimizes even the suffering of ordinary human beings if this proves necessary in order for a great man to achieve his purposes.

26. As Conant (2001, 194) was later to state more precisely, "Specimens are characterized by their *traits*; exemplars (in Nietzsche's sense) by their *excellence*." The current standard English translation published by the Cambridge University Press uses the term "exemplar."

27. For Emerson, human beings are all potentially "great men." But very few become such in fact, that is, bring to full expression their own talents. As Schlegel puts it, formulating a sort of "categorical imperative of genius," "You should demand genius from everyone, but not expect it" (Schlegel, *Critical Fragments* 16, quoted in Conant 2001, 196). Emerson, however, saw this difference in the results actually achieved by different people as something positive: "If men were equals, the waters would not move." It was in "the difference of level" that Niagara Falls originated (LSA, 177; NE 294; Nietzsche marked this passage in the margin with the abbreviation "NB"). In other words, according to Emerson, it is precisely out of the perception of the distance separating the results that one has oneself achieved from the results achieved by those who are higher or more advanced than oneself that there arises the tension that leads to self-improvement.

28. In BGE 257 Nietzsche noted that, historically, every elevation of the type "Man" has occurred where the sentiment of order of rank and differences in value between man and man was clear. Recognizing one's own distance from another is a sort of training for recognizing the distance between one's actual self and the ideal one, from which there follows a need for "self-overcoming." The exact opposite of this "pathos of distance" is the equality of all men before God or the law preached by Christianity and by modern democracy. Nietzsche defines modern democracy as "the historical form of the *decay of the state*" (HH 472), while he speaks favorably on more than one occasion of Athenian democracy at the time of Pericles. Ancient democracy did not foresee equality before the law, since the slaves were not considered political subjects and rights were shared out on the basis of wealth. The nobles held a preeminent position in society and were appointed to conduct the affairs of the state, since they were the only persons free of the need to work (see Van Tongeren, Schank, and Siemens 2004, 578).

29. As has been observed by Siemens and Roodt (2008, 6), in the past 20 years many democratic theorists and thinkers have found in Nietzsche's thought important resources for the rethinking of key democratic ideas. One of the most fruitful of these has been Nietzsche's treatment of the Classical concept of *agon* (see Hatab 2002).

30. With respect to the thesis that Nietzsche was a supporter of moral perfectionism advanced both by Cavell and by Conway (1997, 51), that is, the thesis claiming that, for Nietzsche, "one's primary, overriding—and perhaps sole—ethical 'obligation' is to attend to the perfection of one's ownmost self," let us add that this thesis can only be upheld with regard to the third *Untimely Meditation*. The emphasis on a duty to develop one's own talents to perfection which emerges in this latter text was set aside by Nietzsche from *Human, All Too Human* onward. As I have shown in section 2.2, from this point on Nietzsche was to develop a critique of the notion of the freedom of the will, so that, after the late 1870s he began to consider it completely useless to attempt to establish any "ethical obligation" for the individual. On Nietzsche as supporter (or otherwise) of moral perfectionism, see Fornari 2019.

31. As Stack (1992, 293–294) rightly emphasizes, Emerson—though believing that Nature is pervaded and informed by a great force of cosmic melioration and that Man himself participates in this meliorating force—is not to be described as an "evolutionary optimist." Emerson held, rather, that the individual who wished to participate in and push forward this great work of Nature needed to make a great personal effort of deliberate will if he or she was really to do so.

32. In the essay *Inspiration*, printed in the collection *Neue Essays (Letters and Social Aims)*, Emerson adds that it is necessary to seek out things that stimulate and strengthen one both physically and spiritually. As examples of such things, he cited physical exercise, adequate rest and sleep, the company of intellectually stimulating companions, and occasional refreshing breaks from one's daily routine (LSA, 150–166).

33. Nietzsche explains that "in order to transform the soul, one has to transform the body" (NL 1883 17[6], KSA 10: 535). In some notes from 1882–1883, during a period in which he was reading Spencer and Espinas, Nietzsche gave much thought to the notion of a proper *dressage* of the body that would ultimately lead to a transformation of the soul. "To work directly on the organism instead of indirectly, through ethical education. A different body would *build*

by itself a *different* soul and habits. *Let's turn the relation upside down*" (NL 1883 7[97], KSA 10: 275; see Fornari 2004, 51). In the years 1883–1884 Nietzsche was also passionately engaged in reading Galton's writings on eugenics, a new science aimed at improving the human race by bringing about deliberate changes in the physical conditions under which people lived. According to Galton, every generation displayed a statistical decrease in the probability of its members inheriting exceptional characteristics and an increase in the probability of their inheriting merely average ones. It was as if Mankind were becoming weaker and weaker, and endorsed therefore a morality that favored homologation. Galton's theory of natural selection was instead aimed at enhancing differences (see Stiegler 2001, 110–113; Fornari 2004, 52). He focused his attention on "leading cows," that is, individuals with a particular propensity to independence who do not fear to abandon the "herd" even if this endangers their survival. According to Galton, such superior natures are to be favored through a process of artificial selection in order to promote the progress of the species. Under the influence of Galton's theory Nietzsche noted down in 1885 that these breeding laws should be carefully studied so as not to waste, by permitting erroneous ways of life, all the energies that the species had accumulated (Fornari 2004, 49–53). Nevertheless, Nietzsche finally concluded that the search for the conditions that would best allow one's own nature to flourish was a task purely for the individual, given that every individual is unique.

34. This last sentence is all of the passage that he copies into his notebook: "The tone of seeking is one, and the tone of having is another" (NL 1878 30[98], KSA 8: 539). This is also the gist of a passage from *Spiritual Laws*, heavily underlined and the subject of a marginal comment by Nietzsche: "A broken complexion, a swinish look, ungenerous acts, and the want of due knowledge,—all blab. Can a cook, a Chiffinch, an Iachimo be mistaken for Zeno or Paul?" (E I, 130; V 118; Nietzsche underlined the passage "A broken . . . knowledge"). The passage continues, "Confucius exclaimed, 'How can a man be concealed!' . . . Common men are apologies for men; they bow the head, excuse themselves with prolix reasons, and accumulate appearances because the substance is not" (E I, 130–131; V 118–119; Nietzsche underlines the passage "Confucius . . . concealed!" and "the substance is not"). At the bottom and on the right side of the page Nietzsche appended an annotation: "My philosophy—draw men out at *any* risk from behind appearance [*Schein*, underlined]! And fear not the ruination [*Zugrundegehen*] of life!" (NL 1881 13[12], KSA 9: 620).

35. The passage from Emerson runs, "The world has indeed been instructed by its kings, who have so magnetized the eyes of nations. It has been taught by this colossal symbol the mutual reverence that is due from man to man. The joyful loyalty with which men have every where suffered the king, the noble, or the great proprietor to walk among them by a law of his own, make his own scale of men and things, and reverse theirs, pay for benefits not with money but with honor, and represent the Law in his person, was the hieroglyphic by which they obscurely signified their consciousness of their own right and comeliness, the right of every man" (E I, 52; V, 47).

36. Emerson initially became familiar with the Zoroastrian religion through his studies of the Pythagorean doctrine. Pythagoras claimed to have traveled widely in Asia and to have drawn, in his teachings, in part on the wisdom of the Zoroastrian mages. Other sources from which Emerson drew his knowledge of Zoroastrianism include Plotinus, Goethe, and, last but not least, Anquetil-Duperron's *Exposition du système théologique des Perses* along with this scholar's three-volume edition of the *Zend-Avesta* (Richardson 1995, 351).

37. Nietzsche, who had discovered, during this very summer of 1881, information on the Persian Zerthust as the founder of morality in a book by Ellwald, now encountered this same figure in the pages of Emerson's *Essays*. See the Commentary to volume 4, KSA 14. 279, and D'Iorio 2016.

38. As Nietzsche explains in a letter to Lou von Salomé from 1882, already in his lectures on the Pre-Socratic philosophers given at the University of Basel he had wanted to highlight the personality of each of the philosophers in question rather than his specific teachings. This, he explained, was because, while the systems have only a limited validity and can be disproven, "you cannot disprove the person behind it—the person cannot be killed" (KSB 6: 259, n. 305).

39. As Conant (2001, 232) explains very well, this "unattained but attainable self" is intended as an ideal that poses to us "duties stringent enough to require our transformation, yet not so

stringent as to be unfulfillable." In the margin of the above-mentioned passage from Emerson Nietzsche wrote, "We honour and safeguard every *aggregation of power* because we hope one day to *inherit it*—the *wise*. Similarly, we want to be the heirs of moral systems, after we have destroyed morality" (NL 1881 13[8], KSA 9: 620). This comment opens a new phase of Nietzsche's thought which builds on the position marked out by Emerson but at the same time distances itself from this position in a very significant way. Nietzsche alludes to the fact that the "wise man" (he who, as we saw in section 2.3.5, knows how to take advantage of circumstances and use them to his own advantage) is interested in the manifestations of power that have occurred in the course of history, that is, in "great men," because he knows he will be, or hopes to be, their inheritor. "Inheritor," indeed, not only in the cultural sense but also, as we will see in the following section, in the biological one.

40. In a passage from the *Essays* which Nietzsche summarized in his 1882 notebook of excerpts Emerson argues that "the actions of kings have informed the world"; that is to say, the reverence that kings inspire in us shows "through colossal symbolism what respect a man owes to man" (NL 1882 17[33], KSA 9: 671; see E I, 52; V, 46–47). In other words, the reverence that we feel toward great men shows us what reverence we ought to feel toward every person if that person is giving full and complete expression to his or her own self. In another passage of the *Essays* which Nietzsche likewise summarized in his notebook for 1882 (see NL 1882 17[21], KSA 10: 668), Emerson declares, "In every work of genius we recognize our own rejected thoughts: they come back to us with a certain alienated majesty" (E I, 27; V 33; Nietzsche marked the passage with a vertical line in the margin and the number "25").

41. As pointed out in section 4.2.4, following Hesiod, Nietzsche identified the former, purely destructive envy with the Greek goddess of strife or discord, Eris, and the second, nondestructive envy with the "sister" of this "bad Eris," the "good Eris." This latter form of "envy," and thus *agon* itself, are also characteristic of the relationship between friends in that conception of "high friendship" that Nietzsche derives from Emerson (see section 4.2.3).

42. On April 7, 1884, Overbeck's wife must still have been working on her translation of *Representative Men* because Nietzsche asks, "How goes it with Emerson and your revered spouse?" (KSB 6: 496, n. 504). Ida Overbeck's translation, unfortunately, is not to be found among her husband's *Nachlass* (see Meyer and von Reibnitz 2000, 479).

43. It was Montaigne who, in his own famous *Essais*, had spoken of the friend as a "sibling soul [*âme-sœur*]."

44. Nietzsche copied into a notebook from the year 1878 a passage in which Emerson observes, "People forget that it is the eye which makes the horizon, and the rounding mind's eye which makes this or that man a type or representative of humanity with the name of hero or saint" (E II, 44; V, 328; for Nietzsche's notebook entry, see NL 1878 30[94], KSA 8: 538). This note represents the preparatory version of AOM 398, entitled *Greatness and Those Who See It*: "The finest effect of greatness is that it bestows on those who see it a magnificatory and discriminating eye." (See also NL 1872–1873, 19[50], WEN, 109; NL 1872–1873 19[80], WEN, 118.) In the essay *Self-Reliance*, Emerson explicitly states that the "great man" is a creation of the writers of history books: "There are no such men as we fable; no Jesus, nor Pericles, nor Caesar, nor Angelo, nor Washington, such as we have made. . . . [A great man] is admired at a distance, but he cannot come near without apparing a cripple" (E II, 134; V, 433).

45. In a passage from the *Essays* next to which Nietzsche approvingly noted the word "ego," Emerson says that the self-reliant individual never idolizes the results achieved by others. Rather, he concentrates on bringing his own individual self to perfection and says, "Let me do my work so well that other idlers, if they choose, may compare my texture with the texture of these [i.e., of the great men of the past] and find it identical with the best" (E I, 134; V, 122; Nietzsche marked the passage with three vertical lines in the margin; see Appendix Figure 12).

46. Emerson's notion of an "Over-Soul" drew on multiple sources, while at the same time being an utterly original invention. Among these sources, the principal ones were Schelling's philosophy of Nature, particularly as it was popularized by Coleridge in the *Biographia Literaria* (chap. 12); Neoplatonic philosophy; and the Vedic tradition (Richardson 1995, 334). Emerson possessed a profound knowledge of the sacred writings of the East which, above all during the second phase of his life, became his principal source of inspiration (see Versluis

1993, 52; Carpenter 1930, 257). Another important source for the "Over-Soul" was the Neoplatonic tradition, with which he was familiarized by his Harvard classmate Sampson Reed. In his renowned *Oration on Genius*, delivered in August 1821, Reed raised the question of how genius—that is, an original and revolutionary spiritual force—comes into being. While emphasizing the irreducible uniqueness of each individual, Reed nonetheless held that genius is the capacity to attain to a universal, transpersonal dimension: "The intellectual eye of Man is formed to see the light, not to make it" (quoted in Richardson 1995, 17). Notes on this oration are to be found in Emerson's *Journals* (see Richardson 1995, 17).

47. Emerson, who follows Coleridge in this, understands reason as a faculty higher than the intellect (Richardson 1995, 93). Whereas the intellect is dependent on the input that it receives through the senses—that is to say, is bound to materiality—reason can leave the senses and their input entirely out of consideration. The great man is described by Emerson as "the Seer," not, however, in the negative sense of "visionary." The great man is he who, intuiting the principles that govern the universe—that is to say, the law of cause and effect—succeeds in understanding what it is possible to bring to realization and how to do so.

48. In this note Nietzsche includes a reference to page 201 of the *Versuche* (the German translation of the *Essays*) in which Emerson states that the soul is not subordinated to time like the senses and intellect. Therefore, great men of history are all simultaneously present within the individual soul once he or she accesses the one mind common to mankind.

49. In this period Nietzsche arrived at the conclusion that our mental categories are not, as Kant had held them to be, universal and eternal structures but rather "habits of feeling [*Gewohnheiten der Empfindung*]" (HH 16) acquired over the centuries (see Zavatta 2017).

50. Wilhelm Roux, whose works Nietzsche began to read in 1881, hypothesizes that there exists, besides the struggle for survival between organisms hypothesized by Darwin, also an internal struggle between the various parts of each organism. Such a struggle can also be observed, at the microscopic level, to occur between the various parts of a single cell. According to Roux, it is through this struggle that there are selected which properties of the parts in question are going to most benefit the organism as a whole. This internal struggle, then, no less than the external one, is a motor driving the evolution of the species. What interested Nietzsche in Roux's discourse, besides the fact that it suggested that the capacity for choosing that which is useful is something exercising itself at the organic level, is that the organism conserved memories also of those properties which are defeated in the struggle and overwhelmed. "Assimilation and incorporation is, above all, a willing to overwhelm, a training, shaping and reshaping, until at last the overwhelmed has passed entirely into the power of the attacker and augmented it" (NL 1887 9[151], WLN, 165).

51. In the original English edition this passage reads, "The world exists for the education of each man. There is no age or state of society or mode of action in history to which there is not somewhat corresponding in his life. Every thing tends in a most wonderful manner to abbreviate itself and yield its whole virtue to him. He should see that he can live all history in his own person" (E I, 7). Baumgarten (1956, 23) argues that the passages copied from Emerson's *Essays* were selected on the basis of their usefulness in forming the portrait of the "superior individual" and that Nietzsche wrote the Latin word "ego" at the end of those which best expressed this concept. But, in fact, this term was, for Nietzsche, just a sign of general approval, as it had already been for Schopenhauer in the margins of his books.

52. Lupo (2007, 78–79) notes, "Contrary to all appearances, the so-called 'instinctual judgment' is, in reality, the most fully elaborated and mediated type of judgment, because it is produced by an experience derived from interaction between the organism and the external world in the long course of evolution. In a certain sense, paradoxically, the 'instinctual judgment' is a far more prudent and reflective judgment than is that 'linguistic judgment' that is the representative fruit of rational reflection. In the case of the 'instinctual judgment,' what decides and chooses in a particular contingent situation is not the mere ontogenetic rationality of the single human individual but rather the phylogenetic 'wisdom' already long since accumulated through the entire evolutionary development of the species."

53. The phrase is quoted from *Psychologie des grands hommes* (1883) in which the Positivist psychologist Henry Joly reports a judgment expressed by the French physiologist Flourens regarding Buffon (see Campioni 2001, 32). In the third chapter of this work, entitled "Le

grand homme et le milieu contemporain," Joly discusses an essay of James's that had been published in 1880 in the *Atlantic Monthly, Great Men and Their Environment*. In this essay, James attributes the emergence of the great man to a "spontaneous variation" in the evolution of the species which will be conserved or rejected depending upon the more or less favorable reception accorded to this variation by the social and cultural environment (see Campioni 2001, 32–33). Like Joly, Nietzsche opposed the theory of James and observed that to begin from the ground up is indeed a luxury that mankind cannot afford: "Nothing is more expensive than to begin from the ground up" (NL 1887 10[15], KSA 12: 461).

54. We find evidence of how Nietzsche's position had matured through reflection specifically upon notions that he found in Emerson, while remaining at the same time, quite distinct and distant from the American, in the following reflection: "The actual man is far behind the embryonic, he that emerges from him only in three generations" (NL 1881 13[14], KSA 9: 621). Nietzsche jotted this comment down at the top of page 205 of his German copy of Emerson's *Essays*. This page contains a passage in which Emerson states, "We do not yet possess ourselves, and we know at the same time that we are much more" (E I, 230). Whereas Emerson was speaking here of the potential intrinsic to the individual, Nietzsche appears to draw from the passage inspiration and encouragement for his own theory to the effect that the exceptional individual is biologically the fruit of the work of many generations.

55. I reject, then, Stack's (1992, 326) thesis whereby the *Übermensch* would be an imaginary figure endowed with "all of the noble, heroic, creative, poetic, and venerable characteristics that actual human beings have exemplified in hard-won experience" and would be "venerated and admired" as an example of "alien perfection." I likewise reject Conway's (1997, 23) thesis whereby this figure would correspond exactly to the "representative man" of Emerson. According to Conway, all the great men of history are, for Nietzsche, *Übermenschen*: "The *Übermensch* is any higher human being whose 'private' pursuit of self-perfection occasions an enhancement of the species as a whole, thus contributing to the perfection (rather than the transcendence) of the all-too-human" (23). Van Tongeren (2008, 73) had already raised objections to this claim.

Conclusion

1. Some comments on Emerson appear also in the notes and works of Nietzsche's final active years (i.e., those he wrote between the end of 1887 and the end of 1888). Some time between November 1887 and March 1888 he entered into his notebooks a posthumous note of Baudelaire's in which the French poet ironically suggests that Voltaire was wrongly omitted from Emerson's *Representative Men*. Nietzsche's note is in part a translation, in part a word-for-word transcription, of Baudelaire's: "France bores and annoys me, above all because everyone here resembles Voltaire. Voltaire, or the 'Anti-Poet' (Emerson forgot to include him), *le roi des badauds, le prince des superficiels, l'anti-artiste, le prédicateur des concierges*" (NL 1887–1888 11[200], KSA 13: 82). He also mentions Emerson early in 1888, in one of his draft plans for his book on the "transvaluation of all values," where his name occurs alongside Carlyle's (NL 1888 12[1], KSA 13: 209).

2. In *Twilight of the Idols* Nietzsche portrayed Emerson in the following terms: "*Emerson.*—Much more enlightened, eclectic, refined, much more given to wandering than Carlyle, above all happier.... The sort of person who instinctively lives only on ambrosia and leaves behind anything indigestible. Compared to Carlyle, a man of taste. Carlyle really loved Emerson but still said that 'he doesn't give us enough to chew on': which might in fact be true but does not reflect badly on Emerson. Emerson has the sort of kind and witty cheerfulness that discourages any seriousness; he just does not know how old he already is and how young he will yet become— he could apply Lope de Vega's saying to himself: *Yo me sucedo a mi mismo* (I am my own successor). His spirit always finds reasons to be satisfied and even grateful; and, every once in a while, he touches on the cheerful transcendence of that honest man who came back from an amorous encounter *tamquam re bene gesta* (as if the deed had been done well). '*Ut desint vires,*' he said with gratitude, '*tamen est laudanda voluptas* (though the power is lacking, the lust is praiseworthy)'" (TI, Skirmishes 13). Nietzsche cites Lope de Vega "at second hand" from an article written by Victor Cherbuliez, under the pseudonym G. Valbert, on political life in Spain

(Valbert 1873, 13; see also Azorín 1957, 19; Zavatta 2006b, 296). "Have you never seen an old tree with wrinkled trunk but crowned with budding green?" asks the peasant Belardo of the Emperor Oton in the Lope de Vega comedy quoted by Nietzsche. "With the passing of time, I am my own successor [*yo me sucedo a mi mismo*]" (Valbert 1873, 13). The quotation is from *¡Si no vieran las mujeres!* (1637), act I, scene XI (Vega Carpio 1872, 2.579). Nietzsche recognized in himself this same attitude toward self-renewal. Both in an 1887 letter to Carl Fuchs and in a private note of the same year he applies to himself the very expression of Lope de Vega's that he had applied to Emerson: "I am just now, without really wanting to but in obedience to a pitiless necessity, 'settling accounts' with people and things and 'writing off,' once and for all, all I've experienced up to now. Almost all that I'm currently doing is setting one or another kind of 'full stop.' All these last few years the vehemence of my inward oscillations was something terrible; and now that I must pass over into a new and higher form, I need above all else a new estrangement, a still higher *depersonalization,* the essential thing here being: 'what and *who* remains mine?'—How old am I now? I do not know. Nor do I know how young I will yet become" (KSB 8: 209, n. 963; see also NL 1887 11[22], KSA 13: 14).

3. See Genesis 4:12.

4. Nietzsche reformulates this marginal note in NL 1881 11[258], KSA 9: 539.

REFERENCES

Aaron, Daniel. 1962. "Emerson and the Progressive Tradition." In *Emerson: A Collection of Critical Essays*, edited by Milton Konvitz and Stephen Whicher, 85–99. New York: Prentice Hall.

Abbey, Ruth. 1999. "Circles, Ladders and Stars: Nietzsche on Friendship." *Critical Review of International Social and Political Philosophy* 2 (4): 50–73.

Abbey, Ruth. 2000. *Nietzsche's Middle Period*. New York: Oxford University Press.

Abel, Günter. 1998. *Nietzsche: Die Dynamik der Willen zur Macht und die ewige Wiederkehr*. Berlin: de Gruyter.

Acampora, Christa Davis. 2008. "Forgetting the Subject." In *Reading Nietzsche at the Margins*, edited by Steven V. Hicks and Alan Rosenberg, 34–56. West Lafayette, IN: Purdue University Press.

Acampora, Christa Davis. 2013. *Contesting Nietzsche*. Chicago: University of Chicago Press.

Acampora, Christa Davis. 2015. *Being Unattached: Freedom and Nietzsche's Free Spirits*. In *Nietzsche's Free Spirit Philosophy*, edited by Rebecca Bamford, 189–206. London: Rowman & Littlefield.

Alcott, Luisa May. 1873. "Transcendental Wild Oats." *The Independent* 25 (1307): 1569–1571.

Andler, Charles. 1920. *Les précurseurs de Nietzsche*. Vol. 1 of *Nietzsche, sa vie et sa pensée*. Paris: Bossard.

Ansell-Pearson, Keith. 2015. "The Need for Small Doses: Nietzsche, Fanaticism, and Epicureanism." In *Aurore, tournant dans l'oeuvre de Nietzsche?*, edited by Céline Denat and Patrick Wotling, 193–227. Reims: Editions et presses universitaires de Reims.

Aristotle. 1999. *Nicomachean Ethics*. 2nd ed. Translated by Terence Irwing. Indianapolis, IN: Hackett.

Atwell, John. 1990. *Schopenhauer. The Human Character*. Philadelphia: Temple University Press.

Azorín. 1957. *Dicho y Hecho*. Barcelona: Ediciones Destino.

Bamford, Rebecca. 2015. "Health and Self-Cultivation in *Dawn*." In *Nietzsche's Free Spirit Philosophy*, edited by Rebecca Bamford, 85–109. London: Rowman & Littlefield.

Baumgarten, Eduard. 1938. *Die geistigen Grundlagen des amerikanischen Gemeinwesens*. Vol 2: *Der Pragmatismus. R. W. Emerson, W. James, J. Dewey*. Frankfurt a. M.: Klostermann.

Baumgarten, Eduard. 1939. "Emerson-Nietzsche." *Internationale Zeitschrift für Erziehung* 8: 1–16.

Baumgarten, Eduard. 1956. "Mitteilungen und Bemerkungen über den Einfluss Emerson auf Nietzsche." *Jahrbuch für Amerikanstudien* 1: 1–13.

Baumgarten, Eduard. 1957. *Das Vorbild Emersons im Werk und Leben Nietzsches*. Heidelberg: Carl Winter Verlag.

Beheim-Schwarzbach, Felix. 1943. "Diederich Volkmann." In *Schulpforte und das deutsche Geistesleben*, edited by Hans Gehrig, 23–25. Darmstadt: Hans Buskenachf.

Bercovitch, Sacvan, and Cyrus Patell, eds. 1995. *The Cambridge History of American Literature*. Vol. 2: *Prose Writing 1820–1865*. Cambridge, UK: Cambridge University Press.

Biedenkapp, George. 1902. "Der amerikanische Nietzsche." *Ernstes Wollen* 76: 246–249.

Bremer, Frederike. 1854–1855. *Die Heimat in der Neuen Welt: Ein Tagebuch in Briefen, geschrieben während 2 jähriger Reisen in Nordamerika und auf Cuba.* Leipzig: Brockhaus.

Brinton, Crane. 1941. *Nietzsche.* Cambridge, MA: Harvard University Press.

Brobjer, Thomas. 1995. *Nietzsche's Ethics of Character: A Study of Nietzsche's Ethics and Its Place in the History of Moral Thinking.* Uppsala: Uppsala University.

Brobjer, Thomas. 2008. *Nietzsche's Philosophical Context: An Intellectual Biography.* Urbana: University of Illinois Press.

Brown, Mark. 2009. *Science in Democracy: Expertise, Institutions, and Representation.* Cambridge, MA: MIT Press.

Buell, Lawrence. 1984. "The Emerson Industry in th 1980's: A Survey of Trends and Achievements." In "Emerson/Nietzsche." Special issue of *ESQ: A Journal of American Renaissance* 43: 117–136.

Cameron, Kenneth Walter. 1945. *Emerson the Essayst: An Outline of His Philosophical Development through 1836 with Special Emphasis on the Sources and Interpretation of Nature.* Vol. 1. Raleigh, NC: Thistle Press.

Campbell, Gordon. 2010. "Epicurus, the Garden, and the Golden Age." In *Gardening: Philosophy for Everyone,* edited by Dan O'Brien, 220–232. Oxford: Blackwell.

Campioni, Giuliano. 1987. "Wohin man reisen muß: Über Nietzsches Aphorismus 223 aus *Vermischte Meinungen und Sprüche.*" *Nietzsche-Studien* 16: 209–226.

Campioni, Giuliano. 1992. *Leggere Nietzsche: Alle origini dell'edizione Colli-Montinari.* Pisa: ETS.

Campioni, Giuliano. 2001. *Les lectures françaises de Nietzsche.* Paris: PUF.

Campioni, Giuliano. 2010. "'Gaya scienza' und 'gai saber' in Nietzsches Philosophie." In *Letture della Gaia Scienza / Lectures du Gai savoir,* edited by Chiara Piazzesi, Giuliano Campioni, and Patrick Wotling, 15–37. Pisa: ETS.

Campioni, Giuliano, et al. 2003. *Nietzsches persönliche Bibliothek.* Berlin: De Gruyter.

Carpenter, Frederic Ives. 1930. *Emerson and Asia.* Cambridge, MA: Harvard University Press.

Carpenter, Frederic Ives. 1953. *Emerson Handbook.* New York: Hendricks House.

Cavell, Stanley. 1972. *The Senses of Walden.* New York: Viking Press.

Cavell, Stanley. 1979. "Thinking of Emerson." *New Literary History* 11 (1): 167–176.

Cavell, Stanley. 1990. *Conditions Hansome and Unhandsome: The Constitution of Emersonian Perfectionism.* Chicago: University of Chicago Press.

Cavell, Stanley. 1995. *Philosophical Passages.* Cambridge, UK: Blackwell.

Cavell, Stanley. 2003. *Emerson's Transcendental Etudes.* Stanford, CA: Stanford University Press.

Cavell, Stanley. 2005. *Cities of Words: Pedagogical Letters on a Register of the Moral Life.* Cambridge, MA: Harvard University Press.

Christy, Arthur. 1960. *The Orient in American Transcendentalism.* New York: Octagon Books.

Clay, Diskin. 2009. "The Athenian Garden." In *The Cambridge Companion to Epicureanism,* edited by James Warren, 9–29. Cambridge, UK: Cambridge University Press.

Conant, James. 2001. "Nietzsche's Perfectionism: A Reading of Schopenhauer as Educator." In *Nietzsche's Post Moralism,* edited by Richard Schacht, 181–257. Cambridge, UK: Cambridge University Press.

Constâncio, João. 2012. "A Sort of Schema of Ourselves: On Nietzsche's 'Ideal' and 'Concept' of Freedom." *Nietzsche-Studien* 41: 127–162.

Constâncio, João, Maria João Branco, and Bartholomew Ryan. 2015. Introduction to *Nietzsche and the Problem of Subjectivity,* edited by João Constâncio, Maria João Branco, and Bartholomew Ryan, 1–45. Berlin: de Gruyter.

Conway, Daniel. 1997. *Nietzsche and the Political.* New York: Routledge.

Dewey, John. 1903. "Emerson—The Philosopher of Democracy." *International Journal of Ethics* 13 (4): 405–413.

D'Iorio, Paolo. 1996. "Les Volontés de Puissance." Postscript to Mazzino Montinari, *"La volonté de puissance" n'existe pas,* 119–190. Paris: Éditions de l'éclat.

D'Iorio, Paolo. 2000. "Nietzsche et l'éternel retour: Genèse et interprétation." In *Nietzsche*, edited by Marc Crepon, Jacques Le Rider, Michel Haar, François Chenet, and Marc de Launay, 361–389. Paris: l'Herne.

D'Iorio, Paolo. 2012. *Le Voyage de Nietzsche à Sorrente: Genèse de la philosophie de l'esprit libre*. Paris: CNRS Éditions.

D'Iorio, Paolo. 2013. "Friedrich Nietzsche." In *Méditerranée: Les porteurs de rêve*, edited by Th. Fabre and C. Portevin, 102–117. Paris: Textuel et MuCEM.

D'Iorio, Paolo. 2016. "Génesis, parodia y modernidad en así habló Zarathustra." *Estudios Nietzsche* 16: 27–40.

Danto, Arthur. 1965. *Nietzsche as Philosopher*. New York: Macmillan.

de Goncourt, E. J. Huot. 1887. *Journal des Goncourt: Mémoires de la vie littéraire*. Vol. 2: *1862–1865*. Paris: Charpentier.

Delano, Sterling. 2004. *Brook Farm: The Dark Side of Utopia*. Cambridge, MA: Belknap Press of Harvard University Press.

Derrida, Jacques. 2005. *The Politics of Friendship*. London: Verso.

Dougherty, Carol. 2006. *Prometheus*. London: Routledge.

Emerson, Edward Waldo. 1903. Preface to Ralph Waldo Emerson, *Letters and Social Aims*. Vol. 3 of *The Complete Works of Ralph Waldo Emerson*. Concord Edition, v–viii. Boston: Houghton Mifflin.

Emerson, Ralph Waldo. 1841. *Essays*. Boston: James Munroe.

Emerson, Ralph Waldo. 1857. *Über Goethe und Shakespeare*, translated by H. Grimm. Hannover: C. Rümpler.

Emerson, Ralph Waldo. 1858. *Versuche (Essays: First and Second Series)*, translated by G. Fabricius. Hannover: Carl Meyer.

Emerson, Ralph Waldo. 1862. *Die Führung des Lebens*, translated by E. S. von Mühlberg. Leipzig: Steinacker.

Emerson, Ralph Waldo. 1876. *Neue Essays (Letters and Social Aims)*, translated by J. Schmidt. Stuttgart: Auerbach.

Emerson, Ralph Waldo. 1883. "Historic Notes of Life and Letters in Massachusetts." *Atlantic Monthly* 52: 529–543.

Emerson, Ralph Waldo. 1959. *Early Lectures, vol. I: 1833–1836*. Cambridge, MA: Harvard University Press.

Emerson, Ralph Waldo. 1960–1982. *Journals and Miscellaneous Notebooks*. Cambridge, MA: Harvard University Press.

Emerson, Ralph Waldo. 1964. *Early Lectures, vol. II: 1836–1838*. Cambridge, MA: Harvard University Press.

Emerson, Ralph Waldo. 1972. *Early Lectures, vol. III: 1838–1842*. Cambridge, MA: Harvard University Press.

Emerson, Ralph Waldo. 1980. *Essays: First Series*. Vol. 2 of Collected Works. Cambridge, MA: Harvard University Press.

Emerson, Ralph Waldo. 1984. *Essays: Second Series*. Vol. 3 of *Collected Works*. Cambridge, MA: Harvard University Press.

Emerson, Ralph Waldo. 1971. *Nature, Addresses, and Lectures*. Vol. 1 of *Collected Works*. Cambridge, MA: Harvard University Press.

Emerson, Ralph Waldo. 1987. *Representative Men*. Vol. 4 of *Collected Works*. Cambridge, MA: Harvard University Press.

Emerson, Ralph Waldo. 1994. *English Traits*. Vol. 5 of *Collected Works*. Cambridge, MA: Harvard University Press.

Emerson, Ralph Waldo. 2004. *The Conduct of Life*. Vol. 6 of *Collected Works*. Cambridge, MA: Harvard University Press.

Emerson, Ralph Waldo. 2008. *Society and Solitude*. Vol. 7 of *Collected Works*. Cambridge, MA: Harvard University Press.

Emerson, Ralph Waldo. 2010. *Letters and Social Aims*. Vol. 8 of *Collected Works*. Cambridge, MA: Harvard University Press.

Ezrahi, Yaron. 2012. *Imagined Democracies: Necessary Political Fictions*. Cambridge, UK: Cambridge University Press.

Faustino, Marta. 2009. "Philosophy as a 'Misunderstanding of the Body' and the 'Great Health' of the New Philosophers." In *Nietzsche on Instinct and Language*, edited by João Constâncio and Maria João Mayer Branco, 203–218. Berlin: De Gruyter.

Farias, Victor. 1987. *Heidegger et le Nazisme*. Paris: Verdier.

Ferry, Luc, and Alan Renaut. [1988] 1990. *Heidegger and Modernity*. Chicago: University of Chicago Press.

Foot, Philippa. 2003. *Natural Goodness*. New York: Oxford University Press.

Fornari, Maria Cristina. 2004. "Superuomo ed evoluzione." In *Nietzsche e la provocazione del superuomo*, edited by Francesco Totaro, 45–66. Roma: Carocci.

Fornari, Maria Cristina. 2019 (forthcoming). "Friedrich Nietzsche." In *Autonomieperfektionismus*, edited by Douglas Moggach, Nadine Mooren, and Michael Quante, Munich: Fink.

Francis, Richard. 2007. *Trascendental Utopias: Individual and Community at Brook Farm, Fruitlands, and Walden*. Ithaca, NY: Cornell University Press.

Francke, Kuno. 1907. *German Ideals of To-Day and Other Essays on German Culture*. Boston: Houghton and Mifflin.

Frothingham, Octavius B. 1959. *Transcendentalism in New England*. New York: Harper & Brothers.

Gerratana, Federico. 1988. "Der Wahn jenseits des Menschen. Zur frühen E. v. Hartmann-Rezeption Nietzsches (1869–1874)." *Nietzsche-Studien* 17: 391–433.

Giamatti, Angelo Bartlett. 1981. *The University and the Public Interest*. New York: Atheneum.

Gilman, Sander. 1980. "Nietzsches Emerson-Lektüre: Eine unbekannte Quelle." *Nietzsche-Studien* 9: 406–431.

Gilman, Sander. 1987. *Begegnungen mit Nietzsche*. Bonn: Bouvier.

Goethe, Johann Wolfgang von. (1808) 1949. *Faust: An American Translation of Part I*. New York: New Directions.

Goethe, Johann Wolfgang von. (1810) 1840. *Theory of Colours*. London: Murray.

Goethe, Johann Wolfgang von. 1948–1971. *Gedenkausgabe der Werke, Briefe und Gespräche*. 27 vols. Zürich: Artemis.

Golden, Mason. 2013. "Emerson-Exemplar: Friedrich Nietzsche's Emerson Marginalia. Introduction." *Journal of Nietzsche Studies* 44 (3): 398–408.

Golomb, Jacob, and Robert S. Wistrich, eds. 2002. *Nietzsche, Godfather of Fascism? On the Uses and Abuses of a Philosophy*. Princeton, NJ: Princeton University Press.

Goodman, Russel B. 1998. "Moral Perfectionism and Democracy: Emerson, Nietzsche, Cavell." In "Emerson/Nietzsche." Special issue of *ESQ: A Journal of American Renaissance* 43: 159–180.

Grimm, Herman. 1874. *Fünfzehn Essays*. Berlin: Dümmler.

Grimstad, Paul. 2013. *Experience and Experimental Writing: Literary Pragmatism from Emerson to the Jameses*. New York: Oxford University Press.

Gsell-Fels, Theodor. 1878. *Süd-Frankreich, nebst den Kurorten der Riviera di Ponente, Corsica und Algier*. Leipzig: Bibliographisches Institut.

Gundolf. 1908. "Emerson." *Preußische Jahrbücher* 131: 252–259.

Harcourt, Edward. 2011. "Nietzsche and the 'Aesthetics of Character.'" In *Nietzsche's On the Genealogy of Morality: A Critical Guide*, edited by Simon May, 265–284. Cambridge, UK: Cambridge University Press.

Harcourt, Edward. 2015. "Nietzsche and the Virtues." In *The Routledge Companion to Virtue Ethics*, edited by Lorraine Besser-Jones and Michale Slote, 165–180. New York: Routledge.

Hartmann, Eduard von. 1869. *Philosophie des Unbewussten*. Berlin: Loewenstein.

Hatab, Lawrence J. 2002. "Prospects for a Democratic Agon: Why We Can Still Be Nietzscheans." *Journal of Nietzsche Studies* 24: 132–147.

Hegel, Georg Wilhelm Friedrich. (1837) 1975. *Lectures on the Philosophy of World History*. Cambridge, UK: Cambridge University Press.

Heidegger, Martin. 1961. *Nietzsche*. Frankfurt a. M.: Klostermann.

Holls, Frederich William. 1903. "Emerson's Correspondence with Herman Grimm." *Atlantic Monthly* 91: 467–479.

How, Lawrence. 1911. "Emerson and Nietzsche." *Reedy's Mirror* 12: 6–9.

Hubbard, Stanley. 1958. *Nietzsche und Emerson*. Basel: Verlag für Recht und Gesellschaft.

Hummel, Hermann. 1946. "Emerson and Nietzsche." *New England Quarterly* 19: 63–84.

Hurka, Thomas. 1993. *Perfectionism*. New York: Oxford University Press.

Hutter, Horst. 2006. *Shaping the Future: Nietzsche's New Regime of the Soul and Its Ascetic Practices*. Lanham, MD: Lexington Books.

Janaway, Christopher. 2007. *Beyond Selflessness: Reading Nietzsche's Genealogy*. New York: Oxford University Press.

Jensen, Anthony. 2013. *Nietzsche's Philosophy of History*. Cambridge, UK: Cambridge University Press.

Jensen, Anthony. 2018. *An Interpretation of Nietzsche's "On the Uses and Disadvantage of History for Life."* New York: Routledge.

Kant, Immanuel. (1787) 1999. *Critique of Pure Reason*. Cambridge, UK: Hackett.

Kateb, George. 1992. *The Inner Ocean: Individualism and Democratic Culture*. Ithaca, NY: Cornell University Press.

Kateb, George. 2002. *Emerson and Self-Reliance*. New edition. Lanham, MD: Rowman & Littlefield.

Kateb, George. 2006. "Friendship and Love." In *Emerson's* Essays, edited by Harold Bloom, 191–226. New York: Chelsea House.

Katsafanas, Paul. 2013. *Agency and the Foundations of Ethics: Nietzschean Constitutivism*. New York: Oxford University Press.

Katsafanas, Paul. 2016. *The Nietzschean Self: Moral Psychology, Agency, and the Unconscious*. New York: Oxford University Press.

Kaufmann, Walter. 1950. *Nietzsche, Philosopher, Psychologist, Antichrist*. Princeton, NJ: Princeton University Press.

Kaufmann, Walter. 1974. "Translator's Introduction" to Friedrich Nietzsche, *The Gay Science*, 3–26. New York: Random House.

Kazin, Alfred. 1982. "The Father of Us All." *New York Review of Books*, January 21: 3–6.

Keane, Patrick. 2005. *Emerson, Romanticism, and Intuitive Reason*. Columbia: University of Missouri Press.

Kerkering, John. 2003. *The Poetics of National and Racial Identity in Nineteenth-Century American Literature*. Cambridge, UK: Cambridge University Press.

Kristeva, Julia. 2002. *The Powers and Limits of Psychoanalysis*. Vol. 2: *Intimate Revolt*. New York: Columbia University Press.

Lane, Melissa. 2007. "Honesty as the Best Policy? Nietzsche on Redlichkeit and the Contrast between Stoic and Epicurean Strategies of the Self." In *Histories of Postmodernism: The Precursors, the Heyday, the Legacy*, edited by Mark Bevir, Jill Hargis, and Sara Rushing, 25–51. New York: Routledge.

Lasch, Christopher. 1991. *The True and Only Heaven: Progress and Its Critics*. London: Norton.

Lecznar, Adam. 2013. "Aryan, German, or Greek? Nietzsche's Prometheus between Antiquity and Modernity." *Classical Receptions Journal* 5 (1): 38–62.

Leiter, Brian. (1998) 2001. "The Paradox of Fatalism and Self-Creation in Nietzsche." In *Nietzsche*, edited by John Richardson and Brian Leiter, 281–322. New York: Oxford University Press.

Leiter, Brian. 2007. "Nietzsche's Theory of the Will." *Philosophers Imprint* 7 (7): 1–15.

Leopardi, Giacomo. (1834) 1983. *Operette Morali: Essays and Dialogues*. Berkeley: University of California Press.

Lysaker, John T. 2008. *Emerson and Self-Culture*. Indianapolis: Indiana University Press.

Lopez, Michael. 1996. *Emerson and Power: Creative Antagonism in the Nineteenth Century*. Dekalb: Northern Illinois University Press.

Lopez, Michael. 1997. "Emerson and Nietzsche: An Introduction." In "Emerson/Nietzsche." Special issue of *ESQ: A Journal of American Renaissance* 43: 1–36.

Lupo, Luca. 2007. *Le colombe dello scettico: Riflessioni di Nietzsche sulla coscienza negli anni 1880–1888*. Pisa: ETS.

Maeterlinck, Maurice. 1987. "Emerson." In Ralph Waldo Emerson, *Repräsentanten der Menschheit*, 267–280. Zürich: Oesch Verlag.

Malory, Thomas. [1485] 1976. *Morte d'Arthur*. London: Scolar Press, in association with the Pierpont Morgan Library.

Marcuse, Ludwig. 1951. "Nietzsche in America." *South Atlantic Quarterly* 50: 330–339.

Matthiessen, Francis Otto. 1941. *American Renaissance: Art and Expression in the Age of Emerson and Whitman*. New York: Oxford University Press.

May, Simon. 1999.*Nietzsche's Ethics and His War on "Morality."* New York: Oxford University Press.

McCrae, Robert, and Paul Costa. 1994. "The Stability of Personality: Observations and Evaluations." *Current Directions in Psychological Science* 3 (6): 173–175.

Meyer, Julius Robert. 1845. *Die Organische Bewegung im Zusammenhang mit dem Stoffwechsel*. Heilbronn: C. Drechsler'sche Buchhandlung.

Meyer, Katrin, and Barbara von Reibnitz, eds. 2000. *Friedrich Nietzsche / Franz und Ida Overbeck Briefwechsel*. Stuttgart: Metzler.

Meysenbug, Malwida von. 1898. *Der Lebensabend einer Idealistin*. Nachtrag zu den *Memoiren einer Idealistin*. Berlin: Schuster & Loeffler.

Meysenbug, Malwida von. 1900. *Stimmungsbilder*. Berlin: Schuster & Loeffler.

Michaud, Régis. (1910) 1924. *Autor d'Emerson*. Paris: Bossard.

Mikics, David. 2003. *The Romance of Individualism in Emerson and Nietzsche*. Athens: Ohio University Press.

Miller, Perry. 1950. *The Transcendentalists*. Cambridge, MA: Harvard University Press.

Miller, Perry. (1953) 1962. "Emersonian Genius and American Democracy." In *Emerson: A Collection of Critical Essays*, edited by Milton Konvitz and Stephen Whicher, 163–174. New York: Prentice Hall.

Miner, Robert. 2010. "Nietzsche on Friendship." *Journal of Nietzsche Studies* 40:47–69.

Montinari, Mazzino. 1996a. *Nietzsche*. Roma: Editori Riuniti.

Montinari, Mazzino. 1996b. *"La volonté de puissance" n'existe pas*. Paris: Éditions de l'éclat.

Müller-Lauter, Wolfgang. 1998. *Volontà di potenza e nichilismo: Nietzsche e Heidegger*. Trieste: Parnaso.

Müller-Lauter, Wolfgang. 1999. "On Judging in a World of Becoming: A Reflection on the 'Great Change' in Nietzsche's Philosophy." In *Nietzsche, Theories of Knowledge, and Critical Theory*. Vol. 1 of *Nietzsche and the Sciences*, edited by Babette Babich and Robert Cohen, 165–186. Dordrecht: Kluver Academic.

Nehamas, Alexander. 1985. *Nietzsche: Life as Literature*. Cambridge, MA: Harvard University Press.

Nicoloff, Philip L. 1961. *Emerson on Race and History*. New York: Columbia University Press.

Nietzsche, Friedrich. 1962. *Philosophy in the Tragic Age of the Greeks*, translated by Marianne Cowan. Washington, DC: Regnery.

Nietzsche, Friedrich. 1967a. *The Case of Wagner*, translated by Walter Kaufmann. New York: Vintage Books.

Nietzsche, Friedrich. 1967b. *Werke, Kritische Gesamtausgabe*. Berlin: de Gruyter.

Nietzsche, Friedrich. 1975. *Briefwechsel, Kritische Gesamtausgabe*. Berlin: de Gruyter.

Nietzsche. Friedrich. 1986a. *Assorted Opinions and Maxims*, translated by R. J. Hollingdale. Cambridge, UK: Cambridge University Press.

Nietzsche, Friedrich. 1986b. *Human, All Too Human*, translated by R. J. Hollingdale. Cambridge, UK: Cambridge University Press.

Nietzsche, Friedrich. 1986c. *The Wanderer and His Shadow*, translated by R. J. Hollingdale. Cambridge, UK: Cambridge University Press.

Nietzsche, Friedrich. 1988. *Sämtliche Werke, Kritische Studienausgabe*. 2nd rev. ed. Berlin: de Gruyter.

Nietzsche, Friedrich. 1991. *On Moods*, translated by Graham Parkes. *Journal of Nietzsche Studies* 2: 5–10.

Nietzsche, Friedrich. 1993a. *Fate and History*, translated by George Stack in "Nietzsche's earliest Essays. Translation and Commentary on 'Fate and History' and 'Freedom of Will and Fate'," *Philosophy Today* 37: 153–169, 154–156.

Nietzsche, Friedrich. 1993b. *Freedom of the Will and Fate*, translated by George Stack. *Philosophy Today* 37: 153–169, 156–158.

Nietzsche, Friedrich. 1994. *On the Genealogy of Morality*, translated by Carol Diethe. Cambridge, UK: Cambridge University Press.

Nietzsche, Friedrich. 1997. *Daybreak*, translated by R. J. Hollingdale. Cambridge, UK: Cambridge University Press.

Nietzsche, Friedrich. 1999. *The Birth of Tragedy*, translated by Ronald Speirs. Cambridge, UK: Cambridge University Press.

Nietzsche, Friedrich. 2001. *The Gay Science*, translated by Josefine Nauckhoff and Adrian Del Caro. Cambridge, UK: Cambridge University Press.

Nietzsche, Friedrich. 2002. *Beyond Good and Evil*, translated by Judith Norman. Cambridge, UK: Cambridge University Press.

Nietzsche, Friedrich. 2003a. *Sämtliche Briefe, Kritische Studienausgabe*. 2nd rev. ed. Berlin: de Gruyter.

Nietzsche, Friedrich. 2003b. *Writings from the Late Notebooks*, translated by Kate Sturge. Cambridge, UK: Cambridge University Press.

Nietzsche, Friedrich. 2005a. *The Antichrist*, translated by Judith Norman. Cambridge, UK: Cambridge University Press.

Nietzsche, Friedrich. 2005b. *Ecce Homo*, translated by Judith Norman. Cambridge, UK: Cambridge University Press.

Nietzsche, Friedrich. 2005c. *On the Uses and Disadvantages of History for Life*, translated by R. J. Hollingdale. Cambridge, UK: Cambridge University Press.

Nietzsche, Friedrich. 2005d. *Richard Wagner in Bayreuth*, translated by R. J. Hollingdale. Cambridge, UK: Cambridge University Press.

Nietzsche, Friedrich. 2005e. *Schopenhauer as Educator*, translated by R. J. Hollingdale. Cambridge, UK: Cambridge University Press.

Nietzsche, Friedrich. 2005f. *Twilight of the Idols*, translated by Judith Norman. Cambridge, UK: Cambridge University Press.

Nietzsche, Friedrich. 2006. *Thus Spoke Zarathustra*, translated by Adrian Del Caro. Cambridge, UK: Cambridge University Press.

Nietzsche, Friedrich. 2009. *Writings from the Early Notebooks*, translated by Ladislaus Löb. Cambridge, UK: Cambridge University Press.

O'Brien, Mahon. 2015. *Heidegger, History and the Holocaust*. London: Bloomsbury.

Packer, Barbara. 1982. *Emerson's Fall: A New Interpretation of the Major Essays*. New York: Continuum.

Parrington, Vernon. 1927. *Main Currents in American Thought*. Vol. 2: *The Romantic Revolution in America, 1800–1860*. New York: Harcourt.

Pippin, Robert. 2009. "How to Overcome Oneself: Nietzsche on Freedom." In *Nietzsche on Freedom and Autonomy*, edited by Ken Gemes and Simon May, 69–87. New York: Oxford University Press.

Pippin, Robert. 2010. *Nietzsche, Psychology, and First Philosophy*. Chicago: University of Chicago Press

Porte, Joel. 1988. *Representative Men: Ralph Waldo Emerson in His Time*. New York: Columbia University Press.

Porte, Joel. 1999. "Representing America—The Emerson Legacy." In *The Cambridge Companion to Ralph Waldo Emerson*, edited by Joel Porte and Saundra Morris, 1–12. Cambridge, UK: Cambridge University Press.

Porte, Joel, and Saundra Morris, eds. 1999. *The Cambridge Companion to Ralph Waldo Emerson*. Cambridge, UK: Cambridge University Press.

Quetelet, Lambert Adolphe Jacques. 1842. *A Treatise on Man and the Development of His Faculties*. Edinburgh: Chambers.

Rawls, John. 1971. *A Theory of Justice*. Cambridge, MA: Belknap Press of Harvard University Press.

Rée, Paul. 1877. *Der Ursprung der moralischen Empfindungen*. Chemnitz: Ernst Schmeitzner.

Reginster, Bernard. 2003. "What Is a Free Spirit? Nietzsche on Fanaticism." *Archiv für Geschichte der Philosophie* 85:51–85.

Reginster, Bernard. 2006. *The Affirmation of Life: Nietzsche on Overcoming Nihilism*. Cambridge, MA: Harvard University Press.

Reginster, Bernard. 2007. "The Will to Power and the Ethics of Creativity." In *Nietzsche and Morality*, edited by Brian Leiter and Neil Sinhababu, 32–56. New York: Oxford University Press.

Richardson, John. 2004. *Nietzsche's New Darwinism*. New York: Oxford University Press.

Richardson, John. 2009. "Nietzsche's Freedoms." In *Nietzsche on Freedom and Autonomy*, edited by Ken Gemes and Simon May, 127–149. New York: Oxford University Press.

Richardson, Robert. 1995. *Emerson: The Mind on Fire*. Berkeley: University of California Press.

Ridley, Aaron. 1998. "What Is the Meaning of Aesthetic Ideals?" In *Nietzsche, Philosophy and the Arts*, edited by Salim Kemal et al., 128–147. Cambridge, UK: Cambridge University Press.

Risse, Mathias. 2009. "The Eternal Recurrence: A Freudian Look at What Nietzsche Took to Be His Greatest Insight." In *Nietzsche on Freedom and Autonomy*, edited by Ken Gemes and Simon May, 223–246. New York: Oxford University Press.

Robinson, David. 1993. *Emerson and the Conduct of Life: Pragmatism and Ethical Purpose in the Later Work*. Cambridge, UK: Cambridge University Press.

Robinson, David. 1999. "Transcendentalism and Its Times." In *The Cambridge Companion to Ralph Waldo Emerson*, edited by Joel Porte and Saundra Morris, 13–29. Cambridge, UK: Cambridge University Press.

Rose, Valentin. 1863. *Aristoteles Pseudepigraphus*. Leipzig: Teubner.

Royce, Josiah. 1917. "Nietzsche." *Atlantic Monthly* 119: 321–331.

Royce, Josiah. 2005. *The Basic Writings of Josiah Royce*. Vol. 1: *Culture, Philosophy, and Religion*. New York: Fordham University Press.

Russell, Bertrand. 1945. *A History of Western Philosophy*. New York: Simon & Schuster.

Salter, William. 1917. *Nietzsche the Thinker*. New York: Holt.

Sandberger, Wolfgang. 1997. *Das Bach-Bild Philipp Spittas: Ein Beitrag zur Geschichte der Bach-Rezeption im 19. Jahrhundert*. Stuttgart: Franz Steiner.

Santayana, George. (1900) 1962. "Emerson." In *Emerson: A Collection of Critical Essays*, edited by Milton Konvitz and Stephen Whicher, 31–38. Englewood Cliffs, NJ: Prentice Hall.

Schaff, Philip. 1855. *America: A Sketch of the Political, Social, and Religious Character of the United States of North America*. New York: C. Scribner.

Schneider, Herbert Wallace. 1946. *A History of American Philosophy*. New York: Columbia University Press.

Schopenhauer, Arthur. (1819) 1969. *The World as Will and Representation*. New York: Dover.

Schopenhauer, Arthur. (1840) 1995. *On the Basis of Morality*. Indianapolis, IN: Hackett.

Schopenhauer, Arthur. (1841) 2009. "On the Freedom of the Will." In *The Two Fundamental Problems of Ethics*, edited by Christopher Janaway, 31–112. Cambridge, UK: Cambridge University Press.

Schopenhauer, Arthur. [1851] 2015. *Parerga and Paralipomena*, edited by Christopher Janaway. Cambridge, UK: Cambridge University Press.

Shapiro, Gary. 1983. "Nietzsche on Envy." *International Studies in Philosophy* 15 (2): 3–12.

Sharma, Mahesh. 2005. *Bhagavad Gita: A Journey from the Body to the Soul*. Boomington, IN: Author House.

Siemens, Herman. 2006. "Nietzsche and the Empirical: Through the Eyes of the Term 'Empfindung.'" *South African Journal of Philosophy* 25 (2): 146–158.

Siemens, Herman, and Vaasti Roodt. 2008. Introduction to *Nietzsche, Power, and Politics: Rethinking Nietzsche's Legacy for Political Thought*, edited by Herman Siemens and Vaasti Roodt, 1–33. Berlin: De Gruyter.

Simon, Julius. 1937. *Ralph Waldo Emerson in Deutschland 1951–1937*. Berlin: Junker und Dünnhaupt.

Small, Robin. 2003. "Translator's Introduction." In Paul Rée, *Basic Writings*. Urbana: University of Illinois Press.

Solomon, Robert. 1987. *From Hegel to Existentialism*. New York: Oxford University Press.

Spurzheim, Johann Gaspar. 1832. *Phrenology, or the Doctrine of Mental Phenomena*. Vol. 1. Boston: Marsh, Capen & Lyon.

Sommer, Andrea Urs. 2006. "Nihilism and Skepticism in Nietzsche." In *A Companion to Nietzsche*, edited by Keith Ansell-Pearson, 250–269. Oxford: Blackwell.

Stack, George. 1992. *Nietzsche and Emerson: An Elective Affinity*. Athens: Ohio University Press.

Stack, George. 1998. "Nietzsche and Emerson: The Return of the Repressed." In "Emerson/Nietzsche. Special issue of *ESQ: A Journal of American Renaissance* 43: 37–68.

Steiner, Rudolph. 1925. *Mein Lebensgang*. Dornach: Philosophisch-Anthroposophischer Verlag am Goetheanum.

Stendhal. 1876. *De l'amour*. Paris: Callmann-Levy.

Stern, Madeleine. 1984. "Emerson and Phrenology." *Studies in the American Renaissance* (1984): 213–228.

Stiegler, Barbara. 2001. *Nietzsche et la biologie*. Paris: PUF.

Swanton, Christine. 2005. "Nietzschean Virtue Ethics." In *Virtue Ethics Old and New*, edited by Stephen M. Gardiner, 179–192. Ithaca, NY: Cornell University Press.

Swanton, Christine. 2015. *The Virtue Ethics of Hume and Nietzsche*. Oxford: Wiley.

Thiele, Leslie. 1990. *Friedrich Nietzsche and the Politics of the Soul: A Study of Heroic Individualism*. Princeton, NJ: Princeton University Press.

Tocqueville, Alexis de. 1840. *Democracy in America, Part II: The Social Influence of Democracy*. New York: Langley.

Townsend, Dabney. 2010. *The A to Z of Aesthetics*. Lanham, MD: Scarecrow Press.

Treiber, Hubert. 1992. "Wahlverwandtschaften zwischen Nietzsches Idee eines 'Kloster für freiere Geister' und Webers Idealtypus der puritanischen Sekte." *Nietzsche-Studien* 21:326–362.

Turner, Sharon. 1799–1805. *The History of the Anglo Saxons*. 4 vols. London: Longmann.

Urbinati, Nadia. 1997. *Individualismo democratico: Emerson, Dewey e la cultura politica americana*. Roma: Donzelli.

Valbert. 1873. "L'Espagne politique: Première partie. Le caractère espagnol et la monarchie constitutionnelle." *Revue des deux mondes* 107:5–38.

Van Cromphout, Gustav. 1990. *Emerson's Modernity and the Example of Goethe*. Columbia: University of Missouri Press.

Van Der Zee Sears, John. 1912. *My Friends at Brook Farm*. New York: Desmond Fitzgerald.

Van Tongeren, Paul. 2000. "Politics, Friendship and Solitude in Nietzsche (Confronting Derrida's Reading of Nietzsche in 'Politics of Friendship')." *South African Journal of Philosophy* 19 (3): 209–222.

Van Tongeren, Paul. 2008. "Nietzsche as 'Über-Politischer Denker.'" In *Nietzsche, Power, and Politics: Rethinking Nietzsche's Legacy for Political Thought*, edited by Herman Siemens and Vaasti Roodt, 69–83. Berlin: De Gruyter.

Van Tongeren, Paul, Gerd Schank, and Herman Siemens, eds. 2004. *Nietzsche-Wörterbuch*. Berlin: De Gruyter.

Vega Carpio, Frey Lope Félix de. 1872. *Comedias Escogidas 1853–1860*. Vol. 2. Madrid: Rivadeneyra.

Versluis, Arthur. 1993. *American Transcendentalism and Asian Religions*. New York: Oxford University Press.

Vivarelli, Vivetta. 1992. *L'immagine rovesciata*. Genova: Marietti.

Vivarelli, Vivetta. 1994. "Nietzsche, Goethe und der historiche Sinn." In *"Centauren Geburten": Wissenschaft, Kunst und Philosophie beim jungen Nietzsche*, edited by Tilman Borsche, Federico Gerratana, and Aldo Venturelli, 276–291. Berlin: de Gruyter.

von Arnim, Gisela. 1858. "Vorwort." In Ralph Waldo Emerson, *Versuche* [Essays: First and second series], iii–vi. Hannover: Meyer.

Von Frank, Albert. 1999. "Essays: First Series (1841)." In *The Cambridge Companion to Ralph Waldo Emerson*, edited by Joel Porte and Saundra Morris, 106–120. Cambridge, UK: Cambridge University Press.

Walsh, Anthony. 1972. "The American Tour of Dr. Spurzheim." *Journal of the History of Medicine and Allied Sciences* 27 (2): 187–205.

Wellek, Renée. 1965. *Confrontations: Studies in the Intellectual and Literary Relations between Germany, England, and the United States during the Nineteenth Century.* Princeton, NJ: Princeton University Press.

West, Cornell. 1989. *The American Evasion of Philosophy: A Genealogy of Pragmatism.* Madison: University of Wisconsin Press.

Whicher, Stephen. 1953. *Freedom and Fate: An Inner Life of Ralph Waldo Emerson.* Philadelphia: University of Pennsylvania Press.

Whitman, Walt. (1871) 1945. *The Portable Walt Whitman. Selected and with Notes,* edited by Mark van Doren, 411. New York: Viking Press.

Wienand, Isabelle. 2008. "Political Implications of Happiness in Descartes and Nietzsche." In *Nietzsche, Power, and Politics: Rethinking Nietzsche's Legacy for Political Thought,* edited by Herman Siemens and Vaasti Roodt, 583–604. Berlin: De Gruyter.

Wilbur, Earl Morse. 1952. *A History of Unitarianism: In Transylvania, England, and America.* Boston: Beacon Press.

Williams, Robert. 2012. *Tragedy, Recognition, and the Death of God: Studies in Hegel and Nietzsche.* New York: Oxford University Press.

Wilson, Eric. 1997. "From Metaphysical Poverty to Practical Power: Emerson's Embrace of the Physical World." In "Emerson/Nietzsche." Special issue of *ESQ: A Journal of American Renaissance* 43: 295–321.

Wilson Allen, Gay. 1981. *Waldo Emerson: A Biography.* New York: Viking Press.

Worthington Smith, Lewis. 1911. "Ibsen, Emerson and Nietzsche: The Individualists." *Popular Science Monthly* 78: 147–157.

Zakaras, Alex. 2009. *Individuality and Mass Democracy.* New York: Oxford University Press.

Zavatta, Benedetta. 2006a. *La sfida del carattere: Nietzsche lettore di Emerson.* Roma: Editori Riuniti.

Zavatta, Benedetta. 2006b. "Nietzsche, Emerson und das Selbstvertrauen." *Nietzsche-Studien* 35: 274–297.

Zavatta, Benedetta. 2015. "L'impossibile alleanza tra filosofia e arte." Postscript to Friedrich Nietzsche, *Su verità e menzogna in senso extramorale,* 37–49. Milano: Adelphi.

Zavatta, Benedetta. 2017. "From Pure Reason to Historical Knowledge: Nietzsche's (Virtual) Objections to Kant's First Critique." In *Nietzsche, Kant and the Problem of Metaphysics,* edited by Marco Brusotti and Herman Siemens, 45–70. London: Bloomsbury.

INDEX

Abbey, Ruth, 128–29, 130, 132–33, 134–35,
    137–38, 150, 241n18
abnegation, 88–90, 105–6, 112, 122–23, 189–90,
    228–29n49
Acampora, Christa, 91, 141, 185, 215n42, 231n63,
    235n30, 238n1
accountability. *See* moral responsibility
active forgetting, 71–72, 155–56, 157–58, 163,
    238n1, 239n6
adversary. See *agon*
adversity, 34–35, 53–55, 58, 64–65,
    66–67, 152–53
agency, 17–18, 19, 29–31, 39–41, 43,
    64–65, 72–73, 195–96, 200, 212n21,
    213–14n31, 215n39, 230n60, 231n63,
    240–41n15, 242n25
agent, the. *See* agency
agon, 95–96, 141, 150, 151, 184–86, 198, 228n43,
    234n23, 235n31, 235n32, 237–38n51,
    243n29, 245n41
Alcott, Bronson, 7–8, 145, 206–7n13, 207n16.
    See also Fruitlands
altruism, 114–18, 120, 129, 152–53, 231n1
    non virtuous form of, 117, 125
    virtuous form of, 72, 114–15, 117, 125, 127–28
amor fati, 62–63, 64–65
Andler, Charles, 1–4, 90
aristocracy, 4–5, 15–16, 123–24, 177, 191,
    230n60, 237n47, 242n24
aristocraticism. *See* aristocracy
Aristotle, 131–32, 133, 135, 139, 213n29, 221n4,
    229n54, 238n52
art, 2–4, 42–43, 60–62, 75–76, 158–59, 165,
    173–74, 175–76, 177–78, 180–81, 184,
    187–88, 198, 204–5n2, 219n59, 219–20n60,
    220n61, 220n66, 222n7, 222n9, 231n63,
    239n6, 239n7, 241–42n21
artist. *See* art

ascetic ideal, 41–42, 84–85, 90, 116–17,
    216n46, 230n60
ascetism. *See* ascetic ideal
autonomous individual. *See* moral autonomy

Basel, 141–42, 244n38
Baumgarten, Eduard, 11–14, 51–52, 211n19,
    218n54, 230–31n62, 235n34, 246n51
Bayreuth, 141–42, 178
Biedenkapp, Georg, 5–6, 204n1
Blessed Isles, 141–42, 148, 149–50, 154, 235n33
Brenner, Albert, 141–42
Brentano von Arnim, Bettina, 2–4
Brinton, Crane, 10–11, 13–14
Brisbane, Albert, 8–9, 145, 236n41, 236n43
Brookfarm, 8–9, 144–45, 207n16, 236n42.
    See also George Ripley
Buddhism, 8, 54–55, 208n19, 208n20, 209n4,
    231n5, 245–46n46
Buddhist, the. *See* Buddhism
Buonarroti, Michelangelo, 192–93
Burckhardt, Jacob, 172–73, 191, 228n45, 242n22
Byron, George Gordon, 26–27, 53, 209n4,
    210–11n15, 211n16

Cabot, James Elliot, 207n14, 207–8n18,
    218–19n55
capitalism, 8–9
Carlyle, Thomas, 8, 75–76, 86, 145, 173, 185–86,
    188, 207n14, 242n24, 247n1
Cavell, Stanley, 1, 15–16, 62–63, 175–76, 177,
    226n34, 226–27n37, 243n30
Channing, William Ellery, 6–7
character
    empirical, 30, 32–33, 212n22
    intelligible, 30–31, 32–34, 212n22
child, the, 104–5, 106–8, 111, 159–60, 208n22,
    208–9n2, 229–30n56, 230n58, 238n1